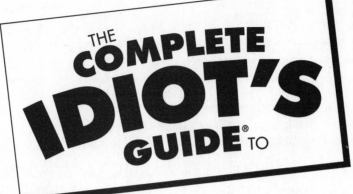

THE COMPLETE **IDIOT'S** GUIDE® TO

Screenwriting

Third Edition

by Skip Press

ALPHA

A member of Penguin Group (USA) Inc.

To my children, Haley and Holly, and to better movies.

ALPHA BOOKS

Published by the Penguin Group

Penguin Group (USA) Inc., 375 Hudson Street, New York, New York 10014, USA

Penguin Group (Canada), 90 Eglinton Avenue East, Suite 700, Toronto, Ontario M4P 2Y3, Canada (a division of Pearson Penguin Canada Inc.)

Penguin Books Ltd., 80 Strand, London WC2R 0RL, England

Penguin Ireland, 25 St. Stephen's Green, Dublin 2, Ireland (a division of Penguin Books Ltd.)

Penguin Group (Australia), 250 Camberwell Road, Camberwell, Victoria 3124, Australia (a division of Pearson Australia Group Pty. Ltd.)

Penguin Books India Pvt. Ltd., 11 Community Centre, Panchsheel Park, New Delhi—110 017, India

Penguin Group (NZ), 67 Apollo Drive, Rosedale, North Shore, Auckland 1311, New Zealand (a division of Pearson New Zealand Ltd.)

Penguin Books (South Africa) (Pty.) Ltd., 24 Sturdee Avenue, Rosebank, Johannesburg 2196, South Africa

Penguin Books Ltd., Registered Offices: 80 Strand, London WC2R 0RL, England

Copyright © 2008 by Skip Press

International Standard Book Number: 978-1-59257-755-2
Library of Congress Catalog Card Number: 2008920824

10 09 08   8 7 6 5 4 3 2 1

Interpretation of the printing code: The rightmost number of the first series of numbers is the year of the book's printing; the rightmost number of the second series of numbers is the number of the book's printing. For example, a printing code of 08-1 shows that the first printing occurred in 2008.

Printed in the United States of America

Note: This publication contains the opinions and ideas of its author. It is intended to provide helpful and informative material on the subject matter covered. It is sold with the understanding that the author and publisher are not engaged in rendering professional services in the book. If the reader requires personal assistance or advice, a competent professional should be consulted.

The author and publisher specifically disclaim any responsibility for any liability, loss, or risk, personal or otherwise, which is incurred as a consequence, directly or indirectly, of the use and application of any of the contents of this book.

Most Alpha books are available at special quantity discounts for bulk purchases for sales promotions, premiums, fund-raising, or educational use. Special books, or book excerpts, can also be created to fit specific needs.

For details, write: Special Markets, Alpha Books, 375 Hudson Street, New York, NY 10014.

Publisher: *Marie Butler-Knight*
Editorial Director: *Mike Sanders*
Senior Managing Editor: *Billy Fields*
Acquisitions Editor: *Tom Stevens*
Development Editor: *Lynn Northrup*
Production Editor: *Megan Douglass*
Copy Editor: *Drew Patty*

Cartoonist: *Steve Barr*
Cover Designer: *Kurt Owens*
Book Designer: *Trina Wurst*
Indexer: *Heather McNeill*
Layout: *Brian Massey*
Proofreaders: *Laura Caddell, Terri Edwards*

Contents at a Glance

Contents

Foreword

Every great movie begins with a screenplay. Whether the writer is a nerd in a closet writing on legal pads or an incredibly successful screenwriter tapping away on his MacBook Pro laptop, great movies are possible only when a writer has fused together one of the most difficult art forms: the written, dramatic word produced for the visual medium.

And yet, success stories come from every part of the country. Anyone who writes is eligible. As one of the judges for the Nicholl Fellowships in Screenwriting, I read scripts written by "nobodies," and I am pleased to report that some of these writers have become incredibly successful.

It is a lonely and difficult vocation. The only way to be a writer is to write and write and write. Whether you want to shock, thrill, or excite your audience, or whether you want to make people laugh or cry, you must have stories to tell.

However, screenplays—like every other art form—need study and technique. Just as each screenplay you write and each story you tell makes you a better writer, developing your knowledge of the art and improving your technique makes you a skilled and more professional writer. The more you read screenplays and books on screenplay writing, the better a writer you will be.

This is why I like Skip's book, *The Complete Idiot's Guide to Screenwriting, Third Edition*. It's about helping writers write. It provokes you into being a little better. And sometimes, it is the little bit better that makes the difference between a rejection and a sale.

My first screenplay was *King Kong Versus Godzilla*. I got the job because a producer had read several of my screenplays, none of which had sold so they were considered "writing samples." The producer never bought the scripts, but he liked the writing and the ideas. Many writers get hired this way. At the time, I was writing cartoons for Beetle Bailey and Snuffy Smith. However, I was writing and studying how to be a better writer, and I got a break.

The good news is that there is a desperate need for writers … and there always will be a need. Movies and television suck up millions of stories annually. I genuinely believe that those who work hard and study hard will get a chance. That door will slip open, which is when you can shove your script through and keep your fingers crossed … and keep writing.

I met Skip Press at a panel that discussed selling to Hollywood, and I could tell he had something to say. Not long after returning to Los Angeles, we made a deal on a project and have since worked on others. I optioned a screenplay he co-wrote, and we became friends.

This is often how it works in Hollywood. You try to associate with people who are competent and work on projects that you think will succeed. It starts with a great script.

Learning to be a screenwriter is not easy. I know how it works because I have been one. I was twice awarded *Fame* magazine's Critic Award for writing and producing the best television detective series (*McMillan and Wife*). I was nominated for the Emmy for best television series (*Ironside*), which won the first Image Award from the NAACP. Regardless of whether it was a long-form drama, a movie, or sitcoms I did—from *Chico and the Man* to *Welcome Back Kotter*—much of the success of these shows was due to the writing.

When Skip and I met, I was senior vice president in charge of production for Viacom Productions, where I supervised eight television series and several television movies including *Sabrina, The Teenage Witch*. If you want to be a producer, read *Producing for Hollywood*, a book I wrote with Don Gold. If you want to be a screenwriter, read this book by Skip Press. There are reasons why the Canadian Writers Guild said the first edition of this book was the best of its kind and why Triumph Publishing in Moscow translated it into Russian. Skip has covered everything a beginning or an intermediate screenwriter needs to know—from story history and psychology to Hollywood "secrets" and insider tips.

There are also things you will not find in other screenwriting books, such as Skip's description of the "Shaping Force" in the middle of Act One, the alignment of the three-act structure of Aristotle's *Poetics* with the five acts of Shakespeare, and the myth theories of Joseph Campbell.

For reasons like these, I hope that a lot of aspiring screenwriters will read this book and learn how to turn out a better script. As I write this, I'm working on a new movie with Richard Gere and Joan Allen called *Hachiko*. I hope it's a big success, and I wish success for you as well.

And who knows? Maybe I will read your script some day. Wouldn't it be wild if I bought it? Good luck, and keep writing …

—Paul Mason, president, BARSTU Productions, was senior vice president of production at Viacom and Showtime from 1992–2002. He has twice been awarded *Fame* magazine's Critic Award for writing and producing the best television detective series (*McMillan and Wife*), has been nominated for the Emmy for best television series (*Ironside*), and produced the series that won the first Image Award from the NAACP (*Ironside*).

Introduction

The one movie that my entire family saw in a theater was *To Kill a Mockingbird*. We saw this Academy Award–winning film in a small East Texas town, and the racial struggle portrayed in the story was going on outside the theater doors. I remember where I was sitting and all the details of the movie.

Unfortunately, my father had problems and was no bastion of sensibility like Gregory Peck's Atticus Finch onscreen. As a child, I grew up admiring movie actors, particularly Jimmy Stewart, and stars of TV shows, such as Ronald Reagan. More than mere actors playing roles, they were father figures who showed me the way a man should live his life.

But there was something deeper in the movies and shows that I admired. The stories etched themselves into memory, and at some point I began paying attention to who wrote those stories. When I saw *Lawrence of Arabia*, while I admired Peter O'Toole's wonderful performance, I was much more impressed by the stunning visuals, the sweeping story, and the glimpse of heroic history.

Still, I wanted to write books. I knew from a very early age that I would write, but it never occurred to me that I might some day write screenplays. When I moved to southern California, I had writing the Great American Novel in mind. I still do!

Then I won a game show and had enough money to take a half-year sabbatical to pursue my writing seriously. I lived in the shadow of the Hollywood sign at the time, and after writing my first novel, I wrote a screenplay. I met people working in "the business" and told them about another script that I wanted to write. Then they shocked me by paying me real money for my story, an "option" that was a rental of the story until they could afford to buy it and make the movie.

From that point forward, I was hooked. And every time I get a check for a script, whether it's for a kids' TV show or another option on a screenplay, I'm hooked again. The basic thought is, "Wow, they pay me to do something that's so much fun?"

Of course, it seems like fun only before the writing begins and after it is done. While the scripting is actually in progress, I can be a bear to live with—a grumpy California bear.

Thankfully, in recent years, I've grown much more congenial. That's because I've learned so much more about the structure of screenplays. I no longer find it so hard to draw up the blueprints to build a new world, you see.

And that's what I've tried to give you here, in this book: a blueprint to build your own cinematic world so that someone will read your blueprint and commission the construction of something that can some day thrill us all. I hope that it helps both you and me see your name on the silver screen, and soon.

How to Use This Book

The Complete Idiot's Guide to Screenwriting, Third Edition, is, like a Shakespearean play, divided into five parts:

Part 1, "The Evolution of Storytelling," takes us on a tour that starts with the Greek playwrights and takes us to the present, stopping to examine the discoveries of Freud, Jung, and others who have impacted cinema. We examine Shakespeare, the birth of the movies and Hollywood, and everything about filmdom, on into the current digital age.

Part 2, "What to Write," explains where to find the best movie ideas, what subjects sell, and how screenwriting differs from other writing forms, and it delves into the unique language of Hollywood that screenwriters must understand. In a few short chapters, you get an education that some writers take a decade to figure out.

Part 3, "How to Write Your Screenplay," is the nuts-and-bolts explanation of putting together a screen story, from premise to outline to completed script, with a complete step-by-step description of the best structure for your movie. And then, just when you think you're done, we cover the secrets of rewriting.

Part 4, "Post-Script Possibilities," provides a Hollywood behind-the-scenes plan for improving a screenplay when it's rewritten and tells you what happens after a script is purchased. It also explains how the film industry works and explains the nuances of writing TV movies and short films for the Internet.

Part 5, "It's All in the Details," explains the things that you learn only by working in Hollywood. For example, use two brads (not three) when binding your script. Amateur technical mistakes, screenwriting gurus, the real deal on selling scripts, and how to plan a screenwriting career are all covered.

 With this book, we're adding something I hope you love as much as I enjoyed putting it together. It's a CD with sample scripts from myself and others, articles and interviews, and demo versions of software, among other things. You'll see an icon of a CD throughout the book when I mention things on the CD.

Extras

The Complete Idiot's Guide to Screenwriting, Third Edition, also features, sprinkled through each chapter, snippets of information in boxed sidebars. These sidebars provide you with additional tips, definitions of key terms, warnings of potential dangers, and additional information that you may find helpful or even amusing. (You *must* have a sense of humor to be a screenwriter!) We call these sidebars:

Script Notes

Hollywood has its own language, so you will need the definitions provided here.

Skip's Tips

These sidebars contain useful tips on the current topic. They may fit with the flow of the page or provide an interesting counterpoint to it.

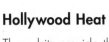

Hollywood Heat

These bits provide the kind of "bet you didn't know" inside information that serve to remind you that you're not the only one troubled and confused by the daunting task of embarking on a career in screenwriting in that wacky place known as Hollywood.

It's Not for Us

When scripts are rejected, writers are often told, "It's not for us." These warnings outline potential pitfalls and mistakes that, if avoided, might help you never hear that troubling, cryptic phrase.

Acknowledgments

Even though this is my tenth book of writing advice, I don't try to be a Hollywood or writing guru. I simply continue to share helpful information with other writers. That now includes readers of the first edition, which was translated into Russian. If I can save any other person anywhere from going through even a small trouble that I've endured, it's worth the effort.

Ironically enough, I was asked to write this book after being referred to my editor by Janet Bigham Berstel, another *Complete Idiot's Guide* author whom I met at a writers' conference. I gave her free advice about Hollywood, and she remembered. And that's how Hollywood success comes about. Someone who can deliver the goods meets someone who gets that person a job. First and foremost, I would like to thank Janet for her graciousness.

With this new edition I would like to thank editors Tom Stevens, Lynn Northrup, Megan Douglass, and all the others who worked to make this third edition an even better book. I don't think writers thank editors enough or realize that just about all editors are writers, too, and need acknowledgement.

Ultimately, a special thanks goes to my children, Haley and Holly, for their continued understanding and love.

I also want to acknowledge every person who ever thought that I couldn't make it as a writer or screenwriter. Almost 40 books and a lot of sold scripts later, I can safely say they couldn't quench my fire.

And that's why I last want to acknowledge every hopeful writer out there whom I'm able to help in any way. I'm glad to do it, folks. It's giving back to people who helped me in the beginning. Keep those great stories coming, and never, ever give up!

Trademarks

All terms mentioned in this book that are known to be or are suspected of being trademarks or service marks have been appropriately capitalized. Alpha Books and Penguin Group (USA) Inc. cannot attest to the accuracy of this information. Use of a term in this book should not be regarded as affecting the validity of any trademark or service mark.

Part 1

The Evolution of Storytelling

Get on the Movietown Bus as we tour through the centuries, starting with the Greek playwrights and other world influences. Then we'll stop to examine the discoveries of Freud, Jung, and others whom you might not suspect have impacted cinema. You'll meet William Shakespeare, attend the birth of the movies in Europe and in Hollywood, and learn how film-dom has become a worldwide art as it speeds into the digital age. Warning! Your driver's name is Oedipus!

History Lessons Make Better Writers

In This Chapter

- It all started with the Greeks
- The three-act structure began with Aristotle
- The influence of Romans, Christians, and Shakespeare
- Our stories and our mentors
- The impact of Carl Jung and Joseph Campbell

In almost any screenwriting class, you will hear discussions about the importance of *conflict:* good guy versus bad guy, good versus evil, or youth versus tradition. It's really the dual nature of the universe, and the struggle of opposing forces, with all sides usually considering themselves "right." Remember this: The "villain" of any film is the "hero" of his own movie. And conflict has been around since the beginning of human storytelling.

Most people in the West know the story of Adam and Eve from the Book of Genesis. But are you familiar with the story of the beginning of life found in the *Brihadaranyaka Upanishad?* Written around 700 B.C.E., this tale from India describes how the original Self divided himself into two parts because he "lacked delight." With his new female half, *conflict* began!

Script Notes _____

When writing a screenplay, **conflict** doesn't have to mean violence. *Webster's New Collegiate Dictionary* offers this definition: "The opposition of persons or forces that gives rise to the dramatic action in a drama or fiction." In action movies, however, some producers want something blown up every 10 minutes.

According to the ancient Chinese, however, the creation of the world came about in 2,229,000 B.C.E., when the first man, P'an Ku, got the universe in shape after working on it for 18,000 years.

The Australian aboriginals disagree. They say the Lord God Baiame made the earth, the plants, and the animals, and created man and woman to rule over them.

Who's right? Who knows, but that's what's great about stories.

How many aspiring screenwriters know the tale of *Gilgamesh*, which began in Sumer, a country that gave us cuneiform writing? The Babylonian historian Berosus (circa 250 B.C.E.) said the Sumerians were a race of monsters led by Oannes, who gave the world all its arts including writing. Are you familiar with the country Media, which gave Persia (now Iran) their Aryan language and replaced writing on clay with pen on parchment? Does the term "media" originate from this ancient land?

The Native American Iroquois believed their race came from women mating with animals. Before you assume they were misogynists, consider that they, like the Seneca "Indians," gave women equal rights in tribal affairs. The Senecas even had women chieftains.

No matter where you are or where you came from, people have stories to tell.

Hollywood Heat _____

Want some conflict? Tell a Hindi director that movies started in Hollywood. You'll probably be told that the subcontinent's movies began in 1896, when the Lumière brothers arrived from France with their Cinématographe, shortly after debuting it in their home country. The Indians' original filmmaker was apparently a fellow named Bhatvadekar, and their first films were of Bombay attractions like wrestling matches. All, you will be told, long before anyone filmed a single frame in Hollywood.

The Greeks Got It Started in the West

It is believed that the Greek poet Thespis founded the art of drama about 600 B.C.E. Plays before his time did not feature an actor who spoke independently of the Greek chorus. Thespis created monologues for actors and gave them dialogues with the leader of the chorus. This innovation signaled the birth of Western drama. It was also Thespis's idea to use masks and makeup, so an actor is also known as a "thespian."

The Greek dramatist Aeschylus introduced a second actor, costumes, and scenery. Sophocles added a third actor, making intricate plots possible; he is usually considered to be the greatest of the Greek playwrights. His contemporary, Euripides, bucked the system, writing about the ordinary person and using more natural dialogue than his contemporaries, who preferred to write about moral and religious themes.

It's Not for Us

A fortune-teller predicts that a prince will kill his father and marry his mother. Abandoned in the woods to die, the boy survives, grows up, meets a king, kills him, and then marries the king's widow. He later discovers that his new wife is also his mother! She commits suicide, and the king blinds himself. That's *Oedipus Rex*, by Sophocles, which the philosopher Aristotle thought was the perfect play.

Think about it: In Western civilization, writers have been devising plots for more than 26 centuries. That fact alone is reason enough to look into history for screenplay ideas.

Aristotle and the Three-Act Structure

If you've ever wondered why we have three acts in modern screenplays, blame Aristotle. He studied with Plato and was the tutor of Alexander the Great of Macedonia, the first Western conqueror of the known world. Aristotle's *Poetics* is still heavily influential among Hollywood writers. Here's what he said about the construction of a dramatic work:

> … the plot manifestly ought, as in a tragedy, to be constructed on dramatic principles. It should have for its subject a single action, whole and complete, with a beginning, a middle, and an end.

Aristotle held that the plot of a story was "the first principle, and, as it were, the soul of a tragedy" and that "*character* holds the second place." He asserted, "A similar fact is seen in painting. The most beautiful colors, laid on confusedly, will not give as much pleasure as the chalk outline of a portrait."

Other Aristotelian observations are particularly applicable to screenwriting: He coined the terms *reversal of the situation*, defined as "a change by which the action veers round to its opposite," and *recognition*, defined as "a change from ignorance to knowledge." Aristotle then pulled the two together for a general conclusion: "Two parts, then, of the Plot—Reversal of the Situation and Recognition—turn upon surprises."

Consider the heroic characters of the *Lord of the Rings* movies and their continuous reversals and recognitions. The classic *Casablanca*, starring Humphrey Bogart, delivers similar twists. It's true, in fact, of all great films.

Romans, Christians, and Shakespeare

Writers in ancient Rome were poets first and playwrights second. The Romans contributed few works that are still performed today, but they provided the preservation of old stories. Because the seat of the Christian church was in Rome, Latin became its language, and Christian monks preserved the past during the Dark Ages by writing things out in Latin. In fact, the Bible translated by Saint Jerome is the Latin Bible in use today.

Unless you were a nobleman in Rome, you could not speak freely, and this early censorship continued for centuries after the fall of Rome, thanks to the Catholic Church. In medieval times, the only plays that were performed in public were those with religious themes, usually staged during church services. Starting in 1487, a work could be printed and distributed only after church authorities had approved it.

That changed drastically by the time of William Shakespeare, and the Romans had more influence on him than one might think. A translation of the Roman philosopher and playwright Seneca's plays was published in London in 1581, not long before Shakespeare came to prominence there. English children of the time studied Latin grammar (not English) in school, and young Shakespeare learned a great deal about writers like Cicero, Virgil, and Ovid. Seneca's dramatic themes had influence upon the Bard of Avon, as did the comedies of Roman playwrights Terence and Plautus. In fact, *Menaechmi*, or *The Twin Brothers*, by Plautus is the play from which Shakespeare took the plot for his *Comedy of Errors*. In his 1598 work *Palladis Tamia: Wits Treasury*, Francis Meres compared Shakespeare's poetry to that of Ovid and his plays to those of Plautus and Seneca. Small wonder that so many of the Bard's great plays have Italian settings.

Classic Stories Are Immortal

As the art of storytelling evolved, epic poets propagated great feats and legends. An epic was a long poem that celebrated the feats of a legendary hero. You may have studied them in school, with *The Iliad* or *The Odyssey*.

How do such classics apply to writing movies? Well, *The Iliad*, set in the tenth and final year of the Greek siege of the city of Troy, has been described as one of the greatest war stories of all time. Maybe you saw the 2004 movie *Troy*? Stories from mythology have long been popular with film audiences. *Jason and the Argonauts*, the 2,500-year-old story of the quest for the legendary Golden Fleece, was filmed in 1963 by Columbia Pictures and remade by Hallmark Entertainment in 2000. And let's not forget *Beowulf*, the Anglo-Saxon epic about battles with demons and dragons dating back to the sixth century. Director Robert Zemeckis made his own big budget version of the tale in 2007.

> **Skip's Tips** _____
>
> Playwrights who adapt their work for the screen must learn proper screenplay format. Most screenwriting software programs will reformat text automatically, and formatting is discussed in Part 3. The next thing playwrights need to do is turn as many speeches as possible into visuals. Moving pictures, remember?

Whether history or fiction, epics done well are often blockbusters. The *Star Wars* movies were all box office smashes. George Lucas has drawn from many stories and legends in creating his films. Perhaps that has something to do with their popularity. And let's not forget Mel Gibson's Oscar-winning *Braveheart* and even more controversial *The Passion of the Christ*, or the giant box office hit *300* in 2007. History dramatized is powerful!

Here's one for you. In a world that is a constant struggle between good and evil, a messiah returns to wage a final battle, after which the leader of darkness is defeated and the Kingdom of God is established on Earth. Is that the plot of the 1999 movie *The Omega Code*, where ancient codes hidden within the Torah reveal the secrets of global events? Actually, it's also a story from the Persian Zoroaster, approximately 3,000 years old.

To write an epic screenplay, study history and mythology, or even your own family history. You might find an undiscovered classic.

Story and the Mind

Movies provide dream fulfillment. A person buys a ticket, sits in a darkened space, and for an extended length of time lives vicariously. As a screenwriter, it is easy enough to learn basic structure, passable dialogue, and clever tricks. The more difficult task is to create a story that will stand the test of the ages, like a Greek classic or a Shakespearean play.

Perhaps that's why, in the late nineteenth century, intellectuals began to steadily examine what makes people tick, their dreams, ambitions, and motivations. This opened the Pandora's box of the human mind and changed storytelling forever.

Hegel, Freud, Sex, and Stanislavsky

German philosopher Georg Wilhelm Friedrich Hegel developed the argument that self-development results from the conflict of opposites. He proposed that any thesis has an incompleteness that causes its own antithesis, or opposition, to arise. When the synthesis of the thesis and antithesis, or third point of view, comes about, the conflict is resolved at a higher level of truth. Then, he said, comes a new thesis and resulting antithesis.

Sounds like conflict and resolution, doesn't it?

Let's use the first *Star Wars* movie as an example. Both thesis and theme come from the same Greek work meaning "something laid down." In other words, an idea proposed. An antithesis would be a force against this, and the synthesis would be what results from these opposing forces. The word *premise* comes from the Latin meaning "to place ahead," so basically it has the same meaning as *theme*. Luke Skywalker (thesis) at first questions "the Force" (antithesis) and then learns to use it to his advantage (synthesis at a higher level of truth). More broadly, the rebel forces (who propose the thesis that people should live freely) use the Force to fight the Galactic Empire and "the dark side" (antithesis). The rebels ultimately win, resulting in a more stable peace (synthesis), and Luke is revealed as a "royal" Jedi (higher level of truth).

In *The Philosophy of History*, Hegel said, "The first glance at History convinces us that the actions of men proceed from their needs, their passions, their characters and talents; and impresses us with the belief that such needs, passions, and interests are the sole spring of actions." Apply that to your characters.

And now to Sigmund Freud, who loved mythology and Greek gods. Athena, the goddess of war and wisdom, was particularly significant to him. Remember Aristotle's favorite play, *Oedipus Rex*? Freud felt that society creates mechanisms for the social control of human instincts and that, at the base of these controlling mechanisms, is a prohibition against incest. Guilt, he said, arose from the symbolic murder of a patriarch by sons ruled by their father's commands even when he is dead. Freud also wrote repeatedly about the biblical stories of Joseph and of Moses, both of whom had troubled family backgrounds.

Freud called the wish to push aside guilt "repression," the act of which instantly creates in the mind conflict, that concept so loved by Hollywood. Freud was absorbed with sex and was obsessed with the "Oedipus complex." He believed that people were bisexual and that individuals have death drives that conflict with their sex drives. Sound like Hollywood, where people often seem obsessed with shattering taboos? Freud believed that all groups prohibit only those things that individuals actually desire.

Skip's Tips

Your Name

In Hollywood, when a screenplay or property is being considered for purchase or has been purchased, and a number of in-demand actors or directors want to be a part of the project, it is said to have "heat." The term implies sexual tension, and that's Hollywood all day (and night) long.

This brings us to Russian actor-producer Konstantin Stanislavsky, the founder of the Moscow Art Theater and the creator of the Method style of acting. Stanislavsky, who produced the first successful performance of Anton Chekhov's famous play *The Seagull*, put great emphasis of the psychological motivation of an actor.

Stanislavsky discovered that, by recalling old, troubled feelings or traumatic experiences while doing a scene, actors could affect a more believable performance. With Stanislavsky, the actor's emotional mindset during a scene was all-important. Here's how his Method affected Hollywood and, as a result, screenwriting. The Actors Studio, a rehearsal group for professional actors founded in New York in 1947 by writer/director Elia Kazan, became the hotbed for the Method. It was the calling card of the Studio's director, Lee Strasberg, who joined in 1948. Many screen legends studied at the Actors Studio or with Strasberg, including Marlon Brando, James Dean, and Marilyn Monroe. Given the life problems of famous Method actors, you might wonder why no one considered the possibility of lasting, deleterious mental effects from using the technique. But, because they emoted so well onscreen, we've had Method actors ever since.

Carl Jung and the Symbolic World

And now to Carl Jung, Freud's most famous associate. In 1909, accompanied by devotees whom he called "The Committee," Freud traveled to Massachusetts to lecture on psychoanalysis. Following this visit, he formed the International Psychoanalytic Association and chose Carl Jung as his successor. Unlike Freud, Jung did not concentrate so heavily on sexuality. He was the founder of analytical psychology, which dictates that mental aberrations represent an attempt by a person to find spiritual wholeness.

Hollywood Heat

Carl Jung believed that men had feminine inner personalities, while women had a submerged animus, or inner masculinity. Similarly, great movie heroes have an inner struggle to overcome, which is as important as their outward struggle. In *Raiders of the Lost Ark*, Indiana Jones battles to keep the Ark of the Covenant away from the evil Nazis. And he has a deathly fear of snakes.

If you've ever seen a movie in which a doctor and a patient are doing "word association," that is a Jungian technique. Jung also coined the terms *extrovert* and *introvert* in his 1921 book, *Psychological Types*. He believed that repressed thought and feelings had great impact on individuals, but he also held that a "collective unconscious" existed that contained "archetypes" symbolically manifested in the great stories of the world.

This becomes interesting when we consider what Jung thought about films. "The cinema," he said in 1944, "like the detective story, makes it possible to experience without danger all the excitement, passion, and desirousness which must be repressed in a humanitarian ordering of life." What do you think?

Here are some excerpts from Jung's *On the Nature of Dreams*, first published as *Vom Wesen der Traume* in 1945, in which he discusses a procedure that he calls "taking up the context."

> … the dream begins with a STATEMENT OF PLACE. … Next comes a statement about the PROTAGONISTS. … I call this phase of the dream the EXPOSITION. It indicates the scene of action, the people involved, and often the initial situation of the dreamer.
>
> In the second phase comes the DEVELOPMENT of the plot. …
>
> The third phase brings the CULMINATION of peripeteia [ed. note: a sudden change of events or reversal of circumstances, a term used by Aristotle]. Here something decisive happens or something changes completely. …
>
> The fourth and last phase is the lysis, the SOLUTION or RESULT produced by the dream-work. … This division into four phases can be applied without much difficulty to the majority of dreams met with in practice—an indication that dreams generally have a 'dramatic' structure.

To a seasoned screenwriter, Jung's four phases of a dream could easily be akin to the three acts of a screenplay, with his "lysis" comparable to the denouement (events following the climax).

Jung observed that the incest theme was found in numerous myths and philosophies of Earth. Whereas Freud concentrated on incest fantasies in the years before the age of six, Jung dealt with the incestuous wishes of adulthood. Jung also felt that every person has a personal unconscious called "the shadow," a primitive, untamed threat. Sounds like the "dark side" from *Star Wars*.

Jung also said, "Eternal truth needs a human language that alters with the spirit of the times." I don't know about you, but to me, that language could very well be motion pictures.

Skip's Tips

Your Name

The film Stanley Kubrick was planning when he died was *A.I.* (for "artificial intelligence"). Director Steven Spielberg picked it up for his next project and even wrote the script. The movie was overly long, even nightmarish, but dreams and psychology have their influence in Hollywood. What did Spielberg name the studio that he formed with David Geffen and Jeffrey Katzenberg? DreamWorks!

Joseph Campbell's Powerful Myths

Author and teacher Joseph Campbell, a great admirer of Jung, spent his lifetime studying the great stories of the Earth. The great stories of humankind, he realized, all had a similar pattern, which he called a "myth structure." He taught this story blueprint in classes at Sarah Lawrence College in Bronxville, New York, and then codified it with the publication of *Hero with a Thousand Faces* in 1949. Thirty years later, Hollywood caught on.

One of those influenced by Campbell's book was screenwriter and director George Lucas, who told the National Arts Club, "It's possible that if I had not run across [Campbell], I would still be writing *Star Wars* today."

Hollywood Heat

YOUR NAME

In 1924, Joseph Campbell met Indian philosopher J. Krishnamurti on a boat trip to Europe and became interested in Hinduism and Buddhism. Later, he worked with Swami Nikhilananda to translate Indian holy texts. He also spent time with the great American author John Steinbeck. No ivory-tower scholar, Campbell wrote about stories and authors he knew firsthand.

While doing European graduate study in the Holy Grail legends of Arthurian mythology, Campbell discovered the work of Freud and Jung. This helped him see the parallels between myths, legends, and dreams. A couple years later, in 1931, Campbell went to California, met then-unknown novelist John Steinbeck, and got to know marine biologist Ed "Doc" Ricketts, a friend of Steinbeck's who was the model for main characters in *Cannery Row* and *Sweet Thursday*. On a coastal journey to Alaska collecting intertidal specimens, Ricketts mentored Campbell in Jungian philosophy. Finally, in 1954, Campbell and his wife Jean met Jung and his wife at Bollingen, Jung's castle on a lake near Zurich.

While Joseph Campbell's work gained a foothold in Hollywood via filmmakers like George Lucas and Dr. George Miller (an Australian Campbell devotee whose *Mad Max* made a star of Mel Gibson), the person perhaps most responsible for the respect given Campbell among screenwriters is Christopher Vogler, who discovered Campbell while studying at the University of Southern California film school (where George Lucas was also a student).

While working as a story analyst, Vogler wrote a memo titled "A Practical Guide to *The Hero with a Thousand Faces*," which convinced Jeffrey Katzenberg, then running Disney, that every Disney project should be compared against "myth" structure. Vogler later wrote *The Writer's Journey* (see www.thewritersjourney.com). Campbell's *The Hero with a Thousand Faces* and Vogler's *The Writer's Journey* are highly worthwhile reads.

Flowing Onward

Isn't it funny that, in 10,000 years of recorded history, a certain kind of story seems to work over and over again? In a way, it makes you feel kind of good about humankind.

Nevertheless, story structure questions linger. The Campbell "myth" structure simply does not work with certain films. And on first glance, it seems that the three acts of Aristotle do not reconcile with the five-act structure of William Shakespeare.

Unless, that is, you take a holistic view not necessarily bound only by the arts. While studying international finance, I came upon the Elliott Wave Principle, named for its discoverer, Ralph Nelson Elliott. (See www.elliottwave.com for more information.) The Wave Principle studies mass psychology to explain a specific up and down natural sequence that forms measurable patterns. While working with students of my "Your Screenwriting Career" course (see www.skippress.com), I was stunned to see how Elliott's pattern perfectly aligned all of the structures championed by Aristotle, Shakespeare, and Campbell.

For example, the five-wave pattern of an Elliott "bull market" perfectly correlates with the story structure that works best for top Hollywood movies. The rising action of the first half of the first act leads to the "shaping force" in the middle of the first act that begins the "spine" of the story. That's the first line or "wave." The downward second line descends into a change necessitating a transition to the "new world" of the second act. The third upward wave leads to the Act Two midpoint change that shows the protagonist may actually win. That drops off into the deepest dilemma of the hero or heroine at the end of Act Two. And the third act is an upward struggle to a conclusion. More on that in Chapter 14.

Meanwhile, let's take a look at the works of the most successful writer in Western history, the Bard of Avon, William Shakespeare.

The Least You Need to Know

◆ Some of the most successful movies of recent years have been derived from ancient tales.

◆ The three-act structure outlined by Aristotle in *Poetics* (beginning, middle, and end) is still a standard in Hollywood.

◆ Stanislavsky's "Method," in which actors mentally dredge up old traumas while performing, has had more influence on film actors than any other acting style.

◆ Hollywood's preoccupation with sex and violence reflects *Oedipus Rex*, Carl Jung, and Sigmund Freud.

◆ Read *The Hero with a Thousand Faces* by Joseph Campbell and *The Writer's Journey* by Christopher Vogler to understand a story structure highly favored by Hollywood.

◆ Hollywood, like filmmaking around the world, constantly changes. Popular new story structures are always evolving.

That Fellow Shakespeare

In This Chapter

- ◆ Love that Shakespeare
- ◆ Shakespeare's many uses
- ◆ What makes Shakespeare special
- ◆ History's a good read
- ◆ Action over words
- ◆ Shakespeare in 25 words or less

If you are an aspiring screenwriter, studying William Shakespeare might seem like the oddest idea in the world. In reality, however, Shakespeare has had a greater influence on motion pictures than any other writer, and yet he has been dead for almost four centuries. You might have seen a movie based on his work without even knowing it. *10 Things I Hate About You*, starring Julia Stiles, was based on *The Taming of the Shrew*.

Other Shakespeare-derived movies included *O*, a modern *Othello* set in a high school (again starring Julia Stiles), and a year-2000 version of *Hamlet*, starring actor Ethan Hawke. As this book was written, four movies based on Shakespearean works were planned for 2008. Four centuries after his heyday, William Shakespeare is still thrilling actors and audiences.

Shakespeare in Love

The most entertaining example of a Shakespeare-based story was 1999's *Shakespeare in Love*, a romantic comedy by Marc Norman and Tom Stoppard that won the Academy Award for Best Writing, Screenplay Written Directly for the Screen. In the script, young Will Shakespeare is broke, has a terrible love life, and has not delivered a promised play, *Romeo and Ethel, the Sea Pirate's Daughter.*

> **Skip's Tips**
>
> You could do a lot worse than basing your screenplay on Shakespearean stories or structure. The Internet Movie Database (www.imdb.com) lists 711 movie-writing credits for William Shakespeare, several in every decade, beginning with the filming of *King John* in 1899.

The situation looks hopeless, but things start to turn around when he meets the fictional Viola de Lesseps, a young and beautiful noblewoman who is desperate to be an actor at a time when women were not allowed upon the stage. Love at first sight leaps to inspiration and, mostly due to Shakespeare's clandestine affair with the soon-to-wed Viola, the Bard of Avon changes his play into a tragedy called *Romeo and Juliet*, which, to his surprise, entertains even the great Elizabeth herself, queen of England.

> **Hollywood Heat**
>
> Beginning screenwriters often hear about the importance of the "first ten pages" of a screenplay. If you can't interest the reader by then, you're sunk. Shakespeare faced an equivalent. Audiences would see the first act for free. If they found it worthy, they would pay to see the play. Otherwise, they could leave.

Using Shakespeare

Shakespeare in Love was great for obvious reasons: the story was clever, the dialogue was delicious, and one of the most popular plays of all time was woven into the plot. Less conspicuous is the fact that William Shakespeare is the most famous writer of the English language, yet little is known about him personally. Therefore, we have at the least a subconscious desire to know.

Shakespeare in Love's concocted character Viola (wonderfully portrayed by Gwyneth Paltrow, who won the Best Actress Oscar) plays on speculation over whom Shakespeare's mistress, the infamous "Dark Lady of the Sonnets," might have been.

In the movie, Viola is also his muse, the inspiration for Shakespeare's Juliet, and a blonde. The "Dark Lady" a blonde? Shocking!

In the script, the writers use Shakespeare's very words and a Shakespearean plot device. Historical characters, very well-known, real life people, are dramatized in a manner that makes us think yet entertains, stirs the blood yet offers laughs, and touches deep passions while commenting on the recurring need to change antiquated societal conventions, even when it means risking everything in the attempt.

Shakespeare's Secret

The secret of Shakespeare's lasting appeal is that *he writes for everyone on a scale bigger than normal life*. When he examines the ordinary, he does so in a fearless yet poetic way that offers a perspective heretofore unnoticed. He takes us to places we have not been and into ideas that we have not examined and that speak to the great questions of humankind throughout the ages.

Writing in a time when actors were looked upon with little more regard than beggars in the street, and when criticism of a monarch or members of the ruling class could result in death, Shakespeare knew that writing about larger-than-life characters would fascinate royalty and commoners alike. He made his own legends.

Queen Elizabeth was a living legend, but no playwright could dramatize the Virgin Queen and survive. This left other royals as subjects for high drama, but many contemporary members of the court were more thin-skinned than their queen. So, Shakespeare drew from history and myth, weaving in characters from his own fertile imagination who, mixed with legendary real people, displayed lusts and lamentations, fears and rejoicings as human as anyone in the audience, regardless of social station. He examined common, deep human passions on tableaus broader than common, everyday life.

Pages from History

Here's an example of Shakespearean technique: There may be no more deathly story than *Macbeth*, drawn from Raphael Holinshed's *Chronicle of the Reigns of Duncan and Macbeth (1034–1057)*. This dramatization of real historical events commented heavily upon Shakespeare's time, without pointing fingers. The real-life corollary? Queen Elizabeth's struggle with her own cousin, Mary Stuart, better known as Mary, Queen of Scots, who was beheaded in 1587 on charges of sedition against the English crown.

How could a playwright in London dramatize great and bitter royal struggles and keep his neck intact? *Macbeth* was likely written in 1606, but even two decades after Mary's death, no one had forgotten her beheading. Shakespeare could, however, safely write about a royal death match set in Scotland 600 years before. Blood lust, the struggle for power, witchcraft, and the psychology of evil are all woven into this great tragedy, a play that casts its own legendary shadow over thespians today.

If you utter the word "Macbeth" in a theater, the superstition among actors is that it will curse the production. Some actors feel the same way on a film set, and call it "the Scottish play." So watch your Mac-mouth.

Skip's Tips

Your Name

Your screenplay is your property until you sell it. When it's sold, your book or story is referred to as a property. This is in contrast to the theater, where a property is any physical thing used during the play.

Dialogue May or May Not Be the Thing

Take a hint from Shakespeare, who knew that when an audience has too much of one thing for too long, you've lost them. Swords and daggers and knives and poisons appear in profusion amongst his great words. People fight and die. They go mad, see ghosts, and hold the skulls of fallen comrades in their hands. They battle for kingdoms, wear disguises, and embark on great follies. "Action!" shouts the movie director. Learn that word from Shakespeare. You may be in love with dialogue, but if you put too much in a screenplay, you most likely will never see that screenplay filmed.

In Shakespeare's time, theaters had two types of patrons. The upper class sat in balconies, while the lower classes stood in front of the stage on a bare dirt floor, and were referred to as "groundlings." The upper class understood the clever turns of phrase and the use of languages other than English, while the groundlings who could not read or write thrilled to the action. Movies are moving pictures. Smart movie actors have used that maxim from the days of silent films. Charlie Chaplin, with his "Little Tramp" character, could convey a universe of pathos with the twitch of a mustache. Buster Keaton, with his ever-mournful face, could hand you a belly laugh and a gasp in the same instant, as when he took a step forward and narrowly escaped being flattened by the front of a falling building. Think of your scripts as moving pictures and you'll write better screenplays.

Still, you should strive for memorable dialogue. Readers tired of poring over dozens of screenplays will often quit reading the description and read only the dialogue to follow the story.

Skip's Tips _____

Beginning screenwriters often forget that movies are moving pictures and write too much stage play-like dialogue. Try this exercise:

1. Write a three-minute scene with all the dialogue you want.
2. Write the same scene, this time without words. Just describe the action.
3. Reread both and decide which one you would be more interested in watching in a movie theater.

Shakespeare's Continuing Influence

Like the Avon River whose banks he knew so well, Shakespeare as a source seems to never run dry. When Akira Kurosawa, arguably the greatest Japanese filmmaker of all time, released his epic battle film *Ran* in 1985, he readily acknowledged that it was based on *King Lear*. Some critics believe that Orson Welles's *Chimes at Midnight* is the greatest *Lear* adaptation, but who is to say?

Why do film artists repeatedly turn back to Shakespeare? It could be that he took care to speak to everyone, and perhaps even to the ages. His friend and contemporary Ben Jonson spoke of the Bard's desire to create art in a time when most playwrights simply wanted packed houses and full purses. Plus, Shakespeare's stories *work*. Hollywood is largely a copycat town.

The long-term view works well in Hollywood. With films being perhaps the most collaborative of all the arts, writers must be willing to listen and adapt, as was true for Shakespeare. Be willing to dig deep, and find out how things really are. It worked for him.

It's Not for Us _____

If you have written plays or acted in them, you're used to stage directions "stage right" and "stage left." Don't use those in a screenplay. The first film actors were from the stage, but screenwriting has its own rules. One big one is that actors and directors don't like the writer telling them where to go.

Shakespeare's Log Lines

When you are asked to describe your screenplay, you will be asked for the "high concept" or (more likely) the *log line*. This means, can you describe what your movie is about in 25 words or less? Generally, if you can't lay out your story in a few sentences, you probably don't have your plot well conceived. This is one reason why in Hollywood it has become common practice to combine two well-known movies in describing a new property. For example, *Freddy vs. Jason* combined two serial killers from separate movie franchises.

It's Not for Us

If you don't think Shakespeare was forced to rewrite, pick up The Oxford Shakespeare *The Complete Works* and study it. The editors, Stanley Wells and Gary Taylor, went to great pains to explain the Shakespearean writing process, and presented text at the end of some plays that had been cut from other versions.

By and large, adaptation from other sources is how many films come about. Someone compares a plot to some successful film and the person who can "green light" the picture (that is, approve the financing) decides that lightning is most likely to strike again in a similar place. They'll tell you they want it to be original, just not *too* original. The box office receipts (they think) depend on it.

The following list shows my interpretation of some of Shakespeare's plays, expressed in log line terms. One of them might help you come up with your own saleable variation or spark a new idea altogether, such as *Two Gentlemen of Venus*. It can't hurt to study the plays; people have successfully stolen from Shakespeare for ages. If you are not familiar with his plot lines, here are some examples:

- *The Taming of the Shrew.* Against a backdrop of social intrigues, a fortune-hunter named Petruchio woos and wins the extremely difficult beauty, Katherine.

- *Richard III.* This play's dark examination of greed and power is based on historical facts of the cutthroat, bloody rise to the throne by a man absorbed in his own insanity.

- *Love's Labour Lost.* Four men, a king and three friends, vow to spend three years improving themselves while avoiding female relationships. The arrival of the princess of France with three of her beautiful ladies complicates this decision in comedic fashion.

- *A Midsummer Night's Dream.* As the duke of Athens prepares to wed the queen of the Amazons, two young men fall in love with the same girl, complicated by another girl jilted by one of the men. Into this mix is a quarrel between the king and queen of the fairies.

- *The Merchant of Venice.* Love is more valuable than worldly things in this tale of a suitor of a young woman required by her father's will either to choose correctly between love and caskets of gold, lead, and silver.

♦ *Julius Caesar.* This study of the assassination of a great leader and the motivations of the conspirators involved was based on histories of the famous Roman general and ruler.

♦ *As You Like It.* This contrast between courtly life and country living centers on two royal maidens, Rosalind (disguised as a boy) and her cousin, Celia, who fall in love with unexpected suitors.

♦ *Hamlet.* To revenge his father's murder by his uncle, a prince feigns madness and kills his uncle's advisor. Caught and banished to England, he alters a letter ordering his execution, resulting in his captors' death instead; then he returns and kills his uncle.

All this brings us once again to the movie *Shakespeare in Love.* At the close of the film, young Will Shakespeare has lost his lover, Viola, after unexpectedly winning the favor of the queen of England, with much thanks to Viola's efforts. As he says his goodbye to Viola, they discuss his next, unwritten play.

When Viola de Lesseps is gone, Shakespeare picks up a pen and begins to write scenes that we see onscreen: a ship goes down and all are lost but one girl, who makes it to shore and walks alone across a wide beach toward a waiting forest. Then we see young Will's handwriting as he gives the heroine of his new play, *Twelfth Night*, the name Viola.

William Shakespeare wrote constantly, despite emotional upsets or successes. He drew from many sources to create his great works—other plays, legends, folk tales, and real history—and he wrote from his own loves, longings, and disappointments. Write, as he did, about things that matter to people, and you're more likely to do well. Otherwise, you may find that people view your work like the line from *Macbeth*: "full of sound and fury, signifying nothing."

The Least You Need to Know

♦ More than 500 films have been drawn from the works of the Bard, so don't be afraid to borrow from Shakespeare. Even if someone has already based a film on a Shakespearean work, you can almost bet it's safe to do so again.

♦ An unexplored facet of any famous person's life is ripe material for a screenplay, à la *Shakespeare in Love.*

♦ Do thorough research before starting a fact-based screenplay, using resources such as the Internet Movie Database at www.imdb.com.

◆ Movies are moving pictures, so in most cases, be sparing on the dialogue and concentrate on the action.

◆ When you can describe your movie in 25 words or less, you probably have a well-conceived plot and can write a better screenplay.

Birth of the Movies

In This Chapter

- ◆ Storytelling traditions around the world
- ◆ Listen to the great playwrights
- ◆ Great storytellers through the centuries
- ◆ The brothers Lumière and other lights of Europe
- ◆ The influence of Thomas Edison
- ◆ How Hollywood was born

In September 2003, Iranian director Babak Payami caused an international controversy at the Venice Film Festival when he arrived with only a digital copy of his *Silence Between Two Thoughts*. Islamic fundamentalist authorities in his country had confiscated the original film, which was about a Taliban soldier ordered to rape a female prisoner so that she could not enter paradise. They also prevented another Iranian director, Abolfazl Jalili, from traveling to Venice to show his film *Abjad (The First Letter)*, which was about a Muslim boy who falls in love with a Jewish girl. Such is the power of film, even over governments. Don't forget that when you write your movie.

Skip's Tips

Your Name

Audiences love to see characters undergo a *catharsis*, a term Aristotle used to describe purification or purging. When characters undergo a transformation in which egocentric notions are shattered and they restructure their lives, it can result in a classic.

In the last few decades, great filmmakers have popped up all over the world. In 1980, an international hit was *The Gods Must Be Crazy*, in which Xixo, a bushman in the Kalahari, sees his village go crazy over a Coke bottle dropped from a passing airplane. He decides to return the bottle to the gods and in doing so encounters an outside world that seems insane. The movie was voted Most Popular Film at the Montreal World Film Festival. It made more than $50 million in the United States, even with a bushman in the lead role who had had no contact with modern civilization before being cast in the film!

The Worldwide Storytelling Tradition

The Australian aboriginals believe in "dreamtime," a spiritual dimension that surrounds all things and creates the reality that we live in. They believe that the creators of the dreamtime project their dream onto our physical dimension, and their dream is our reality. Before writing existed, such stories of origin were passed orally from generation to generation. A great number of top stars and filmmakers have come from Australia and New Zealand in recent years, telling their own stories and others with worldwide impact. Hollywood may still be a geographical location, but as far as filmic storytelling goes, Hollywood is a state of mind akin to the aboriginals' "dreamtime." With the *Lord of the Rings* movies, no one has had a larger impact on international box office than New Zealand's Peter Jackson. Even in animation, it's not just the United States that turns out hits. *Happy Feet* (2006) from Australia's George Miller, made $379 million worldwide.

Hollywood Heat

YOUR NAME

Randall Wallace's script *Braveheart*, about a thirteenth-century Scottish warrior, took in more than $200 million. It won several Oscars, including Best Writing, Screenplay Written Directly for the Screen. And when its director and star, Mel Gibson, made the crucifixion story *The Passion of the Christ*, it was a worldwide success. Who says "period pieces" don't sell?

Influences of the Great Playwrights

Although William Shakespeare (see Chapter 2) has been more influential on movies than any other writer, the work of several other playwrights is worth noting. The satirical plays of Molière, France's greatest comic dramatist, dealt with serious themes and paved the way for experimental theater. His most famous play, *Le Tartuffe*, written in 1664, dealt with religious hypocrisy and got banned from the stage because of the Roman Catholic Church's influence. *Tartuffe* is a five-act play in verse, about a scoundrel masquerading as a holy man who is taken in by a rich family. Tartuffe's real intent is to have an affair with his benefactor's wife and snatch his fortune. Did you see Paul Mazursky's *Down and Out in Beverly Hills* (1986)? It was a remake of Jean Renoir's *Boudu Saved from Drowning* (1932), which came from a René Fauchois play. It seems rather obvious what inspired the play, particularly because Molière is recognized as the father of French comedic theater.

It's Not for Us

Beginning screenwriters *must* learn the differences in format of stage plays and screenplays. Unless you are submitting a stage play to a movie production company for consideration, your work will likely not even be read unless it is presented in accepted screenplay style (covered later in this book). And in case you haven't noticed, a lot less dialogue is used, too.

During the Renaissance and into the nineteenth century, writers rarely specialized. Johann Wolfgang von Goethe was an eighteenth-century German dramatist, novelist, poet, and scientist whose work may have been more influential on early German film than any other. His great dramatic poem *Faust* is about a German doctor who sold his soul to the devil in exchange for knowledge, youth, and magic powers. *Faust* continues to fascinate audiences and has been filmed several times.

As serious dramatists go, however, Norwegian Henrik Ibsen was likely the most influential playwright of his time. One drama researcher claimed that all modern drama owed homage to Ibsen. Perhaps Ibsen's work has had lasting influence because he wrote often about characters who feel that they are missing out on life to such a degree that they feel they are in a living death. His *Enemy of the People* was most recently a feature film in Denmark in 2005.

In *Hedda Gabler*, Ibsen shows us people who trample others to reach their own goals. He creates such deep psychological portraits that he became known as the "Freud of the theater." In fact, Freud himself used Ibsen's character Rebekka West to draw a psychological portrait of a victim of incest.

There's that Oedipus complex again! You can't get away from it. **Voltaire, one** of the great French writers, wrote his first major play, *Oedipe*, while in **prison in 1717.** Guess what it was about.

The most influential Russian playwright in pre-cinema days was Anton Pavlovich Chekhov. (Yes, the character in the original *Star Trek* TV series was named after him.) Like Ibsen, Chekhov's plots deal with loneliness and wasted lives. He also concentrated heavily on internal conflict, an innovation that had worldwide influence. Almost every serious actor has performed in a production of *The Seagull, Uncle Vanya,* or *The Cherry Orchard.* And we shouldn't neglect to mention an earlier influential Russian, Alexander Pushkin, author of *Boris Godunov* and other works. Two centuries before the world saw the award-winning movie *Amadeus,* Pushkin told the story in *Mozart and Salieri.*

> **Skip's Tips**
>
> *Your Name*
>
> Chekhov believed that if you had a gun hanging over a fireplace, the gun should be used during the play. If it is not used, don't write it in. Such attention to detail goes a long way in writing screenplays.

Many influential playwrights were also novelists. Victor Hugo, recognized as the most important French Romantic writer of the nineteenth century, gave us *The Hunchback of Notre Dame* and *Les Misérables,* but how many people can name one of his plays?

The reverse is true for Scottish playwright Sir James Matthew Barrie. Certainly you've seen a movie of his play *Peter Pan,* about the boy who refuses to grow up. If you saw *Finding Neverland* in 2004, you're familiar with this imaginative work.

Last but not least, it's reasonable to say that cinema was influenced by British writer W. S. Gilbert. His comic operas with composer Sir Arthur Seymour Sullivan such as *H.M.S. Pinafore, The Pirates of Penzance,* and *The Mikado* were the precursors of movie musicals. The 1999 movie *Topsy-Turvy,* an improvisation about a strained relationship between the duo, resulted in numerous awards and accolades.

Authors from Centuries Past: The Great Storytellers

Hollywood never tires of classics. A major film from Turner Network Television in 2000 was *Don Quixote,* starring John Lithgow. That didn't stop director Terry Gilliam from planning *The Man Who Killed Don Quixote* later in the year, with Johnny Depp starring as Sancho Panza. Miguel de Cervantes wrote the classic book from which these films were derived 400 years ago. And if you think *Pirates of the Caribbean: The Curse of the Black Pearl* and the two sequels that followed weren't influenced by *Treasure Island,* read Robert Louis Stevenson's great book.

The remainder of this section deals with eighteenth- and nineteenth-century American and European writers who influenced the beginnings of film. Let's start with the author of a book whose theme is by far the most popular in Hollywood. This probably has Freudian implications because the subject is vampires! (After meeting a few Hollywood producers, you'll understand …)

Bram Stoker, the author of *Dracula*, held a number of jobs and was published often before *Dracula* emerged in 1897. It was a worldwide success. Although the author met many famous people, including American presidents and Mark Twain, his name did not gain equal recognition. Perhaps Francis Ford Coppola took that into consideration when he made *Bram Stoker's Dracula* in 1992.

Skip's Tips _____

Want to try adapting a classic novel into a screenplay? You can freely download the full text of many classic books, thanks to Project Gutenberg, at www.gutenberg.org/wiki/Main_Page.

More movies have been made about vampires than any other subject. A search of the Internet Movie Database (www.imdb.com) reveals more than 200 matches that have the word "vampire" in the title, and more than 100 entries with the word "Dracula," including the TV series "Mr. and Mrs. Dracula." Roughly 600 vampire films have been made worldwide. Just because many other writers have used vampires as the subject of screenplays doesn't mean that you should not. You simply need a new twist, like 2003's *Underworld*, which pitted vampires against werewolves, and its 2006 sequel *Underworld: Evolution*.

Ah, but the movies love all monsters, such as Mary Shelley's *Frankenstein*, a novel inspired by a party game. The Frankenstein monster has been the subject of many successful films, but vampire movies are a better bet. For example, the 1994 *Frankenstein* starring Robert De Niro was a box office disappointment.

Even though Jane Austen died in 1817, her novels have been adapted into several miniseries from the British Broadcasting Company (BBC) and films from American movie studios. *Clueless*, the breakthrough movie for Alicia Silverstone, was based on the Austen novel *Emma*. Austen's social intrigues were so popular that she was listed in *People* magazine's "Most Intriguing People" in 1996.

A contemporary of Austen, Scottish writer Sir Walter Scott, is generally regarded as the progenitor of historical novels. His *Ivanhoe*, published in 1819, is a repeatedly popular movie subject. Scott's *Rob Roy* (1818) inspired a 1995 film of the same name. The great Scott must have anticipated Hollywood studio accounting methods when he penned these lines: "O, what a tangled web we weave, when first we practice to deceive!"

Stories from famous authors of the eighteenth or nineteenth century continually resurface on film. Director Tim Burton created a gory visual masterpiece with *Sleepy Hollow* in 1999, based on Washington Irving's *The Legend of Sleepy Hollow*. Walt Disney's earlier animated version fascinated Burton as a child. Similarly, although Herman Melville's *Moby Dick* became a classic film directed by John Huston, it was remade as a 1999 TNT cable movie. Louisa May Alcott's *Little Women* has been filmed eight times and it has been a TV series twice.

Skip's Tips

Film tastes constantly evolve, and you must keep up. As Oscar Wilde said in *Soul of Man Under Socialism*, "The only thing that one really knows about human nature is that it changes. The systems that fail are those that rely on the permanency of human nature, and not its growth and development."

In the 1960s, producer Roger Corman made a mini-industry of films based on Edgar Allan Poe works, such as *The Raven* (1963). Poe's works have been put to film more than 70 times.

One author gave rise to a virtual film studio of material. Sir Arthur Conan Doyle was the author of more than 50 books, not all of them featuring his greatest creation, Sherlock Holmes. The 1905 film *Adventures of Sherlock Holmes* helped establish the detective genre of film, and more than 70 Sherlock Holmes movies and TV series have been made. Holmes is always interesting.

Before reading all the descriptions of great books turned into movies, you may have felt that the classics are what Mark Twain said they are: "Something that everybody wants to have read and nobody wants to read." Almost 60 of Twain's works have been set to film. His *Huckleberry Finn* has appeared in films almost 20 times, about the same number of appearances as Huck's buddy Tom Sawyer, and in 2008 producer Jeff Dowd was planning another one.

The most filmed author who wrote in English is Charles Dickens, with more than 100 novel and story adaptations. His *A Christmas Carol* has been seen onscreen more than 30 times. Much of Dickens's work deals with children in dire circumstances. Paralleling his own life, Dickens's self-made characters triumph over meager beginnings, and his novels offer poignant commentary on society.

The works of other English authors contributed greatly to film because they were works of high adventure that adapted well. The works of Robert Louis Stevenson, author of *Treasure Island*, have been filmed almost 80 times. Stevenson's *The Strange Case of Dr. Jekyll and Mr. Hyde*, first filmed in 1908, has inspired more than 20 films, including the Julia Roberts movie *Mary Reilly*.

Rudyard Kipling, an Englishman born in Bombay, India, had an Indian nurse in his youth who taught him the language and folklore of India. Kipling shared these stories with the world and inspired the massive Indian film industry, known today as "Bollywood." Kipling's characters have appeared in almost 30 films, including a new *Gunga Din* in 2000. Remember the most popular subject for films? The first Kipling property filmed was *The Vampire*, in 1910.

In the adventure vein, several French authors were influential on early films and have continued influence. The works of Victor Hugo have been put to film almost 50 times, most noticeably his *The Hunchback of Notre Dame*. Even more successful is Alexandre Dumas père. (His son, known as Alexandre Dumas fils, gave us *The Lady of the Camelias*, a.k.a. *Camille*, which has been filmed more than 20 times in several different languages.) Alexandre Dumas the father is perhaps most popular for *The Count of Monte Cristo* and *The Three Musketeers*. More than 70 films have been made from the elder Dumas's works.

Skip's Tips

The great thing about a modern adaptation of a classic book is this—you don't have to pay anyone for the rights. That's one reason why the Hallmark Company has adapted so many classics and why you see stories adapted from Shakespearean plays and classic novels. Just don't think it guarantees you an automatic audience. It all depends on the script, and how it is filmed. And then, on distribution and audience whims.

H. G. Wells produced more than 80 books, including science-fantasy novels that became films, such as *The Time Machine* and *The Invisible Man*. More interesting as far as Hollywood is concerned is his 1898 novel *The War of the Worlds*. When it was dramatized on radio in 1938, a panic was created on the east coast of the United States when thousands believed that an alien attack was actually occurring. The incident propelled producer, director, and writer Orson Welles into a Hollywood contract. And you've probably seen Steven Spielberg's more recent version.

Speaking of science fiction, let's "cut" back to France. More than 50 movies have been based on the works of Jules Verne, who is the father of the genre. You're probably familiar with his *Journey to the Center of the Earth* or *20,000 Leagues Under the Sea*. Both have been filmed more than once. You may know his *Around the World in 80 Days* or *Mysterious Island*, but how about *Le Voyage dans la Lune* (*A Trip to the Moon*)? This 14-minute 1902 short, directed by fellow Frenchman Georges Méliès, came from a Verne novel about a group of men who travel to the moon in a capsule shot from a giant cannon. That film marked the birth of "special effects."

European Originals: The Brothers Lumière and Other Lights

Who invented "the movies"? Well, the experience might have begun on December 28, 1895, in a basement in Paris, France, that held an audience of 35 people. This is where two brothers, Auguste and Louis Lumière, debuted the Lumière Cinématograph, the first machine to combine the functions of camera and projector in one, allowing the projection of film onto a screen. Ten short films, each less than a minute, were screened for the unsuspecting first movie patrons. The first film seen was *The Shift Ends at the Lumière Factory in Lyon*, and the last was *La Mer* (*The Sea*). In two years, the Lumières made more than 1,000 documentaries.

Skip's Tips

Your Name

Don't be satisfied with a thimble-size version of film history. To learn more about the Lumières and their other inventions such as the 3D cinema, see www.lumiere.org. The website is only in French, but you can translate it via the Web.

Perhaps the most important person that the Lumières impressed in 1895 was a professional magician who fell in love with the new "moving pictures." As Georges Méliès began filming he discovered, by accident, moviemaking techniques such as dissolve, fade-in, and fade-out, and special effects such as double exposure and superimposition. This helped the documentary style give way to narrative films. Méliès, who was trained in classic eighteenth-century theater and so composed his films in scene form, made more than 500 films that influenced filmmakers around the world. Charlie Chaplin called Méliès "the alchemist of light," while the most important of early American directors, D. W. Griffith, said that he owed Méliès "everything." In 1931, France recognized Méliès with the Legion of Honor and a rent-free apartment in Paris, where he and his actress wife, Jeanne, lived happily ever after.

Pathé, one of France's first film companies, was initially formed by Charles Pathé and his brothers Émile, Jacques, and Théophile to sell phonographs. Charles began producing short films in 1901, and by 1902 he had an assembly-style movie studio. By 1908, the company had facilities in Budapest, Calcutta, Kiev, and Singapore and was selling twice as many films in the United States as all the American companies combined. Although the 1953 American movie *Houdini* starring Tony Curtis was a hit, we know what the real master of escape looked like in action thanks to *Houdini, the Handcuff King and Prison Breaker*, a Pathé film. The Pathé brothers also created the world's first weekly newsreel, a weekly filmed summary of news events that was shown in movie theaters.

Thomas Edison and the Monopoly That Didn't Work

"I am experimenting upon an instrument which does for the eye what the phonograph does for the ear, which is the recording and reproduction of things in motion," said Thomas Alva Edison in 1888. But did he really invent the medium of film?

We read mentions of early projectors such as Skladanowsky's bioscope and the Eidoloscope (developed by Dickson, Lauste, and Rector, used for paying audiences in Chicago four months before the initial Lumière screening in Paris). Thomas Edison's laboratory was responsible for the Kinetograph motion picture camera and the Kinetoscope motion picture viewer, with Edison's assistant William Dickson doing the most work. But that's like saying that Mickey Mouse became popular worldwide thanks to someone other than the mouse's originator, Walt Disney.

Dickson also constructed the "Black Maria," a tar paper-sealed studio structure with a large skylight that sat on a revolving track to follow available sunlight. In West Orange, New Jersey, the Edison Manufacturing Company built the machines and produced films that set the world standard. The studio was the first to use the 35mm film from George Eastman with four perforations on each side of each frame, still in use today. Lastly, with regard to the question of "first," a Library of Congress "American Memory" collection of Edison films includes a camera test made in 1891.

Edison was early to realize the drawing power of celebrity. One early film made at his Long Island estate featured Mark Twain, but the first famous person he put on film was strongman Eugene Sandow in 1894. Edison filmed Native American performers from Buffalo Bill Cody's "Wild West Show" and a famous pair of boxing sisters. His company made what may have been the first commercial, for Admiral Cigarettes in 1897. Edison's portable camera made it possible to film action scenes and news events, such as the first war films covering the Spanish-American War that made Theodore Roosevelt and his Rough Riders famous. Edison also first brought film into the home with his Home Projecting Kinetoscope in 1911.

When the public appetite for narrative films grew, Edison's assistant, Edwin S. Porter (the first American studio director), gave the company the classic *The Great Train Robbery* (1903) and other dramas. Under Porter's guidance, when foreign films began flooding the American market, The Edison Company concentrated on American stories such as *Uncle Tom's Cabin* and kept actors busy. Porter's contributions are as important as any. For example, he gave us the close-up and pioneered film editing techniques.

Production companies in the early days often specialized; for example, the special effects "trick" movies came from Vitagraph. Edison, who held more than 1,200 patents, could not dominate the film business. The competition was fierce, and by 1909, Edwin S. Porter was out of a job, mostly because Edison and some others made a big mistake, one that led to the birth of Hollywood.

A Place Called Hollywood: How Tinseltown Was Born

In 1909, Edison and several other companies formed the Motion Picture Patents Company trust to thwart independent producers. This resulted in a government antitrust action that broke up the monopoly in 1917. The Edison Company went out of business. William Selig of Chicago owned one company that survived the monopoly's pressures. In 1909, Selig faked a film about President Theodore Roosevelt's safari to Africa and released a film of "Teddy" killing a lion that coincided with news of the real event in newspapers. Selig also gave us animated cartoons, Westerns with early cowboy movie star Tom Mix, and the first movie serial, *The Adventures of Kathlyn*. In 1907, he moved part of his company to Hollywood, and in 1909, opened the first L.A. studio.

The words *Hollywood* and *film* are synonymous, however, due to Cecil B. De Mille. In 1913, De Mille planned to shoot *The Squaw Man*, from a Western novel, in Phoenix, Arizona. The snow-capped mountains there didn't fit the story, so De Mille and his codirector, Oscar C. Appel, took the train west. The line ended in Hollywood. When they got off, a legend got going.

The Least You Need to Know

- Great film stories can come from anywhere in the world.

- Mythologies of indigenous peoples and tales of ancient history can be the source for highly successful films.

- The most popular subject of movies is the vampire.

- The works of eighteenth- and nineteenth-century playwrights and authors offer a seemingly endless supply of movie source material.

- Science-fiction films hold the majority in all-time box office bonanza movies, a trend that may not end soon.

- No one is truly certain who invented the movies, but we do know how Hollywood was born.

Chapter 4

From Scenario to Screenplay

In This Chapter

- ◆ Scenarios before screenplays
- ◆ Women writers once ruled Hollywood
- ◆ When sound came
- ◆ Everyone moves to Hollywood
- ◆ The genre evolution
- ◆ Hollywood's greatest year

On Highland Avenue in Hollywood, across from the Hollywood Bowl, sits a historical landmark, the studio used by Jesse L. Lasky and Cecil B. De Mille when they made *The Squaw Man*. Down at the corner of Highland Avenue and Hollywood Boulevard is the Academy of Motion Picture Arts and Sciences and its Kodak Theatre. Across the way is Disney's refurbished El Capitan movie theater, and farther along is the Roosevelt Hotel; the first Academy Awards were held in the hotel's Blossom Room.

Hollywood takes itself seriously these days, with a billion dollars spent on renovation in recent years. When you watch the Academy Awards on television in the Kodak Theatre, it's Hollywood at its best like never before. (For your own guided tour of ceremonies past, see www.oscars.org.)

Hollywood Heat _____

Deida Wilcox and her husband divided their southern California ranch into parcels, and in 1903, a village was incorporated under the ranch's name, Hollywood. The Hollywood sign, however, was not their doing. Reading "Hollywoodland," it was built to advertise a real estate development. When a despondent actress committed suicide by jumping from the final "d" (the thirteenth letter), the last four letters were torn down. And that's the story of Hollywood and its sign.

The Scenarists: How Screenwriting Began

Before silent films, crank-operated machines called mutoscopes used the same eye-tricking principle employed by flip books. A customer dropped a nickel in a slot and turned the crank, and photographs mounted on an axis turned, giving the illusion of motion. They lasted about a minute. A manufacturer of the devices, The American Mutoscope and Biograph Company, was an early antagonist of Thomas Edison when he refused them a regular supply of film, but they later joined him in the Motion Picture Patents Company that was broken up by government antitrust actions.

William Dickson, so instrumental in Edison's success, joined the American Mutoscope and Biograph Company in 1896, and the New York company became a spawning ground for silent film greats. Dickson helped develop the company's American Biograph, which used nonperforated film of a larger size than was customary, resulting in a sharper image. This drew talent to the studio that included director D. W. Griffith, director and producer Mack Sennett, actress Mary Pickford, and many others.

In 1920, seven years after De Mille made his first film there, Hollywood turned out 800 films a year. Because of the difficulties in handling non-perforated film, the most important person in those days was the camera/projector operator. What mattered most was the filming and handling of the film, a series of scenes on a "one-reeler" that averaged about 10 minutes. It wasn't until 1911 that directors began pushing for two-reel films.

When writers were employed, they described the scenes and were known as "scenarists." Other duties included composing snips of dialogue or description that was displayed on cards interspersed in the film. The writer wasn't that important. Of course, these days some producers and directors say the same thing!

Women Writers Ruled: Frances Marion and the Scenario Queens

Women screenwriters have complained about a lack of opportunity in a business whose main consumers are purported to be males aged 18 to 34. Oddly enough, in early Hollywood, women screenwriters ruled.

Cecil B. De Mille has been called "the most successful filmmaker of them all." He knew what stirred emotions. This "founder of Hollywood" discovered stars such as Gary Cooper, Paulette Goddard, Gloria Swanson, and Charlton Heston. Remember Swanson's "I'm ready for my close-up, Mr. De Mille!" from *Sunset Boulevard?* De Mille's films are legendary, but did you know about his "harem"? Every important creative person on De Mille's production staff was a woman. Actress/scenarist Jeanie Macpherson was known as De Mille's "write hand." De Mille hired her as his stenographer, but it wasn't long before they cowrote a script, *The Captive* (1915). They collaborated for 30 years, through silent epics such as his first (silent) *The Ten Commandments* in 1923 and into the sound era.

Skip's Tips

Hollywood has terms for everything. You might think that *Enchanted* was simply a great "date movie," but chances are good that Hollywood movie executives would call a funny, touching movie like that one a "chick flick." If you add in the "women in jeopardy" genre, chick flicks have their own cable networks such as the Lifetime Network.

If Cecil B. De Mille was the founder of Hollywood, Alice Guy Blaché was the Mother of Cinema. She was the first female producer and film director. Some believe she, not Georges Méliès, directed the first narrative film. Blaché was involved in almost 700 films, 400 in Europe and 300 in the United States. Her first, a one-minute fairy tale called *La Fée aux Choux* (*The Cabbage Fairy*), was apparently made a few months before Méliès's first movie.

Blaché got into film early, working for the Gaumont organization as a secretary. Seeking funding, Louis Lumière introduced his motion picture camera to Gaumont, but Blaché was the only staff member who could see any use for the gadget. Her first film was popular, and she became *the* filmmaker for Gaumont, developing many "trick" film techniques. By 1912, she had moved to the United States and formed the Solax Company, which turned out more than 300 films. Blaché left the United States and went back to France in 1922. With no copies of her films, she had trouble working in Europe. When Blaché was almost 80, France recognized her as the first woman filmmaker and gave her the French Legion of Honor.

Skip's Tips

Your Name

If you find women screenwriters fascinating, read the memoirs of Frances Marion, *Off with Their Heads! A Serio-Comic Tale of Hollywood* (Macmillan). Another great read is *Without Lying Down: Frances Marion and the Powerful Women of Early Hollywood* (Lisa Drew Books/Scribner), by Cari Beauchamp. And don't miss the great website at www.reelwomen.com.

As writers go, Anita Loos was Hollywood's first golden girl. After she wrote a hit for actress Mary Pickford, director D. W. Griffith assigned Loos to silent star Douglas Fairbanks. She wrote a number of hits for Fairbanks. In 1925, she wrote *Gentlemen Prefer Blondes*, a hit novel about a "flapper" party girl. A stage version and the script for a Paramount movie followed. When "talkies" began, Loos wrote memorable films such as *San Francisco*, starring Clark Gable, and Jean Harlow's last film, *Saratoga*. Her last script was a 1953 musical remake of *Gentlemen Prefer Blondes*.

Someone with similar sentiments but more important to film history was writer/director Lois Weber. She made sensational films such as *Hypocrites* (1914), which featured a nude woman as "Naked Truth." If a movie had no moral point, Weber wasn't interested. She was the first woman to write, produce, direct, and star in a major feature. She mentored many filmmakers, including director John Ford. Unfortunately, she finished her career as a script doctor.

Frances Marion was the most prolific screenwriter of all time. Introduced to films by Lois Weber in 1915, Marion became a close friend of superstar Mary Pickford and wrote 10 Pickford movies, including *Rebecca of Sunnybrook Farm* (1917). She may have written as many as 200 films, but we don't know for sure because she wrote under pseudonyms. Marion wrote silent classics such as *The Wind* (1928), starring Lillian Gish. When sound arrived, she penned the Garbo starrer *Anna Christie* (1930) and won Academy Awards for writing *The Big House* (1930) and *The Champ* (1931). Frances Marion wrote 137 produced screenplays. For a long time, she was the highest-paid screenwriter in history. It is almost certain that no screenwriter will surpass her credits.

The Transition to Sound

Al Jolson made a name for himself wearing "blackface" makeup (meant to look like an African American but, in reality, a slur). He starred in a number of Broadway musicals and was a popular radio performer and recording artist. Warner Brothers hired him to sing three songs in the experimental sound film *April Showers* and then again in *The Jazz Singer* in 1927 (the first feature film with synchronized sound). When he began speaking onscreen, audiences gasped. Jolson's phrase "You ain't seen nothin' yet!" became the popular slogan of the day. Stunned by "talkies," one screenwriter remarked that the "international language" of silent films was dead. Charlie Chaplin, known worldwide as "The Little Tramp," hated talkies. In 1929, Chaplin said: "Talkies are … ruining the great beauty of silence. They are defeating the meaning of the screen." Chaplin, who made his first film for Mack Sennett in 1913, was so opposed to sound films that he didn't make one until 1940, when he gave us *The Great Dictator.* Playwright George Bernard Shaw called Chaplin "the only genius developed in motion pictures," but Buster Keaton and even Harold Lloyd were equally inventive. If you want to learn how to convey an emotional arc in a film sequence with pictures alone—which is technically the proper use of a *montage*—study some Chaplin silent films.

After Chaplin died, his fourth wife, Oona, revealed that her husband had rehearsed all his bits on film before shooting them "officially." It was the precursor of training by video playback. Chaplin scrupulously preserved all his films, including the rehearsals and outtakes. Any writer wanting to write comedy would be wise to study Chaplin's films.

Skip's Tips

If you want to write an action comedy, study Charlie Chaplin, Buster Keaton, and Harold Lloyd, who all methodically planned their stunts. Turn on a camera, act out a scene, and then play it back with the sound off. If you don't laugh, it might not be funny.

Script Notes

A **montage** is a series of images without dialogue. Russian Sergei Eisenstein used his "montage of attractions" to elicit emotions on several levels. To him, the clash of two images resulted in an unseen third emotion (such as thesis, antithesis, and synthesis).

Understanding film history is imperative to good writing. At one time, the "hats" of stars, directors, and producers could be one and the same. With the advent of digital filmmaking, that day has to some degree returned. Study the classics of early stars, and you'll write better films, no matter who shoots them.

Hollywood Heat

Hollywood filmmakers continually rework old scenes into new scripts. In *The Untouchables* (1987) when a baby in a carriage goes jolting down a flight of steps during a shootout. It's taken from Eisenstein's classic "Odessa Steps" scene from *Bronenosets Potyomkin* (*The Battleship Potemkin*, 1925).

These days, as in early Hollywood, you get more notice if you do more than write screenplays. Beginning writers rarely look at history to see that long careers happened because of flexibility and a thorough knowledge of the entire moviemaking process.

Perhaps the greatest director who ever lived, John Ford, made more than 600 films. He was also a director, producer, and writer, but when he first came to Hollywood, he toiled as a cameraman and a film editor, and even did stunts. Classic Ford films include *Stagecoach* (1939), starring John Wayne; *The Grapes of Wrath* (1940), starring Henry Fonda; and *The Quiet Man* (1952), also starring John Wayne. The last script credit Ford received was for *3 Bad Men* (1926). Ford must have seen the writing in the sand. After 1926, he mostly directed and produced. Like other Hollywood pros such as Raoul Walsh, Tay Garnett, and Frank Capra, Ford made a smooth transition from silents to sound by being flexible *and* talented. Others, such as Chaplin, did not fare well because they were convinced that the art of film should not be sullied by synchronized sound. Now, with digital filmmaking and movies shown on the Internet, inflexible writers unwilling to learn new media may not survive.

Hollywood, the World, and Migrating Writers

As the movie industry grew in Hollywood, Germans made silent classics such as the vampire thriller *Nosferatu*, by F. W. Murnau (1922), and the futuristic *Metropolis*, by Fritz Lang (1926). Lang's *Dr. Mabuse, der Spieler* (*The Gambler*; 1922) was likely the first "film noir." It was produced by Erich Pommer, who also produced the joint English/German 1925 production *The Pleasure Garden*, directed by the young Alfred Hitchcock. Germans with the biggest impact on Hollywood were good friends Ernst Lubitsch and Billy Wilder, who became legends when they migrated to the United States.

European filmmakers pushed their American counterparts to higher levels. In France, director Abel Gance worked with a 103-year-old collaborator named Simon Feldman to craft his masterpiece, *Napoleon* (1927). Having had the pleasure of seeing a restored *Napoleon* in its complete, 17-reel, triple-screen "Polyvision" accompanied by a full symphony orchestra, I can tell you personally that it has held up magnificently.

Skip's Tips

Many common terms originated in Hollywood. The word "corny" was coined in the pages of *Variety*. To better understand Hollywood expressions, see the "Slanguage" dictionary (do a search to find it at www.variety.com).

Audiences in India saw silent movies to live Indian music, perhaps because dancing often fit into the film's story. Current Indian movies still have plenty of dancing, too. In fact, they sometimes look like old MGM musicals, a form that Hollywood has mostly abandoned.

Scandinavian filmmakers gave us moody lighting from Hamlet's home, Denmark. Swedish filmmakers, perhaps influenced by their Norwegian neighbor Henrik Ibsen, made socially conscious movies, which influenced the young director-to-be, Ingmar Bergman. They're still dark; the most prominent Scandinavian filmmaker today is Lars von Trier, who repeatedly chooses America-bashing as a theme.

Musicals, comedies, gangster flicks, and horror movies dominated U.S. screens in the 1930s under the "star system" of actors on contract with U.S. movie studios. In Europe, influential filmmakers fell under the domination of political tyrants. Adolf Hitler used Leni Riefenstahl's *Triumph of the Will* (1935) to glorify the Nazi Party, while Sergei Eisenstein exalted Russian communism under the iron fist of dictator Joseph Stalin. A mass migration of European talent fled to the United States. Brave French filmmaker Jean Renoir made the antiwar *Grand Illusion* (1937), while English directors turned out documentaries, sharing with the world the mounting troubles on the continent.

Hollywood Heat

In the days before air conditioning, transom windows were built over office doors for air circulation on hot days. These windows were left open when doors were locked. Aspiring writers would throw scripts over the transom. Scripts from unknowns are still occasionally referred to as "coming in over the transom."

Great American writers migrated to Hollywood to cash in on easy money. Broadway playwrights and working journalists made the journey west and struck gold. One of the most successful was Ben Hecht.

In 1925, he began turning out screenplays for Paramount every two to eight weeks, at $50,000 to $125,000 a script. In his 1954 book *A Child of the Century*, he said, "Hollywood held this double lure for me, tremendous sums of money for work that required no more effort than a game of pinochle."

Hecht's frequent writing partner, Charles MacArthur, also started as a journalist and later wrote plays. One of their most notable collaborations was *Twentieth Century* (1934), directed by Howard Hawks. One of the unaccredited writers on *Twentieth Century* was Preston Sturges, a former playwright whose name is synonymous with the term "screwball comedy." (More on that in the next section.)

It's Not for Us _____

Before you adapt a famous work into a screenplay, do some research. I know one writer who wrote an updated version of Fitzgerald's *The Great Gatsby* without gaining permission. His timing was unfortunate: a new production was already in progress, scheduled to air on a cable channel. You can often find out how to reach an author via www.authorsguild.org.

One great American writer notably never wrote directly for Hollywood. Eugene O'Neill is regarded as the father of modern American drama. He won the Nobel Prize for literature in 1936, and four of his plays won Pulitzer Prizes. Hollywood liked him immediately. O'Neill's play *Anna Christie* (1922) was made into a film in 1923 and again in 1930 with Greta Garbo starring. Perhaps O'Neill was simply too thoughtful a writer to work in Hollywood, or he might have stayed away because his daughter, Oona, married Charlie Chaplin!

After the Depression, Hollywood hit a boom that some refer to as its Golden Age. Primary among famous authors who arrived at this time was William Faulkner, winner of two Pulitzer Prizes and the Nobel Prize for Literature. Faulkner worked on many films, including five with director Howard Hawks. Their most interesting project was derived from the Ernest Hemingway novel *To Have and Have Not*. This 1944 film marks the only time in history that two Nobel Prize–winning authors have had their names onscreen in the same picture. The screenplay came about when Hawks bet Hemingway that he could make a good film out of Hemingway's worst novel.

Like William Faulkner, F. Scott Fitzgerald could not support himself with stories and novels. Much of Fitzgerald's Hollywood work went uncredited. For example, he was paid $2,904 for work on *Gone with the Wind* (1939). Fitzgerald detested Hollywood but liked its money.

How Genres Evolved: What's a Screwball Comedy, Anyway?

In 1935, when money was scarce, Hollywood studios that owned their own chains of theaters offered double bills with "A" films (the feature) and "B" films (cheaply made with lesser-known stars). Any script that could be shot with a minimal amount of locations and costume changes might make a B movie, and the Bs were a godsend to writers. Writing them was easy; competence was expected, not genius, and working writers didn't complain.

The screwball comedy was named after a baseball pitch that breaks the opposite direction of a curve ball. This type of 1930s picture had slapstick physical humor, sarcastic barbed dialogue, and wacky romance between the hero and the leading lady, who loathe each other in the beginning. Writer/director Preston Sturges, credited with films such as *Sullivan's Travels* (1941), is considered the screwball master. Post-Depression America loved seeing acerbic dialogue duels between stars, like William Powell and Myrna Loy in *The Thin Man* (1934), a B movie that turned into a giant hit, prompting several sequels and elevating its stars to A status. When World War II began, however, the world grew too serious for the screwball comedy.

> **Hollywood Heat**
>
> Are *El Mariachi*, *Reservoir Dogs*, or *Napoleon Dynamite* B movies? Most film-makers would say yes. These days, $10,000 buys you the equipment to make and edit a digital feature. Some of today's B films, like *The Blair Witch Project*, are multimillion-dollar moneymakers.

The Impact of 1939, Possibly Hollywood's Greatest Year

No year epitomizes Hollywood's Golden Age like 1939. There was a World's Fair in New York that year, showcasing the new wonders of television. At the movies, some of our greatest films were playing. The Academy Awards of 1940 did not limit its Best Picture category to five, so there will never be another lineup quite as great as the choices of 1939. In a ceremony hosted by Bob Hope in Los Angeles, the Best Picture category included these nominees:

Picture	Producer
Gone with the Wind	David O. Selznick
Dark Victory	David Lewis
Goodbye, Mr. Chips	Victor Saville
Love Affair	Leo McCarey
Mr. Smith Goes to Washington	Frank Capra
Ninotchka	Sidney Franklin
Of Mice and Men	Lewis Milestone
Stagecoach	Walter Wanger
The Wizard of Oz	Mervyn LeRoy
Wuthering Heights	Samuel Goldwyn

Gone with the Wind, set against the American Civil War, won Best Picture and seven other statuettes, including Best Writing, Screenplay. But to get there, producer Selznick went through 3 directors and 15 screenwriters!

But all things must pass. World War II was beginning, and the world would never again be the same. Writers from all over the world had helped create the Golden Age, but it was quickly gone.

The Least You Need to Know

- Compose your scenes as if they were for a silent movie. You'll get stronger action.

- The most successful screenwriter of all time was a woman, Frances Marion.

- People in Hollywood who have the longest and happiest careers are those who can adapt to changes.

- Hollywood's Golden Age owed much to the infusion of ideas from talented authors, journalists, and playwrights.

- 1939 is generally regarded as Hollywood's greatest year.

From the Big Screen to the Computer Screen

In This Chapter

- ◆ Post World War II: worldwide changes
- ◆ Television and *I Love Lucy* transform Hollywood
- ◆ Antiheroes and oddities
- ◆ Genres don't change but outlets do
- ◆ Hollywood in the digital age
- ◆ Short films as a route to success

In 1999, the American Film Institute (AFI) published "America's 100 Greatest Movies." The top two films were World War II–era movies, but only one had a wartime setting. Number one was *Citizen Kane* (1941), the Orson Welles masterpiece based on the life of newspaper magnate William Randolph Hearst. *Casablanca* (1942) was number two. Written by twins Philip and Julius Epstein, with Howard Koch, the Academy Award–winning *Casablanca* was directed by Michael Curtiz and produced by Hal Wallis, who would make Elvis Presley a movie star. *Casablanca* was based on an unpublished play, *Everybody Comes to Rick's,* by Murray Burnett and Joan Alison. Burnett and Alison made $20,000, but have you ever seen another movie with their names on it? Hollywood has many "one hit wonders."

Hollywood Heat

World War II audiences saw classic movie musicals such as *Yankee Doodle Dandy* (1942), with James Cagney; the all-black *Cabin in the Sky* (1943); and *Meet Me in St. Louis* (1944), with Judy Garland. Live-action musicals in recent years were box office disappointments until Australian director Baz Luhrmann's *Moulin Rouge* (2001) and the 2003 Oscar successes of *Chicago.* Writing and selling an original movie musical today remains difficult, but unique innovations like *Once* (2006, Best Song Oscar winner in 2008) make you wish for more.

Hollywood has changed mightily since the 1940s. The town pitched in heavily during World War II. Movie star Jimmy Stewart flew real-life bomber missions over Europe. Clark Gable and other stars joined the service, while Hollywood directors made training films and documentaries. Germany lost more than just the war. Universum-Film AG (UFA), the Berlin studio where classics such as *Metropolis* and *The Blue Angel* were made, saw an exodus of talent that included all-time great writer/director Billy Wilder.

The year 1946 rivaled 1939 for classic films. *The Big Sleep, Gilda, Henry V* (starring Laurence Olivier), *It's a Wonderful Life,* and *The Postman Always Rings Twice* debuted in 1946. Americans wanted more realistic stories, which is why Frank Capra's *It's a Wonderful Life* was dismissed by moviegoers as overly sentimental "Capra-corn." William Wyler's *The Best Years of Our Lives,* about three GIs who have trouble adjusting to postwar life, won a number of Oscars, including Best Picture and Best Director.

Movies After World War II: The Whole World Changed

Bette Davis in *Now, Voyager* (1942), represented resilient women who had worked men's jobs in factories during the war and liked their new freedom. After the war, Hollywood softened a bit; wholesome films such as *The Bells of St. Mary's* (1946), with Bing Crosby, were popular, but "film noir" fare was also very popular. *Key Largo* (1948), with Edward G. Robinson, and *Treasure of the Sierra Madre* (1948), with Humphrey Bogart playing a man driven crazy by greed, are still classics, as is Billy Wilder's *Sunset Boulevard* (1950).

Skip's Tips

Film noir often means "memorable." With its femme fatales, "hard-boiled" detectives, 1920s German lighting techniques, and 1930s gangster movie plots, the "black film" genre never dies. Examples through the years are *The Maltese Falcon* (1941), *Chinatown* (1974), *Body Heat* (1981), *L.A. Confidential* (1997), and *Mulholland Dr.* (2001).

Minority roles also began to change. Other than all-black "race movies" by Oscar Micheaux and other independents, black roles in films were few. When Bill Robinson tapped out rhythms on a staircase with Shirley Temple in *The Little Colonel* (1935), he did so as a servant. Buckwheat in Hal Roach's *Our Gang* comedies was an equal, and so was Eddie "Rochester" Anderson on the popular Jack Benny radio show, but otherwise, black people were not treated equally. In 1949, director Stanley Kramer bravely broached the subject of military race bias in *Home of the Brave*, much as Elia Kazan tackled anti-Semitism in *Gentlemen's Agreement* (1947). Hollywood became the focusing lens for national problems.

Everyone in Hollywood shared a common enemy in the Hays Office. The Hollywood Production Code was devised in 1922 by Will Hays to make sure that movies did not anger government censors. The code was not always logical; a man and a woman could lie on a bed together, as long as there was no nudity and they kept one foot on the floor. Then director Howard Hawks made *Scarface* in 1931. Hawks refused to comply with Hays's editing demands. Only the intervention of producer Howard Hughes allowed the picture to go forward. The film angered citizen groups, causing studios to cut down on violence and emphasize sex. This prompted the Catholic Church to form the Legion of Decency and threaten boycotts. In 1934, a strict Roman Catholic named Joe Breen took over for Hays and even rewrote scripts if he thought it was warranted. Although it sounds odd today, some have speculated that Breen's efforts helped bring about the Golden Year of 1939.

Hollywood Heat

The films of the 1930s and 1940s have often been favorites for remakes. *Here Comes Mr. Jordan* (1941), starring Robert Montgomery, became Warren Beatty's *Heaven Can Wait* (1978) and received several Oscar nominations. A remake called *Down to Earth* (2001), starring Chris Rock, was a box-office disappointment.

In 1943, Howard Hughes pushed the morality envelope again with *The Outlaw*, which starred the amply endowed Jane Russell. Had we not been at war, Hughes might not have been able to release the film (lonely GIs loved it). Alcoholism, mental illness, and rape were also written about. Then, in 1947, the masters of morality zeroed in on Hollywood. With Stalin in power in Russia and Mao in China, communism was a world threat, and the House Un-American Activities Committee (HUAC) wanted to ferret out Communist operatives in Tinseltown. The hearings led by Senator Joseph McCarthy resulted in a polarization of the country. Were there Communists in Hollywood? Well, actors studying at the Actor's Lab, behind world-famous Schwab's Drugstore, sang the Communist anthem "Le internationale" in the parking lot after classes. A screenwriter, John Howard Lawson, probably sealed the fate of the accused when he chastised HUAC members. The "Hollywood Ten" (directors, producers, and screenwriters who refused to answer questions) were held in contempt of Congress and were blacklisted from working in the industry by Louis B. Mayer and 49 other film executives. More than 200 people in the movie business had their careers ruined. Top playwright and director Elia Kazan also named names, and was ostracized by many.

Affected screenwriters simply wrote under pseudonyms. Hollywood Ten member Dalton Trumbo won Best Original Screenplay for *The Brave One* at the 1957 Academy Awards as "Robert Rich." In 1960, in open defiance of the blacklist, actor/executive producer Kirk Douglas hired Trumbo to write *Spartacus* under his own name, and that served to break the blacklist. Even today, the McCarthy Era is a source of contention for filmmakers. In 1945, a union strike raised the price of making films, and as television caught on, movies had less appeal. By 1948, one out of every eight American families owned a television. Even more threatening to Hollywood was a 1947 Supreme Court decision against the five major and three minor studios, which forced them to sell off theater chains. After that, marketing films on a theater-by-theater basis meant cost-cutting and the end of B pictures and serials. In October 1948, the five majors were again ordered to give up their interests in more than 1,400 movie theaters. Howard Hughes caved in first, declaring RKO would sell its almost 250 theaters within a year. Other studios fell in line, and the vast studio system was dead.

How Television and *I Love Lucy* Transformed Hollywood

In 1946, 80 million people went to the movies each week. By 1948, that was down to 60 million. Moviegoing offered less "bang for the buck" without B pictures and serials, and TV shows were free. People stopped going to the movies, and Hollywood paid the price.

Variety shows were popular on early TV. For example, singing superstar Patti Page had her own variety show on all three major networks. The writers turned out skits and jokes that hearkened back to vaudeville. The most memorable of the variety breed was Sid Caesar's *Your Show of Shows*, from New York. It debuted in 1949 as the *Admiral Broadway Revue*. (Admiral was the name of the sponsor.) Writers who became Hollywood superstars, including Mel Brooks, Neil Simon, Woody Allen, and Larry Gelbart, were staff writers for Caesar.

Advertiser-supported television brought about censorship called "Standards and Practices." Sponsors knew that if a show offended, the all-powerful consumer could boycott products. As television expanded into a writer-consuming behemoth, supporting 80 percent of the registered members of the Writers Guild of America, TV writing was regulated by moral standards that gave us shows such as *Leave It to Beaver*, which celebrated the status quo.

Lucille Ball and Desi Arnaz did more to change television history than anyone else. Lucy was almost 40 when she was approached about moving her hit CBS Radio *situation comedy My Favorite Husband* to television. She agreed, but she refused to move to New York. The network agreed to let her film the 1951 show in Los Angeles and caved in to her demand that her Cuban bandleader husband, Desi Arnaz, play her show husband. Within six months, more than 30 million Americans tuned in each Monday night to watch the number 1 hit *I Love Lucy* on CBS.

Script Notes

A **situation comedy,** or **sitcom,** about characters caught in comedic situations, is structured like any other story. With a beginning, middle, and end, characters struggle to reach goals, encountering obstacles and conflict. The solutions that they devise result in even more complicated, funny situations.

Instead of doing the show live, Lucy and Desi wanted to film it, which cost a lot more. The cigarette company Philip Morris was the only sponsor they could find. The couple took less money in exchange for producing the show and keeping the negatives. By filming, reruns could be aired across the country, and the shows could be dubbed in other languages. Eventually, *I Love Lucy* was seen in more than 80 countries.

Desilu Productions developed a major TV innovation. Working with Academy Award–winning cinematographer Karl Freund, Desi devised the three-camera filming technique to allow for better editing. It became the standard for all TV sitcoms, and Hollywood's television industry was born.

The Birth of the Antihero and the Death of Feel Good

In October 1947, the Actors Studio was founded in New York by Cheryl Crawford, Elia Kazan, and Robert Lewis. Two years later, Lee Strasberg joined this bastion of Method acting, which was derived from Konstantin Stanislavsky, author of *My Life in Art*. Strasberg learned Stanislavsky's "system" from Richard Boleslavski, a defected member of the Moscow Art Theatre. When the Actors Studio began, the founders invited 50 young actors to join the company and recruited teachers such as Kazan and Sanford "Sandy" Meisner, who went on to great success teaching in Hollywood.

Twenty films from the 1950s are listed in the AFI's "Top 100" film list, making the 1950s the movies' most influential decade. The only actor to star in two of the top 10 films is Marlon Brando, who studied at the Actors Studio. Number 8 on the list, *On the Waterfront* (1954), starred Brando and was directed by Elia Kazan. Number 14, *Some Like It Hot* (1959), starred Marilyn Monroe, a Studio alum. The Studio also had a playwrights wing, and one of that group's founding members, Tennessee Williams, wrote number 45 on the list, *A Streetcar Named Desire* (1951), Brando's greatest early role. Studio alumnus James Dean starred in two movies on the AFI list: number 59, *Rebel Without a Cause* (1955), and number 82, *Giant* (1956). Studio members also included Paul Newman and Joanne Woodward. The Studio's influence on Hollywood is enormous.

When the Korean War was over, even though the atomic bomb and communism were real threats, life in America was peaceful. Young men who didn't have to go to war idolized rebellious "antiheroes" who challenged middle-class values. They talked tough, looked cool, and, in James Dean's case, died young.

Studios still made plenty of "family fare" movies during the 1950s, with great musicals such as Gene Kelly and Stanley Donen's *Singin' in the Rain* (1952). When rock 'n' roll exploded mid-decade, however, it was inevitable that music stars such as Elvis Presley would appear in films, and most definitely not in the traditional musical. No musical ever made had a sequence as electrifying or overtly sexual as the title scene in Presley's *Jailhouse Rock* (1957). Presley films produced by Hal Wallis influenced movies for decades.

With B movies and serials gone, film stars moved to TV. Gene Autry, the original singing cowboy, got his own series, as did "The King of the Cowboys," Roy Rogers. Their success motivated Warner Brothers to produce a number of made-for-TV Westerns, the most popular being *Maverick* (1957), starring James Garner. Other studios followed suit.

Skip's Tips

Ride your modem on over to www.cowboypal.com, pardner. You'll find Western comics, B Westerns, and Warner Brothers TV series. You can watch the "Double Trouble" episode from the *Cisco Kid* TV series, learn about *Zorro* serials, or listen to a *Hopalong Cassidy* (William Boyd) radio show. See ya there, buckaroo!

As television climbed and film declined, studios fought back with sweeping epics and gimmicks such as Cinemascope and 3D. Filmmakers took chances by putting previously taboo content in movies. In 1953, Otto Preminger's *The Moon Is Blue* was deliberately released without the Production Code seal of approval and was condemned by the Legion. When Preminger made *The Man with the Golden Arm* (1955), starring Frank Sinatra, the film was denied a production seal because it dealt with heroin addiction. This prompted United Artists to resign from the association of studios that upheld the Code and set in motion a Hollywood rebellion. The film that brought the confrontation to a head was Elia Kazan's *Baby Doll* (1956), written by Kazan's friend Tennessee Williams. The openly sexual content caused the film to be banned by the Legion.

With the studio system broken, some productions went overseas for cheaper labor. Additionally, movie theaters in major cities began importing and exhibiting foreign films that had great impact on young filmmakers. No foreign moviemaker was more influential than Japanese writer/director Akira Kurosawa. *The Magnificent Seven* was an American remake of Kurosawa's *The Seven Samurai* (1954), and Kurosawa's favorite American director was John Ford, who made many great Westerns. Kurosawa's heroes were often antiheroes, particularly when his favorite, Toshirô Mifune, starred. If you've ever seen a *Star Wars* movie in which the existing scene is wiped away by the next, that's a Kurosawa technique. *Star Wars* is based on Kurosawa's *The Hidden Fortress* (1958). Asian films such as *Ringu* (1998, remade in the United States as *The Ring* in 2002, have had heavy impact on Hollywood in recent years, and Kadokawa USA, the American arm of the major Japanese media company, has sold dozens of properties to Hollywood to remake.

⭐ **Hollywood Heat** _____

In the January 1954 issue of *Cahiers du Cinema*, French critic François Truffaut held that the director was the *auteur* (author) of a film because he controls the *mise en scène* (placing of the scene). Truffaut loved mainstream American directors, B pictures, and English director Alfred Hitchcock. (He married Hitchcock's daughter, Patricia.) Truffaut also directed the Oscar-winning *Day for Night* (Best Foreign Film, 1973). In homage to the author of *auteur*, Steven Spielberg cast Truffaut in *Close Encounters of the Third Kind* (1979). In case you ever wondered, the "A Film By [Director]" in the opening credits is Truffaut's idea.

Hollywood Genres Don't Change, but the Outlet Does

Another influence on young filmmakers in the 1950s was the plethora of classic science-fiction films as *The Day the Earth Stood Still* (1951) and *Forbidden Planet* (1956). Many films mused on horrors resulting from atomic bomb tests. In Japan, where atomic explosions had destroyed cities, audiences loved the mutated giant lizard *Godzilla*, and other atomic mutant films followed. Roger "King of the Bs" Corman got his start during this time with low-budget knockoffs such as *Not of This Earth* (1957). By the mid-1960s, however, the genre was relatively dead. Many films during the 1960s were about social issues, not the future dreams of science fiction. Which is odd, given the 1960s American race to put a man on the moon in that decade.

In 1968, Stanley Kubrick made perhaps his best film, from a book by science-fiction futurist Arthur C. Clarke. Kubrick's *2001: A Space Odyssey* was a social drama about a machine as Frankenstein's monster, with technology defeating its creators.

Hollywood grasped for substance and meaning in the 1960s, a time of turbulence, confusion, and a sexual explosion that resulted from the appearance of the birth control pill. In an attempt to get a grasp on public desires, Hollywood adopted a new film rating code almost identical to the one we have today. There was not yet a PG-13, and X was reserved for films suitable to viewers 16 years and older. That is precisely how *Midnight Cowboy* (1969), starring Jon Voight and Dustin Hoffman, became the first (and likely the last) X-rated film to win the Best Picture Oscar.

When Baby Boomers came of age, most Hollywood studios were slow to pick up on their rebellious tastes. That changed after Columbia took a chance on an independently made low-budget film called *Easy Rider* (1969). The box office results and soundtrack album sales quickly opened everyone's eyes.

Skip's Tips

For a script with the highest chance of getting made as a studio feature, don't write anything rated above PG-13. There's a saying in Hollywood that you can make $100,000,000 with an R-rated film, but it's hard to make any more than that. Of the Best Picture–nominated movies in 2008, the only one that made more than $100 million was the family-friendly *Juno*. To better understand movie ratings, go to www.mpaa.org and www.filmratings.com.

Almost all remnants of the studio system were gone by the end of the 1960s. Most of the participants in Hollywood's Golden Age had either died or retired. Actors worked independently, not on contract, a trend begun when Jimmy Stewart took a cut in pay for a share in the profits of two films that he made in 1950.

When the Baby Boomers began making feature films, Steven Spielberg and George Lucas quickly moved to the forefront. College dropout Spielberg sold a cowritten feature in 1973 (*Ace Eli and Rodger of the Skies*) and wasn't happy with the filmed result. So, he directed his next feature, *Sugarland Express* (1974). After winning several awards in film school at the University of Southern California, Lucas became the protégé of Francis Ford Coppola and directed his first feature, *THX 1138*, in 1971. His next feature was *American Graffiti* in 1973. Its box office success helped him get financing for his next film, *Star Wars*. Lucas got rich largely due to retaining most of the merchandising rights on items from that movie. These Boomers well remembered their Hollywood lessons. When Spielberg and Lucas teamed up to do the Indiana Jones films, they did so in homage to the great serial films.

Spielberg and Lucas contributed to the field of screenwriting in other ways. Spielberg's third acts tend to be longer than usual, while Lucas's support of the myth story structure outlined by Joseph Campbell resulted in a paradigm shift in Hollywood stories. Even so, they have their flops. Lucas had *Howard the Duck*, and Spielberg's *A.I.* (which he co-wrote) was much too long.

A Hollywood World in the Digital Age

"Experts" predicted that both the Cable News Network (CNN) and Music Television (MTV) would fail. Independent filmmakers offer similar surprises. Low-budget films have had big impact in recent years. They include films that make a lot of money, such as Daniel Myrick and Eduardo Sanchez's *The Blair Witch Project* (1999), which

Skip's Tips

HDTV is an abbreviation for High-Definition Television. Video is replacing 35mm film in making movies, but getting a true "film look" from video cameras has not been easy. When George Lucas used a Panavision-modified HD video camera from Sony to shoot the live-action scenes of *Star Wars: Episode II,* that told people that video's day had finally arrived.

initially cost around $8,000 and eventually made more than $140 million in the United States alone; and *Napoleon Dynamite* (2004), made for $200,000 initially and grossing over $44 million. Ever consider shooting your own script? After Apple Computer concentrated on easy-to-use software products like Final Cut Pro and QuickTime, lots of other companies jumped on the bandwagon. I wrote a full chapter on the subject in my *Ultimate Writer's Guide to Hollywood* (Barnes & Noble Books, 2004), and it is often discussed by members of "Skip's Hollywood Hangout" on Yahoo! For Web, print, and real world resources to get you started, check out www. videomaker.com, www.digitalfilmmaker.com, and www.actioncut.com.

Screenwriting and filmmaking have come a long way in 100 years, and now we have massive Internet distribution. See www.cinemanow.com for an example. For writers, there are more outlets and opportunities than ever before. With digital filmmaking and the Web, you can get noticed quickly, worldwide. It's easy to upload a short film on www.youtube.com and similar outlets. The catch is knowing what goes into a good short film. If you haven't seen "405" yet, surf to www.405themovie.com and see one that furthered the filmmaking careers of its makers in a big way.

Devorah Cutler-Rubenstein, filmmaker and Adjunct Professor, USC-Film TV Summer Program, author of *What's The Big Idea? Writing Shorts* and CEO of www. thescriptbroker.com, says this about shorts:

> Short films can open up a moment, describe a problem, or give a solution to a problem. As art, they have to create emotion either by being dramatic or thematic or technologically dazzling. The three C's must be there—character, challenge and change. They may be little fish as films go, but they still have to swim. They should be painfully, ruthlessly *honest*. Like short stories, every moment must be a sculpted truth. Make them. They are good for your soul and great for learning about craft.

These days, you can write and market one-minute movies for cell phone comedies, like tiny TV commercials. See www.funlittlemovies.com for examples.

Another interesting take on shorts and movies in general in our digital age comes from the Celtx company. See http://celtx.blip.tv, where the premise is "We watch because we like to worry." You don't have to agree, but that's the screenwriting and Hollywood world these days—wild new ideas can come from anywhere.

 For examples of short films scripts, see the CD that came with this book for examples from Devorah Cutler-Rubenstein, Dawn Natalia, and Gavin Heffernan—all fine successes in their own right.

The Least You Need to Know

- Movies after World War II reflected a desire for equality of women and minorities who had contributed to the war effort.

- For decades, unknown actors in film noir movies have become stars; a first script in that genre is a good idea.

- Attempted censorship of Hollywood movies and creative people is a highly volatile issue.

- Lucille Ball and Desi Arnaz are responsible for the television industry being centered in southern California and the three-camera situation comedy format.

- In the past decade, the success of inexpensive independent films has made it more attractive than ever before for writers to become successful filmmakers, particularly with digital cameras.

- You can learn all about making and uploading short films for worldwide viewing at www.youtube.com and all over the Web; it's share and share alike these days!

Part 2

What to Write

Great ideas and how to sell them, writing forms, and other oddities are all explained here as you learn the unique language of Hollywood that screenwriters must master to succeed. You'll get an education that some writers take a decade to figure out (the ones that don't give up, that is). The shortcuts and the detours are mapped out here in full. You'll learn why a quality called "Kids Love It" may be the key to box office success, with a step-by-step plan to make you a successful screenwriter.

Chapter 6

Sources for Movie Ideas That Will Sell

In This Chapter

- ◆ News stories as story sources
- ◆ Old movies make new movies
- ◆ Scripting true stories
- ◆ Qualifying original ideas
- ◆ Movies to comics to TV shows to video games to movies
- ◆ Understanding movie demographics
- ◆ Video games bigger than movies

Freelance journalists like myself have to come up with story ideas that editors will buy, or we won't get paid. The first time I sold something to Hollywood I only knew that I had pleased the two producers who *optioned* my story. I didn't have an overall idea of what producers consistently bought. Thankfully, I soon learned. I also learned the power of networking, and I never hesitated in passing a good story that was unsuitable for me on to someone I thought could use it.

Script Notes

When a production company thinks that your property would make a good movie, they make an **option** deal. You're paid something now (usually 10 percent of the total price) or nothing if you allow it, and the rest when the movie is made. Usually, the remainder is due on the first day of principal photography.

One day I came across the story of a psychiatrist in Australia who drugged patients and raped them. I passed it on to Michael Rymer, a then-unproduced Australian screenwriter living in Los Angeles. He wrote a screenplay, sold it to Village Roadshow, and gave me a finder's fee. His movie *Dead Sleep* was a thriller starring Karen Black and Linda Blair. He went on to also direct movies like *Angel Baby* and *Queen of the Damned* and the redo of the *Battlestar Galactica* TV series. It's good to help others, particularly in a "people business" like Hollywood.

Reading the Newspaper Like a Screenwriter

Showbiz veterans develop a sense of good movie stories, which can be an interesting news story. Writer/producer Mary Sweeney was reading *The New York Times* one day in 1994 when she came across the story of Alvin Straight, a 73-year-old man from Laurens, Iowa. When he found out that his estranged brother in Mt. Zion, Wisconsin, was ill, Straight, who no longer qualified for a driver's license, rode his lawn mower to see his brother. When Sweeney looked into optioning the story, however, highly successful producer Ray Stark had already grabbed it.

Sweeney didn't forget the story. When Alvin Straight died in 1996, she contacted his children and found out that the option had lapsed. She made a deal with them for the story and she and John Roach wrote (and rewrote) a screenplay, and then Sweeney gave it to director David Lynch, her partner in the Los Angeles production company, The Picture Factory. Lynch and suggested that they recruit acclaimed actor Richard Farnsworth to play Alvin Straight, and Farnsworth came out of retirement to do the part. Filming of *The Straight Story* resulted in a Best Actor Oscar nomination for Farnsworth in 1999.

Read your local newspaper. Is something unusual happening? Can you get the film rights? Dig up famous local stories. A story doesn't have to be in *The New York Times* to make it to Hollywood. Remember, *The Blair Witch Project* was inspired by a local legend of Burkittsville, Maryland.

Recycling Old Movies

As the story goes, George Lucas, who loved the old serial movies, wanted to do a remake of *Flash Gordon*. Unfortunately, producer Dino De Laurentiis had already secured the rights. So, Lucas wrote *Star Wars*. People who grew up loving a film or TV show often think of new twists. Producer David Permut was flipping back and forth between cable TV channels one night and saw Dan Ackroyd in an old movie and then Jack Webb in an old *Dragnet* TV show. Ackroyd. Webb. The next day he called Ackroyd's manager and pitched his idea for a new, comic *Dragnet* feature. The manager signed on and Permut made the quickest deal of his life with the president of Universal. Remakes are often successful. In case you didn't know, the 2006 movie *The Departed*, which won Martin Scorsese the Oscar, was a remake of the 2002 Chinese film *Mou gaan dou*.

How do you ascertain whether someone in Hollywood is already doing the remake you've picked? In recent years top Hollywood websites have begun listing films *in development*. For a monthly fee to www.hcdonline.com, inhollywood.com, or www.showbizdata.com, you can get all the Hollywood contacts you need and read development listings.

True Stories: How to Secure the Rights and Where to Sell Them

I'm not a lawyer, and I don't play one on TV. I don't intend to offer you legal advice or to try. But I will give you some tips:

◆ You cannot write a screenplay based on a true story of a living person or persons unless you secure the rights from one or more of the involved parties. Use legal representation to help you with finalizing any agreement(s).

◆ You can write a screenplay based on documents in the public record, such as a trial transcript, but if you have not secured rights from people, usually you must use dialogue as reflected in the court record.

◆ You can base a screenplay on a true story if the parties involved are no longer living, unless they have descendants whose interests might be infringed. Consult an attorney if you have *any* questions.

For entertainment business legal advice, I recommend *Business and Legal Forms for Authors and Self-Publishers* (Allworth Press, 2005) by attorney and publisher Tad Crawford, and *The Writer Got Screwed (but didn't have to): A Guide to the Legal and Business Practices of Writing for the Entertainment Industry* (Harper-Perennial, 1997) by Brooke A. Wharton. Both are excellent resources. You might also sign up for the free e-mail reports of entertainment attorney Gordon Firemark at www.firemark.com.

Skip's Tips

If you're serious about selling screenplays, keep up with what is being sold. Get a subscription to *Daily Variety* or *The Hollywood Reporter*. You can read portions of each magazine free online at www.variety.com or www. hollywoodreporter.com, or you can subscribe to the complete versions online. The site www. donedealpro.com also tracks recent sales.

If you secure the rights and decide for some reason that you do not want to write a screenplay, some producers may be interested in obtaining the rights from you via a pitch. For more information on how to do that, read my *Ultimate Writer's Guide to Hollywood* (Barnes & Noble Books, 2004) and take a look at the site of Bob "Pitch King" Kosberg at www. moviepitch.com.

Do your research and learn how to legally secure rights and then move quickly as soon as you decide that a story is good. How much should you pay to secure the rights? That is entirely between you and the person(s) with the story. You could pay as little as $1 in some states to make an agreement legal. A great reference for such transactions is *Producing for Hollywood: A Guide for Independent Producers* (Allworth Press, 2004) by Paul Mason and Don Gold.

You can secure the rights of a hot true story even when many other people want it. American Billy Hayes was caught attempting to smuggle drugs out of Turkey and was put in prison. After Hayes made a daring escape and returned to the United States, one of the first things he did was acquire a literary agent. He had been home only a few days when producer Peter Guber flew to Long Island, New York, to meet with Hayes and his parents. Hayes told me that Guber made an offer that he would have been a fool to refuse:

> And when he flew me out to LA first class to meet with the Columbia brass, he pulled up in front of the hotel with a shiny new Mercedes and a lightning bolt with the word "FLASH" emblazoned across the front of his sweater. I was impressed. Of course, I'd been in jail for five years, so I was easily impressed. But I knew Peter was going places, and his driving energy got my movie made, and made well, so I have nothing but good things to say about Peter. I even took his producer class at UCLA one year, when he used *Midnight Express* as the model deal discussed that semester. Made for fascinating view of my project from the other side.

The critically acclaimed *Midnight Express* was one of the hits of 1978. If you're as creative a producer as Guber, you might be able to secure the rights to an equally compelling story.

How to Know If Your Original Idea Is Truly Original

In 1981, I cowrote a screenplay called *Fair Game*. It was an action film about a man seeking revenge on modern-day pirates who kill his wife while stealing his yacht. "Fair game" referred to a law of the sea that states that you are within your rights to kill someone who attacks you on waters outside the territorial limits of seaside nations. Not long after we wrote the script, it was optioned by a successful producing duo. Then we learned of a movie starring Gary Busey that sounded very much like our story. We hired a detective, who got a copy of the script before the movie finished production. He concluded that the scripts were different. Since that time, there have been at least four other *Fair Game* movies. None of these movies came from our original script; we later changed its name to *South China Sea* and sold it to an American producer living in Thailand.

You can't copyright a title. If you wrote a screenplay called *Star Wars*, though, you might be in trouble. The term is trademarked, and the George Lucas franchise is firmly established. (Confused? The "All About Trademarks" page at www.ggmark.com is a good place to begin learning about trademark law.) You can also read a lot about what can and cannot be copyrighted at the U.S. Copyright Office home page at www.copyright.gov.

How do you know if your movie idea is truly original? You don't. You simply have to do the best research you can. Check the Internet Movie Database at www.imdb.com. You can search by keywords there; it's a fairly complete database, but it's not perfect. There are also many books covering every movie ever made, and television shows, too. Look into Leonard Maltin's movie guides at www.leonardmaltin.com, and try *Total Television* (Penguin Books, 1996) by Alex McNeil to research TV. If you really want to be a successful screenwriter, you need to watch a lot of movies. Successful screenwriters can rattle off lines and scenes and obscure bits of film trivia (which is precisely why I can write this book). They know the medium, and you should, too.

> ### Skip's Tips
>
> Time after time, I've seen Hollywood folks get interested in an idea and say, verbatim, "Hey! Nobody's ever done a movie about [insert idea here]." If you're musing over possible screenplay ideas, it might help to use, "Nobody's ever done a movie about ..." as a starting point.

No matter how much research you do or how many movies you watch, you can't be sure that your idea is truly original. You simply have to exercise what attorneys call "due diligence." That is, put forth the effort that an average, sincere, energetic person would exhibit. If you come up with a well-written script with a truly original story in a recognized movie genre, you might be surprised how well you'll do with it.

> ### It's Not for Us
>
> Mum's the word. When you've decided on a story for your screenplay, watch who you discuss it with. Even when you are protected, there can be trouble. A story of mine about Shakespeare and his "dark lady of the sonnets" was once optioned by a famous actor. He got nowhere with it, but I never heard where he took it. Then came the very similar, Oscar-winning *Shakespeare in Love*. In September of 2003, I attended a photo exhibition by his wife. Two of the photos were of a producer of *Shakespeare in Love*, and a co-writer of the movie. Talk about your stranger things in Heaven and Earth, Horatio ....

Comics to Movies to TV to Video Games to Movies

Filmmakers often do remakes of things that made a strong impression on them in their youth. For young males in the Unites States, perhaps nothing makes a stronger impression these days than video games, which really got their start in comic books. Superman debuted in a comic book, and that's where he stayed for years. In 1941, the first animated Superman cartoon by Dave Fleischer debuted. *The Mad Scientist* featured the Man of Steel fighting a mad scientist intent on destroying Metropolis with an energy cannon styled on the legendary "death ray" supposedly invented by Nikola Tesla. Bud Collyer voiced Clark Kent and Superman in the cartoon, while Joan Alexander was the voice of Lois Lane.

The first time an actor played Superman on film was in 1948, in serials featuring Kirk Alyn as Clark Kent/Superman and Noel Neill as Lois Lane. Another 15-chapter serial was made in 1950. *Atom Man vs. Superman* also featured Alyn and Neill. When the *Adventures of Superman* TV series began in 1953, with George Reeves as our favorite man from Krypton, Neill once again played Lois Lane.

And then came Christopher Reeve as Superman with a number of movies in the 1970s and 1980s. And just when we thought that was the last of it, *Lois and Clark: The New Adventures of Superman* was a hit on ABC starting in 1993; then came the 2001 WB Network hit, *Smallville*, starring Tom Welling as Superman in high school. You can't kill Superman.

Can you think of another character who first appeared in movies, then on television, then back again to film? *Batman*? That's easy. How about one that began in novels? *Tarzan of the Jungle*, from the original books by Edgar Rice Burroughs. As popular as Superman is, Tarzan rules, with well over 100 onscreen portrayals including a new TV series on the WB Network in 2003 and three video games.

> **Skip's Tips**
>
> One script element that *must* be present in an adventure is the "character arc." While fighting a villain equal in power to his own, the hero changes inside while changing the world outside. This transformation of inner nature during the story is his character arc. The villain, on the other hand, does not change and, by keeping static, remains a villain.

The lone hero, with special powers or abilities far beyond that of the normal man, follows an ethical code, either acknowledged or innate. Would that describe Superman and Tarzan? Batman, certainly. How about Hercules? And let's not forget the swashbuckling Zorro, first seen in the silent *Don Q Son of Zorro* (1925), with silent film superstar Douglas Fairbanks as Don Cesar de Vega/Zorro. Including the excellent *The Mask of Zorro* (1998) with Antonio Banderas, Zorro also has been onscreen more often than Superman.

A solitary hero, with superhuman skill or abilities, who follows an inner ethical code and can be played by any number of handsome actors, is a winner time after time. And all these characters have one more thing in common: Either their family structure was heavily threatened, or they were orphaned at a very early age.

How we interpret that I'll leave up to you. To me, it's too reminiscent of the Oedipus story, and utterly Freudian!

Meanwhile, it's now easy to make your own comic books, right there on your computer. Check out My Comic Book Creator at www.mycomicbookcreator.com and Comic Life software at http://plasq.com.

Turning a screenplay into a comic can pay off in big ways. In 2007, Stephen L. Antczak did that with *Nightwolf*, published by Devil's Due, a story about a werewolf turned anti-hero. The comic book was discovered by producer Marty Adelstein in a comics bookstore and the comic book series was put into development as a TV series with Adelstein and 20th Century Fox Television. Adelstein, one of the executive producers of the hit television series *Prison Break*, knew a good story when it flipped through his hands.

Anything the Whole Family Likes

You've probably never heard of the *Statistical Abstract of the United States*, a reference book of vital U.S. statistics compiled by the Bureau of the Census in the Department of Commerce. It comes out annually and is available to anyone via the U.S. Government Printing Office. It's also available online at www.census.gov/compendia/statab. (You'll need Microsoft Excel software to read some of the information.) I doubt that anyone in Hollywood ever read it, but from somewhere, the idea of males between the ages of 18 to 34 keeps coming up. Supposedly, that is the number-one demographic movie audience.

Whoever determined that hasn't researched the demographics of the American population. At the census site, in a spreadsheet entitled "Resident Population by Age and Sex: 1980 to 2005," I learned that the four-year age groupings were relatively the same in size for males ages 10-34, while in 2005 the segments were relatively equal from ages 5-49. For females in 2005, segment sizes were about the same from toddlers to age 54.

U.S. citizens can vote at age 18. In some states, they can drink alcoholic beverages. By the time they're 34, males are usually married, have usually finished college, and have been earning a living (we hope) for a number of years. And best of all, they have the most disposable income!

Movies are where young men most often take their dates. If they're traveling in packs, they often go to the movies together. Thus, the magic age group of moviegoers that you hear about in Hollywood over and over is 18 to 34. That continues with new media. When I created an original animated cartoon series for the Web, the core demographic target was males 18 to 34.

Nevertheless, the real numbers of entertainment consumers are spread across generations. I researched the top grossing movies of all time when writing the first edition of this book and discovered a different, more important, demographic.

I'll tell you more about my demographic discoveries in Chapter 8. Meanwhile, you should know this: while the "conventional wisdom" of Hollywood is that males ages 18 to 34 are the core moviegoers, the real story is that the majority of the development executives I've met are males aged 18 to 34. Despite these executives' prejudices, the majority of entertainment viewers and participants comprises a much wider swath of the population.

The Real Hollywood Boom Is in Video Games

In the September 2, 2003, issue of *Fortune* magazine, Peter Lewis reported that three weeks after the August 14 debut of *Madden NFL 2004*, the game grossed $100 million, which was two million copies at $50 each. Only the biggest movie blockbusters rack up numbers like that. The 2002 global video game market, Lewis said, was $28 billion, but everyone expected it to keep growing exponentially.

I got an idea of how big video games in 2003 were when producers I knew left Hollywood to get into making video games. Then there were my kids, Haley and Holly, who spent endless hours in the summer of 2003 playing video games. Then, on September 6, 2003, Sony announced that sales of its PlayStation 2 console had reached 60 million units. In showbiz terms, that's a lot of "butts in seats."

If you want to pick up movie ideas from video games, forget it—Hollywood is already there. In November 2002, the major Hollywood agency International Creative Management formed a department to sell video games movie rights to studios. You can't compete with that. You can, however, begin to learn by visiting the following sites:

◆ International Game Developers Association: Student & Newbie Outreach—
www.igda.org/students.

◆ Gamasutra publication and forums—www.gamasutra.com.

◆ Author, design workshop leader and lead game designer Ernest W. Adams—
www.designersnotebook.com.

◆ Develop magazine, European trade monthly for everyone in game development—
www.developmag.com.

◆ Heather Grove's role-playing games and writing advice—www.errantdreams.com.

◆ International Hobo script samples—http://ihobo.com/samples.

◆ For software with which to write these games, your best bet is Storyspace from
www.eastgate.com. This company also has a popular games magazine and other
helpful products.

The absolute best way to get started in video games, however, is via the book *The
Ultimate Guide to Video Game Writing and Design* (Lone Eagle, 2008) by Flint Dille
and John Zuur Platten. I should know, I put together the deal and edited the book.
You can also reach them at www.filmandgames.com. Good gaming to you!

The Least You Need to Know

◆ A story in your local newspaper, if well scripted and filmed, might make a movie
good enough to earn Oscar attention.

◆ Recycling old movies into modern scripts is best left to established producers,
but sometimes you can get lucky.

◆ The basic plot of a classic movie can easily be adapted to a different time or setting to form a new screenplay.

◆ The right kind of heroic character could turn into a franchise, resulting in dozens
of movies and TV series.

◆ Males aged 18 to 34 are considered to be the primary movie-going audience.
Whether or not they really are, male movie development executives *do* fit that
demographic.

◆ Video games offer financial and storytelling possibilities on a level with writing
movies.

7

Movies Are Not Books or Plays

In This Chapter

- ◆ Screenplays are not stage plays
- ◆ Novels are more flexible than scripts
- ◆ Television and movie scripts are different
- ◆ Screenwriting points to remember

A sculptor I know, Chuck Johanasen, often raved about *The Natural Way to Draw*, by Nicolaides. I read it because I knew Robert Redford was a talented artist who painted in Europe before coming home to Hollywood. Redford sketched out scenes before directing people. I thought some day I'd like to be able to do that, too. Nicolaides insisted you practice drawing six hours a day, until technique becomes effortless. I got the point. With any art, you have to learn the basics of the form, or you will always be handicapped.

Beginning screenwriters not only need to write, they also need to read scripts, particularly those of recent movies. You can download scripts at these sites:

- ◆ www.scriptcrawler.net
- ◆ www.simplyscripts.com
- ◆ www.dailyscript.com
- ◆ www.script-o-rama.com
- ◆ www.iscriptdb.com

Skip's Tips _____

Busy producers have projects "covered," meaning someone they trust does the initial reading. The reader provides a synopsis of the story, along with a "pass," "consider," or "recommend." A "recommend" is rare. The reader's job could be on the line if they recommend and the resulting movie flops.

If you live in southern California, it's easy to get copies of TV show and feature film scripts at a number of stores. If you don't live here, Newmarket Press (www.newmarketpress.com) has a Shooting Script Series that includes supplementary notes, still photos, and credits of scripts. You'll find, for example, *Chicago* (the only book on the movie, with a DVD), classics like *Cast Away* and *Cold Mountain: The Journey from Book to Film*, which tells how Oscar-winning director Anthony Minghella adapted Charles Frazier's award-winning novel for the big screen. Newmarket is also one of the few companies offering "novelizations" of some movies.

The script that you want to submit for consideration will not be a shooting script. A shooting script is a specially formatted script with numbered scenes and is not the "master scene" script that you will write. Scripts written by those who also direct the film, however, can look very different than a normal script. For example, John Milius's *The Wind and the Lion* (1975) had the scene descriptions in *past* tense, like a novel, rather than standard present tense.

Why You Don't Write a Screenplay Like a Stage Play

Hollywood owes a great debt to Broadway. Unique connections still exist between playwriting and screenwriting, with a number of notable playwrights making a mark in Hollywood in recent years. If you attempt to write a screenplay like a stage play, however, you should never expect to quit your day job.

In the theater, the playwright is god. The words are performed as written. Changes in the script are made only in the presence of the playwright, with the permission of the playwright, or *by* the playwright, who also has final say on casting. Changes are rarely made after the play has opened, with the exception of preview performances in some place other than New York (and, these days, in London, where New York stage hits increasingly originate).

In moviemaking, the prevailing rule is that the film director is god, the *auteur* of the movie. Often enough, if the screenwriter and the director are still speaking by the time the film wraps, chances are the screenwriter is also producing the picture. Catch the difference? Writer for the stage = god. Writer for Hollywood = not even a demi-god. That changes if you also direct your movie.

Hollywood Heat _____

Body heat! In recent years, Hollywood movie stars have taken off for and taken it off on the stage. When Nicole Kidman did *The Blue Room* in London, performances were sold out because she appeared *au naturel*. Similarly, sultry Kathleen Turner wowed audiences with an in-the-buff exhibition as Mrs. Robinson in a Broadway version of *The Graduate*, and Daniel Radcliffe was nude onstage in *Equus* in London while still starring in the *Harry Potter* films.

And now to format. Unless you're one of those exceedingly talented souls who can capture people's attention whether you write on napkins or fine stationery, you must learn the proper format of screenplays. Don't turn in a stage play expecting the reader to transpose it in the mind to "see" the movie version. Following you will find a short example of the difference in an opening of a script, both in stage version and screenplay. This script started as my stage play *Fourth World*. Its premise is that true love may arrive when you least expect it.

After writing the play, I submitted it to national competitions. The play was a finalist in two and a semifinalist in two others. People who read it, however, kept telling me that it would be better as a movie. So I wrote the screenplay, which I titled *Walking After Midnight* (inspired by the great country music hit). The great actor Ben Johnson wanted to play one of the main roles and was telling other top actors about it before he died. Later, a neophyte producer optioned the screenplay for a sizable sum, but then had family troubles and abandoned the project. Here's how my play opened. Note the format, which is the standard recommended by the Dramatists Guild of America. If you are not familiar with it, the "AT RISE" means "at the curtain rise":

ACT I

SETTING: We are in a small diner just outside Gallup, New Mexico. The counter features stools with red vinyl seats. Stage right are two booths with Formica table tops and overstuffed red vinyl seats. This place saw its best day 30 years ago, but it is well kept, clean, and functional, a sparse statement of the desert Southwest.

       A clock on the wall has simple, big hands. It reads 12:30. Between the booths and to the left of the counter is a door with a "RESTROOMS" sign. A window in the wall features an order ticket carousel, with the kitchen beyond.

The entrance to the diner is stage left. A bell on the door jingles when someone enters. An ancient coat rack stands next to the counter, near the door. On a back shelf, behind the counter, is a half-empty display of handmade turquoise and silver Indian jewelry. To the side of the jewelry is a tiny crystal unicorn.

The diner has the necessary accouterments: a malt and shake mixer, glasses, menus, a John Deere tractor calendar behind the counter, and a pay phone near the door leading to the restrooms, where the counter joins the wall. Sometimes people sit at the counter and talk on the pay phone. High on the back wall are two fairly modern-looking speakers that serve both the radio and the old Wurlitzer jukebox positioned in a corner.

AT RISE: There is no music. Sitting in a booth, drinking a cup of coffee, is an older African-American man, JAKE PARSONS. Jake is trying to read a newspaper.

Behind the counter is MIRABELLE FLOWERS, known to all her friends and most of her customers as "MIRA." She inherited the diner from her mother and is working the graveyard shift while trying to figure out her life. Tonight is Mira's 30th birthday. She may not look 30, but she's feeling it.

Using the mirror in her compact, Mira puts on lipstick, humming along to herself. She takes one final look, smacks her lips loudly and faces Jake, who grins a drunken grin.

MIRA
(hopeful)
How do I look, Jake?

JAKE
(slowly, kind of drunk)
Not bad, for a woman turnin' 30.

MIRA
Jake, it's never hard to find an asshole with an opinion.

> JAKE
> Don't start with me, Mirabelle. You know the spiritual
> turmoil I'm goin' through.

Imagine that a theater audience viewed the preceding scene. All they would notice would be the general layout of the stage and the two main characters. They would notice Mira with her compact and lipstick, and Jake with his coffee and newspaper. And they would listen to the spoken lines, all of which would take about 20 seconds.

Now let's look at the opening of the screenplay, which was rewritten from the play. The screenplay was optioned for $5,000 the same year the first edition of this book came out. See whether you can guess how much time elapses.

It's Not for Us

PASS Cut the "CUT TO." In some books on screenwriting, you will be advised to insert "CUT TO:" on the right side of the page at the end of a scene, signifying a switch in location. The majority of people who make movies no longer see a need for it. So cut it out.

FADE IN:

EXT. MOONRISE STREET - NIGHT

MUSIC OVER, on a lonely New Mexico street in the small town of Moonrise. A wind kicks up dust and a tiny piece of paper dances.

> PATSY CLINE
> (V.O., singing)
> I go out walking, after midnight
> Out in the moonlight
> Just like we used to do
> I'm always walking, after midnight
> Searching for you …

Following the paper is lusciously beautiful MIRABELLE FLOWERS, almost 30, in cowboy boots, a long billowy skirt, a Mexican peasant blouse, and Southwest Indian silver conch belt and jewelry. She adjusts the CD player and then studies the moon.

In the distance, a COYOTE HOWLS. Mira sees a bright light streak across the moon. A comet? Blink, it's gone. Mira walks on.

INT. MOONRISE DINER - NIGHT

30 years past prime. Ancient wooden coat rack. Red vinyl stools and booth seats. Booths with Formica table tops. A pay phone.

A clock ticks over to 12:01. Flanking the clock are two speakers **that serve the** radio and the old Wurlitzer jukebox.

In a wall opening behind the counter, an order carousel has no **tickets**. Nearby, some Indian jewelry, and a tiny crystal unicorn.

Beneath a John Deere calendar, pouring himself a cup of coffee, is an old black man, JAKE PARSONS, ruining a song like "Amen."

Mira steps into the open doorway of the diner.

                    MIRA
          Hi, Jake.

Jake jumps like he's been shot at, spilling coffee on himself.

                    JAKE
              (drunk & in pain)
          Yowly shit! Woman, don't put the spook on me
          like that!

                    MIRA
          What's the name of that spook, Jack Daniels?

It's Not for Us

Don't cheat a script. Some screenplay formatting programs offer you the option of "cheating" a script, or squeezing the space between lines and letters so that, for example, what should be a 130-page screenplay looks like 120. Don't do it, because it breeds distrust. They'll find out sooner or later. Make your script the right length.

A screenplay with proper margins and tabs runs *roughly* one minute of onscreen time to screenplay page, with great variations, depending on how much action, how much dialogue there is, and so on.

Note that the set description in the screenplay opening above is broken up into short paragraphs. That's the way the great Billy Wilder and his partner I. A. L. Diamond wrote screenplays such as *Some Like It Hot*, which Wilder directed. Each of the previous paragraphs could be a single camera shot. When you write a script like that, you don't have to worry about camera directions that are the director's job, anyway.

Although theater patrons would not notice much that is described on the page, movie-goers *will* see most of what is written on the screenplay page, with the exception of song lyrics. I added those in case the reader of my screenplay was unfamiliar with the song and would not get the intended mood. I ended on "Searching for you" because it's relevant to the plot.

As in the stage play, I try to use a single thought in each dialogue exchange, and as few sentences as possible each time. In most successful movies, that's how it's done.

Compare stage plays that have been made into films to screenplays of the movies. With most successful stage plays that have been made into movies, the playwright usually writes the screenplay alone or participates in its writing. As I mentioned earlier, in the theater, the playwright is god, a sentiment that is respected even in Hollywood. David Mamet's book *On Directing Film* (Penguin, 1991) explains his thoughts on stage to script to screen very nicely.

What a Novel Can Do That a Movie Cannot

Great novels are movies on paper. By triggering mental pictures in our minds, they stimulate senses that a film may not. We can taste the chocolate, smell the frangipani, feel the delicate warmth of an aroused sexual partner, and be privy to something difficult to portray onscreen. Namely, a character's *thoughts*.

I remember seeing the promotional spots for the TV series *Ally McBeal*. When a man whom Ally admired revealed he was spoken for, arrows thudded into her chest. Her thoughts were literalized in a very clever way, a difficult thing for a screenwriter to do. Even an adequate novelist could simply describe how she felt.

It's hard to write visually sometimes. *I, Robot*, from classic stories by Isaac Asimov, was not adapted to screen for a long time. The stories were very mental. For example, how do you show a robot reading a human mind in an entertaining fashion? Nevertheless, some top screenwriters worked out the problems, and 2004 gave us the movie starring Will Smith.

Thought-heavy books can be filmatically problematic, but books dealing with mental patients often make compelling films. That's because we see outward behavior, not what goes on inside heads. One good one is *Freedom Writers* (2007) based on *The Freedom Writers Diary: How a Teacher and 150 Teens Used Writing to Change Themselves and the World Around Them*. Another example is *Girl, Interrupted* (1999), from the book of essays by Susanna Kaysen about her own

> **Skip's Tips**
>
> Don't confuse a "log line" with a "tag line." The former is a *TV Guide* description of a screenplay, a one- or two-sentence summary. Tag lines are advertising "teasers" often seen on movie posters. Two tag lines for *300* listed on the Internet Movie Database (www.imdb.com) are: "Prepare for glory!" and "Spartans, tonight, we dine in hell!"

18-month stay at a mental hospital in 1967. Another great one is *One Flew over the Cuckoo's Nest* (1975), from the book by Ken Kesey. Kesey derived his novel from his experiences on staff at an institution in San Jose, California. The film was the first since Frank Capra's *It Happened One Night* (1934) to win the five top Oscars: Best Picture, Best Director, Best Actor, Best Actress, and Best Screenplay. And let's not forget Ron Howard's great film, *A Beautiful Mind* (2001), which won four Oscars and gleaned four more Oscar nominations.

Why are some great books made into films and some not? It usually boils down to action. Try showing chapter-long thought processes on film, and it becomes difficult.

As you begin to outline a big story, you should ask yourself whether you want any of the principal characters to do a lot of important thinking on the page. If you do, you have a novel.

The Differences in Television and Movie Scripts

Unless you are an established screenwriter, it is difficult to sell a script that will air on a major network. It's much more likely to get a movie on a cable channel. MTV is in the movie business now, as is Nickelodeon. VH-1, the History Channel, the Science Fiction Channel, The Lifetime Movie Channel, and many others make movies for their channel. I knew a previously unproduced writer living in New England whose manager arranged a script sale to the Disney Channel, and the manager didn't even live in the Los Angeles area. That's television today.

> **Hollywood Heat** _____
>
> YOUR NAME
>
> You might hear about TV queue, referring to actors so popular TV audiences would form a queue (line) to see them. If an actor with sufficient queue wants to do a project, the network may green light it. Networks also keep lists of "approved" writers. Neither type of list is supposed to exist, yet they do.

Films made for American TV (movies, not miniseries) are generally filmed for $3 million or less. By its nature, this limits the amount and types of locations, special effects, costumes, and other things.

TV movies also have a seven-act structure instead of the normal three-act structure, but that is easily explained. How often do commercials air during a two-hour TV movie, leaving out the commercials before the movie begins and after it concludes? Let's say that we see a commercial break every 15 minutes.

If a TV movie budget rarely goes over $3 million, with the writer getting 5 percent of the production budget, that's only $60,000. A studio feature writer generally makes a lot more money. Go to www.wga.org and search for "Schedule of Minimums" and you can find exact minimum figures.

Hollywood Heat _____

YOUR NAME

The first feature version of the *Charlie's Angels* TV series was plagued with problems but did great at the box office. The feature of *The Brady Bunch* cost only about $12 million to make and produced a nice profit. You see old TV movies made into features because they require less advertising. Fans of the TV series are certain to show at the box office.

So now let's take a quick look at what a situation comedy script looks like. Let's imagine my *Walking After Midnight* was a sitcom. (I'll cross my fingers, hoping for a three-year run.) About ⅗ of the way down the page we would see:

WALKING AFTER MIDNIGHT

"Episode title would go here"

ACT ONE

A

FADE IN:

INT. MOONRISE DINER - DAY

(MIRABELLE, JAKE)

JAKE IS SITTING AT A BOOTH WHEN MIRABELLE ENTERS. (In sitcoms, action is written in uppercase.)

MIRA

Hi, Jake.

JAKE JUMPS LIKE HE'S BEEN SHOT AT, SPILLING COFFEE ON HIMSELF.

JAKE

Woman, you put the spook on me!

MIRA

What's that spook's name, Jack Daniels?

AS JAKE CLIMBS OUT OF THE BOOTH AND HURRIES TOWARD THE BATHROOM IN THE BACK, WE …

CUT TO:

NOTE: There are parts to a sitcom script, hence the "A" underneath "ACT ONE" above.

As you can see from the different format examples, you need to read *current* scripts to see how it's being done. I highly recommend formatting programs for various kinds of scripts, as they offer samples from real shows and movies.

Elements to Remember When Writing a Script

Great scripts often have a main setting or tackle a subject that you don't expect. Watch as diverse a diet of movies as possible; you want people to say "Ah, we've never seen *that* before!"

The main secret of a great script is to write something that you would dearly love to see onscreen or that you can *get* onscreen yourself. Kevin Smith's hilarious *Clerks* is a good example of a great script that anyone could film. I've heard from famous film-makers repeatedly that when they reach a point where they can make their choice of scripts, they film the ones that they want to see or the ones they think they can make better than anyone else can.

If you decide that your story idea should definitely be a screenplay, before you commit yourself to weeks, months, or years perfecting it on paper, ask yourself this question: Do I *really* want to see this?

The Least You Need to Know

- It is essential that you perfect the basics of any art before you attempt to deviate from established norms, but breaking the rules could make you famous.

- For beginning screenwriters, it is wise to read as many scripts as possible, particularly scripts of recent movies.

- Stage plays and screenplays have distinctly different formats and approaches to dialogue; if you like long, eloquent speeches, you're probably better off as a playwright or a politician.

◆ If you want to spend much time revealing a character's thoughts, you're better off **writing** a novel.

◆ The format of TV movie scripts and feature films is not that dissimilar, but it's generally very difficult as a first-timer to make a TV movie sale.

◆ One-hour TV scripts are much like feature films. Sitcom format is very different. Either way, series are where the big TV money is made.

Chapter 8

What Your Audience Really Wants to See

In This Chapter

◆ What sex and violence really mean

◆ Escape from reality

◆ Genre success

◆ Writing for the world

◆ The kids have it

Writers for television sooner or later realize that certain types of programs repeatedly get on the air. One-hour cop shows and one-hour medical dramas will most likely be with us for the foreseeable future. It's pretty much the same year after year. Family comedies were a staple of early television and still work today, with "family" having increasingly diverse definitions. But how about features?

As a screenwriter, you should basically write a story that *you* want to see onscreen. Nevertheless, to remain ignorant of established genres, box office successes, and market preferences is screenwriting suicide. Do yourself a favor and study what has done well, with an eye toward what may remain popular in the future. When you've mastered the basics, then innovate.

Hollywood Heat

YOUR NAME

The surprise hit of the summer of 2003 was the PG-13 *Pirates of the Caribbean: The Curse of the Black Pearl.* Derived from a ride at Disneyland, the movie was written by Terry Rossio and Ted Elliot, who readily share all they know about their craft at www.wordplayer.com. They also wrote another surprise blockbuster, *Shrek.* If you write a family-friendly PG-13 movie, that could be the hottest ticket in Hollywood.

There will always be artists and intellectuals in any art form. They'll whine about commercialism and bemoan the low or "unenlightened" tastes of the masses. History has a keener eye. Often enough, some of the most popular works of entertainment manage to become classics. The most successful screenplays and films remind me of Mark Twain's comparison of his writing to more literary works. The others were like fine wine, he said, while his books were like water—and a lot more people drank water. They still do.

Sex and Violence Sell: What That Really Means

I once dated a girl who helped me see why so many people like the horror genre. She led a humdrum life and worked at a job she didn't like. People have lives full of frustration and mental demons they can't conquer. The thrill of horror makes them feel better, and the demons on the screen get conquered! This is precisely why teenagers love horror, see these films in packs, and make huge hits out of movies like the *Saw* series (2004–2006).

It's Not for Us

PASS

Thinking that I was very clever, I once began a feature script with a weightless sex scene in space. Six months later, I discovered that someone had already filmed one—in a porno movie. Never write a scene merely for the "wow" factor. Besides, if it doesn't fit the flow of the story, you may jar the reader or viewer out of getting through your script.

For a long time, movie people had told me that "sex and violence sell." They never qualified it much, and I had trouble with the idea. Did I have to write bloodily violent films or push the bounds of sexual content in scripts to get noticed? Having grown up admiring Walt Disney movies and with Jimmy Stewart as my favorite movie star, I've felt that I would be betraying my heritage in writing overly salacious and grossly violent movies.

I love Clint Eastwood films, particularly the *Dirty Harry* stories. I'm not a regular viewer of porno, but I've seen a few. I just wasn't inclined to write either type of material. So how could I use the "sex and violence sell" dictum?

Eventually, I realized that my Hollywood mentors were talking about an *increased sense of living* comparable to sex. Your heart races, your senses are enhanced, and you breathe more deeply. Hopefully, when it's over, you're left with a memorable emotional experience, and you simply feel more alive. What teenager doesn't like the excuse a horror movie gives him or her to cling to a date for security?

Now let's look at violence. Have you ever been in a fight or been attacked? Your heart races, your senses are enhanced, and you breathe more deeply. When it's over, you're left with a memorable emotional experience, whether it's positive or negative.

In terms of Hollywood movies, sex and violence can be metaphorical. What is sex but attraction and interaction between potential sexual partners? What is violence but conflict between two opposing forces? With that in mind, let's examine *Gone with the Wind* (1939), for a long time the all-time box office champion. There was never a more sexually charged relationship onscreen than that of Rhett Butler (Clark Gable) and Scarlett O'Hara (Vivien Leigh). We never see them naked, together or alone, but even today a lot of people prefer that movie to the nakedly graphic *Basic Instinct* (1992).

Skip's Tips _____

Ah, the "sexy" opening. Starting a script with a sexual or violent scene will likely grab a reader's attention and get them past the first few pages, but you should ask yourself two questions: First, is this incident a major turning point in your main character's life? Second, does it immediately propel your main character into the heart of the story?

In any number of Clint Eastwood films, someone is brutally victimized by a very evil person or a pack of evil people. Eastwood's character suffers through much travail to finally wreak even greater revenge on the bad guys at the end of the film.

So how about a less graphic arc of violence? Let's take the suffering of Gary Cooper's character in *High Noon* (1952). We don't see much graphic violence in that movie, but Cooper suffers wound after emotional wound as the townspeople cowardly refuse to help him defend the town against approaching thugs. At the end, just as in the much more violent Eastwood films, there is great relief as we experience a sense that rightness has prevailed and that justice has once again won out. Don't take my word on this. See which movie you find more appealing, Eastwood's *Unforgiven* (1992) or *High Noon*.

Sex in Hollywood does not have to equal sweat and skin. Beautiful leading ladies and handsome leading men help us live vicariously and fulfill our fantasies. When movies are truly entertaining, they make us feel better, more alive. Similarly, bad guys who live by violence only respect a stronger force, in real life and in the movies. If you

Skip's Tips

Most scripts begin with "FADE IN:" (note the colon). This means that a picture gradually appears from a black screen. Scripts end with the opposite, "FADE OUT." (note the period). Think of these editing actions in terms of being born and dying, with varying shades of sex and violence in between.

cannot combat them, an onscreen hero who smashes thugs into oblivion helps fulfill a desire for justice.

You don't have to write graphic sex and violence to sell. If a movie engages your intellect, makes your blood race, and leaves you feeling better or more thoughtful when it's over, you've done your job as a screenwriter. The real test is whether the movie makes someone feel more alive. And here's one more tip. Both words, sex and violence, denote *action*. In a business built around "moving pictures," they imply a connection and movement between opposites and an interesting story moving forward.

Helping Your Viewer Escape from Reality

If you are around a shopping mall with a multiplex movie theater, spend some time there, but don't watch a movie. Sit outside and watch the people. Or try a video store. Go browse the hundreds of videos and DVDs, but don't rent anything. Watch the other people who are renting. Watch the teenagers, the working adults, the parents with kids, the couples on a date, and the seniors, too. Try and figure out what they're spending their money on.

How good are you at reading people? Can you read faces? Do you know when someone is overworked? Can you tell when someone's eyes are sad, even though they're smiling? See if you notice a change in their demeanor, perhaps a quickening in their step, after their ticket is purchased or their video is selected.

It's Not for Us

In *Adventures in the Screen Trade: A Personal View of Hollywood and Screenwriting* (Warner Books, 1983), screenwriter William Goldman offered a single axiom about Hollywood: "Nobody knows anything." This gets misinterpreted to mean that you can break any rule at will. What Goldman really meant is that someone always comes along who successfully defies conventional film wisdom. But those mavericks know the rules they break. Learn the rules.

I don't know about you, but for the time I'm watching a video, a movie, or a theatrical or musical performance, I forget about my cares and escape from reality. I think you'll discover it's much the same for everyone. In recent years, the graphic carnage and high emotions of graphic novels by Frank Miller like *Sin City* and *300* have easily translated to film, partly due to the fact that the world is so exaggerated from our own, it's obvious that it's just escapism.

Movies provide this escape for anyone, anywhere, no matter what their social station or location. If you saw the delighted young Dalai Lama in *Seven Years in Tibet* (1997), you know what I mean. Even a spiritual leader needs relief from life. Long before that movie was made, Preston Sturges emphasized this in his *Sullivan's Travels* (1942), about a disheartened "fluff" movie director who thinks that his work is meaningless. Dressed as a hobo, he sets off to research a socially relevant movie called *O Brother, Where Art Thou?* and, through a series of circumstances, ends up on a criminal chain gang in the South, where life seems very bleak. Then, on a Saturday night, the hardened criminals are treated to a Hollywood movie, projected with rudimentary equipment. As he watches the delighted laughs of his fellow chain gang members, the director realizes the true service that he provides his fellow human beings by creating escapist entertainment.

The Coen brothers' *O Brother, Where Art Thou?* (2000), which is *Ulysses* set in the U.S. South in the 1930s, took its title and inspiration from Sturges's great film.

If your screenplay is made, you have no idea who will see it. It may be the Dalai Lama or a man on a chain gang. They both have their everyday burdens, and each equally welcomes the escape that a good movie provides. For your script to be made (unless you film it yourself), you will have to please, at minimum, a producer, a director, and someone who finances the filming of your script. Just don't get lost in trying to be so "Hollywood" you forget your eventual audience.

Remember the story about Shakespeare, who had to please the commoner "ground-lings" as well as the royals in the balconies. If your movie is made, you have a chance to be important in all sorts of lives. Your words may someday echo through the heavens, but not until they pass the high test of the common man.

Pick a Genre and Pick Success

In the first class on writing that I ever taught at the Extension Writer's Program at the University of California at Los Angeles (UCLA), I had my students go to a bookstore and report on all the categories they found. At first they thought it was dumb, but then I asked them where the manuscript they would work on in class would be filed. As the light dawned in their eyes, I explained that *when* (not if, when) they sold their work, the first thing they would be asked about was the genre of the piece.

Skip's Tips _____

Your Name

Because of the dynamic nature of the World Wide Web, you can find more up-to-date information there than anywhere else, as long as you know where to look. For a very thorough listing of top movies by genre, do some browsing at us.imdb.com/chart. It's an education in itself on what is successful in Hollywood.

A trip to the video store should give you a general idea about what has been popular in the past few years. Will those tastes continue? Generally, yes. Anomalies such as *The Blair Witch Project* or *My Big Fat Greek Wedding* come along, but there is no category for "Unexpected Success."

Many authors attempt to distill plot lines into repeating formulas. Eugene Polti's *Thirty-Six Dramatic Situations* is one of the oldest. Genres and subgenres are covered in Robert McKee's *Story* (Regan Books, 1997), but not exactly in the type of classification that you see at a video store. In this book, I'd rather list genres as you would hear them mentioned by Hollywood development executives and producers, and also give you some indication of how popular they are currently. This is a primer, alphabetically listed shorthand, with examples from recent years. If you think I've left out any important genres, let me know.

- **Action.** This is most often a cross-genre description. A crime drama such as *The Untouchables* might be considered action by some, but epic historical dramas such as *Braveheart* or *Gladiator* or *300* or *Beowulf* are also action movies. In definite action movies, monumental forces clash in an almost continuous and unrelenting fashion. Action movies usually involve big stars.

- **Adventure.** Anyone who favors the Joseph Campbell myth structure is a fan of adventure movies. The main character almost always deals with some kind of new and amazing world. The *Lord of the Rings* movies fit this genre, which can also be referred to as epic or myth, due to the Campbell influence.

- **Animation.** With the advent of computer animation with Pixar's *Toy Story*, this genre is very sophisticated. One look at the amazing action in the 2007 blockbuster *Ratatouille* will show you that. It's a hard genre to break into, but it's not impossible.

- **Anime.** Although this Asian "adult cartoon" type of movie has legions of followers, at the time of this writing you probably wouldn't get far in Hollywood with an original anime script, but that could change.

- **Chick Lit.** This genre sprang up after the first edition of this book. "Chick literature" features smart, often funny women and are hot movie properties. Think *The Devil Wears Prada* (2006, novel by Lauren Weisberger), and you've got it.

Hollywood Heat

Jennie Lew Tugend had worked on a number of the *Lethal Weapon* films when she found *Free Willy*. The powers-that-be at Warner Brothers liked the script, but they suggested that it be rewritten to accommodate an action star such as Mel Gibson. Many producers would have overlooked this family favorite, but Tugend insisted that the star was the whale and convinced Warner to fund the movie. The original cost $10 million to make, grossed $100 million, and was followed by two sequels. Not bad for an unknown cetacean.

♦ **Comedy.** This is a broad genre that skews toward the bizarre, with the successes of Jim Carrey, Will Ferrell, Adam Sandler, Ben Stiller, and the Farrelly brothers. A maxim in Hollywood is, drama is easy, comedy is hard. If you have the talent to write broad comedy such as *Analyze This* or family comedy like *Big Fat Liar*, you'll get rich.

♦ **Coming of age.** Also known as "rites of passage," this genre is a reflective drama requiring skillful and insightful writing. When it works, it works well, as in *The Cider House Rules*. When it doesn't work, it is maudlin. If you aspire to win an Oscar, this could be your genre. This type of movie, like *To Kill a Mockingbird* or *Forrest Gump*, is often a classic.

♦ **Crime/detective.** This once-prolific genre has been largely hijacked by television. Crime features now are usually cross-genre thrillers, as in *L.A. Confidential*, or are mixed with love stories, as in *Ghost*. One neglected subgenre was the "caper" film, until the remake of *Ocean's Eleven* with an all-star cast was a big hit spawning sequels.

♦ **Drama.** This very broad category is generally used to refer to a story about some social issue or struggle, as in *A Beautiful Mind*. If you're intent on sending a message in a script, this is your genre. Dramas are generally a hard sell, however.

♦ **Dramedy.** Rapidly becoming its own genre is this combination of drama and comedy in which serious issues are dealt with in a comedic fashion, as in *Juno*.

It's Not for Us

PASS If you find it hard to pin your script down to one genre, don't worry. Just don't use more than a couple of genres to describe it, and use popular genres in the description. For example, a "mystery musical comedy" is certain to get your script tossed, unless you are an established writer/director.

◆ **Ensemble.** This type of drama is usually made by actors as first-time directors who also write. The emphasis is on a central issue, not a central character. You must be able to write interesting dialogue to make this one work. An example is *The Anniversary Party.*

◆ **Fantasy.** This genre is one usually derived from hugely best-selling novels, like the *Harry Potter* movies. Even then, those books were a hard sell at Warner Brothers. Original fantasy screenplays are tough to market unless they're meant for animation.

◆ **Film noir.** This stylized crime drama is great for launching a career or even *making* a career. The Coen brothers broke in with *Blood Simple*, while *Chinatown* was considered for a long time to be the greatest script of the latter twentieth century. *L.A. Confidential* won an Academy Award. A dark movie with a unique twist, like *Memento*, can be a breakthrough for a writer-director.

◆ **Horror.** This one seems easy, but you need a twist, such as *The Blair Witch Project* (promoted on the Internet in a way that made it initially seem like real people died on camera). If you are original, you'll get rich because horror movies can be made with unknowns and be big at the box office, as 2002's *28 Days Later ...*, from the U.K.

◆ **Independent.** If you don't understand this genre, just read up on the Sundance Film Festival or watch a lot of movies on The Sundance Channel. These films, formerly known as "art films," involve quirky subjects and low budgets, and can be a fine way to launch a career. Robert Rodriguez's *El Mariachi* is a great example.

◆ **Musical.** The successes of *Moulin Rouge* and *Chicago* changed Hollywood's perception of musical possibilities in recent years, and on television Disney's *High School Musical* (2006) and its 2007 sequel were *huge.*

◆ **Mystery.** It's sad to say, but this genre seems like a remnant of another age. Was *The Usual Suspects* a mystery, a crime drama, or a thriller? These days, mysteries mostly work on television.

◆ **Outdoors/wildlife.** Most beginning screenwriters don't consider this genre, but *Homeward Bound* and *Babe* were big hits. If you have a script in which kids interact with animals, you usually can get it read. This type of film is visually rich and usually inexpensive to make.

◆ **Romance.** There aren't enough good romances around, which is why it's hard to find a good "date movie." They're much tougher to sell than "chick lit" or romantic comedy, however.

◆ **Romantic comedy.** Also known as "romcom," this is a completely separate genre from comedy. In a romance, there's more drama than comedy. In the latter, it's reversed, and the way the couple fumbles toward their inevitable result is hilarious, like *Wedding Crashers.*

◆ **Sci-fi.** The science-fiction genre needs no explanation, and with computer-generated film technology and the megasuccess of *The Matrix* movies, this one's a winner. Take a look at the top 10 moneymakers of all time, and you'll see a lot of sci-fi titles.

◆ **Thriller.** Alfred Hitchcock virtually invented this genre. To master it, see all his films. Usually, the hero is an innocent and the enemy is seemingly unbeatable. *Silence of the Lambs* is a great example, as is *The Firm* or *The Brave One* with Jodie Foster. Authors of thrillers make big bucks, and movies of their novels draw big stars and big box office success.

◆ **War.** For some reason (looming mortality, perhaps) the Baby Boomer generation has rediscovered the war movie. *Saving Private Ryan* was a success and many imitators followed. War movies are expensive, but sometimes they hit the public mood just right, as *300* did in 2006.

◆ **Western.** A long-time Hollywood staple, this genre gets neglected until someone makes one and generally always has a hit. *Last Stand at Saber River* with Tom Selleck was Turner Network Television's top movie of 1997. Then Kevin Costner had a nice comeback with *Open Range* in 2003. Robert Duvall's *Broken Trail* (2006) topped all TV networks in the rating and won Duvall an Emmy. The remake of *3:10 To Yuma* in 2007 was a hit, too.

I've listed only fictional genres here. Documentaries are worthy of another book and generally are not as profitable; they're not so much written as made. Whatever genre you pick, remember that Hollywood people who are genre-savvy mix them in description all the time. For example, *Ace Ventura, Pet Detective,* can be described as an action comedy mixed with outdoor/wildlife. I hope that you find a genre at which you excel.

It's Not for Us _____

Don't force trying to write for a certain genre just because you like it. Sometimes the proper genre finds you. Stephen King has had more books, stories, and scripts made into films than any other living writer, but the King of Horror started out wanting to be a great Western writer like Louis L'Amour!

Writing for the Worldwide Audience

To get an introduction to the tastes of audiences worldwide, remember the word _action_. Wordy movies are generally not popular overseas. People understand moving characters; moving lips that don't speak your language are harder to understand. Roberto Begnini understood this well when he made his hit _Life Is Beautiful_ (1997) in his native Italian; Begnini's onscreen characterizations and pratfalls are right out of silent Buster Keaton films.

You might want to keep the mores of other cultures in mind. The R-rated _The Matrix: Reloaded_ was banned in Egypt in 2003 because the censors there felt Neo, the protagonist, was antagonistic to three main religions: Judaism, Christianity, and Islam.

For more insight into non-American, international tastes, pay close attention to the yearly Golden Globe winners selected by the Hollywood Foreign Press Association. The HFPA is an association of journalists in southern California who write for foreign media. HFPA members tend to like rebels and those who challenge the societies in which they live and/or have great internal struggles, at least when they select the Best Screenplay. Winners in this decade have included _About Schmidt_, _Lost In Translation_, _Sideways_, _Brokeback Mountain_, and _The Queen_.

If you want to write for an international audience, think action, watch the Golden Globes, and pay attention to events at the annual Cannes Film Festival. And don't forget, action and a truly great story appeal to people across time and culture. The massive success of movies by Chinese directors have proven this over and over in recent years.

The Kids Have It: Write with Children in Mind and Win

While researching the original version of this book, I studied the top-grossing movies of all time and discovered something that amazed me. Rather than any particular genre being dominant, it seemed that the most money has been made in the movie business based around a kid factor. That has particularly been true in the past decade.

Hollywood Heat _____

The most successful cable television network is Nickelodeon, thanks to "Nick at Nite" reruns of Baby Boomers' favorite old shows and new animated programs such as *Rugrats*, which spawned several animated features. The recent Hollywood animation boom was so enormous that it generated a foreign reaction against animation. Successes in recent years like 2003's *Finding Nemo* and other Pixar films like 2007's *Ratatouille* flattened that antagonism. Count on increased opportunities for screenwriters who write films the whole family likes.

The kids have it. Starting with a breakdown of the 250 top all-time box office leaders (using gross domestic box office only), I broke down successful elements of these films into some very interesting categories. I did not pay attention to the conventional wisdom that movies should generally be geared to the 18 to 34 male age group demographic, nor did I pay any attention to movie ratings (G, PG, PG-13, and so on). I listed the top 250 movies in categories that I developed (listed alphabetically, not by importance) as follows:

A	action
CA	college age character(s)
CH	childlike main character(s)/learning like child
E	epic/grand in scope
GC	group situation, comedy, or caper
K	prominent kid character
KL	kids love it
L	love/matters of the heart
NH	strong animal or non-human character
S/T	suspense/thriller
T	teen character(s)/coming of age
YP	young professionals in lead roles

Skip's Tips _____

Although I've included a lot of material here, I have a discussion about "kids love it" that I am happy to share with any reader. Contact me via my website, www.skippress.com, and I'll get it to you, or you can find a document about it on the CD that comes with this book.

I found that the most important element, by far, of highly successful movies is a kid connection. Whether it is simply that "kids love it," that there is a childlike main character (which Tom Hanks has excelled at playing), or that it includes nonhuman characters that children love, real box office success more often than not derives from one or more elements in a film that all add up into *something that kids love*. Often these films are not those that you would suspect small children would love, such as *Titanic*, which my (then) six-year-old daughter wanted to see repeatedly because of the love story. Naturally, movies with a prominent kid character appeal to young children, but other successful films with a youth element reach viewers of an age much *less* than the conventional wisdom 18 to 34 demographic.

Having published a number of novels and nonfiction books for young adults (generally considered to be ages 12 to 18), I know that if you write a 12-year-old main character, that character will normally appeal most to kids who are two to three years younger. If you write high school kids in the lead, junior high students find them appealing. If movies have teen characters in the lead roles, that means they will not only appeal to teen moviegoers, but also strongly to kids as young as nine. Similarly, if movies have a young professional in the lead role, teens strongly identify with them. Again, this means that the appeal is much younger than 18 to 34. Six of these 12 categories listed relate to kids. Kids want to emulate the actions of older people with whom they can identify. With a little bit of child in all of us and the childhood years so formative in our minds, it is little wonder that a main character with childlike qualities is so popular. *Forrest Gump* is a good example. Of the top 25 movies of all time, most have the main quality of "kids love it." This means that a family can take the kids to see these movies, and these films get a lot of repeat business (kids like to see things over and over). In the summer of 2003, *Finding Nemo* became the most successful animated film of all time, and outgrossed *The Matrix: Reloaded* domestically by $48 million. The PG-13–rated *Pirates of the Caribbean: Curse of the Black Pearl*, sunk *Bad Boys 2*. *Pirates* cost less and made almost double at the box office. In 2002, the "kids love it" idea truly ruled. In 2007, Dwayne Johnson, a.k.a. "The Rock," was on top of the box office two weeks in a row with his family-friendly comedy *The Game Plan*. In March 2008, *Horton Hears a Who* with Jim Carrey was #1 for three weeks.

Take a look at the following table for the Top 20 All-Time Worldwide Box Office movies as of October 2007, courtesy of www.imdb.com:

Rank	Title	Worldwide B.O.
1.	*Titanic* (1997)	$1,835,300,000
2.	*The Lord of the Rings: The Return of the King* (2003)	$1,129,219,252
3.	*Pirates of the Caribbean: Dead Man's Chest* (2006)	$1,060,332,628
4.	*Harry Potter and the Sorcerer's Stone* (2001)	$968,657,891
5.	*Pirates of the Caribbean: At World's End* (2007)	$958,404,152
6.	*Harry Potter and the Order of the Phoenix* (2007)	$936,040,445
7.	*Star Wars: Episode I—The Phantom Menace* (1999)	$922,379,000
8.	*The Lord of the Rings: The Two Towers* (2002)	$921,600,000
9.	*Jurassic Park* (1993)	$919,700,000
10.	*Harry Potter and the Goblet of Fire* (2005)	$892,194,397
11.	*Spider-Man 3* (2007)	$885,430,303
12.	*Shrek 2* (2004)	$880,871,036
13.	*Harry Potter and the Chamber of Secrets* (2002)	$866,300,000
14.	*Finding Nemo* (2003)	$865,000,000
15.	*The Lord of the Rings: The Fellowship of the Ring* (2001)	$860,700,000
16.	*Star Wars: Episode III—Revenge of the Sith* (2005)	$848,462,555
17.	*Independence Day* (1996)	$811,200,000
18.	*Spider-Man* (2002)	$806,700,000
19.	*Star Wars* (1977)	$797,900,000
20.	*Shrek the Third* (2007)	$791,106,665

Even movies that are not in that type of income category, if they have a high cost-to-profit ratio, are usually family-friendly. This includes movies like *Snow Dogs* in 2002 and *Snow Day* in 2000. *Snow Day* was produced by Ray Wagner, a savvy producer who has run more than one studio in his many years in Hollywood. Just like Garry Marshall with *Princess Diaries*, Wagner wanted to make a film that the whole family could see, and it paid off with a massive cost-to-profit ratio.

Nia Vardalos's *My Big Fat Greek Wedding* (2002), which began as a one-woman show and was made for $5,000,000 with no big stars, went on to become the most successful romantic comedy of all time. The profit listed for it at www.imdb.com shows a 50-to-1 return.

At the movies, the kids have it, and something tells me they'll keep it. I told my readers about this in 1999, and Hollywood finally came around.

The Least You Need to Know

- ◆ "Sex and violence sells" is really about the manner in which movies provide the viewer with an increased sense of living.

- ◆ The screenwriter's number-one job is to write a movie that will, at least for a time, help the viewer escape everyday reality.

- ◆ Writers who do not fully understand movie genres are greatly handicapped and may overlook success opportunities.

- ◆ A truly great story with lots of action is guaranteed to appeal to movie audiences across time and culture.

- ◆ In recent years, movies about rebels who challenge the societies in which they live have been popular worldwide.

- ◆ The predominant element, by far, of the majority of highly successful movies over the past few decades can be simply qualified as "kids love it."

Chapter 9

Defining Your Movie

In This Chapter

- ◆ Premises first
- ◆ Messages are for e-mail
- ◆ Pre-script documents
- ◆ The movie's basic idea
- ◆ What a "log line" means
- ◆ Making a storyline work

New screenwriters ask the same questions and inevitably get confused because the definitions and "rules" in the movie world change whimsically. There is no Hollywood dictionary that defines terms for everyone, and every screenwriting teacher tries to come up with something different to make his or her philosophy stand out. That's why, when someone produces a standard, logical observation that defines something about the business, it is adopted in chokehold fashion. That's what happened with Syd Field's "paradigm" of screenplay structure after his book *Screenplay* burst upon the scene. Hollywood readers would check scripts to see whether each act and plot point ended where Field said it should, and some development people actually rejected a script if it didn't match the Field schematic. The practice was maddening to writers.

As you think through the story line of a script, what page an act turns on should not be that much of a consideration. You start with an idea, or maybe a dozen ideas, and then settle on one that you think is most viable. Then you determine what you're really trying to say, and you outline the scenes. And sometimes you throw it all away and start over. You really must be willing to do that. Now let's talk about how to shape a movie story.

Skip's Tips

It costs two people in my neighborhood $30 to go to a first-run movie theater and buy popcorn and sodas. Would you spend the $30 on your idea? Would the poster of your movie prompt you to commit the next hour or two of your life? When I'm selecting possible ideas, I pop the $30 question.

First, a Premise

The root definition of *premise* is "to place (or send) ahead." In *Webster's New Collegiate Dictionary*, one definition is "to set forth beforehand as an introduction or postulate." What's a *postulate?* The word comes from a very ancient root, *prcchati*, a word from Sanskrit, perhaps the most ancient language of Earth. It means, "he asks." A postulate is a question asked, a "What if?" You could say it's a prayer (that your script will be bought!).

Here's another definition of premise: "to presuppose or imply as preexistent." What would that mean in a screenplay story? It means that within our pages, we want to create a world that, even if it reflects a familiar reality, envelopes viewers so that they feel as if the world onscreen has always existed. I don't know how you feel about *Star Wars: Episode I: The Phantom Menace* as a movie, but if you're like me, the idea of living on a planet like Naboo was a thrilling idea.

Hollywood Heat

Writers and writing teachers borrow from each other all the time and sometimes forget that they've borrowed. That might have happened when Irwin R. Blacker wrote *The Elements of Screenwriting: A Guide for Film and Television Writing* (Macmillan, 1986). In Chapter 2, he defined *premise* as the basis of the conflict and then gave examples of *King Lear* and *Macbeth* almost word for word the premises given by Lajos Egri in *The Art of Dramatic Writing* (Wildside Press, 2007).

It's a daunting task to create a world. According to the Bible, it took God six days to accomplish the task, and then he rested. If you spend a week thinking about the premise of your movie, you're right on schedule. Unless you're God, the script usually takes longer.

In *The Art of Dramatic Writing*, Lajos Egri (writing mostly about playwriting) says there is a premise for every life, every second of every day. To him, a premise is something proposed that will lead to a logical conclusion. A number of writers I know object to Egri's proposition because they think he is telling the writer to start with a message and then make the story prove it. Have they read the entire book? Shortly after Egri gives his definition, he lists other writers who talk about things such as theme, root idea, goal, subject, thesis, and other things. All of them, Egri says, are talking about the premise.

Let's examine this premise business with Adam Sandler's *Happy Gilmore. What if* a hockey player took up professional golf? Don't you instantly see some of the scenes, such as Sandler slamming a drive using a hockey stroke? Or the fight on the golf course? We instantly have what Lajos Egri called the "unity of opposites"—the rowdiness and raw power of hockey pitted against the gentility and precision of professional golf. *Happy Gilmore* was a good idea and a very funny movie that started with a great premise. Sandler often makes "What if?" movies, such as *Click* (2006), about a magic remote that controls everything.

A great premise immediately sets up the conflict to come. That applies in all genres. In the romantic comedy *My Big Fat Greek Wedding*, a shy Greek girl blossoms when she meets a great guy. But he's not Greek, so how can she possibly be with him? Her father will kill her! Even if you haven't seen the film, I'm sure you can see what might happen when someone outside a tightly knit ethnic community seeks to marry into it.

Later in this book, we'll discuss pitching your screenplay to producers and writing effective query letters. If you start out with a premise like I've described here, it will be much easier to tell people what your movie is about, and I think you'll find that your screenplay will be easier to write.

Skip's Tips

Pitching a screenplay or screenplay idea goes on in Hollywood all the time. Proven screenwriters (those with a track record or whose writing readers and producers respect) are frequently invited to "come in and pitch." That's when you need to be able to easily describe what your movie is about. You might be asked to "just tell me the beats," which means the high points of the story.

Both Lajos Egri and Irwin R. Blacker define the premise of Shakespeare's *The Tragedy of King Lear* as "Blind trust leads to destruction." If you don't know the story, it's about a monarch who turns everything over to his three daughters, with disastrous results. Let's describe it this way: "*What if* an angry patriarch turns over the family farm to his three daughters and their husbands, prompting the family's dark past to boil over?"

That's the plot of *A Thousand Acres* (1997), starring Michelle Pfeiffer, Jessica Lange, and Jennifer Jason Leigh as the Cook sisters, and Jason Robards as their father, Larry Cook. It's *King Lear* set on a farm in Iowa. If you were searching for screenplay ideas, you could say, "What if *King Lear* took place on a farm?" I prefer the "What if?" approach. Everyone understands it. If you want to look deeper into your story, you might find a *theme*. That isn't the same as a premise, really, unless you're talking about an Egri premise. You can use a theme as a guidepost or a landmark as you write your story. Think of Indiana Jones hacking through a jungle with a machete to get to the top of a mountain always visible above the jungle canopy. There's a cave in the mountain full of golden treasure. Let's say that his theme is "Persistence on a straight path leads to wealth." He can always look up and see whether he's getting closer. Then a new character pops up, a beautiful temptress who beckons him to a river barge. If he strays to one side, pursuing some theme such as "Beauty has its own reward," he'll never reach that cave, will he? He has to stick to his original theme to do that.

> **It's Not for Us**
>
> Don't waste time in arguments with other writers about how to "properly" write a screenplay. Everyone goes about necessary tasks in their own way. Try to get your hands on scripts going into production, written by top screenwriters. Emulate the best whenever you can. Top screenwriters do!

"What if?" defines the story and is true to the original "he asks" definition of the root word of premise itself. When you come up with the right "What if?" question, it can have magical results. When a Hollywood executive, who is usually knowledgeable of movies and TV shows of at least the last five years, hears the right "What if?", the reaction is predictable. "Wow!" this executive will say, with his face lit up. "No one's ever done that before!" (Take my word for it, Hollywood executives are big on "*No one's ever done that before.*")

If You Want to Send a Message, Use E-Mail

Speaking of executives, there probably never will be a more colorful Hollywood character than producer Samuel Goldwyn. He was one of the Hollywood originals, the Goldwyn in Metro Goldwyn Mayer (MGM), and notorious for his nutty statements such as "A verbal agreement isn't worth the paper it's written on." One of his statements is particularly true with regard to writing movies. "Pictures are for entertainment," Goldwyn said. "Messages should be delivered by Western Union."

You've probably never sent a message by Western Union. You might not even know what a telegraph was, and you might not ever have had anyone wire you money to a Western Union office. Western Union no longer sends telegraphs, but in Goldwyn's day, telegraphs were sent all over the world, in a time when international phone connections were often chancy.

If Goldwyn was alive today, his statement might be "If you want to send a message, use e-mail."

When I think of movies of great social conscience that I've admired, I think of films such as *Gandhi*, Sir Richard Attenborough's great triumph. Well, guess what? Mahatma Gandhi changed the world, but it took Attenborough as a highly experienced director and show business veteran 25 years to bring this story to the screen.

One of my favorite screenwriters, Robert Bolt, thrilled me with *Lawrence of Arabia*, *A Man for All Seasons*, and *Dr. Zhivago*. He turned great true stories into works of art. All these Bolt movies were based on true stories on a world stage, in times of great social change, but I'm not sure that Bolt or anyone else who writes movies like these sets out to send a message. I think, rather, that they tell the story and let it pose questions.

The great Greek philosopher Socrates asked questions to elevate consciousness. By posing the proper questions and having people answer them (known as the Socratic method), he led them to conclusions, but they discovered those conclusions on their own.

If you hit people over the head with an idea, they won't appreciate it. If you use a feather to tickle their imagination, they'll be pleasantly stimulated. Don't send a message—get your viewer to ask a question.

Hollywood Heat

If you feel you want to say something meaningful in a script, take a clue from the prolific Philip K. Dick. The movie *Blade Runner* (1982) came from a Philip K. Dick novel titled *Do Androids Dream of Electric Sheep?* Another Dick story was the basis of *Minority Report* (2001). These days, one of his properties goes for $1,000,000 for movie rights. Dick wrote about what he cared about.

Outlines, Synopses, and Treatments

You may feel confused when you start asking about "treatments" in Hollywood because you'll run into so many differing opinions. Some folks will tell you that you can never sell a treatment. They're sold every year, but usually only by experienced screenwriters who are then hired to deliver the script. At least 10 times as many pitches are sold, however, which should tell you something about the importance of relationships in Hollywood. If your work is known and respected—which almost always comes only from completed screenplays—you can pitch a story and get paid to write a treatment, or perhaps a synopsis first and then a treatment.

Skip's Tips _____

If you want to fully understand the process of coverage, read *Reading for a Living: How to Be a Professional Story Analyst for Film and Television,* by T. L. Katahn (Blue Arrow Books, 1991). It's a how-to book that includes coverage samples.

Let's start with a synopsis first. When you mail someone a completed "spec" screenplay—meaning that it was not written as a paid assignment, but on the speculation that you would sell it—that person gets it "covered." That means someone is paid to read your work and comment in writing. This reader might do only a "top sheet," which is one page. Most likely, the reader also will do full coverage, which runs two to three pages. The description of your work will be a synopsis. Should you provide one? Usually not, unless a producer asks to see one to decide if they want to read the script.

In doing coverage, the reader describes what the story is about and offers one of the following recommendations: recommend, consider, or pass. The first thing the reader is interested in is the commercial potential of the material (after all, it is show *business*). If it's commercial, you'll likely get a consider vote. Recommends are rarely given. What if the reader recommends your script, the producer or studio makes the movie, and it bombs? Who gets the blame? The reader is the lowest person on the production company totem pole and the easiest to fire.

The reader might also give your work a consider vote just because he or she likes the quality of your work, so don't fret if you don't think that you write material that would readily be considered commercial. They might hire you to rewrite something, based on quality work.

Now to treatments. If you've ever written a book, or if you had a good composition teacher in school, you probably learned to outline a story. Think of an outline as the skeleton of a treatment. It describes what Hollywood veterans called the "beats" of the story. A real "treatment" is a *tool* that studios, production companies, and screenwriters have used for years. It is simply a description, scene by scene, of the movie, minus most or all the dialogue. If you were writing *Casablanca* you might include Bogart's line about "Of all the gin joints in all the world …." Any strong line that illustrates a crucial part of the story might be included.

Sometimes these days, people (particularly development executives) think of a treatment as 10 to 25 pages (or more) that describe the story. I've heard a development exec say that if he's pressed for time but interested in an idea, he'd rather read the treatment to see if he wants to read the script.

Skip's Tips

Your Name

You go to a pitch meeting hoping to sell something to the company where you're auditioning. If the company is interested, sometimes you'll be asked if you have a "leave-behind." That usually means a two- to three-page synopsis, or a one-pager. But pitch kings will tell you to never, ever leave anything behind. If they can't remember your story, that's a problem. You need "word of mouth" excitement.

I use a treatment only as a tool for telling yourself what your screenplay is about, scene by scene. I've had treatments optioned, and there was a time when treatments sold regularly, but I discovered that producers generally got burned with this practice. They saw a good story on paper but didn't get the goods delivered when the screenplay was done. If you're not a known quantity, don't try to sell a treatment or get hired to write a screenplay based on a treatment. Oh, it could happen, but usually the only thing that proves your screenwriting ability is a completed screenplay. Use a treatment as a tool to help you get that accomplished.

High Concepts and Mixed Ideas

If you mention the term "high concept" in Hollywood these days, it sounds dated. I first heard it while trying to sell a TV miniseries idea to Twentieth Century Fox. I didn't know what it was. Luckily, the TV executive was a friendly one who explained that she meant a couple of sentences that described the story or at least the elements of the miniseries. Sometimes you get that with just the title, as with *Ghostbusters*.

People still use the high concept, but mostly in mixing a couple of known movies to describe the script that they want to sell. Sometimes the combinations seem natural, but often they don't—and they can't help but sound derivative—so this practice is falling out of favor. You're better off just being able to describe it without comparisons to other films. Then it might actually sound original!

I try to be as nonderivative as possible in describing my projects, but if I have to, I'll do a high concept comparison. Because executives already know the hit movies, you don't have to worry about figuring out the high concept for them. They did that before you arrived.

It's Not for Us _____

Don't be ruled by fear. The first question I usually hear from writers is "What if they steal my idea?" Legally protect yourself as well as you can, but at some point you simply have to trust God or Providence or karma or whatever you call it, and simply tell people about your idea.

Try the following exercise:

1. Write down a number of ideas for screenplays that you might write.

2. Give each of these ideas titles, if you can. Try to come up with titles that reveal what the movie is about or are intriguing enough that you want to know what the movie is about.

3. Try to describe the high concept of each idea.

4. If applicable, come up with a couple movies that, mixed together, might match your idea.

5. Now see if you can apply the "What if?" principle to them.

6. See which ideas sound clearest to you and are the most easily described.

7. Pitch the winners to some friends you trust, and see what they think of the ideas. Ask whether they'd pay to see those movies.

Hollywood Heat _____

John Grisham is one of the most successful authors of our day, and most of his books have been made into films. He even started his own movie production company. I was once intrigued by an interview in which he said he would come up with a dozen or more fully fleshed-out ideas for novels, and present those to his New York agents to see which they thought were most commercial. I've known of screenwriters who do the same thing with trusted friends (working Hollywood professionals, usually).

The Log Line: The All-Important Twenty-Five Words or Less

These days, screenwriters are asked for the log line instead of the high concept. Where did the term originate? Imagine a busy production company. Even if the company doesn't actively solicit screenplays, it gets dozens every week. From agencies it gets scripts, books, and writers to pitch ideas.

If the company is active on the Internet (and most are these days), it also gets e-mails. It might even have a website where it solicits properties, and it'll read your work after you've signed a release form posted on the site.

Skip's Tips

A release is a legal document that producers and production companies have unrepresented writers sign for protection. These can be very problematic. I've seen language that says, "We might have received a property that matches yours word for word," which asks you to hold them harmless if they buy that other supposed property. Before you sign any release, you might want to show it to an attorney.

In addition to this, writers with whom the company has worked are phoning, e-mailing, faxing, and mailing about new screenplays, books, and ideas. Those writers have friends whom they are introducing to the production company.

And when the boss comes in on Monday morning, he might be carrying a book or screenplays (or several) that people have recommended but that he hasn't had the time to read. And why should he read them, when he has a secretary or assistant to read them for him?

So here's where the log line comes in. Someone has to keep a record of everything received, for the production company or producer's own legal protection. What if the company makes a movie and someone says that it stole the idea or script? The production company keeps a written log of properties received so that it can show what came in and what did not.

Skip's Tips

Try pitching movie ideas out loud into a mirror or, better yet, to a video camera. You never know when you might get a chance to tell someone influential about your screenplay. Do it with as much emotion as possible, but don't fake it. (If you have to fake it, the passion isn't in the story.) Watch yourself as you tell the story—you might be surprised what you'll learn.

And in that log, each property is described in a sentence or two, usually with where it came from. Think of the description of a movie that you see in the magazine *TV Guide*. It's the old "25 words or less." It's easily written down in a log, or typed in. That's a log line.

When you've fully worked out your premise, you should be able to describe it to anyone in 50 words or less (25 words or less is hard to do for some beginning writers). If you find it difficult to explain your story in so few words, it's my guess (and the guess of many other experienced pros who agree with me) that you might not have your story fully worked out.

If you want to write a Hollywood movie, you should be able to succinctly state the log line. That's what they'll use in formulating an advertising campaign, and it's what you'll see in a *TV Guide* listing, if you get lucky enough that your movie is seen in both theaters and on television.

Honing Your Idea into an Exciting Storyline

Earlier, I gave you an exercise to test your screenplay premise. Then I stressed the importance of having a 25 words or less "log line" that you could pitch to anyone who asked what your script is about. Later in this book I'll explain all the elements of a hit script, including some things you won't find anywhere else. For now, let me give you some questions to ask yourself if you find your premise isn't thrilling anyone:

- Is this a movie you'd personally pay to see?

- Does the title alone evoke images and suggest a movie poster, "tag line," or even a marketing campaign?

- Does the premise suggest continuing conflict that must be resolved, like the revelation of false identities in *Wedding Crashers*?

- Is your movie based on a "What if?" that immediately causes people to start imagining what might happen?

- If a movie like yours has been seen before, is your twist sufficiently original to make people want to produce it?

- Can you easily envision an exciting incident to begin the film and irrevocably propel the protagonist from Act One into a "new world" that must be conquered in Act Two?

- Is there sufficient built-in conflict to the situation that your hero or heroine will constantly have to overcome obstacles to reach his or her goal?

- Is there an antagonist powerful enough to defeat the protagonist entirely and ruin his or her hopes?

◆ Will the ending you have in mind thrill your audience?

◆ Is your story so entertaining people will talk about it the next day and tell their co-workers about it?

◆ Are you willing to spend months or maybe years writing and selling this story?

If you can answer "Yes!" to all those questions, you're probably on to something. If not, keep working at it. When you have a script that will sell, you'll probably be able to answer all of the above in the affirmative. And when you have something that will create continuous "word of mouth," that's a story worth telling.

The Least You Need to Know

◆ It's easy to formulate movie story ideas with the "What if?" approach—for example, "What if aliens invaded tomorrow?"

◆ A great premise immediately sets up the conflict to come.

◆ The theme of a movie is different from a premise; a theme describes the overall lesson that can be learned from the story.

◆ Don't send a message in a movie. Instead, pose situations that cause your viewers to ask themselves questions.

◆ The true definition of a "treatment" is a scene-by-scene description of the plot. It is a screenwriting tool, an outline expanded to serve as a guide while writing a screenplay.

◆ A high concept and a log line both describe the same thing, 25 words or less that say what your movie is about. The log line is the preferred term in Hollywood these days.

10

What's Hot, What's Not, and What's in Your Heart

In This Chapter

◆ Changing tastes

◆ What goes around …

◆ Different strokes for different blokes

◆ Predicting Hollywood's future

◆ Write what you want to see

Eric Hoffer, philosopher and author of *The Passionate State of Mind* (1955), said, "Man staggers through life yapped at by his reason, pulled and shoved by his appetites, whispered to by fears, beckoned by hopes. Small wonder that what he craves most is self-forgetting." Sounds like a screenwriter, doesn't it?

People watch movies to escape their troubles, to travel to different worlds, to vicariously live great adventures, and to forget themselves. Nevertheless, the movies they like most are about characters to whom they can relate. Perhaps that's why we see so many films about underdogs, people who suffer in everyday life but find a way to overcome their circumstances and triumph.

You can generally count on a great screenplay about an underdog to be popular, in almost any country. From 1976 to 2006, Sylvester Stallone scored a worldwide success with the *Rocky* movies. George Lucas had almost as long a run with the *Star Wars* films (1977 to 2005) and made a lot more money. The heroes of those films were always the underdog, even when Rocky was the heavyweight champion, and whether the focus was on Luke Skywalker or the young Darth Vader.

Underdogs will always be popular. They have been since the beginning of film. Remember Charlie Chaplin's great silent film "Tramp" character? But a screenwriter picking a genre can't simply write about an underdog and count on an audience. What other themes can a screenwriter trust? Let's take a look.

Tastes Change with Generations

When Walt Disney was alive, he recycled his films. As every new generation of children arrived, Disney features made their way back to the theater. And why not? Disney's first feature, *Snow White and the Seven Dwarfs* (1938), is just as fresh today as it was when kids first sang along to "Whistle While You Work." When videocassette players came into vogue, the company Walt left behind was in a quandary. Should it issue the movies to video like every other studio and risk killing its generational golden goose? Eventually, the company compromised by releasing some films for a short period of time and then cutting off production, making them more valuable in the public mind. Then digital media came along, and there went the repeat video sales idea. DVDs are virtually eternal, compared to videos. As a writer, you can drive yourself crazy trying to write for the largest moviegoing audience bloc (teens) if you're not a part of that audience. You can get desperate if you don't have teenage kids or know people who do. You might hang around a video store, trying to chat up the clerks. That could get the cops called on you. Or you could take a clipboard down to the local mall to interview moviegoers about their likes and dislikes. They'll instantly know you're old if you do that. Take your cellphone with built-in video instead.

Skip's Tips

Teenagers today know so little about history that you could assume that a historical movie might not be popular. Here's the catch. If you have actors they like, such as Tobey Maguire, Shia Lebouf, Sophia Bush, or Hayden Panettiere, they'll probably be there. Not knowing their tastes is one thing; not knowing their favorite actors is inexcusable. How do you know whom they like? See who they pick as nominees and winners at the Teen Choice Awards (see http://en.wikipedia.org/wiki/Teen_Choice_Awards for more information).

You've seen generational taste changes dramatized on TV season after season. Shows that played on the generations became popular in the late '90s. *Dharma and Greg* (Dharma, child of hippie parents) had a good run before being cancelled. *That '70s Show*, about teenagers in the 1970s, made stars of Ashton Kutcher and others. Naturally, the people who create such shows know something about those time periods, and if a TV show becomes popular, old fashions come back into vogue, just because the new generation thinks they look so weird and cool (or "bad," I should say). Of course, the time period has to have some kind of personality. If someone wrote *Acing the '80s*, what horrible fashions would we see back in vogue?

It's Not for Us

In Hollywood, a town obsessed with youth, it's better not to reveal your age, unless someone asks. If you are not in your 20s but look like you are, let folks think it. Life experience makes better screenwriters, but people in neurotic Hollywood often don't think that idea through. They generally look for younger writers to speak to younger viewers. It's generally held that if you want to write for sitcoms, you'd better not be over 30. Writers have sued over this, but rarely won.

If you're not a Generation Y writer but want to appeal to a younger generation, look for stories that play to (or on) the *clashing* of generations. If you know what Baby Boomers are like, you probably know or can easily find out what their kids are rebelling against. Anyone who knew the 1950s parents from shows such as *Leave It to Beaver* knew exactly what Baby Boomers as teenagers were rebelling against. And when Michael J. Fox as Alex Keaton was a straight-laced Reagan Republican teenage son of former hippie parents in *Family Ties*, that was hilarious.

So why am I discussing TV when this is about screenwriting? Because that's what demographics experts study. Television has immediate impact and a broader reach than film. Plus, TV is so much less expensive than moviegoing, so it's easier to figure out what audiences like by simply watching television ratings.

If you, as a screenwriter, can successfully predict what movie audiences will see, based on generational tastes, you're way ahead of most screenwriters and, if you're right, on your way to being a highly successful producer or even running your own movie studio. The one thing you can count on is that tastes will change over the generations, usually toward the more outlandish. Do your best to keep up with current tastes, but don't drive yourself crazy with it. A solid story works across generations and gets remade again and again.

What Goes Around Comes Back Around

In recent years, the 1960s and 1970s have been back in vogue. We can attribute part of that to the colorfulness of the times, and also the music, but the biggest factor has been the coming of age of the children of Baby Boomers as moviemakers. It should come as no surprise to you that Michael Myers's parents were a very big influence on his very successful *Austin Powers* character.

The real reason that many movie trends come back around is a very simple one. It's somewhat like the Disney generational recycling mentioned previously. Savvy producers know that a new generation has never seen certain films because they weren't playing on TV as the generation grew up. There's the "we can do it better" factor in Hollywood. Even though Gene Wilder was magnificent in *Willy Wonka & The Chocolate Factory*, which is available and very popular with today's kids, that didn't stop anyone from green lighting a new version starring Johnny Depp (which grossed almost half a billion dollars).

Skip's Tips

When you spend millions to make a movie, you hedge your bets. That is why agents and producers "package" a project. They assemble a complete package of the most important elements: the script, the lead actor or actress, and a suitable director. Based on past revenues from the stars, director, or writers, the studio or financier can get some idea of expected revenues.

If you study Hollywood film history, you'll find lots of examples of types of films that might be revived. It simply takes a smart person to realize what hasn't been around in a while and develop a project. Just as people in Hollywood love to say, "Wow, no one's ever done *that* before!" they also love to say, "Hey, nobody's done anything like *that* in a while!"

Just be prepared. If you didn't live through it and have to educate yourself on past film favorites that might work anew, expect that with at least one under-30 or in his or her 30s executive, you'll have to recite the story of the original film, no matter how legendary.

Different Strokes for Different Blokes: What They Like, Around the World

Unless you want to be a film distributor, you should concentrate on the North American audience and let the rest of the world take care of itself when you are considering what screenplay to write. There are, however, some basic things you should know.

Action plays well around the world, which probably comes as no surprise. Mel Gibson was a worldwide star in *Mad Max* before Hollywood paid much attention to him. The film did okay at the box office in the United States, but it made more than $100 million foreign. An action film usually works no matter what language it is originally written in, as *Runaway Train* proved in 1985 and Asian-derived films have proven ever since. Even if you write comedy, think action. Jerry Lewis's slapstick comedy movies of the 1950s and 1960s have made him a virtual cinema god in France. This was not lost on director Tom Shadyac and the other writers on the remake of *The Nutty Professor* (1996). This Eddie Murphy comedy comeback vehicle was so successful that it led to a sequel, *Nutty Professor II: The Klumps* (2000). Murphy scored just as big with the *Dr. Dolittle* remake and its sequel. There's gold in the remake hills, folks!

English-language remakes of foreign comedies, particularly French comedies, translate well for North American audiences. A successful example was *Three Men and a Cradle* (*Trois hommes et un couffin*; 1985), which became the very popular *Three Men and a Baby* (1987) and a sequel as well. If you never saw Tom Selleck, Ted Danson, and Steve Guttenberg in the American movies, they were a trio of swinging bachelors who became unwitting custodians of an infant. The secret of foreign remakes, at least with comedies, is that the situations play just as well to American audiences as they do to Europeans. A great example of this is the NBC TV series *The Office* starring Steve Carrell, which came from a BBC show of the same name that was a hit in England.

Hollywood Heat

Written and directed by Guy Ritchie, the low-budget but multi-award-winning number-one English film *Lock, Stock and Two Smoking Barrels* (1998) was shot on 16mm to give it a grainy look. The movie was respectable at the box office in England and abroad. The American remake rights to this comedy thriller shoot-'em-up about four young men who get into serious debt (£500,000) after a crooked card game reportedly sold to Tom Cruise's production company for $1.7 million (probably more than the original production cost). Action sells, big time.

If you consider yourself to be a serious screenwriter not given to writing action of the dramatic or comic nature, you probably won't care about the possibilities of your film or TV show being seen by audiences around the world. You'll simply go for the artistic merit of what you write, and let the popcorn boxes fall where they may.

Action plays everywhere. Comedic human situations play everywhere, but only situations that could take place anywhere. A comedy about a man with a hot dog stand might not work well in a country where few people have ever seen a hot dog.

And comedy translates most easily around the world when a lot of funny physical things happen, such as three men trying to change a baby's dirty diaper.

When they begin filming a scene in Hollywood, most directors start with "Action!" It's a word the whole world understands.

Predicting the Future by Demographics

I previously illustrated how movie popularity has a lot more to do with the age of the main characters than anything else. So let's now discuss the Baby Boomers, who are the most influential filmmakers today and a huge movie audience. What's a "Baby Boomer"? It's anyone born between the years 1946 and 1964, almost one third of the U.S. population and 78 million U.S. citizens. Why "Boomer"? Because, after World War II and the Korean War, although the Cold War was in progress, the world was relatively at peace, and people got married and had babies. Those babies are the Boomers, the first generation to grow up watching television. Elvis Presley and the music of the 1960s are important to them.

A large number of Baby Boomers never plan to retire, and many of them are now experiencing or will soon experience a midlife crisis, that mental malady of people between 35 and 50 (males mostly) in which they get very neurotic as they feel the last of their youth evaporating. Does that give you any ideas for movies? Baby Boomers are almost a third of the U.S. population, and approximately 30 percent of them have "empty nests" so they have free time on their hands. They like to go to movies. If they don't go out, they have an expensive home theater on which they watch movies, and they buy lots of DVDs.

Skip's Tips

Whether you're a Baby Boomer or not, you might want to check out the website www.bbhq.com. It's a chatty, witty site full of interesting tidbits and opinions (like Baby Boomers are). Another great site covering all the generations is www.freedemographics.com.

Lawrence K. Grossman, a former president of NBC News and PBS, wrote in the *Columbia Journalism Review* January/February 1998 issue that "TV time buyers pay $23.54 per thousand to reach 18-to-35-year-olds and only $9.57 per thousand for those over 35, according to industry sources." That meant a sizable, well-to-do market had been somewhat neglected. That's changed a little recently, but not much.

You probably know that Generation Xers are the offspring of the Boomers, those born between (roughly) 1961 and 1979 (an 18-year gap, with age 18 being adulthood). The generations are quite a contrast. Whereas the Baby Boomers admired Marilyn

Monroe, a lot of Gen-Xers admired Marilyn Manson. But, more Xers graduated college and are into their careers now, even if they're a more pessimistic crowd than their parents. While Boomers in the 1960s might have complained about getting a bad "rap" (treatment) from police whom they called pigs, Xers can be absolutely piggish about rap music. Xers are more tolerant racially and are concerned about the environment, but they've also been called the "Baby Gloomers" because of their attitudes.

Like the Baby Boomers, Gen-Xers seem to marry later in life. What does that mean, movie-wise? More "guy movies" for the males, perhaps? And more "date movies" to suit the females? If that notion doesn't seem very different, just remember that the Baby Boomers grew up enjoying a lot more movies that were about social issues (such as *To Kill a Mockingbird*), world figures (such as *Lawrence of Arabia*), or their generation (such as *The Graduate*). Movies about "social issues" today are usually about issues between sexes.

It's Not for Us

If you study demographics and use your findings as a guidepost to pick which screenplay you choose to write, don't expect to use that as a bargaining tool to sell your script. You'd better be prepared to present charts and graphs and visual evidence. Or even real life; *The Fast and the Furious* (2001) was made because of real-life illegal street racing going on in southern California.

Have you ever heard of a rapper named 50 Cent? If not, you're probably out of touch with Generation Y (also called the Echo Boom), the kids born from 1978 or so to around 1999. There are about 70 million of them and a lot of their attitudes are influenced by their Baby Boomer parents. Older journalists thought they had Generation Y figured out, until the Y-ers started getting married. Suddenly, people noticed that they were more serious about relationships than the previous generation. They'd grown up in broken homes and seen too many divorced parents or even grandparents. They wanted more stable relationships, even a soul mate. A Gen-Y favorite is Drew Barrymore, who loves to do all sorts of films: romantic movies that have fairy tale–like plots, serious dramas, and action films. Another is Liv Tyler, daughter of the lead singer of the rock group Aerosmith. Both of these successful actors grew up with parents who had 1960s values (and not very good ones).

There's another big difference between Generation X and Generation Y. A whole lot of the Gen-Yers grew up around computers. They're a big reason video games are so huge. They're big into downloaded MP3s and don't hesitate about finding friends via e-mail, chat rooms, or instant and text messaging. The current trend toward desktop moviemaking (wisely embraced by Steve Jobs and Apple) fits perfectly with

Generation Y, many of whom are starting their careers right now. And Gen-Yers as a whole seem to have a more positive attitude than Gen-Xers, while sharing the Gen-Xers' tolerance for others.

Hollywood Heat

Ken Kesey, famous for books that became movies—*One Flew Over the Cuckoo's Nest* and *Sometimes a Great Notion*—engineered a 1964 LSD-inspired bus trip across America that was immortalized in Tom Wolfe's *The Electric Kool-Aid Acid Test*. Kesey shot film on the trip but could never get the audio in sync—until, that is, Simon Babbs, the son of Kesey's old friend Ken Babbs, transferred the film and audiotape to a digital editing system. If you ever wondered what the hippiest hippies were all about, look for *Intrepid Traveler and His Merry Band of Pranksters Look for a Kool Place* and other "groovy" items at www.key-z.com/video.html.

This brings us to the younger kids in the theater, which we've covered pretty well in an earlier chapter. There might be something else worth mentioning with regard to kids and movies, though. Did you ever know someone who as a kid saw *Titanic* several times? Do you think it was only because they loved the movie that much? In case it has been a while since you were a kid, here's another reason they see certain movies: *popularity*. Kids like to be respected by their peers, and by seeing a popular movie the most times of anyone in their peer group, they feel that they've accomplished something. Not good for parents, but great for Hollywood. If you write a screenplay that a kid will like, chances are good that they'll see that film not just once, but several times. And if you don't believe me, ask James Cameron, of *Titanic* fame, or George Lucas, of *Star Wars*, for their opinions on the subject.

Skip's Tips

If you communicate with Hollywood executives but are not younger than 35, just know they're heavily electronic. They correspond and even transmit scripts via e-mail (PDFs are the norm), and mostly use "smart" phones like the Blackberry or iPhone. They like "texting" as much or more than calling. You need to speak the generally younger "language" of Hollywood. By that, I mean the types of things on *their* minds, not yours.

Does it seem like we've left someone out? Ah, that's right, the parents of the Baby Boomers, known in demographic parlance as "Matures." Of course, a lot of Boomers are grandparents these days, so the line blurs. Matures are a big segment of the population, and it's a bit of Hollywood's fault that they don't see more movies at the theater. Here's an example. Bobby Vinton, a singer you've probably never heard of, had a big hit song in the 1960s called "Blue Velvet." It was a lush, romantic, feel-good ballad. When David Lynch's *Blue Velvet* movie came out in 1986, many seniors paid the price of admission, thinking that they would see a romantic "song title" movie that followed at least to some degree the lyrics of the song. Brother, were they surprised when they saw a scene in which a man finds a severed human ear in a field and another about the perverse sexual habits of an evil man played by Dennis Hopper. Just keep this in mind: Hollywood favorites run in *cycles*. If it's not popular today but has been in the past, it will probably come back around.

> **Script Notes**
>
> According to the Foundation for the Study of Cycles (foundationforthestudyofcycles.org), a **cycle** is "a rhythmic fluctuation that repeats over time with reasonable regularity. When it is sufficiently regular and persists over a long enough span of time, it cannot reasonably be the result of chance." Take a look sometime at the movie release patterns over the decades. You'll find definite recurring trends.

A more recent example of "what you think you're gonna see ain't what you get" is *American Beauty* (1999). A lot of older moviegoers weren't terribly happy about a middle-age married man's sexual lust for a teenage girl. It's not that they were opposed to the story; they just didn't like being fooled by the advertising. Experiences like that can dissuade seniors from returning to the movies, period.

Perhaps demographics seem too esoteric for someone studying screenwriting, but I've always believed that the better you understand your fellow human beings and the forces with which they deal, the more likely you are to write something notable that will stand the test of time and generations.

Here's an example. How you ever heard of the Elliott Wave? I learned about it from Edward Hunt, a writer/director/producer who retired from making movies to profitably play the stock market. An "Elliott Wave" structure has to do with the natural rhythms of nature. Discovered by R. N. Elliott, it's a favorite of some people who play the stock market and touted by Robert R. Prechter Jr. in many books and articles. R. N. Elliott was an accountant who published his first book on the stock market at age 67. By chance, I once lived briefly in a house at 833 Beacon Avenue in Los Angeles, where Elliott resided from 1927 to 1938. It's a small world with a lot of intersections.

Elliott discovered a five-wave pattern in big upward stock market moves. In story terms, you could consider each wave a surge of action. According to Elliott, this five-wave-up or "bull" pattern would be followed inevitably by a three-wave down trending pattern referred to as a "bear" market. According to him, there's no getting around that cycle in life.

Shortly after I read about these "cycles" I realized that in my career I was at the end of a down trending "bear market" and that things would quickly be on the upswing. Two days later, I received a royalty check for thousands of dollars that was unexpected. Other boons followed. In short, the ease of contact-and-sale that I'd experienced at previous career peaks returned in the beginning of my own new "bull" market. And it made me a lot more relaxed about my writing and writing ability.

It reminded me of Ben Johnson, a great actor I had the pleasure to meet. When there were lulls in this Academy Award winner's career, he wouldn't worry. He'd just say "Let's sit here a spell. Something will come along."

I'll cover the Elliott Wave with regard to screenwriting further in Chapter 14. The point is this: As a screenwriter, you need to stay open to anything, because it might improve your writing in ways that you don't see, initially.

Write What You Want to See on the Screen

If you've never heard of *Being John Malkovich* (1999), *Buffalo 66* (1998), or *Happiness* (1998), or their directors—Spike Jonze, Vincent Gallo, and Todd Solondz, respectively—chances are you shouldn't be writing for Generation X or Y. The class act of Gen-X directors is arguably Alexander Payne (born in 1961) with hit after hit including the small budget but mega-successful *Sideways* (2004).

If you write a teen movie that's cheap to shoot (less than $15 million, a low budget for a studio) and has some new angle on a proven genre, you might do well. You'd just better have a great story. With an original movie for teens, if you come up with a new twist on an old standard, you could win big, as Disney's massive *High School Musical* (2006) and its 2007 sequel proved.

You can get a degree in demographics. You can study the Elliott Wave, or you can graduate summa cum laude in psychology. All these things might help in determining what the public will respond to in a screenplay. The best answer to that question is always this: *a great story.*

Great screenwriters work hard to learn the craft of screenwriting, to supplement any natural writing talent that they have. Once you've learned the craft, though, the best way to determine what to write is simply to write something that you would really like to see on the screen.

If you want producers, directors, and stars to commit life years to something you've written, you need to be very passionate about it. I always advise writers to complete that thing they would write if they had only six months to live and wanted to leave as their legacy. They usually have only one of those.

Hollywood Heat

As soon as you make a script deal, you'll probably hear the term "development hell." The person controlling your script has to "get it in shape" to attract the financing to get the film made. You might earn money in development hell like I have, only to get kicked off the project or eventually get it back in "turn-around." Why? Because "that's Hollywood."

If you're lacking in a plot or simply can't decide on the right one, you might follow the example of the late English novelist Barbara Cartland. She held the *Guinness Book* world record for "Top-selling living author of all time," with her 723 books exceeding one billion copies worldwide in 36 languages. Asked how she could turn out so many books, Cartland told the Associated Press: "I say a prayer. I really do. I say, 'Please God, get me a plot.' It's absolutely extraordinary: then a plot comes."

Whether by prayer, persistence, or perspicacious foresight, I hope you come up with something that you love and that a producer loves enough to get it made, allowing us all to love it just as much as you do.

The Least You Need to Know

- With Hollywood movies, what goes around comes back around. The only question is, "When?"

- No matter what generation you're from, if you write about the clashing of generations, you're probably on the right track.

- Action plays well around the world, whether in drama or comedy, for obvious reasons—language barriers.

- There are more Baby Boomers in the United States than Generation Xers or Generation Yers.

◆ Understanding demographics and the cycles of nature can put you ahead in the screenwriting game.

◆ Ultimately, the best screenplay for you to write is the one that you most want to see onscreen.

Chapter 11

Your Screenwriting Schedule and Why It Is Essential

In This Chapter

- ◆ Three pages at a time
- ◆ A workable schedule
- ◆ Living your schedule
- ◆ Graduation day

Pro screenwriters can write 10-15 pages of screenplay (or more, if necessary) in a single day. It wasn't always that easy for me, before I was writing for a living. When it becomes your job and you get paid for delivering, writing is different. Early in my Hollywood career, I had a major epiphany when I read a story about how writer/director John Milius claimed to write two screenplay pages per day and only two pages per day. Thus, at the end of two months he had a completed 120-page screenplay. Of course, he probably had to rewrite it, but a four-pages-per-day rewrite would mean that he would have a polished second draft in roughly three months.

At the time, I was working as a word processor for law firms to make a living, and so the idea of writing at night after typing all day was not something that I relished. Two pages, however, were manageable. That was the first time I ever realized how much mental impact a writing schedule can have, positive or negative. I've kept a regular schedule ever since, and it has made all the difference.

Getting It Done by Scenes

The general length of a Hollywood screenplay these days is around 110 pages. In the previous edition of this book (2004), I said 114 pages. In the first edition (1999), I said it was 120 pages. I'm sure you see the trend. Why has it changed? Generally, one page of single-spaced script with 1-inch margins on 8½×11-inch paper works out to one minute of onscreen time. That means that a movie from a 110-page script will run a little less than two hours; comedy scripts tend toward the shorter side, 90 to 110 pages, and in action scripts a single script line might take minutes onscreen. A caveat on this: you'll see screenplays that were filmed that are 130+ pages. In every case I've seen, these scripts were written by established pros, and there is a reason why they're that long. Screenplays that long are not a good idea for beginning screenwriters.

A movie scene used to run around three minutes. Some older movie stars have complained about the lack of longer scenes (Paul Newman comes to mind), but MTV music videos and fast-paced TV commercials and shows have changed movies. If you're paying attention at all to popular culture, you should be able to gauge how long a scene should be before it verges on being boring. Most movies seen on YouTube are under a few minutes, and cell phone movies are about a minute. These things affect viewing habits. Still, if it takes five minutes to make a crucial scene work, don't worry about it, just write it.

Skip's Tips

Here's something I use daily. When I was a kid, I drew pictures to entertain my younger brothers. Later in life, I realized that I had mentally "seen" those pictures on the paper and then traced around them. When writing these days, I keep the wall in front of my computer bare so that I can more easily "see" the scenes I envision.

Your Name

You'll find goofy definitions of *scene* in some books. The word comes from the Greek *skene*, which is a temporary building or stage where a play takes place or where the action occurs. The key words are *temporary* and *action*. In a screenplay, a scene is *a transitory sequence, usually in a single location, where something takes place that advances the story.*

This means that in a two-hour movie, you would have 30 to 40 three-minute scenes, give or take a longer or shorter scene here and there. With 110 minutes, you'd have 44 scenes of 2.5 minutes. Isn't that interesting? Sit down with a stopwatch and time out a heavy action movie, like one of the *Bourne* films, you might be surprised how many scenes there are, and how long they last. But back to easy three-minute scene calculations. If you wrote one scene per day, you could finish your first draft in the length of time that it took God to flood the world in Noah's time. (Forty days and forty nights, if you haven't read the *Book of Genesis*.) Does that sound manageable? (The scenes, not the flood.)

Now, what's in each of those three-minute (or less) scenes? Choose from the following:

A. Two people screaming about something on their minds

B. A car being chased by a tractor-trailer down a mountain road

C. A young woman holding a man around the waist, crying as she tells him how she loves him and never wants to lose him

D. Torrents of rain, high winds, and giant bolts of lightning ripping an environment to pieces as people scurry to safety

The one you picked might say something about your film preferences. Choice A could be a scene from *Who's Afraid of Virginia Woolf?* (1966). Choice B might be taken from the TV movie *Duel* (1971). Choice C could have come from any number of films or soap operas, and choice D might be a scene out of *Twister* (1996). Or, they could all be one scene, cutting back and forth from the exterior of and into the interior of a car driving pell-mell in a tremendous thunderstorm down a mountain road, followed by other cars also fleeing to shelter. Just behind the car in which our heroes ride is a tractor-trailer in which the driver is riding the brakes, so heavy sparks are flying everywhere and the brakes are almost burned out. The driver of the car yells at his passenger to get back and give him some room; he can't drive with her crowded so close. She pushes back angrily, and then screams at him that it was his idea to come on this camping trip in spite of heavy storm warnings. She wishes they had never gotten engaged!

This prompts him to return a sharp remark that stuns her. She looks around just in time to scream at something ahead—he's about to miss a turn and drive off the side of the mountain! Her fiancé reacts, jerking the wheel to the left. They slide into a rest stop on the left, against the mountain—safe! The tractor-trailer, however, can't make the turn. It crashes through the metal barrier and plummets off the mountain. Watching, horrified, the woman breaks down in tears. She holds the man around the waist, blubbering that she's sorry for what she said. She loves him and never wants to lose him.

He hesitates and then pushes her away. She looks stunned until **she sees what** he's staring at out his window. Up the mountain, a muddy rivulet is **about to turn** into a flooding avalanche as boulders are being dislodged by the awful **storm.**

"I hope I never lose you, either," he says, stepping on the gas. "So let's get out of here!"

And her eyes well up with a new kind of tears, those of admiration for a man saving their love from disaster.

Then a new scene begins as they escape the watery avalanche just in time and barely miss getting hit by another car as they roar back onto the mountain highway.

This scene, like a screenplay, has a beginning, a middle, and an end. There's a twist at the end. You think that the characters have seen death and realized the folly of their argument, and then suddenly it seems like he has turned cold toward her. Only he's merely getting some physical maneuvering room so that he can pilot the car away from more impending danger. There is an emotional arc in the scene, and we learn something about the characters' relationship. We might not get a full idea of what the movie is about from this one scene, but the scene certainly moves the plot forward—whatever it takes, they have to get out of danger.

This scene, written by a pro, could be done in a page, or two, or three. It's all one scene because it takes place roughly in the same location, the mountain road. As the scene begins, the characters are in danger. As it ends, it seems they have escaped danger. Then a new scene begins, placing them once again in harm's way.

The continuous driving heartbeat of a story that is kept alive when strong scenes flow together is what keeps us going back to the movies. Two of the films that I mentioned previously, *Duel* and *Twister*, had Steven Spielberg involved, directing and executive producing, respectively. Whether you like his films or not, one thing is certain: He knows what makes a scene work and will often move you breathlessly into the next scene.

Hollywood Heat

Diane Thomas was an unknown waitress in Malibu when Michael Douglas bought her script *Romancing the Stone* (1984). Unfortunately, she was tragically killed in an automobile accident just as her career was getting started. Now UCLA Extension Writers Program, where Thomas was a screenwriting student, holds a screenwriting competition in her name for people who study at its program. One of my readers sold his first screenplay after taking a course there. The program offers "land" courses as well as over the Web. See www2.uclaextension.edu and search for "Writers Program" for the link.

Whatever your daily schedule, you should be able to get your screenplay done if you approach it one little movie at a time. We'll delve into screenplay architecture later. When you start your first draft, only worry about it a scene at a time.

Great movies are composed of great scenes, and great scenes always have some element of the unexpected. Go on, surprise yourself. Write a great scene. Do it at least 30 times, and you have your movie.

Setting Up a Schedule That Works

Hollywood doesn't have room for excuses. It's a high-stakes game, and the script is crucial. "If it ain't on the page, it ain't on the stage" is an old theater maxim that you'll hear repeated among movie folk. They don't really care about how you had to take your kids to soccer practice and couldn't finish the script, or how those finals took precedence, or how many deaths there were in your family this week. All that matters is the script you turn in.

Similarly, to most people the idea of writing a screenplay and having it turned into a "real Hollywood movie" is such a far-fetched notion that you're an extremely lucky soul if you have someone in your life who supports you, either financially or mentally, while you crank out your magnum opus. Your friends and family have their needs, and if you turn down a trip to the local amusements with them often enough, they'll get edgy.

The way around that is to establish a writing schedule. You have to set a regular time during the day or even once a week in which you write your script and do nothing but write your script (with due regard to bodily functions and emergencies). You'll find that when you start respecting your own schedule and maintaining it, the cynical jokes will fade away and people will start taking this notion of yours more seriously. You don't have to be nasty about it, just firm. After a while, you'll find people coming around with little things that help—a back rub, a hot cup of coffee or tea, a pillow, or a brighter light for your lamp.

It's Not for Us

Don't be a schedule slave driver. If you're a stubborn sort, you might have a tendency to overdo it in one sitting. Just as you can overwrite a scene, you can overdo a writing period. Stick to your schedule, even if it means stopping a sentence in the middle. Ernest Hemingway used to do that on purpose, and he did all right. (Plus, that makes it easy to get started next time.)

To set up a schedule that works, you need to do an assessment of your life. The following ideas might help:

- What do you do after you get home from work? Time it. If you're spending an hour with your friends or on the Web, cut that in half and gain writing time. Or, drop all that until the script is done. Of course, you could get up a little earlier each morning, too.

- Do you have everyday chores, such as feeding a pet? Do it first, instead of before bed. Get all your chores out of the way.

- Turn off the phone ringer or turn on the answering machine. Put your cellphone on silent or at least on vibrate.

- Hide the remote control for the TV.

- Eat what you need to before writing.

- Find another time to check your e-mail and regular mail.

- Lock the door and set yourself up with some kind of alarm clock, timed to help you take a break from writing at least every 45 minutes (or whatever works for you). Or use software on your computer that makes you do the same thing. If you don't take breaks you can grind yourself down (this is the voice of experience speaking).

The best writing—at least for myself and every other pro writer I know—takes place when there are few or no interruptions. If you find that next to impossible due to your own living conditions, I suggest that you find a way to fix that, or get yourself some comfortable earplugs. With kids in the house, I sometimes put on earphones and listen to music as I write. I have a piece of software on the computer that I can set to remind me to take a break. I know other writers who do things like this, but you might need complete peace and quiet to write.

There is no set schedule when you are a freelancer writing a screenplay on the speculation that you'll sell it. A "spec" screenplay writer is the master or mistress of his or her own universe, or needs to be. Because you need to develop a certain frame of mind to be a professional writer, it's something that you'll have to work out on your own. You'll find that some pros work late at night, when the rest of the world is sleeping. Others have a set schedule that begins early in the morning and finishes at noon or so. It's your call.

When writing, you use your body, your mind, and at least a little bit of your soul. After all, you're not just working in a world; you're working as you build a world! Putting a schedule in place that works, one that you can keep in place, is the foundation upon which that world is built.

Taking Your Schedule Seriously

If you're like 99 percent of all other humans, you're at least a little disorganized. You'll find it hard to get going on your screenplay every time you're supposed to be writing copiously. So what do you do?

If you're a lawyer, you already know this trick. It's called "billable hours." You keep a running record of the time you're actually working for money: when you start, when you stop. If anyone questions the bill you send, you show them the log.

Of course, that might seem a bit over the top, or even ridiculous, to keep a log of the times you spend on the script, but after you've done it a while, you'll be surprised at the time you spend actually writing.

By the time you forget about your screenwriter's log, I'll bet you'll have established a schedule pattern that will get you through your first screenplay and your next one. And when someone hires you to write a screenplay, if you're so inclined, you'll be able to figure out your hourly rate.

Writing every day feels good, particularly when you can do it full-time. Living in Los Angeles, or in any filmmaking center, might help you get lucky. When I first started writing screenplays, it was because I went on a game show and won more than $14,000 in cash and prizes. That allowed me to take off from work and write full-time. If there is any way you can do that, even for a month or two, I suggest that you make the arrangements. There is absolutely no substitute for a concentrated, full-time writing schedule, particularly while learning.

If you can take a vacation or a sabbatical to get your screenplay done but find that you have trouble disciplining yourself to maintain a writing schedule, it might be time for outside help. Don't get downhearted about it; writing is a lonely discipline and a hard one.

I've long maintained there is no such thing as "writer's block" but there certainly is burnout, and there certainly are mental blocks to working on certain projects. How to deal with them? If it gets really bad, take a look at my friend Jerry Mundis's advice at www.unblock.org. Jerry is a genius at dealing with "writer's block" and the cassette series he offers is truly amazing.

Back to the trouble-free life. If you're serious about movies, you must come to Los Angeles some time, right? Yes, whether you like it or not, you probably should, but not as soon as you finish your screenplay.

Let's say that you manage to put in a screenwriting schedule, maintain it, crank out pages that you think are very good, and get a screenplay completed within the time period that you originally projected for yourself. Or maybe just a little longer …

When your script is done, the immediate gleeful instinct is to show it to your best friend. Or, if your best friend happens to live with you, to yell "Yahoo! Look at this!"

Don't show off a first draft. Put it aside. Stick it in a drawer or somewhere safe. Forget about it for at least a couple days. Don't show it to anyone or admit that it even exists.

When Act Three is finished, when you've typed "FADE OUT" on the right side and "THE END," centered, put that script away. Let it sit, like a fine wine needing to mature. Take at least a couple days before you look at it again.

If you work like me, and read the thing you wrote the day before (a chapter or a scene) and correct it before going on, you'll probably have an inclination to come back the next day and read through the whole screenplay and make corrections to everything. If you do that, you'll probably feel like chucking the entire thing because you've been too immersed in it for too long.

Hollywood Heat

YOUR NAME

Because it seems that he could write a grocery list and get it published and made into a movie, I don't mind telling stories about author Stephen King. Hey, he's even directed movies, if you count *Maximum Overdrive* (1986). He does something you might try: When a piece is done, he gives it to a number of trusted friends. If they all have different comments, he might ignore them. If they all offer the same comments, he'll take the comments seriously and consider changes. It's a bit like the old adage that if enough people tell you that you're drunk, you'd better sit down.

What if you swam the English Channel? It's a momentous accomplishment that few people can accomplish. But how soon do you think swimmers who achieve that mark want to get back in the water? Similarly, few people can accomplish writing a really good screenplay on their first attempt, but beginning screenwriters all too typically dive right **back into** that world they've been living in for X number of months. They don't give themselves time to gain perspective on the writing so that they can approach it with an exterior, less emotionally involved set of eyes.

Do yourself another favor. If you've written your screenplay on a computer or word processor, do *not* read it afresh on a screen. Print it out, grab a red pen or pencil, find a quiet place, and go through the script methodically. Take your time. Hollywood won't go bankrupt waiting for you to deliver your superstar screenplay. They might be in the middle of a labor strike and not want to talk to you, anyway. Your script needs to be as perfect as possible before you present it, and the rewrite will go much better if you create that last little bit of scheduling that allows you an unhurried time to page through your script with fresh, non-blurry eyes.

It's Not for Us

These days, you almost can't log onto the Web without running into a script consultant. I know, or know of, just about all of them. Forget them when all you have is a first draft. The two- to three-page evaluation they'll give you may have insight, but you're wasting your money. Beginners learn to write by rewriting, not by reading paid opinions. When I evaluate a script, my opinion usually runs 8-10 pages, single-spaced, but I do not really want to read first drafts. I *will*, but it's usually not the best you can do.

If you're happy with your first draft and you have a friend whom you trust to read it over and give you an opinion, that's up to you. I would urge you to only let fellow screenwriters read it, but not anyone who might be jealous or hypercritical. As far as your own reread of it, make sure that you schedule your own uncluttered time—after a break of at least a couple days—to peruse your script from start to finish. Trust me on this one. I've made the mistake of not doing it more than once, and my scripts suffered accordingly.

Skip's Tips

Your Name

A "page one" is what happens when a screenwriter rewrites someone's script so completely that it's like starting at the first page and creating a new screenplay. It's the kind of rewrite that you hope never happens to your own script, but it probably will. Hang in there—you might get to return the favor someday.

The Day You Become a Screenwriter

If you want to stir up some heat, just go to a party and, when asked what you do, say, "I'm a screenwriter."

When you've answered all the questions that will inevitably follow and they have determined that you're merely an *aspiring* screenwriter, expect some fallen faces and quick moves to the other side of the room, unless the person you're talking to is a writer who understands. Only the most cynical (those you don't want to associate with, anyway) will fault you for identifying yourself as an "aspiring screenwriter." What are you saying about yourself? First, that you have goals. Second, that you're honest and open. In a screenwriter—or in anyone, frankly—those qualities are admirable. Don't say that you're "only" aspiring, just "aspiring."

Just Write (1997), written by Stan Williamson, and starring Sherilyn Fenn as movie star Amanda Clark and Jeremy Piven *(Entourage)* as tour bus driver-turned-screenwriter Harold McMurphy, is a great romantic comedy about the social intrigues that go on with aspiring screenwriters in Los Angeles.

Call me a hard liner, but I don't consider people to "be" their profession until they have received recognition from working professionals in their chosen activity. Usually, that comes in the form of money. When you have been paid for screenwriting, you are a screenwriter, at least in my opinion. Others may have an even harsher definition, believing that you are not a screenwriter until something you have written has been seen on more than just a computer screen in a word-processing program. Purists think that you're not *really* a screenwriter until a feature film—not a movie of the week or a cable movie—that you wrote has been seen in a movie theater.

It's not worth debating. If you want to call yourself a screenwriter as soon as you start writing your first script, that's your business. If it helps you assume the right attitude to get the script done, good for you.

If you're not bothered by cynics or the sour comments of others who wanted to achieve something like selling a screenplay but failed, you could even insist that you're a screenwriter at a social gathering, with supreme confidence in your new craft. I just wonder how you'll handle the question: "So what have you written that I've seen?" That question always amazes me, just like the book question, "So what have you written that I've read?" As if I can climb into their minds, take inventory of their entire literary and filmic experience, and report!

I didn't truly consider myself to be a screenwriter until I sold a cowritten feature screenplay to a company that had just made a movie and I had the check in my hand. I'd had plenty of scripts "optioned." A one-hour video I'd written had won a national award, and I'd written some television.

To me, though, a sold feature script meant that I was a screenwriter. I was eligible to join the Writers Guild of America, too, which is the top screenwriters' organization in the world.

You'll know you're a screenwriter the day you meet your own criteria of the definition of "screenwriter." Whatever that may be, I assure you that it's a very good feeling when it arrives. Meanwhile, don't worry about it. Just get your schedule in order and keep writing until the script is done.

Then comes the real writing, which is rewriting. You'll know that's done when someone buys it. At least until they start giving you "notes" on the rewrite. That's when you *really* need to be on top of your schedule!

The Least You Need to Know

- The standard length of a feature screenplay for Hollywood is roughly 90-120 pages.

- If you can't establish and keep a regular writing schedule that works, it might not be the right time for you to write.

- Few people will take your writing aspirations seriously until you do so yourself; keeping a schedule can help with that.

- A good scene has all the elements of a complete screenplay: a beginning, a middle, and an end with a tag.

- A system of rewards and penalties built around your writing helps; so does keeping a log of your time spent working.

- Don't expect everyone to consider you to be a screenwriter until you are recognized as such by working professionals.

Part 3

How to Write Your Screenplay

Want the nuts-and-bolts explanation of putting together a screen story, from premise to outline to completed script, with the best structure for your movie? You got it! We won't give you an office at a Hollywood studio when you're done, but you'll be convinced you deserve one! And then, just when you think you're driving the smartest new vehicle on the block, you learn the secrets of rewriting. Did you know there is a "Shaping Force" of all great movies that can even be applied to your career? Buckle your seat belt, we'll show you!

Preparing Your Outline and Reordering Scenes

In This Chapter

- Getting your premise right
- How does your log line read?
- "Masterminding" your screenplay
- 3×5 cards make it easy
- Two or three minutes at a time
- Anything less than a script
- Blueprinting for perfection

Are you a part of an electronic backlash? Have you grown tired of working in front of a computer screen and watching television at night? If you've said "Enough!" and evaporated from the electronic stream, you're not alone. I know of a number of successful writers who eschew computers, preferring to write out their work on yellow legal pads, which someone else transcribes.

I also know a lot of writers who work on a laptop, sitting in their local coffee shop, surfing the Internet or checking e-mail as necessary, via a wireless network.

However you choose to work, there's no set way to come up with great ideas. There are software programs to help you formulate your premise, but most of them are built around some formula. There are programs that suggest structure, and others that let you type out your scenes on the electronic equivalent of a 3×5-inch card, which you can then electronically shuffle onscreen.

I prefer to reshuffle real cards and whenever I can I like to disconnect from the electronic world. Call me antiquated, but there's something magical to me about a pen, paper, a cup of coffee, and a seat outdoors.

Hollywood Heat

In 1990, I directed a 48-hour marathon screenwriting fundraiser for the Independent Writers of Southern California. It got TV coverage on Showtime and (by a stroke of luck on a slow news day) appeared on West German TV. Using a story outline formulated by others and myself, people donated money, sat at a keyboard at the Century City Shopping Center near Beverly Hills, and wrote a scene based on the next available scene. In all, we ended up with around 100 writers. The result? Too many screenwriters = garbage.

Sorting Out Your Premise

See if you like this premise. Think of a mountain lake. The water is clear and still and you can see, at the bottom of that lake, a chest full of treasure. The chest is open, and you're amazed by gold coins and red rubies sparkling in the sunlight that illuminates the lakebed. You're in a small rowboat, looking down at the treasure, wondering how you will retrieve it. It seems like this vision of treasure was meant for you and you alone, but the water looks deep and cold, and so you're not sure.

There are logistical problems. Is there so much treasure that it would sink your small boat? If you left it there and came back, could you find it again? What if someone else in a large boat came along and got it? What if someone was netting fish and pulled it up, or raked a bunch of debris on top of it? You'd need expensive equipment to locate it again. Where would you get that? As you continue worrying, you begin to wonder if it's really treasure down there at all.

But what if you had a global positioning device that would lock in the coordinates via orbiting satellite? No matter what conditions were in the future, you could locate the treasure again.

That's how certain you need to be about the premise of your film. Any writer who is any good suffers from uncertainty, but there are ways to build certainty about your premise.

Comparing Your Log Line to Other Movies

To succeed at writing movies, you need to watch a lot of movies, from all eras and as many countries as possible. The greatest movie education comes from the movies, period. If you haven't grown up watching a lot of film, a number of books offer capsulized descriptions of movie plots, probably the best being *Leonard Maltin's Movie Guide* (Signet, latest edition is 2008). On the Internet Movie Database (imdb.com), which is owned by Amazon.com, you'll find plot summaries, but those in Maltin's books are always more complete.

Keep a book like this by your side, and don't rely on being able to check a plot on the Internet. Sure, you can search by keywords at imdb.com, but you'll find that it can become a laborious process to figure out whether someone has matched or approximated your premise. A look through a book is usually much quicker.

> **It's Not for Us**
>
> Just as there are copycat killers, there are copycat moviemakers. When a movie is as successful as *Titanic*, someone will make a similar movie, and there also will probably be a porno "version." Do yourself a favor and don't write a copycat unless you truly have a new twist.

There's nothing like seeing a lot of movies. I can't imagine how I would have been able to search web pages to determine where I had seen the "Odessa Steps" sequence that I recognized in *The Untouchables*. I suppose that I might have located a paragraph stating it came from *Battleship Potemkin*, by Sergei Eisenstein, but because I'd seen the original, I realized fairly quickly what the "inspiration" of the scene had been.

You simply need to see a lot of movies so that you can compare your movie ideas against those that have already been made. The only ways around that are to consult with a very knowledgeable person or to participate in a group of writers whom you can trust. But not just any group.

Skip's Tips _____

Your Name

"What if they steal my idea?" I hear that from neophyte screenwriters time after time. I reply, "They might." It's the "one-baby syndrome." If you only have one child, you worry over it endlessly. If you have a large family, bloody noses are not national emergencies. Take precautions, but at some point, you simply have to send your baby out into the world.

The "Mastermind" Method

In his _Keys to Success_ (Plume, 1994), the great Napoleon Hill advises the reader to "form a mastermind alliance with yourself." He tells a story of a woman he convinced to stop dwelling on her problems so that she could concentrate on the "other" her, a positive, successful person. What you dwell upon, you get more of, Hill believed. In the book, this author of _Think and Grow Rich_ describes how, after you have a definite purpose about what you're doing, if you maintain a positive attitude toward attaining your goal, you can attract other like-minded people. He also stressed the importance of maintaining harmony in your home and environment, to more easily achieve your aims.

In describing how to build an alliance of "masterminds" (people who think like you do), he cautions against teaming up with people just because you like them and they like you. Hill suggests teaming with people only if they have the ability to do the job in question and can get along with others. I highly recommend both of his books, as well as anything else he has written. Napoleon Hill was the original positive thinking guru, so if any of his suggestions sound old now, just know that he wrote them first.

I've seen this method work over and over in Hollywood. People who succeed rapidly in show business actively seek out and ally themselves with like-minded people of similar or higher ability. They are firm in what they are trying to accomplish. This is most often true with producers I've known, who are bound and determined to get a certain screenplay made. It's like they have blinders on, like a horse in a harness. They see only what is in front of them and don't get distracted by diversions.

Judd Apatow, who has shown himself to be a box office comedy king in recent years with movies like _The 40-Year-Old Virgin_ and _Knocked Up_, is part of a group of about 10 screenwriters who get together and go over each other's scripts. You might try it.

It took me a long time to accomplish it, but I was finally able to put together a mastermind group for writers thanks to Yahoo! My "Skip's Hollywood Hangout" has specific rules which include no political discussions, no personal attacks, and a continual concentration on writing and selling. Browse over to it at groups.yahoo. com/group/hollywoodwriters and see what you think. Just be sure to provide the information I ask for; I keep my group screened of troublemakers this way.

If you have a great premise for a screenplay, you will listen only to suggestions that move you toward your goal. Confident people of like mind will not try to distract you with odd ideas. And if it's a great idea, the pros will tell you that. It may surprise you to know that professional screenwriters are often eager to pass on their knowledge. Hollywood people are big on the idea of "giving back." It's an old tradition that I hope never dies. You can see some evidence of it with the free mentoring program of the Writers Guild of America (see www.wga.org for more information). Highly successful screenwriters, directors, and producers may not have the time or inclination to write a book, but they're often happy to talk with an aspiring writer.

Hollywood Heat

Although he knew aspiring screenwriters before he began writing screenplays, no one had as much early influence on David Ayer (*U-571*, *Training Day*, and *S.W.A.T.*) as Wesley Strick (*Arachnophobia*, *Cape Fear*, *The Glass House*). While doing electrical work at Strick's Hollywood Hills home, Ayer showed Strick some stories about his naval experience. Strick liked them and kept after Ayer to write a screenplay. Ayer told me that he was at a crossroads; if a writer that successful took him seriously, he felt that he should do something about it. Ayer is now an "A-list" screenwriter and a director, too.

I've had some success in a number of areas of writing, and I'm happy to pass on information to anyone—but then, I've always been that way. Some writers have to face mortality before they realize that they won't be around forever. That's when they start thinking about their legacy and passing on wisdom.

The criterion that I recommend in selecting other writers with whom to commune about movies and movie ideas is Napoleon Hill's: *Do they have the ability to do the job in question?* If they do not, I'm not sure why you would be talking to them about your screenplay premise, unless you simply want to test it out on "common folk." I've seen more than one competent writer (including myself) chopped to pieces in a writing workshop by angry, cynical people. You should be very careful about picking your writing friends.

The Beauty of the 3x5 Card

Before you piece together your plot, you need to decide which 3×5 card you plan to use—electronic, card stock, or Post-it note. It really depends on your mentality. If you like working at a computer, you can find a number of software programs that have this facility. Some screenwriting format programs feature the ability to switch from 3×5 format to screenplay format, and back. But with Post-its on a blank wall, there's no glare.

If you use Post-it notes on a big blank wall, you can arrange your scenes, moving them around as you want so that you can read your entire movie at eye level, hands-free. I suppose you could do the same thing with index cards, but it would take a lot of tape or pushpins to hold them on the wall.

My favorite is a stack of index cards held together by a rubber band. It's pocket-portable, and you can hike to the top of a mountain and outline your script, if you want. You could do that with a stack of Post-its, but they're harder to move back and forth, with that sticky stuff on the back.

Try it some time. Grab some index cards and go find a quiet place outdoors. Close your eyes, and start visualizing your movie. Let it unfold before you; when you see a full scene, write a description of it on an index card and then repeat the process. It's an intuitive way of putting together scenes that works for a lot of people I know.

Before you embark on that journey, fill out another card, the one that expresses the premise of your movie, your "What if?" I suggest using a different color card, or one with some colored tape on it, to make it stand out in a stack. Take your time on that card, which I call a *pitch card*, because it would be the one I'd have in my hand if I went in to pitch the story to a producer. Try to make it a clean, clear statement of what you want to say. Then, while you're outlining, if you hit a snag, you can check your progress against your pitch card. If you've gotten off-track, you can thumb back through the cards, and I'll bet you'll find a card/scene that shouldn't be there, one that doesn't forward the story. I usually set that one aside—it might work later. Even when I'm done with a script, I'll keep those cards if they look like good scene ideas.

It's Not for Us

If you have a pitch card, a main card that expresses the premise of the script that you're working on, don't show it to anyone, no matter how clever you think it might be. I'm not paranoid, but I've learned the hard way that sharing your central idea before it's written and legally protected is a bad idea.

Outlining by Two- to Three-Minute Scenes

Usually, when I conceive of an idea for a book or movie, I try to encapsulate the entire premise into the title. Sometimes the title tells you what the story is about, and sometimes it only alludes to it. I've found that this process works differently for everyone. Some people (like me) often get the beginning and ending of the story in a flash, along with the idea, leaving them to explore the details, the process of getting from A to Z. If you have trouble plotting out a movie scene by scene, plot it backward. That's easier than it sounds. Think about it, though. Didn't *The 40-Year-Old Virgin* make you laugh as a concept?

Why am I spending so much time on this? Because ideas are a dime a dozen, but great ideas are one in a million. When you pitch an idea in a producer's office and they buy it, it's usually an idea that people will repeat with enthusiasm around the office. It's usually a simple premise that happy moviegoers will share with their friends, creating solid-gold "word of mouth."

Do your best to perfect your premise. Don't start off trying to do one scene after another in sequence. After you have a clear premise, it's better to outline the overall highs and lows of the story—the peaks and valleys that the main characters race up and down on the way to their destination.

Let's take the premise of a screenplay that started out as a stage play. I originally called it *Parts of a Hole* because a girl in a restaurant/bar one night said that the place where we hung out was a real "hole" (a dive, a lackluster establishment) and we were all parts of it. I had to layer in something more esoteric, so the play evolved into something called *Fourth World*, which is the Native American Hopi tribe's description of the Paradise to come, with the present being the Third World. By the time it had reached a second draft with that title, the play was in good enough shape to become a finalist in two national competitions and a semifinalist in two others. If not for *Starman* (1984), starring Jeff Bridges, which came out just as my play was making the rounds, or the TV series derived from it (1986–1987), my play might have been staged in Los Angeles.

Or maybe not. Ten years after I wrote the play, I figured out what it was all about. That's right, I finally came up with a workable premise. I rewrote the play and titled it *Walking After Midnight*, using the title of an old hit country classic by Patsy Cline. My "What if?" went like this—*What if your Prince Charming finally arrives, only he's an alien?*

I did a staged reading of the new play, and two people in one week told me that it should be a screenplay, so I wrote the script. Because I had added a "time clock" of sorts to the script, of a girl turning 30 and worrying about her biological clock and the fact that she'd never been married, the story had more tension and started getting more notice. But, because of paying projects that got in the way, it would be another 10 years before I picked up the script again.

> **Skip's Tips** _____
>
> Someone might ask you to tell the story of your screenplay, but he or she doesn't have time for a long description. This person might ask you to just "hit the beats." A "beat" has two meanings in Hollywood. One is a pause that an actor takes while delivering dialogue. The other (the one that a producer wants) is *a high or important point of a story.*

When I had the premise in shape, the rest of the "world" of the script became more clear. I saw "beats" I would need—a birthday party planned for the heroine, a plan to build an amusement park called "Spaceland" in the UFO-friendly New Mexico setting of the piece, and a clash between the "maybe alien" boyfriend and the local deputy sheriff boyfriend. After working out the major beats of the story—about a dozen, or one every 10 minutes or less—it was easier to fill in the scenes between the beats. When I had all the cards filled out (35 as I recall), I could sit down and write out a treatment to follow, scene by scene, or I could simply write the screenplay from the 3×5s.

One-Sheets, Synopses, and Treatments

Here's a "one-sheet" of my script *Walking After Midnight*, which was optioned in 1999 for $5,000 for a one-year period. I'm revealing how much I made so that you'll understand that someone took this script quite seriously.

WALKING AFTER MIDNIGHT
©1999 by Skip Press

How long would you look for a lost love? Would you travel across a galaxy? Would you search through a dozen lifetimes? What if you found your lost love, only to discover that you were not remembered?

Mirabelle Flowers isn't concerned with such far-flung ideas. The owner of an all-night diner in Gallup, New Mexico, she busies herself with her Midnight Poetry Society. Her odd collection of local poets includes Jake, a drunken church deacon; Rob, a gruff old rancher; Joseph, a Hopi chieftain; and anyone else who shows up.

Tonight, however, only Jake has come around, which is doubly perplexing because this is Mira's thirtieth birthday. She is openly anxious about the course of the rest of her life. This is not a night she wants to feel lonely.

Lloyd Buxtrum, a deputy sheriff who covers the night shift, drops by to flirt. He's had a relationship with Mira but blew it. Before they get much of a chance to talk, Lloyd is recruited by his current lover, Muriel, and her cousin Ramona to investigate what they say is a flying-saucer crash on a nearby mesa.

Busying herself with sobering up Jake, Mira is startled by the arrival of a stranger who introduces himself as Kett Dakota. The man is handsome, charming, and eloquent, with an air of mystery. As the night unfolds and the regulars arrive, Kett changes each person's life in remarkable ways. When Jake is struck by a car outside the diner, Kett revives him by a laying-on of hands. When Lloyd returns to the diner almost naked, the victim of a revengeful trick by Muriel and Ramona, Kett helps avert a violent confrontation. When pressed to tell the group a story, Kett spins an entrancing yarn about lost love across eons and galaxies. Listening breathlessly, Mira has the oddest feeling that Kett is telling the story about her.

Finally, we learn of a plot between Lloyd and Japanese businessman Jakuro Ohito to use the body of an alien being as the centerpiece for a new amusement park called Spaceland. We also meet the loneliest lady ostrich in the world, who threatens to ruin their plans entirely.

Through a night of poetry, drunkenness, and outrageous behavior, Mira grows more enamored of Kett, only to see him suddenly disappear when her interest in him reaches a crescendo. Everyone around her has made a major change in their life on this night, but Mira has been abandoned to contemplate her future all alone. Or has she? As the movie closes, Mira learns that, despite all her fears, things work out for the best, as soon as you discover what the best really is.

***

If you were looking for the premise in the first line, you didn't see it. I'm not saying that's a perfect one-sheet, but it's the one I sent to the lady who ended up writing me a sizable check—and after reading it, she was sold, even before reading the script.

One-sheets are single-spaced. Usually writers cram as much on that one page as possible. You might also have deduced that a one-sheet made double-spaced would pretty much match the one-and-a-half- to two-and-a-half-page synopsis that most people expect in Hollywood when they ask for a synopsis.

Hollywood Heat

YOUR NAME

Joe Eszterhas, a native of Hungary, is famous for violent and sexy screenplays. His *Basic Instinct* sale caused the spec screenplay market to go nuts when it sold for $3 million. Eszterhas once sold a four-page outline called *Trapped* for up to $5 million (with the amount depending on whether the movie was produced with A-list talent). After a number of his scripts (such as *Showgirls*) became flop movies, however, Eszterhas backed off from Hollywood. He went on to write the nonfiction book *American Rhapsody* (Knopf, 2000), a tell-all about Tinseltown, and the eye-opening *The Devil's Guide to Hollywood: The Screenwriter as God!* (St. Martin's Griffin, 2007), about screenwriting and more.

It's Not for Us

PASS

You might be told to never share a one-sheet or a synopsis with a producer. However, it could be a mistake to *not* share this selling tool. If you fax it to someone, you have a record of the transmission, as you do with e-mail "headers." You're protected in those instances, so go for it.

I might share a one-sheet or a synopsis (also called a "leave behind" by some), but I try not to show anyone a treatment. I use a treatment only as a guide for myself, a typed-out elaboration of my 3×5 cards, or to show to another writer with whom I might want to collaborate on the script. Other writers sell treatments and synopses, but they're usually very well-known screenwriters.

Can you as an unknown writer sell a treatment? Maybe, but it's highly unlikely. Lots of producers have lost by spending money on nonscreenplays from proven writers, so why should they trust a neophyte? Someone has to write a script that can be filmed.

Building the Perfect Blueprint

Okay, class of one, let's review. First, if anything I've explained to you here doesn't resonate with you, that doesn't surprise me, and I would never argue with you about it. Screenplays have definite, accepted formats that you can't deviate from as a beginner, and not even as a veteran unless you also plan to direct. In contrast, premises, log lines, outlines, one-sheets, synopses, and treatments are things that you have to work out for yourself. My suggestions are merely intended to give you some ideas of ways that I have been able to better work out screenplay stories. You will find, though, that "coverage" throughout the film industry is fairly standard. Correspondingly, so is the way people write out log lines.

Here's the long and the short of it. If someone in Hollywood asks you "What's this about?" and you can't clearly and quickly tell them, *you're dead in the water.* More to the point, you don't really have your story figured out yet. If someone asked you what *Talladega Nights* was about, for example, couldn't you easily say "It's about the dumbest NASCAR driver on Earth"?

I've known of successful writers who simply start off with an idea and see where the page takes them. Not just poets—authors, playwrights, and screenwriters, too. Some of them are very successful working that way, but that approach might not work for someone new to screenwriting.

Would you build a house without a perfect blueprint? I wouldn't, but then I grew up around the construction business. A great palace starts with a vision, which someone describes to an architect, who makes some sketches, revises them to suit himself, and then presents them to his client. The client makes a decision, the architect finalizes the plans, and the construction process gets under way. No one truly knows what the final product will be until it is nearly done.

It's pretty much the same with a movie, and a screenplay is a blueprint. When the movie is being filmed, the director might change that blueprint. The editor might even suggest changes that are implemented in the cutting room.

Think about movies you've loved and see if you can easily describe them. *It's a Wonderful Life* is about a guy failing in business who wishes he were never born, only to learn how everyone in his town would suffer if he never existed. *Clerks* is a very funny look inside the life and loves of a convenience store clerk in New Jersey. *About Schmidt* is about a boring insurance salesman who retires and finally learns what life is about. *Sideways* is about a loser novelist who learns how to win at life just when he thinks it's impossible.

Get the idea? I purposely used examples from some of my favorite movies that have people in jobs they don't like, just to show you that great movie ideas can be about anyone, anywhere.

The Least You Need to Know

- The more clearly you can state your premise or log line, the more likely you are to write a coherent screenplay.

- There are resources to help you compare your movie idea to existing films, but none as good as personal knowledge of movies.

◆ In forming a "mastermind" peer group of screenwriters, choose only those who also have the ability to write a good script.

◆ A pitch card on which you've written your log line is a tool that you can use to keep yourself focused on your writing mission.

◆ It's okay to share a "one-sheet" synopsis of your screenplay with a potential buyer; unless that person specifically asks to read a synopsis or treatment, make him or her read the screenplay.

◆ In the end, the only correct method of getting your screenplay figured out and on paper is the one that works best for you.

The All-Important First Ten Pages

In This Chapter

- ◆ Back story is for the writer
- ◆ The life of a script reader
- ◆ Unforgettable opening scenes
- ◆ The digital age and screenplay openings
- ◆ A sample opening

Fair Game, a script that I wrote with Michael Sean Conley, impressed director John Badham at Columbia in 1984. At the time, Badham had just come off the success of a cop movie and was one of the hottest directors in town. Our script was about modern-day piracy in the Caribbean. As it worked out, an article in *Variety* had reported that the director's next movie would be about that subject. Producers Ron Hamady and George Braunstein, who had optioned our script and knew Badham from days when he made commercials, called him up and asked if he had a script. He didn't, so he read ours.

The first 10 pages of our script (and the whole script) impressed the director, but he chose to do a sports movie instead, which bombed. We later sold our script, after the setting had been changed to the South China Sea. It still hasn't been made.

The point is this: if you can hook the reader long enough to get them to read the first 5 pages, or the first 10, that reader is much more likely to read the rest of the script. The reader knows that the movie might hook the viewer with a quality opening. If the rest of the script maintains that quality, it's a hit movie.

Back Story Is for the Writer, Not the Viewer

The late Steve Allen, a multitalented funnyman who wrote scores of songs and books, said to start a story where it begins. Allen pointed out that it often takes some writers 20 pages to get to the place where the story really starts. The best movies are not constructed in a way that you have to use multiple flashbacks to show the psychological evolution of a character's life so that we understand their current motivation. Reveal it as we follow them along. How much "back story" was there in the original *Star Wars?* As it turns out, three movies' worth, but we didn't know that or care to know that with the original film.

Beginners seem to love to "flash back" from the present time of the story to some place in the past. Not only is it hard to follow onscreen, but it often disrupts the flow. I find that they usually do this only because they haven't figured out their plot and are trying to "think on paper." Only master screenwriters such as Richard Matheson can pull off the use of the flashback, as in *Somewhere in Time* (1980). Ryunosuke Akutagawa (from the stories *Rashomon* and *In a Grove*), Shinobu Hashimoto, and Akira Kurosawa also did it excellently with *Rashomon* (1950).

Skip's Tips _____

Can't figure out the beginning of your script? Divide your story into two worlds— the world in which your character starts and the one your character is in at the end. Even in the same environment, the character's outlook on it and place in it will have changed. If you know what the movie's about, you have some idea what has to be overcome. What would it take to get this person started and keep him or her from turning back?

When filmmakers make flashbacks work, the essence of the movie usually has to do with time itself, or some very troubling incident that needs psychological resolution. Examples you might recognize are the rape of Sondra Locke's character in Clint

Eastwood's *Sudden Impact* (1983) or the short-term memory loss device used in Christopher Nolan's *Memento* (2000).

Every great story has an *inciting incident*, the event that irrevocably propels the main character into the flow of the main story. Think of it as the character stepping into a whole new world. This incident is not always the first one we see in the film. Sometimes it takes place after the movie starts, and other times it takes place before. In *Star Wars*, the inciting incident is when Luke Skywalker's aunt and uncle get massacred by the overwhelming force of the Galactic Empire. Luke is forced to make his way in the world alone (albeit with robot R2-D2).

In *The Wizard of Oz* (1939), the incident is when Dorothy Gale (who, not so coincidentally, lives with her aunt and uncle) is threatened by Miss Gulch, who wants to take away Dorothy's dog, Toto. Some might argue that the inciting incident is the tornado that sweeps Dorothy off to Oz, but the key word is *inciting*, something that puts the main character on an irrevocable course of action that will lead him or her to a new maturity and a true place in the world.

In *Mad Max* (1979, the movie that made Mel Gibson a star), Gibson is a cop in a post-apocalyptic world who loses his family. Like Luke and Dorothy, he has no choice and his life has changed.

And how about *300*? The Persian empire led by emperor Xerxes is approaching Sparta and intent on conquering it. If the Spartans want any hope of freedom, they simply must fight.

In all these examples, the inciting incident is *not* the first scene of the film. In others it is, like the attack on Clint Eastwood's family in *The Outlaw Josey Wales* (1976).

It's Not for Us

Don't make the mistake of not figuring out a back story for your main characters. The more you know about them, the better. That includes the villain. The more you fully understand the physiognomy, psychology, spiritual composition, and environmental influences of all characters, the better your script will be.

Many movies these days follow the Joseph Campbell "myth" structure. Two of those mentioned previously—*Star Wars* and *Mad Max*—were made by devotees of Campbell. Campbell had not even formulated his theory, however, when *The Wizard of Oz* was made. Myth structure or not, every movie worth anything has an inciting incident that gets the ball rolling. Sometimes it is an action scene, sometimes not. Are you thinking of Indiana Jones being literally chased by the giant rolling ball of rock in *Raiders of the Lost Ark* (1981)? That is not the inciting incident. It's merely an exciting opening that establishes his character. The real inciting incident takes place back at his university, where government officials inform "Indy" that the Nazis are about to grab the lost Ark of the Covenant, the all-powerful instrument of God mentioned in the Old Testament. It's a dialogue scene in an academic setting, yet it is clear to Indiana that he has no choice but to accept the mission. Truly, the fate of the entire world hangs in the balance.

For Tippi Hedren's Melanie Daniels in Alfred Hitchcock's *The Birds* (1963), the inciting incident comes when she flirts with Rod Taylor's Mitch Brenner in a pet shop in San Francisco. She pretends to be a shop girl, to help him pick out a pair of lovebirds for his sister. Then he reveals that he knows who she is and knows some of her past. He's seen her operate in court. Doing what, we don't know; it doesn't matter—she's hooked. When he leaves, she tracks him down via his license plate, buys a pair of lovebirds to give him, and drives an hour north of the city to deliver them.

With none of these great movies did the writers or directors see any need to do a long, slow pictorial build that paints a picture of the setting, the characters, or the story. People just don't take the time for things like that. In the days of the big bands, there would often be a minute or more of instrumental lead-in to a big hit song. People took time to savor the appetizing melody while preparing for the main course to come. Not any more. This is a culture with an expectance of instantaneous fulfillment. The ride must start now. Not that I agree with the way it is—I'm just telling you how it is. Personally, I dig a big band.

Hollywood Heat

Harry Cohn ran Columbia Pictures in the days of the studio system, when studio bosses were akin to gods (or wanted you to think they were). As the story goes, Cohn would use the "butt twitch" method while watching movies. That is, when he squirmed in his seat, something about the movie bothered him. And that's what the filmmakers would fix. See how often you react nervously to something in your script. That's probably what you need to fix.

The Life of a Script Reader and What It Means to You

There are websites called "tracking boards" where script readers, development executives, and producers at top Hollywood companies engage in online discussions about articles, stories, books, screenplays, and any other possible sources of hit movies.

Hundreds of the very top production companies in the business stay on all day, conferring with each other about what might be hot. When a reader or development person finds something good, that person tells the boss (the producer) about it, and the ball starts rolling. If the tracking board members find something that they know is right for another company but not for them, they might pass it on. This type of community-mindedness is a relatively new thing in Hollywood, which I credit in large part to the instantaneous nature of the Internet. What this should tell you is that, these days, word on a good screenplay or a hot new writer gets around *very* fast. Similarly, if a writer is troublesome, that can also get around quickly.

Let's say the average successful production company gets 25 potential submissions per day. (Fifty would be a better estimate, but I don't want to scare you too much.) Twenty-five per day equals 125 per workweek. Let's say that they actually agree to read around half of those, or 65. That's more than a dozen scripts per business day. How many people do you know who could read 12 scripts in a day and report on them intelligently? If you were a kind soul (and most readers are, no matter what you've been led to believe), wouldn't you at least give the writer the benefit of the doubt and read the first 10 pages? But if you weren't hooked on those pages, or if you were put off by bad spelling, typos, coffee-stained

pages, and other evidence of a sloppy mind, what would you do? I know exactly which round file I would put it in. And if the office policy was to not return any script that had no self-addressed, stamped envelope (SASE), I wouldn't think twice about trashing that script. Can that office get through a dozen scripts a day? Maybe the company utilizes three readers who can cover three scripts a day, each being paid $50 a script for "coverage." That leaves 15 scripts not read at the end of the week. And that's what the development executive might take home to read on the weekend. Or, that stack might be split up with a producer in the office.

With that kind of reading burden, do you see how important it is that you follow acceptable etiquette in contacting a company, present your script in the proper format, and have a very impressive first 10 pages? And that comes only after you've impressed someone with a log line, and then perhaps a treatment, to get them to even read your screenplay.

Now let's examine the opening scenes of some top movies, to see just how amply the writers of these screenplays delivered the goods that got their movies made.

Opening Scenes We Don't Forget

The scripts of great movies keep you reading even today, even if you've seen them repeatedly, because they're so well constructed. Let's start with a movie that almost all children see, *The Wizard of Oz* (1939; screenplay by Noel Langley, Frances Ryerson, and Edgar Allen Woolf). In the script, we find references to camera moves such as MS (medium shot), LS (long shot), and CU (close up), which screenwriters don't use anymore because that is considered the domain of the director and the director of photography.

> **It's Not for Us**
>
> Don't get so bound by current form that you're afraid to stretch the boundaries. When Judy Garland's Dorothy Gale interacts with Professor Marvel (Frank Morgan) in the beginning of *The Wizard of Oz,* the four-and-a-half-minute sequence is crucial to the film. If it takes five minutes to get the scene done right, do it.

As the film takes off, we learn that someone tried to hurt Dorothy's dog, Toto. She is running from the camera, to the farm where she lives. She finds Aunt Em, who is taking care of chicks, carefully counting them and bothered by Dorothy's interruption, even when Dorothy complains that mean Miss Gulch hit Toto with a rake. When Uncle Henry confers with Aunt Em, we learn that Dorothy is an orphan. Then Em responds: "We all got to work out our own problems, Henry."

And with that line, we have the theme of the movie.

Next we meet Zeke, Hunk, and Hickory, farm workers who will become the Cowardly Lion, the Scarecrow, and the Tin Woodsman, respectively. We learn that Dorothy doesn't have anyone to play with. When she asks Zeke (Bert Lahr) about Miss Gulch, he chickens out of offering any advice. He says he's gotta get those hogs in. Hunk (Ray Bolger) tells Dorothy that she isn't using her head, has no brains at all. "Well," he says, "your head ain't made of straw, you know." And in the barn, oil spurts in the face of Hickory (Jack Haley) as he works on his wind machine contraption, which is supposed to break up winds so that they won't have any more dust storms that ruin the crops. He says he feels like his joints are rusted and suggests that Dorothy try to have a little more heart.

All the advice from the farm workers, of course, is a projection of their own problems. When Dorothy talks with Zeke at the pigpen, he says that she should have more courage. When Dorothy falls in, he rescues her, only to reveal his own terror.

Seamlessly, all these things happen by page five, setting up so much that we'll see later in the movie. The fretting, childlike Dorothy at the beginning rises to maturity by the end by being repeatedly forced to conquer attempts to keep her locked in childhood. Unlike the book, the film is a deep psychological study. For example, she wears red slippers. They were silver in Baum's book, in which Dorothy was half the age of the 12-year-old depicted in the film. Red is equivalent with blood, menstruation, and the ascent to womanhood.

When Aunt Em brings crullers for everyone, she advises Dorothy to find some place where she won't get into any trouble, which sets up Dorothy singing "Over the Rainbow," the signature song of the film. The lyrics are featured in the script, another thing that you never see today. And as soon as that wonderful sequence is over on page 8, Miss Gulch shows up to take Toto away. At the top of page 10, when Gulch grabs Toto, Dorothy calls her a wicked old witch, and everything in the movie that follows has been established. Despite the inclusion of what would be considered "clutter" today (the dedication, mention of shots, and song lyrics) this is an amazing but subtle first 10 pages.

Hollywood Heat

In the seventh minute of *The Wizard of Oz*, Judy Garland sings "Over the Rainbow." Maybe that minute was lucky—the song almost wasn't in the movie! I had dinner one night with Hy Kantor, who was in charge of music at MGM when the film was made. When they were debating whether to leave the sequence in the film, Kantor put his job on the line, saying that the song would make as much money as the film, which was almost as expensive to make as *Gone with the Wind*. He insisted that they leave it in. His bosses were glad they took that bet, and so are we.

Now let's look at a sexually charged mystery/thriller, *Chinatown* (1974), with a screenplay by Robert Towne that has long been considered to be one of the very best, if not *the* best, ever written. It starts with an office scene, as a fisherman named Curly looks over surveillance pictures of his wife having sex with another man, accompanied by an audio recording of the lovemaking. Private detective Jake Gittes (Jack Nicholson) is not happy showing this to Curly, who cries knowing that his wife is having an affair.

We learn that Gittes pinches pennies because he gives Curly the cheap whiskey out of a desk drawer, when he could have chosen a more expensive brand. We then see his cohorts, Duffy and Walsh, in an outer office, with a woman who is ostensibly married to Hollis Mulwray, the powerful head of the Water and Power Department in Los Angeles. When she hears the audiotape, she thinks that Gittes is having sex with a woman. Gittes is a clean freak: He wipes Curly's sweat off his desk with a handkerchief.

Curly wants to kill his wife, but Gittes angrily admonishes him, saying that you gotta be rich to kill somebody and get away with it. And when we learn that Curly hasn't paid Gittes off, and Gittes lets it slide, we're only four pages in. As Curly departs, we see lettering on Gittes's outer door that reads "Discreet Investigation." This, we now know for sure, is the only kind of detective work that Gittes and company do.

Within 10 pages, we've learned that Gittes thinks it's best for most women to forget their husband's indiscretions if they love them because that's simply the way men are. But money doesn't matter to "Mrs. Mulwray" (whom we later learn isn't who she claims to be), so Gittes takes the job. He goes to a City Hall meeting, where the former mayor, Sam Bagby, is pitching a dam project to bring badly needed water to the desert community of Los Angeles, but Mr. Mulwray (whom we learn is 60 years old) says that the Van Der Lip dam gave way and that this one will, too. Mulwray refuses to build the project. When a farmer brings in a flock of sheep, disrupting the meeting with a claim that Mulwray is stealing water from the valley, we have all the elements in the movie (including an implication of kinky sex that will play out later). Once again, the first 10 pages establish everything in the film.

> **Skip's Tips**
>
> In preparing the opening of your screenplay, think of one perfect picture, which is the essence of the film contained in one scene. We find that in *Raiders of the Lost Ark,* and it is reflected in the movie poster. It's the same with *Jaws.* You needn't make up a poster, but every little bit helps. Set the scene, and they might keep it.

Let's switch gears to the amazing and refreshing *The Sixth Sense* (1999), by M. Night Shyamalan, who also directed the movie. In the first few pages, we learn that something weird is going on in the basement of Anna Crowe (Olivia Williams) as "dripping black" devours the room when she leaves. Her husband, Malcolm (Bruce Willis), has been recognized with the Mayor's Citation of Professional Excellence from the City of Philadelphia for his work in child psychology. We know where we are and who they are, and by end of page five, their celebration has taken them to bed. But there is an intruder in the house, hiding in the bathroom off the master bedroom. He's 19, with a patch of white in his hair, a drugged-out psychotic whom Malcolm worked with when the man, Vincent Gray (Donnie Wahlberg), was a child of 10. Vincent says that Malcolm has failed him, and he's still terrified. He shoots Malcolm and then blows his own brains out on page nine. After a fade to black, and then a title card of "Two Years Later," we find Malcolm sitting on an outside bench, looking over Vincent's file. The "Two Years Later" is a classic misdirectional touch that isn't revealed until the end of the film, and we have all this by page eight.

As Good as It Gets (1997), by Mark Andrus and James L. Brooks, is one of my all-time favorite scripts. In the first *six* pages, we learn that writer Melvin Udall (Jack Nicholson) is an ass, starting with his dumping a small dog named Verdell (who looks like Toto's cousin) down an apartment building garbage chute. We know that Melvin is a homophobe because he goes out of his way to insult the owner of the dog, across-the-hall neighbor Simon Bishop (Greg Kinnear). And, not surprisingly, Melvin is also a racist, as we learn when he insults the man who sells Simon's paintings, Frank Sachs (Cuba Gooding Jr.). As Melvin retreats into his apartment, we find out that he is incredibly superstitious as he locks and unlocks his door several times. Then we see that he's a germophobe as he washes his hands (but only with the third bar of soap that he unwraps). Then, and all within six pages, we learn that this inhuman insult machine writes romance novels! I can't imagine any reader not stamping "Recommend!" on this script, based on the first few marvelous pages.

My Big Fat Greek Wedding (2002), with a budget of $5 million, was a very small movie by Hollywood standards. It was very large by box office standards, though, and is the reigning all-time romantic comedy champion. It begins with a nighttime view of Chicago in the rain. Mousy Toula (Nia Vardalos) and her father pull up to a stop light and wait. It's 5:00 A.M. and she's tired. Her father tells her she's looking old and better get married soon. (She's 30.) From there, with some narration by Toula, we flash back to elementary school and family scenes that establish how different life was for her, growing up Greek. It thoroughly sets up all the quirks of her family and her background. It's a perfect setup for the great conflict of the main movie story, grown-up Toula wanting to marry a man who is not Greek. It's a longer "back story" but it's necessary, to show us the hilarious differences of her Greek American life. Within the first 10 minutes we are pulling for Toula while laughing heartily.

The box office hit *Wild Hogs* (2007) is about four middle-age men who are "weekend warrior" motorcycle riders who all feel in different ways that they are spinning their wheels in life. The one they all think is ultimately successful, Woody (played by John Travolta), is actually in the deepest trouble, facing divorce and bankruptcy. They decide to take a road trip from Ohio to the Pacific Ocean to boost their manhood. As the tagline says: "A lot can happen on the road to nowhere." By the time we've seen the first ten minutes of the movie, we know exactly how tough life seems to all four guys.

Not all the movies discussed here have won Academy Awards, but they have been box office successes, and are loved by audiences around the world. They are different types of films, from different time periods. What they have in common is stellar writing that, in 10 pages or less, sets up the entire movie in excellent fashion. As you might have noticed from these examples, more gets done in fewer pages these days than in the past, but things haven't changed that much. We can still tell a great script early, and readers (and audiences) are suckers for great openings.

So do yourself a favor—*read every top script you can get your hands on.* Your own writing will improve, I promise you. And do yourself another favor, pay for a script if necessary. Reading a first draft you can download for free is an education, but it helps to have the script they used to shoot the movie, and to read it while watching the movie. It's a great education.

How the Digital Age Affects Screenplay Openings

At one time, some B-movie producers with a track record for delivering movies that made money would come up with an idea for a film, and have a poster made up. They would then present the poster at film markets as a supposed product in their pipeline. Foreign distributors who responded to these posters would spend money to pre-buy the "movie" and the producers would then have the cash to commission the writing of the script and production of the picture. The money a producer gets from an overseas source prior to delivery of a movie is called *foreign pre-sales* and has traditionally been important to the moviemaking.

As computer graphics have proliferated and made the production of artwork much cheaper, making up posters of nonexistent movies to raise money is a practice that may still go on. It's similar to a producer using a "one-sheet" of text that you supply to try to generate interest before committing to buying the project from you. Unfortunately, writers don't often manage to get paid on the "back end" (from profits) like these producers do, so if you encounter someone using methods like this, watch out. And if any of this sounds unethical, welcome to Hollywood at the independent level.

> **Script Notes**
>
> **Foreign pre-sales** are how many movies have been made, using advances from foreign distributors. That means that only the North American market is left to produce a profit. It's yet another reason why screenwriters very rarely make any money on the back end (post-expense profits). Actor Eddie Murphy calls net profit participation "monkey points" because only a monkey would expect to be paid.

Hollywood Heat _____

Supposedly, director John Huston asked reclusive novelist B. Traven to script his own novel, *The Treasure of the Sierra Madre* (1948). Traven turned him down, as he did when asked if he wanted to visit the set. Huston suspected that Traven did show up, posing as "Howe Crows-Translator, Acapulco," who served as technical adviser on the film. Now here's the Hollywood legend. Perhaps frustrated with Traven, the story goes that Huston told his secretary to turn the book into a script, and that's what he shot. Because Huston won the Oscar for Best Writing, Screenplay, on that film, the story is probably just gold dust in the wind.

Writers can combat this by becoming digital filmmakers. For around $10,000, you can buy a high-end Apple computer, editing software, and a high-quality digital camera that would allow you to make a movie. I wrote an entire chapter about this in the third edition of my *Writer's Guide to Hollywood*. Rather than simply trying to get your script read, you might think of shooting a key scene of your script. Try to pick a scene that might be a small movie all its own, or rewrite a portion of your script as a small film that, expanded, would be your screenplay. Hollywood filmmakers do this type of thing all the time. The evolution of Billy Bob Thornton's *Sling Blade* (1996) is an example.

Here's a fact: if you shoot something really funny and put it on YouTube.com, or even "serialize" a story you made up that seems real, you can get noticed by Hollywood *very* quickly. This was proven in June 2006 when a supposedly 15-year-old teenager named Bree began appearing on YouTube talking about her life into a Webcam. It later turned out that her life was fictional and scripted and she was an actress named Jessica Rose. The short shows got endless views and the story of the fakery became famous around the world.

An Opening Page for You

Here's a suggestion. Get some of the scripts mentioned above and rewrite the first 5 or 10 pages. If you like the results, share those pages with some friends. If they agree that yours are better, send them to the persons who produced and directed the original (if they're still alive, of course) and see what happens.

Who knows? They might be impressed and offer that Hollywood catchphrase that means you have their interest—*What else you got?* Believe me, stranger things have happened.

Meanwhile, here's an opening page from *Alien Creeps*, a script by me and Ed Hunt. It was optioned in 2002 but hasn't been made.

FADE IN:

EXT. NIGHT SKY - NIGHT

A night sky full of stars. A glowing UFO moves across a full moon.

WE FOLLOW this saucer-shaped UFO as it descends on a small town in the Midwest, Melonville.

EXT. WHEAT FIELD - NIGHT

The UFO circles the large wheat field then descends and begins "zapping" with low frequency waves. Patches of wheat collapse.

The UFO produces a crop circle that is a masterpiece of advanced geometry. The UFO hovers over the crop circle.

INT. UFO - NIGHT

Two aliens, the PILOT and the CO-PILOT, are at the high tech controls. They have large gray heads, no hair, large teardrop-shaped black eyes, small bodies covered by blue bodysuits. They're about four feet tall.

They look at the crop circle on the high-tech screen. Both aliens speak by telepathy and use facial expressions to match their thoughts. We hear them in English although they don't actually move their mouths.

> PILOT
> (counting on fingers)
> CNN, ABC, NBC, CBS ... even PBS.

> CO-PILOT
> (cocky)
> Watch this one. Fox Special!

EXT. UFO AND WHEAT FIELD - NIGHT

INTERCUT: In fast motion, the co-pilot takes the controls, whips the saucer to the opposite end of the wheat field, descends, and much to the pilot's silent dismay, makes an even more impressive crop circle.

INT. UFO - NIGHT

The co-pilot grins. The pilot knows he's been whipped. He hands over four huge diamonds. The co-pilot puts them in a belt pouch, then holds out his hand again.

CO-PILOT
Double or nothing, remember?

[End of page.]

NOTE: "INTERCUT" means that we leave it to the director how the scenes inside and outside the saucer are shot.

Do you get the idea on what the script is about? Aliens and fun at the same time? Did you laugh? Would you want to see more?

We hope so, and one of these days we'll get it made, even if we have to film some scenes and put them on YouTube!

The Least You Need to Know

- Using flashbacks to show your character's back story is usually the mark of an amateur.

- Every decent movie has an inciting incident that irrevocably propels the main character into the flow of the main story.

- The average successful production company learns of 25 to 50 potential submissions per day, so yours had better be special.

- With many great films, the entire framework of the movie is set up within the first 10 pages—these days, usually less.

- A short film, shot digitally, might get you a major deal more quickly than a screenplay alone.

- You become the best by studying and competing with the best, and you must keep track of what other upcoming talent is doing.

Chapter 14

The Structure of Hollywood Movies

In This Chapter

- ◆ Three acts and 2,500 years
- ◆ The myth structure
- ◆ Syd Field's influence
- ◆ New ideas
- ◆ The ultimate screenplay

I've never seen anyone who didn't have to learn the craft of screenwriting to make it in Hollywood. I've been an entertainment journalist, a novelist, a magazine editor, a playwright, and an actor. I helped get the Hollywood Film Festival started, but never once have I met a natural storyteller who just ventured into screenwriting and sold a screenplay without learning basic film structure. Then there's the fact that the craft continues to evolve. Read on, I'll explain.

Three Acts and Thousands of Years Later

At some point in your writing career, you absolutely *must* read Aristotle's *Poetics*. These days, you can even download it from the Internet. It's a very short work, although you'd better have your poetry dictionary by your side, to look up terms such as *anapest* (a metrical foot composed of two short syllables followed by one long one, as in the word *seventeen*). Although it is a treatise on the elements of poetry—the method of dramatic presentation in Aristotle's time—it is filled with principles that rule dramatic structure even today.

The three-act structure comes from an Aristotelian observation. In speaking of drama, Aristotle says: "It should have for its subject a single action, whole and complete, with a beginning, a middle, and an end. It will thus resemble a living organism in all its unity, and produce the pleasure proper to it."

Skip's Tips

If you're good at conversation, you might use a technique that some screenwriters use to test their story ideas. It's called "I knew this guy …." Here's an example: "I knew this guy whose grandfather found the real Ark of the Covenant." And they say with enthusiastic interest, "Really?" (the reaction you want). And you tell them your Indiana Jones story. If the story bombs, maybe it's a bad movie idea.

Ever wonder why movie stars are generally much better looking than normal people and character actors are often very odd-looking? Perhaps this quote from Aristotle explains it: "Since the objects of imitation are men in action, and these men must be either of a higher or a lower type (for moral character mainly answers to these divisions, goodness and badness being the distinguishing marks of moral differences), it follows that we must represent men either as better than in real life, or as worse, or as they are."

Reading *Poetics*, you realize that the basics of entertainment haven't really changed that much in the past few thousand years. Oh, you'll find other screenwriting books that claim to be the latest, hippest thing, but movies will still be primarily made on the three-act structure, except in places like Japan, where some movies have only two acts. See if you think Aristotle's definition of comedy would apply to *Superbad*: "Comedy is, as we have said, an imitation of characters of a lower type—not, however, in the full sense of the word *bad*, the ludicrous being merely a subdivision of the ugly. It consists in some defect or ugliness which is not painful or destructive."

Hollywood Heat

Here's Aristotle on how comedy got its name: "[C]ertain Dorians of the Peloponnese … appeal to the evidence of language. The outlying villages, they say, are by them called *Komai*, by the Athenians *demoi*: and they assume that comedians were so named not from komazein, 'to revel,' but because they wandered from village to village (*kata komas*), being excluded contemptuously from the city." (Funny, I know some comedians today who should be excluded from cities ….)

Does the following seem applicable, in comparing filmmakers who want to ennoble culture to those who simply want a reaction? "Poetry now diverged in two directions, according to the individual character of the writers. The graver spirits imitated noble actions and the actions of good men. The more trivial sort imitated the actions of meaner persons, at first composing satires, as the former did hymns to the gods and the praises of famous men."

The elements of drama according to Aristotle: "Every Tragedy, therefore, must have six parts, which parts determine its quality—namely, Plot, Character, Diction, Thought, Spectacle, Song." He defines these at length in a few short pages. For example, diction is "the expression of the meaning in words." Movie stars who do that best, such as Jack Nicholson, inevitably become legends. "You want the truth!? You can't handle the truth!" (From *A Few Good Men*.)

If you think there is too much emphasis on structuring a screenplay before you begin writing, consider this: "But most important of all is the structure of the incidents …. For Tragedy is an imitation, not of men, but of an action and of life, and life consists in action, and its end is a mode of action, not a quality. Tragedy is an imitation of an action that is complete, and whole, and of a certain magnitude; for there may be a whole that is wanting in magnitude." How many movies have you seen that don't seem to be about anything?

If no one has ever defined "beginning, middle, and end" for you, here it is, in Aristotle's words:

> A whole is that which has a beginning, a middle, and an end. A beginning is that which does not itself follow anything by causal necessity, but after which something naturally is or comes to be. An end, on the contrary, is that which itself naturally follows some other thing, either by necessity, or as a rule, but has nothing following it. A middle is that which follows something as some other thing follows it. A well-constructed plot, therefore, must neither begin nor end at haphazard, but conform to these principles.

Get out your dictionary and read *Poetics*, if you have not. There is a reason this essay continues to be so influential long after the glories of Greece are dust.

The Influence of the Myth Structure

I could list a number of movies that have followed the Joseph Campbell "myth structure," which he derived from stories and legends that he studied from around the world. Even though George Lucas is the most well-known proponent of Campbell and *Star Wars* is a very well-known movie, I'd rather use *The Wizard of Oz* to outline the basic Campbell "Hero's Journey" steps. Like all great myth structure stories, it starts in an everyday world, Dorothy Gale's farm home in Kansas: Dividing a story into Aristotle's three acts, the following steps fit into Act One:

> **The Call to Adventure.** Miss Gulch is coming to take Toto.
>
> **Refusal of the Call.** Dorothy runs away from home with Toto.
>
> **Supernatural Aid.** The tornado transports them to Oz and Glenda the Good Witch comes in.
>
> **The Crossing of the First Threshold.** Dorothy and Toto discover Munchkinland.
>
> **The Belly of the Whale.** Dorothy and Toto travel to Oz on the Yellow Brick Road.

Here are the steps that fit into Act Two:

> **The Road of Trials.** Dorothy accumulates allies on the way to Oz.
>
> **The Meeting with the Goddess.** Dorothy and friends meet the Wizard.
>
> **Woman as the Temptress.** Surrender, Dorothy!
>
> **Atonement with the Father.** Dorothy destroys the Wicked Witch.
>
> **Apotheosis.** Dorothy is immediately celebrated and elevated.
>
> **The Ultimate Boon.** Dorothy captures the Wicked Witch's broom.

Act Three would break down this way:

> **Refusal of the Return.** Dorothy has second thoughts on leaving Oz.
>
> **The Magic Flight.** The Wizard's balloon leaves without her.

Rescue from Without. Glenda arrives to explain the way.

The Crossing of the Return Threshold. Dorothy uses the ruby red slippers.

Master of the Two Worlds. She's no longer worried in Kansas.

Freedom to Live. There's no place like home!

Skip's Tips

Reading Joseph Campbell is a storyteller must. Read *The Hero with a Thousand Faces* (Princeton University Press, 1972), but also study *An Open Life: Joseph Campbell in Conversation with Michael Toms* (Perennial Library, 1989); *The Hero's Journey: Joseph Campbell on His Life and Work* (Harper and Row, 1990); and *Joseph Campbell and the Power of Myth,* the interview series done by Bill Moyers for PBS (Mystic Fire Video, 1991). You'll find his organization's website at www.jcf.org.

In "The Meeting with the Goddess," remember that "the Goddess" symbolizes the world in which the story takes place. When Dorothy and friends meet the Wizard, they are conferring with the person whom they think is the spokesperson and ruler of the world of Oz. In the "Woman as the Temptress" step, as the Wicked Witch of the West skywrites "Surrender, Dorothy!" in black smoke over the Emerald City, we literally have a woman who is tempting Dorothy to stop on her adventure, to give up her quest.

Nevertheless, the "Atonement with the Father" is when Dorothy destroys the Wicked Witch. The "Father" in this story is the thing that gets the story started, namely the dual Miss Gulch/Wicked Witch of the West played by Margaret Hamilton. To *atone* means "to make amends, as for a sin or fault." What's Dorothy's sin or fault? She keeps running away from growing up. In the opening, she wants her Aunt Em and Uncle Henry to handle a situation that she got herself into (Toto chasing Miss Gulch's cat). By the time she kills the Wicked Witch (while defending her friend the Scarecrow), she has grown up and will stand up to Miss Gulch/Wicked Witch of the West, with no concern for the consequences. After all, she has no idea that water will kill the witch. Thus, Dorothy has made amends for not handling her own problems in the beginning, and we know that she'll be able to do so from there onward.

In films built on the myth structure, Act Two is generally twice as long as either other act. In Hero's Journey storytelling, Act One has to do with the mental and spiritual preparation before getting started on the journey. Act Two is concerned with all the obstacles that must be overcome to reach the elevated state of being that rescues these characters from the problems they had in the beginning. In Act Three, their new knowledge or ability allows them to function in the world in which they began, as well as the one to which they traveled.

Syd Field's Paradigm

Hollywood screenwriting has two time periods: B.S. (before *Screenplay*) and A.S. (after *Screenplay*). *Screenplay*, of course, is Syd Field's *Screenplay: The Foundations of Screenwriting, A Step-by-Step Guide from Concept to Finished Script* (Dell, 1994). When the first slim edition appeared in 1979, it took the industry by storm because no one had codified the basic structure of a screenplay in such a simple manner. His "paradigm," the skeletal structure of scripts, was photocopied and hung on walls of readers and development executives. Some critics (there are always critics in Hollywood) wondered, however, what Field's own writing credits were. Why was he qualified to comment on how to write a screenplay?

Subsequently, Field cleared that up, revealing that he had been a writer/producer for David L. Wolper, a well-known producer. He explained that he had been the head of the story department for Cinemobile Systems for around two years, during which time he read more than 2,000 scripts but recommended only 40.

Field used the word *paradigm*—an example that serves as pattern or model—to describe the structure that he saw at work in screenplays that sold. Act One was the beginning, the setup for the action that followed, and ended on page 30. Act Two was the middle, the major conflict of the film (he calls it "confrontation"), and ran to page 90. Act Three, the end, was where all the major conflicts were resolved, and this act ended on page 120.

Hollywood Heat

When you truly know how things work mechanically, it's a lot shorter route to realization in the physical universe, and recognition from others comes more quickly. Nikolai Tesla, the discoverer of alternating current, would build a complete working model of something in his mind before he even attempted to build it in the real world. When Syd Field published *Screenplay* it codified a screenplay structure others had worked with mentally for years. Thus, when he spoke about it at the Writers Guild of America, he got a standing ovation.

Field added a new term to the schematic structure of a successful screenplay—the plot point. One is in the first act, between pages 25 and 27, and another toward the end of the second act, between pages 85 and 90. A plot point is an event that anchors the story line and spins it around in another direction. He gives the example of *Chinatown*, in which Jack Nicholson's Jake Gittes meets Faye Dunaway and discovers that she is the real Evelyn Mulwray. The one who came to Gittes's office to have her husband investigated was an impostor.

The plot point in Act Two (I hope you've seen the movie) comes when detective Gittes discovers the glasses of the murdered Hollis Mulwray in a saltwater garden pool behind Mulwray's house. Suddenly he realizes why Mulwray was found to have salt water in his lungs. He was not murdered where it was thought he was murdered. All the unanswered questions that Gittes has start to unravel. Because of the new direction in which the movie has been spun—while remaining true to the premise of the film, "People with enough money and power can get away with murder or anything else"— Gittes is able to uncover the incest and murder at the root of the mystery.

Field's philosophy of plot points was seen as a revelation for aspiring screenwriters, but the fact is, Aristotle had already mentioned such reversals. He called them "peripeteia." Don't believe me? Read *Poetics*.

Skip's Tips

The secret to learning Hollywood secrets is to accumulate knowledge over time, from as many sources as possible. One of the best places for that is the Sherwood Oaks Experimental College. Working pros such as James Cameron started there and come back to do seminars. Contact director (and founder) Gary Shusett at Sherwood Oaks Experimental College, 323–851-1769; or see www. sherwoodoakscollege.com.

When the first edition of *Screenplay* came out, it was adopted so broadly across Hollywood that writers adjusted their screenplays so that the plot points—which screenwriters had been calling "twists" for years—landed on exactly the same pages that Field said they would land.

Why? Because readers looked for them, and if the scripts did *not* fit Field's paradigm, particularly Plot Point I, scripts would be rejected right there. Writers learned quickly what the new rules in town were, those outlined in *Screenplay*. For some writers, though, Field's paradigm seemed like a cookie-cutter approach, and it drove them crazy.

New Approaches and Other Ideas

A number of people in recent years have decided that, for whatever reasons, all or part of existing story structure is antiquated and somewhat irrelevant. One of them is John Truby (see www.truby.com). I like him because he emphasizes studying the masters to gain an understanding of the craft of screenwriting. Truby offers books, software, and seminars to support his theories, and he has a theory and a book or software module for just about everything.

Perhaps the most influential recent guru is Robert McKee (see www.mckeestory.com), the author of *Story* (ReganBooks, 1997). McKee's main pitch is the "Classic Five-Part Narrative Structure," consisting of: (1) inciting incident; (2) progressive complications; (3) crisis; (4) climax; and (5) resolution. Studying McKee, it is obvious that Campbell and classical sources influenced him.

In *Alternative Scriptwriting: Writing Beyond the Rules* (Focal Press, 1991), Ken Dancyger and Jeff Rush reviewed existing theories and went to elaborate lengths to describe almost everything within the purview of screenwriting in their own terms. For example, they call a plot point a "turning point," which is a minor or major reversal.

One refreshing new addition to screenwriting books is Blake Snyder's *Save the Cat* (Michael Wiese Productions, 2005). Rather than try to describe it, let me simply say that Blake is a continually working screenwriter, wrote a big hit with Disney's *Blank Check*, and is very good at telling you what screenwriting looks like from the inside in Hollywood. He isn't simply theory with a Ph.D. attached, he's someone who does it successfully. I found many things in common with this book and I like his style.

I covered (or tried to cover) all the main gurus of Hollywood and screenwriting in three editions of my book *The Writer's Guide to Hollywood Producers, Directors, and Screenwriter's Agents* (Prima Publishing) and in my *Ultimate Writer's Guide to Hollywood* (Barnes & Noble Books, 2004). I've either met or studied them all, and so these are not just offhand observations.

The Ultimate Screenplay Design

Film is a constantly evolving medium, and if you're not actively in the heart of Hollywood, you need to keep up as best you can, at least until you break into the business.

Then you have to do better than keep up—you have to forge new trails to stay noticed. When developing my "Your Screenwriting Career" course, which was available in more than 1,400 schools on three continents, I did not want to simply regurgitate what every other screenwriting teacher was saying. So I looked deeply into structure and studied a lot more successful movies. One of the first things I realized was that the Campbell "myth" structure, with its heavy emphasis on a "mentor," does not work in lots of films. In many movies, there is *no mentor*.

It's Not for Us

Do yourself a big favor. Don't get cute with your first screenplay, or even your third. Pick an established genre and come up with an original story that fits the parameters of that genre. If you experiment before you master the basics, it might blow up in your face.

Instead, there is almost always in the middle of Act One of a good movie something I call the "Shaping Force," which can be anything. Sometimes it is a mentor who unleashes a power, like Obi-wan Kenobi in *Star Wars*. It could be a concept like Time in *Cast Away*. It could be what everyone wants, that which Hitchcock called the "Macguffin," like in *The Maltese Falcon*. Or it could be a villain like "Hans Gruber" in *Die Hard*. There are hints of it before it arrives in mid-Act One, and it reappears at crucial times during the course of the film.

I also noticed that in almost all films, there is a distinct *midpoint change*, roughly in the middle of Act Two, where the main character, who has been the effect of events that he or she is battling against, becomes more positively causative over the opposing force. This usually coincides with Joseph Campbell's "Woman as the Temptress" Hero's Journey step. By "woman," Campbell means life, with the hero "its knower and master." It is the moment when the hero becomes determined or empowered to do what it takes to achieve the goal.

I taught the Shaping Force and the Midpoint Change in my course (with references to Aristotle, Campbell, and other story gurus) for some time before I learned about the Elliott Wave. When writing the first edition of this book, I knew there had to be some connection between the three acts of Aristotle and the Greeks and the five acts used by Shakespeare. The Elliott Wave helped me see it. (As it turns out, those five acts were not "gospel" during Shakespeare's time, but that's how his plays were printed.) Rather than telling you, however, let me show you.

Pictorial depiction of the Shaping Force story matrix.

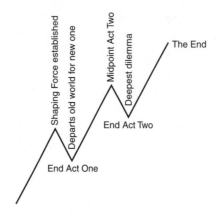

Pretty simple, wouldn't you say? Try it out, but don't take it as gospel. Here's another tip: in some movies, there isn't really a villain, simply an "opposing force." That force will always be visually represented, however, by a person who downplays the hero or heroine doing something about it. Disaster movies often have this kind of setup. Study structure by watching lots of successful movies, but never get locked into an "only way to do it" structure. Film and storytelling are evolving media, as you'll discover throughout your career.

Hopefully by now you have a screenplay idea in mind. I hope that you've tried it out on friends or professionals, that you have winnowed this idea out from at least a dozen other ideas, and that you're convinced that you have the right one for you to write. If you have done this, move to the head of the class. For everyone else, provided that you've done your homework, the following steps should put you well on the path to a professional screenplay:

1. Develop a premise whose "What if?" question personally excites you. Write your premise down on a "pitch card" and keep it posted nearby.

2. Determine whether you have a theme for your movie. If you do, write it down. If you don't have a theme, don't worry about it. It will emerge on its own, or not. The Shaping Force will help you find it.

3. Try to give your movie a title that provides the reader/viewer with a good idea of what the movie is about, as in *Cast Away* or *Knocked Up*, or alludes to the subtext and theme, as in *My Big Fat Greek Wedding*.

4. Figure out where your story begins. You're looking for the inciting incident from which the main character will not be able to turn back. If your movie is an ensemble piece, you will still have an inciting incident that will propel the group

into some irreversible course of events. If you have "back story" beginning scenes, set them aside for reference.

5. If it has not already occurred to you, try to establish an ending to your film, the logical progression from the beginning point of your movie.

6. Lay out a rough description of the scenes in your movie, describing the major action of each scene.

7. Divide your scenes into acts, with Act Two being roughly twice as long as either Act One or Act Three. It might help if you use actual index cards, which you can sort into stacks.

8. Try to locate where your plot or turning points are located, usually a scene or two before the end of Acts One and Two. These are events that accelerate the story by sending it in a new direction, which may even be a full reversal of events up to that time.

9. Find a scene roughly in the middle of Act One that is your *Shaping Force* that establishes what the movie is about. You might discover you've hinted at it a few pages into the script.

10. Find the scene roughly in the middle of Act Two that is your *midpoint change*, where the hero makes a shift, however subtle, from being more the effect of the "new world" to being more causative over it.

11. Flesh out your scenes on index cards, if the scenes are not already fully described. Do your best to add a denouement, or tag, at the end of Act Three.

12. Write out a treatment of your screenplay, using your cards to describe your movie scene by scene as they flow. Then set it aside for a few days or a week.

Your Name

Skip's Tips

Don't leave out the denouement, the icing on the cake of a great screenplay that provides a final clarification of what the hero has accomplished. Think of the wonderful ironic twist at the end of *Raiders of the Lost Ark*, as the Ark of the Covenant is filed away to be forgotten in a U.S. government warehouse. Audiences expect it, so give it to them.

Let's take the three-act structure and assume that there is an inciting incident that starts us off, followed by a shaping scene in the middle of Act One, and then a turning point before the end of Act One. Then in Act Two a midpoint change in the middle, and a turning point before the end of Act Two. I think you'll find that matches the illustration provided. Of course, I don't show a denouement or "tag" with one of the "waves" but it's not a major part of a film, just a nice touch that audiences expect.

In any event, I hope all this helps you write a script that keeps them coming back for more. And please, don't just rely on what I tell you; read any book you think might be helpful. Good screenwriters *never* think they know it all.

The Least You Need to Know

♦ The beginning, middle, and end dramatic structure described in Aristotle's *Poetics* remains the predominant storytelling framework today.

♦ The myth structure outlined by Joseph Campbell in *Hero with a Thousand Faces* is crucial to understanding epic stories.

♦ The "paradigm" story schematic in Syd Field's *Screenplay*, with its change of direction plot points before the ends of Acts One and Two, should be studied by all screenwriters.

♦ By using the idea of a "Shaping Force" in the middle of Act One, you are much less constrained to rigid structures such as the "myth" theory.

♦ In almost all films, a midpoint change occurs in which the main character transitions from being mostly the effect of the opposing force to a causatively positive state.

♦ In 12 short steps, you can create all the necessary elements for writing a professional screenplay.

Chapter 15

Writing the Feature Film

In This Chapter

- Beginning, middle, and end
- First acts and shaping forces
- The second act is it, the second act needs fixing, and Spielberg's second acts
- The midpoint
- The crucial third act
- Post-story extras

You don't have to work from an outline. You may choose to simply start from an opening scene and wing it. Some writers will tell you to do that. The successful writers I've known, however, start with structure.

After you've outlined your scenes, pick a couple that you think are crucial. Start with the one that interests you most and see whether you can determine if that scene begins where it should. That is, does it open with a specific action, or are you "thinking out loud on paper" and writing down back story that isn't relative to the current scene? Find the middle of the scene, where it turns in another direction. When the scene ends, you should want to know what happens next. If you aren't feeling compelled to

Skip's Tips _____

Some critics maligned writer/director/producer James Cameron's *Titanic* script, but he does something at the end of many scenes that propels you into the next one. Read the script sometime, and you'll see what I mean. You'll find little scene-ending "tags" that move the story. The movie was a blockbuster, but not merely because people liked watching a ship sink.

read on, there could be something wrong with the ending. Then try the same process with the other scene you selected. Does it have the same problems (if any) the first one had?

As you can see, I'm saying that every scene usually has a three-part structure, just like you find in a good screenplay.

Scenes in a well-constructed screenplay are like the many layers of an onion, organically connected one to the other at a base that we might compare to the premise of the story. If one scene is removed, it collapses those above it, and the overall look is a hollow one. With no base, the layers go everywhere.

Making the Beginning, Middle, and End Work

At the end of the previous chapter was a 12-step program (no jokes, please) prescribing a path to a full treatment (expanded outline) from which to write your screenplay. Let's assume you wrote it and rewrote it, starting off with the *inciting incident*. Here are some examples of the type of scene you should have:

♦ A beautiful young female swimmer is eaten by the great white shark in *Jaws*. This danger to the community must be dealt with so that the bay is safe and the tourist season is not harmed.

♦ In *The Sixth Sense*, an intruder kills child psychologist Malcolm Crowe. Although we don't know it until the end, Crowe must (like other ghosts) attempt to finish the cut-short efforts of his life.

♦ In *As Good as It Gets*, ultimate grouch Melvin Udall tries to hurt an innocent little dog. When the dog's owner challenges him, it is karma's first demand that Melvin face his own flawed character.

♦ In *Finding Nemo*, a mother fish and all but one of her many babies are eaten. When the survivor, Nemo, is captured by fishermen, his father will do anything to find him and bring him back.

♦ In *300*, the Spartans are the toughest of Greek fighters, some raised from birth to be warriors. When the Persian hordes approach, threatening Sparta and all of Greece with overrun, that's definitely an incitement to war.

If you're not sure whether you have your inciting incident, think about the ending that you have in mind for your screenplay. If you know where you're going, ask yourself this question: *Will this event put my main character on a path to his ultimate goal from which there is no turning back?*

A question like that makes you think about structure. In the 2003 animated blockbuster *Finding Nemo*, kids naturally identified with the cute young fish named in the title. His father will not turn back from rescuing his son, and Nemo will not turn back from adventure. They ultimately reach the same conclusion about balancing security and adventure, but who is the protagonist?

Lajos Egri believed in the "unity of opposites." He thought that the villain had to be the equal of the hero, the yin to the hero's yang. They oppose each other in a life-and-death struggle that one must lose. Like an electric motor, their opposite poles drive the engine of the story, based on that premise. Does your inciting incident place your hero and villain in irreversible conflict?

Who is the villain in *Finding Nemo*? It's the dangerous outer world, which we might describe as "anti-family." (Remember what I said in the last chapter about an "opposing force"?) Nemo's mother and siblings are eaten. Nemo is captured. He ends up in a fish tank far from his home, which he may never escape. By teaming up with other fish in the tank (a substitute family), just as his father teams up with other sea creatures (a larger family), Nemo's rescue is achieved and their family harmony restored and enhanced. Since Nemo is the one who learns the most and returns from the "new world" with that knowledge, that makes him the hero of the movie, even though he has put himself and his father in great danger by letting himself be captured.

Let's take a look at the various *signposts* you'll have in your outline. Remember, they're just there to guide you, not to bind you to a rigid, inflexible structure.

It's Not for Us

Never tailor your scenes to fit some rigid skeletal structure. That takes away the intuitive nature of great storytelling. When you've fixed your story in your mind, by whatever method works for you, just write. Let it flow. Use the scenes that you've outlined as *guideposts* on your journey. If a more appealing direction appears, don't be afraid to take it.

First is your inciting incident (which may occur before the movie begins, as in *The Wizard of Oz*). Then the Shaping Force in the middle of Act One, which firmly establishes what your movie is about. In *The Wizard of Oz* (as in *Finding Nemo*), the Shaping Force is the importance of home and family, which is represented by Dorothy seeing the picture of Auntie Em in the crystal ball. Then comes the first big break as Act One ends, which comes when your main character has undergone all the steps necessary to *set up* the major conflict that is the extended Act Two. In *The Wizard of Oz*, that twist is the tornado lifting Dorothy, her dog Toto, and the house into the sky. And once she lands in Oz (where Act Two begins) it seems there's no turning back.

> ### Script Notes
>
> If you think audiences these days are intellectual and thus demand mind-challenging plot points, consider this. Aristotle used the term "peripeteia" to refer to a moment of reversal in the plot. In the magic of writing from a good premise, peripeteia will often arise naturally. Peripeteia also refers to Aristotle's habit of teaching while walking about with his students.

Here's something to remember about Act Two: it's usually twice as long as the other acts, roughly a 1:2:1 ratio. If your script is 120 pages, the acts will likely be 30:60:30 minutes long. If your script is 110 pages long, the acts will be 27.5:55:27.5. Because comedy scripts are generally shorter, let's say that you have a 90-minute comedy, so the acts will be 22.5:45:22.5. (Remember, these are simply guide-posts, not absolutes.)

Let's say you write a 120-page script, roughly 40 three-minute scenes. (That's about five pages too long by today's standards, and many scenes would be shorter than three minutes, but it's an easier length for doing the math.) When you reach the *midpoint change* in the middle of Act Two, has your main character undergone some change that will shift his or her focus slightly so that he or she becomes more the attacker than the attacked? Is it clear that the protagonist, while not being in control, is more in control than not? In *The Wizard of Oz*, Dorothy leads her friends off to get the broom of the Wicked Witch of the West.

At the end of Act Two should be a scene that will again send your main character in a new direction and prepare him or her for the resolution of the conflict. At this second turning point, you're on the brink of the place where, in rapid succession, the hero defeats the villain and reaches the goal that began with your inciting incident. In certain films, particularly those by Steven Spielberg and James Bond movies, this sequence will be more extended, providing more room for exciting action. In *The Wizard of Oz*, Dorothy defeats the Wicked Witch fairly quickly after being captured.

By now you're probably wondering what to do with 10 three-minute scenes that make up a 30-minute Act Three. Chances are, your third act will be shorter. That has been the trend of movies for some time now. If you had seven scenes in Act Three, with your other acts roughly the "normal" length of 30 minutes and 60 minutes, you'd end up with about 110 minutes, which is very normal for a Hollywood drama these days. In *Men in Black*, by my count, Act Three is only eight minutes long.

Then comes the tag at the end of Act Three, the denouement. How long should it be? Well, how long was the scene in which Dorothy woke up in her home in Kansas? Denouements in uplifting films are short and to the point, and inevitably provoke a smile. In dramas, they provoke irony, and in horror films another little shock. In many comedies, we are shown the outtakes from filming.

First Acts Don't Last Forever but a Shaping Force Endures

Syd Field puts the end of Act One at page 30 and puts his first plot point between pages 25 and 27. Former UCLA screenwriting department co-chairman Lew Hunter feels that Act One, which he calls "The Situation," usually ends around page 17. I asked Lew about that one day over lunch, and he replied that he simply noticed that with most good scripts, you know what's going on by page 17. I've observed roughly the same thing, which means that you have to get going fast, on the first page. Here's an example from a thriller that I wrote and sold with Peter Flynn. The premise of *Allure* is this: *What if models in lingerie commercials started getting killed in real life?*

FADE IN:

EXT. DOWNTOWN LOS ANGELES STREET - NIGHT

SEXY SAXOPHONE MUSIC COMES UP as LOIS CHAMBERS, a beautiful model, drives a white Pontiac Fiero through downtown Los Angeles streets toward the Static Club, the hottest spot in the downtown L.A. scene.

Lois slows and starts to turn into the parking lot, but the ATTENDANT flashes a sign that says "Lot Full!"

Lois looks around, but the streets are packed with cars.

Skip's Tips

If you've never seen a screenplay before, I should clue you in that the first time we see a character's NAME it is ALL CAPS. Similarly, SOUNDS are capitalized only if important to the action or to denote sounds from a character, such as Lois's nervous LAUGH.

And lots of young, hip people are going into the club, laughing, and having a good time. It's the place to be.

Lois GUNS the Fiero down the street. Gotta find some parking.

EXT. ANOTHER DOWNTOWN LOS ANGELES STREET - NIGHT

Lois finally finds a place to park, only it's in a very shabby, downright frightening neighborhood.

INT. LOIS'S FIERO - NIGHT

She checks the rearview mirror and sees nothing. These streets are more or less deserted this late at night. She checks her lipstick and then, satisfied, grabs her purse and gets out.

SAXOPHONE FADES IN as she walks along slowly, sensually, all business and in no hurry. Suddenly, she hears a MOTORCYCLE ROAR and turns to face it.

As it comes her way, her pace quickens, but it's only a PIZZA DELIVERY BOY on his way somewhere in a hurry. She LAUGHS to herself at her alarm, and then slows down.

But on the night streets there is something else, and she hears it and turns again. It is a black car, with darkened glass windows, going very slowly, as if following her. It is between her and her car—there's no going back there. Lois turns and tries to ignore it, her pace quickening. Behind her, she hears the black car speed up.

She gauges the distance to the brightly lit main street up ahead. There are no police, not even other people headed to the club. She starts trotting, her breath coming hard. She looks back, and the car is closer and closer, edging close to the curb, definitely following. She begins to run, SCREAMING at the black car.

***

We sold that script before anyone aired lingerie commercials on television. I saw that day coming, so I incorporated it into the script. The screenplay was shelved and then resold. It might get made someday—who knows? I would write some of the description differently now, to suggest (but not describe) more shots. I would rewrite the last two paragraphs of page one like this:

Something else. She hears it, turns. A jet-black car, darkened glass windows. Moving slowly. Stalking. Between her and the Fiero, there's no going back. Lois turns, speeds up, tries to ignore it. The black car speeds up.

The brightly lit main street. She gauges the distance. No police. No one. Her feet quicken, then trot. Her breath, coming hard. She looks back. The black car closes. It's edging the curb. She's running, SCREAMING. Dying.

Some people would advise you to be less specific than "SAXOPHONE FADES IN" and say only "MUSIC UP"—if you say more, you're attempting to do the job of the composer or soundtrack supervisor. A saxophone usually evokes a sexy vibe, though, so I put it in.

Lois isn't the only model for the "Allure" line that gets killed. Who is doing it and why is the plot of the movie. On page two, Lois is hit by the car and killed, and the pizza delivery boy returns and finds her. In the next scene, we are introduced to the male lead, JOHN PALMER, as he drives from downtown Los Angeles toward Hollywood. This was done to establish for the audience what city we are in. (They don't see the EXT. LOS ANGELES STREET on the script, so how could they know?)

The next scene features another beautiful model in a fancy, high-rise, West Side apartment building. She is alone, wearing an emerald green lingerie ensemble. She finds a handsome cat burglar in her apartment and starts to fight him, and then they discover an instant animal attraction. As she pulls off his mask and the wind blows her sheer robe around her body, we hear a sultry, female narrator say: "Allure. There's danger in the night."

And then APPLAUSE as we see that this has been a commercial on a TV monitor in a television studio where the director of the commercials, John Palmer, is the guest on a morning talk show. The commercials are controversial (maybe because they're a bit corny?), and people are protesting them. But not half as much as they will after they learn that Lois has been murdered.

By page five of *Allure*, we've met CYNTHIA NIELSEN, the creator of the Allure lingerie line and the one who hired John to direct when no one else would hire him to do film. You see, John has a bit of a past. We know that because CAPTAIN CONLEY and his partner, LIEUTENANT FROMER, show up at the TV studio to ask some questions about Lois. When John learns what happened to Lois, he is reminded of the death of LAUREN ASHLEY, a supermodel that he was dating when they were both on top of the world, success-wise.

By page 10, it's clear that John is a suspect in Lois's murder, and then Cynthia lies, saying he was with her the night before, providing him an alibi for reasons that John doesn't understand.

Then we see John's studio and watch him work a commercial photo shot. His assistant, BETTY, obviously has some issues with him, but we don't know if it's because his client has been waiting and is upset, or some other issue. And we see John's assistant, BOBBY, a wisecracking Lothario capable of anything.

And even though I didn't know about the principle at the time, there was my "Shaping Force," namely Betty. Since that script was purchased but will probably never get made, I'll give away the ending. Betty was, unbeknownst to John, the sister of his model girlfriend who died mysteriously years before. Betty was jealous of her sister and killed her, and being psychotic she has "projected" that onto John, and is now trying to kill him.

The Shaping Force usually has hints that it's coming, like all the concerns over *time* in Act One of *Cast Away*, leading up to the firm establishment of that Shaping Force when Helen Hunt gives Tom Hanks a pocket watch containing her picture, at dinner.

Skip's Tips

Producer Joel Silver, with pictures to his credit such as *The Matrix* trilogy, the *Die Hard* movies, and the *Lethal Weapon* series, has often said that in action films, some major shoot'em-up or explosive event should occur onscreen about every 10 minutes. Watch one of his films some day and time it out. He's not kidding, and neither are his box-office figures.

By the top of page 17 in *Allure*, we've met all the important characters in the screenplay, and John Palmer is propelled into a murder mystery in which he'll have to prove his own innocence and determine who the real killer is. Our script is 102 pages long. There's a turning point on page 20, introducing the undercover policewoman who cracks the case, but the point wasn't written very well, frankly. It did send the story in another direction, but not as effectively as I could do it today.

Hopefully this example gives you some idea of at least a decent first page and Act One. The people who bought *Allure* told me that they considered 250 feature scripts before picking ours.

The Second Act Is the Movie

In case you didn't know it, the biggest box office star of the last few years is Will Smith. My favorite Smith film is *Men in Black*, a masterful script written by Ed Solomon (with some unaccredited help from others) from a hit comic book by Lowell Cunningham. (Of course, I loved him in the much more serious *Pursuit of Happyness*, too.)

Act One of the script ends when Smith's James Edwards goes with Tommy Lee Jones's Kay into a pawnshop owned by a fellow named Jeebs. When Kay blows off Jeebs's head with a "Cricket," a strange futuristic pistol, Edwards knows that they aren't in Kansas any more because Jeebs, the alien, grows another head immediately. Everything in this 98-page script is set up by page 18. But guess what? It is not until the end of page 93 that Act Two ends. That comes when Edwards distracts the giant alien bug intent on destroying the galaxy long enough for Kay, who has tricked the bug into swallowing him, to blast his way out of the bug's belly with a gun that the bug ate.

Did you remember that general 1:2:1 pages-to-act ratio that I mentioned earlier? Try to apply it to *Men in Black*. Obviously, it would be way off. The ratio in *MIB* would be 18:75:5. That's because *Act Two is the movie*, particularly true in an all-out action movie like *MIB*. When the action is finished, the movie is basically over. In a pure drama, an Act Three usually lasts longer. There are issues to be handled, things to be worked out and wrapped up.

When you're writing your second act, you're really writing the movie. The first 10 pages are essential in grabbing the readers/viewers and keeping them with you, and the act break that happens between pages 17 and 27 or so (depending on the length of your script and how you write) is crucial, as are any turning points that you have in the first act.

Hollywood Heat

W. C. Fields's Hollywood career was a great second act. He was in his mid-30s when he starred in a short entitled *Pool Sharks* (1915). Because he was a star on Broadway, it was nine years before he starred in the feature *Sally of the Sawdust* directed by D. W. Griffith. Fields's last feature was in 1941, the classic *Never Give a Sucker an Even Break*. He wrote the story of that film as "Otis Cribblecoblis." He wrote a lot of his own material, with screenplay credit for his famous film, *The Bank Dick* (1940, writing as "Mahatma Kane Jeeves").

Usually, the Second Act Most Needs Fixing

The late great Diane Thomas, who wrote *Romancing the Stone*, was loved by producers because she believed so much in making sure that the second act was top-notch. According to a producer I talked with, when they started talking story problems, she would immediately zero in on the second act and go fix it. Thomas was right. Think of all the things that happen in Act Two:

♦ The main character engages in the immediate conflict of the movie. If it's a comedy, some of the more outlandish things happen that truly establish the pickle that the main character is in, such as Jim Carrey in *Bruce Almighty* learning just how difficult it can be, being God.

♦ Act Two events lead to a midpoint change, such as when Carrey realizes that he's stuck with hearing the incessant stream of prayers of people in the world and he has to do something about them.

♦ With the new empowerment that came at the midpoint change, the struggle intensifies, crescendoing at the end of the act. In *Bruce Almighty*, Carrey sees that it's quite a job being God and that the troubles he was screaming at God about in Act One were pretty unimportant, given all that God has to deal with.

Bruce Almighty is a good one for pointing out how the hero can use personal weaknesses established at the beginning of the film to defeat the bad guy in Act Two. In this case, the bad guy is himself. Carrey is a villain to his career and relationships because he's so self-centered and jealous he has to blame God when he fails. So, Carrey has to conquer himself.

Script Notes

You'll often hear the term "character arc" in Hollywood. I like to think of that as a golf shot to an uphill green. The hero's journey in the story rises to an apex and then descends to its final destination. The apex is the midpoint change, where the necessary (inner) "motion" has taken place. The ball (hero), now mid-action, completes the journey with accelerated force.

In most movies, there is an "A" story in which the hero battles outer villains, like the Nazis in *Casablanca*. There is also a "B" story in which the hero struggles within himself. In *Casablanca*, Humphrey Bogart's Rick has a weakness for Ilsa, played by Ingrid Bergman. But Ilsa is married. Rick has a deeper weakness as well. He is running his club and staying neutral in the struggle of World War II, and so he's somewhat of a coward. In contrast, Ilsa's husband, Victor Laszlo (played by Paul Henreid), is a freedom fighter. By making the decision in Act Two to help Ilsa and her husband escape, Rick conquers his weaknesses and sacrifices his own desires for a greater cause. By doing so, he brings the local police chief over to his side.

In movies like *Bruce Almighty* where the main struggle is within the main character, there is still a "B" story, but it's the one on the outside. In this case, it's what happens with the protagonist's career at the TV station.

Steven Spielberg's Second Acts

Using the example of the original cut of *Close Encounters of the Third Kind* (1977) as an example, Syd Field feels that Spielberg created a new storytelling form, with acts of that screenplay of roughly the same length—a 1:1:1 ratio. While this could be debated, the fact remains that the film (as with many Spielberg films) is longer than the "normal" two hours. If you're a fan of Spielberg, as I am, you probably already know that he dwells long on the action of a movie and doesn't spend much time wrapping things up once the story is done. To me, he does that with an extended Act Two. *Saving Private Ryan* is an example, as are the *Jurassic Park* movies and the *Indiana Jones* films. He did the same thing with *Minority Report*.

The Midpoint and the Hero's Orientation

Rather than provide you with further examples, it's best that you do your own homework. Do the following with at least a dozen films, and see if the midpoint change happens, ratio-wise, at roughly the same time in all movies. Try this:

1. In the first act, spot what you think is the main weakness of the protagonist, at the very least with regard to dealing with the main villain.

2. Locate examples of how this protagonist's weakness is exploited by the villain, keeping the hero or heroine at effect.

3. Spot the point in the movie where a change comes over the hero or heroine in which he or she will do whatever is necessary to defeat the villain, no matter what might happen to him or her personally.

Great films are really about personal transformation, and understanding what personal transformation your protagonist undergoes is crucial to telling your story effectively. While you don't have to preach, the more movie audiences relate to that struggle, the better off you are at the box office.

The Short but Crucial Third Act

At the end of *Men in Black*, there are five pages for the last five steps of the Joseph Campbell myth structure to work out—only five pages to conclude the entire screenplay and add a tag at the end. How was this done? Assuming that you've read the screenplay or seen the movie, let's take a look:

◆ **Refusal of the Return.** Kay (Tommy Lee Jones) won't reveal to Jay (Will Smith) whether getting eaten by the bug was part of his plan; he merely shrugs and says "Worked."

◆ **The Magic Flight.** Zed (Rip Torn), their boss back at headquarters, tells them that the aliens who live on Earth are returning, now that it's safe again.

◆ **Rescue from Without.** Laurel (Linda Fiorentino), a coroner whom they rescued from the giant alien bug, saves Kay and Jay as they argue by blasting the menacing front half of the still-menacing alien into oblivion with an "atomizer."

◆ **The Crossing of the Return Threshold.** Back at the MIB building, Kay reveals to Jay that he hasn't been training a new partner. He's been training a replacement. Kay wants to quit and go home.

◆ **Master of the Two Worlds.** Jay is reading a tabloid that includes a picture of Kay with the woman he left to join the Men in Black. The headline reads "MAN AWAKENS FROM 30-YEAR COMA: Returns to Girl He Left Behind." Jay now understands fully how some of the outlandish stories in the tabloids are actually real.

◆ **Freedom to Live.** At the curb in the LTD is Elle (formerly known as Laurel). She is now a Woman in Black, Jay's new partner. When Jay returns, she tells him that Zed has called, wanting tickets to a New York Knicks vs. Chicago Bulls basketball game. Jay can get them because Dennis Rodman (then playing for the Bulls) is an alien. Jay is now truly the master of two worlds.

This all takes place in about eight minutes.

Although third acts are shorter these days, they are not dispensable. For the foreseeable future, third acts will still be with us because they wrap up the psychological package that the audience has spent the last hour or two of their lives purchasing.

Hollywood Heat _____

Daniel Petrie Jr. (*Beverly Hills Cop*) once had an office in Beverly Hills in the same building with Billy Wilder. Petrie told me that Wilder was always concerned that the third act be just right. The endings of his films always wrap up nicely. My favorite Wilder movie is *Some Like It Hot* (1959), which the American Film Institute voted greatest comedy of all time. Get your third acts right, and you might become a legend.

In the highly entertaining *Adaptation*, written by Charlie Kaufman, an actor playing screenwriting guru Robert McKee tells Nicolas Cage (playing Charlie Kaufman, you need to see it) that if you have a good ending, audiences will pretty much forgive you for other things. That may or may not be true, but Billy Wilder didn't fret over third acts just to hear himself grumble.

Tag, You're a Denouement with a Coda

The dictionary definition of a *denouement* is "the final outcome of the main dramatic complications in a literary work." That's a bit misleading with regard to movies. The root of the word literally means "to untie." The tag at the end of a film is that bit which, if a thriller or horror movie, gives us one additional hesitated beat of the heart.

What the denouement actually does is allow us to let go of the movie, to mentally return to our own world. Remember when Jody Foster's Clarice Starling gets the phone call from the escaped Hannibal Lecter (Anthony Hopkins) at the end of *Silence of the Lambs?* When Hannibal the Cannibal then loses himself on the street, it's a thrilling little scene that would go well with a glass of Chianti. There is another item to consider writing. It's called a *coda* in Hollywood. The American Heritage Dictionary definition is a musical term: "A passage at the end of a movement or composition that brings it to a formal close." Directors love them. They're placed after the credits have rolled and are only seen by people remaining in the theater. Why? Because they create "buzz" and some people will see the movie again just to see the coda they walked out before seeing! A good example is at the end of *Pirates of the Caribbean: Curse of the Black Pearl*. The pet monkey of the villain runs off with a cursed gold coin, reviving a curse that made unkillable ghosts of the villainous pirates in the movie. That scene set up the sequel.

The Least You Need to Know

- Every good movie begins with an inciting incident that places the hero and villain in irreversible conflict.

- Generally, the acts of a screenplay have a 1:2:1 length ratio, but that can vary greatly.

- Even if you don't know it exists, if you write a good screenplay you may create a "Shaping Force" mid–Act One.

♦ Good screenplays have a midpoint change, an event where the hero shifts to being more causative than effect of the villain.

♦ The second act is so important that you can say it *is* the movie.

♦ Third acts and the denouement, or "tag" at the end of the act, wrap up the movie for the audience and allow them to mentally return to the real world. Additionally, a "coda" at the end of the credits may get them to see the movie again.

Chapter **16**

The Screenplay, Step-by-Step

In This Chapter

- ◆ The initial concept
- ◆ The proper treatment
- ◆ Drafting mastery
- ◆ Importance of format
- ◆ The Hemingway trick

 If you do your writing on a computer, I strongly suggest that you invest in a screenplay-formatting program. If you want a full description of all the available programs and add-ons to existing software programs. You will also find demo versions of some software programs and listings of websites for others on the CD that accompanies this book.

The All-Important Initial Concept

In his intriguing book *Blue Highways*, Native American author William Least Heat Moon describes a process that the Hopi Indians call "sitting in pictures." The Hopi are perhaps the most peaceful of all indigenous American tribes and have inhabited their land for as long as they have had legends. They are one of the very few Native American groups (if not the only one) never displaced from their homeland. That speaks of some kind of power.

When the Hopi sit in pictures, they engage in creative visualization. They close their eyes and evoke the help of their departed ancestors when, for example, they "see" in their minds thunderclouds forming on the horizon to bring needed rain. The mental pictures that Least Heat Moon painted in my mind were so vivid that I wrote a scene into a published novel featuring my character Alexander Cloud, who is half-Hopi, sitting with his grandmother to bring rain. I also incorporated the scene into an earlier screenplay featuring an older Alex that I wrote for a producer and director.

Hollywood Heat

The amazing documentary *Koyaanisqatsi* (1983) sprang from Hopi words meaning "life out of balance." Directed by Godfrey Reggio, the film lists four writing credits, to Ron Fricke, Michael Hoenig, Alton Walpole, and Reggio (who also produced with Francis Ford Coppola). Featuring an original score by composer Philip Glass, the movie was made without a script. Producer Lawrence Taub of the Institute for Regional Education in Santa Fe, New Mexico (see www.koyaanisqatsi.org), told me that all the credited writers were "dramaturgical contributors" who helped piece together a treatment as the film was made. Such is the power of a powerful idea; many people can get behind it.

I hope that when you receive or conceive of your initial concept, it is like a flash of invigorated life that causes scenes to unfold before you, as though you are sitting in pictures watching the movie that you will soon be writing. Many screenwriters have told me the process happens that way for them.

I often get ideas whose logical conclusion appears almost simultaneously with the beginning. If you find it hard to visualize scenes based on your concept, I have a suggestion. *Throw the idea away.* Accept nothing but the most intriguing concepts, those that will keep you excited through the long, hard process of writing a screenplay. Believe me, it's like driving a luxury car for the first time—you don't know what you're missing until you get the real thing in your hands.

Giving Yourself the Proper Treatment

Some writers don't write a treatment. They would rather just write the script from a brief outline or from cards. The truth is that treatments will change while you write the screenplay. That's normal—don't worry about it. When you breathe life into your characters, they will, like children gaining powers of independence, start saying things and doing things that you did not think about when you slaved over your rough out-line (which some call a "beat" or "step" outline). Roll with what works for you.

Most pro screenwriters I know work from a treatment so they can follow the flow of the story more easily. Unfortunately, there is no clear consensus in Hollywood about what constitutes a treatment. Some will tell you that it's 10 pages or less. Others will insist that it's the script minus all or almost all the dialogue, which could be 75-80 pages. Still others will say that 20 to 30 pages should do it. Whatever you favor, it is usually double-spaced, written in prose style, in present tense, and maintains as much dramatic tension in the narrative as possible. Check out Terry Rossio and Ted Elliott's treatment of their *Sinbad* comedy script at www.wordplayer.com for a pro example.

Let's hope that you get into the position where you're doing business with a produc-tion company and the company asks for a treatment. Because you don't know what that particular company expects to see, say, "Great. What format do you prefer?" They'll probably expect you to simply tell the story as I've outlined already. They may ask for headings such as Setting or Main Character. If they are that specific, how-ever, they'll probably have a treatment in the office from someone else that they've adopted as their preferred style. Ask if they do have one.

Don't use treatments as a selling tool unless specifically asked for them, because sharing treatments with others can make you crazy when you get feedback. With a script, they generally have to be more specific with "notes."

> ### It's Not for Us
>
> Never assume that just because one production company does things a certain way, others will, even if they are on the same studio lot. Production companies move all the time, change personnel a lot, and are largely personality-driven. If the Director of Development today loves to read treatments, the one next week may think you're an amateur if you even mention one.

Drafting Beats Dreaming

Screenwriting seems like a sexy occupation. In reality, it's hard work and often abused in Hollywood to the point that writers have gone on labor strikes. Studio executive Irving Thalberg reportedly said, "The screenwriter is the only absolutely essential element in this town, and he must never find out." His granddaughter, whom I met in Aspen, Colorado, agreed that's what he said.

Keep your true value in mind as you set up a schedule that you can live with, and stop waiting for your "muse." The muse is busy—there are a lot of aspiring screenwriters these days. Even if you don't feel like it, there comes a day when you simply have to sit down and start typing out the scenes.

> **Script Notes** _____
>
> *"CUT TO:"* means to abruptly switch from one scene to another. *"DISSOLVE TO:"* means that one scene fades as another scene comes into focus and traditionally denotes passage of time. These are essentially camera and editing decisions (and a director or cinematographer's job), so scene changes are increasingly left out of professional scripts. On the other hand, some top writers use them.

I started making money in Hollywood by having a treatment optioned. I generally wouldn't try to do that today. If I feel strongly enough about a story to ask people to spend millions making it, I'll try to sell it via a script I've written.

The Importance of Being Formatted

It's different keystrokes for different key folks with regard to treatments, but script formats are much more standardized. Even so, you'll still find some disagreements. (We'll assume here that you are not using a screenplay-formatting program.)

Some people advise a margin of 1 inch on both the top and the bottom of your 8½×11-inch page, but one popular script formatting software program uses a text margin of 1.12 inches at the top and 0.75 inches at the bottom, with .5 inches from the top of the paper to the page number, and .5 inches from the bottom of the paper to footers such as (CONTINUED). Such a footer indicates that a scene is continued on the next page. Because (CONTINUED) is falling out of favor, however, you're best counting on a .75-inch margin on the bottom of the page.

Another popular program uses a left margin set at 10 and a right margin at 75. I prefer this one.

The left margin should be 1.5 inches because scripts are copied onto or printed on three-hole paper. If you use a lesser margin, it might be hard to read the left side of your script after it is bound. Many people advise a right margin .5 inches from the edge of the paper, but in the Final Draft program, the default margins are set at 12 and 72, which is a wider right margin.

Use a 12-point Courier font. Courier New is fine also; the point is that it looks like it was typed on a typewriter. (That's Hollywood longing for a simpler time, I suppose.)

There's another reason for Courier 12. It is a fixed-pitch font with 10 characters per horizontal inch and 6 lines per vertical inch. That means that what you see is what you get, and a page will roughly add up to one-minute screen time. Do not use a proportional font or a justified right margin. The first line of text on the first page, which has no number, should begin 0.75 inch from the top.

Starting on the *second page*, the distance from the top to your page number should be three carriage returns, or .5 inches. Then a single blank line separates the page number and the body of the script, which begins at .75 inch from the top of the page. Numbers should align aesthetically past the right margin. (*Note: There is a period after the number and no "Page Number." For example, page five would be written 5.*)

The bottom page margin should be at least .5 inch (three carriage returns) or the end of a scene. If you leave a 1-inch margin (six returns) at the bottom, no one will complain.

There are three other format spacing concerns for a script. A character's first name is in all capitals, as in "SKIP." We usually do not use both names, unless the person has a title in front, such as "COL. PRESS." A character's name begins at 37 spaces over from the left margin of 10. The first letter of all character names in the script starts at 37.

Dialogue appears two tabs, or 10 spaces, over from the left margin. The right margin for dialogue is two tabs, or 10 spaces, in from the right margin. *Parentheticals* (dialogue directions) appear one extra tab over from the left, as in the following example:

SKIP

(quietly)
How does it look so far?

Scene transitions, such as …

CUT TO:

… should be aligned against the right margin. (Note the colon that follows any indication of scene change.) These are generally left out these days because it is considered obvious that the scene has changed when we see a new location listed below a scene.

When someone speaks off-screen but is in the scene, write this:

SKIP (O.S.)

When someone speaks off-camera but is not in the scene, write this:

SKIP (V.O.)

V.O. is an abbreviation for "voice over."

It is a time-honored tradition to begin each script with:

FADE IN:

I don't expect a change of that norm anytime soon, but some writers leave it off. The title of the script is generally left off the first page. If you add it, and it's likely that no one will complain, center it:

<u>My Screenplay</u>
by Joe Screenwriter

Note that the title is underlined. However, you must still put the title and byline on a separate title page preceding the script. In Hollywood, simplicity is the best policy. If there's a doubt, leave it out. That's why, when you break dialogue at the bottom of a page, you should break it only at the end of a complete sentence. Do not add "(MORE)" centered beneath the line to indicate that more dialogue follows on the next page. That has fallen out of favor. Instead, on the following page, type "(CONT'D)" directly after the character name. Example:

SKIP
You must get your format right.

-----------------------page break-----------------------

SKIP (CONT'D)

If you don't, you'll just look foolish, and
your script may be rejected.

Do not break dialogue with hyphens. Use whole words only, and keep the parts of hyphenated words together on the same line, if at all possible. You don't want anything in the format to distract the reader from following the story in your script.

Hollywood Heat

In 1982, Chuck Ross wrote an article for *American Film* magazine, the official organ of the American Film Institute. He described how he retyped the screenplay of the immortal *Casablanca* and titled it *Everybody Comes to Rick's*. He submitted the script to 217 agencies, but only 85 of them read it. Thirty-eight agencies rejected it completely, and 33 thought that it seemed familiar, but only 8 recognized it as *Casablanca*. All told, only three agencies thought that it was saleable, and one suggested that it be turned into a novel!

When breaking the narrative, the convention is generally to break it only at the end of a complete sentence or even a paragraph, because action description is best done in short paragraphs of only a few lines. The convention of breaking only at the end of a complete sentence is wavering somewhat, but you're better off adhering to it. Just don't leave a one-line "widow" hanging at the end of a page or on the beginning of the next page.

Don't worry about a "CONTINUED" to show that an action description has been broken up. Just let the lines flow, as in this example:

Tarzan chases Jane across the floor of the valley, grinning as he watches her dart in and out of the long grass. She's stunning.

------------------------page break----------------------

CRACK! Too late, he stops. He's stepped onto a thatched lion trap. Only this one is meant for a man. Down he plunges, YELLING.

Shot headings, also known as "slug lines," show where the scene is located, the time of day or night, and if it is an inside shot or an outside shot. Use two blank lines between the end of one scene and a new slug line. Some authorities will tell you to use three lines, but two is still broadly preferred.

"EXT." is for "EXTERIOR" shots, and "INT." is for "INTERIOR" shots. If you have any "trick" locations, such as in the ocean or out in space, simply state where you are and don't worry about it. Only differentiate the time of day if it is absolutely essential (examples follow) and if we can see sunlight.

Note the spacing and punctuation in these examples:

EXT. PARAMOUNT STUDIOS - DAY

INT. PARAMOUNT STUDIOS - NIGHT

100 FEET BELOW OCEAN SURFACE - DAY

EXT. SPACE STATION

With the slug line denoting that we are under the ocean, I wrote "DAY" assuming that the next scene will be on the surface during the day, or that we can see at the top of the water that it is daylight.

Because day or night is not a consideration in space, I left off the time. The previous slug line indicates that the point of view is outside a space station. If we were inside, it would be this:

INT. SPACE STATION

The first time we see a location, it is necessary to establish it with an "EXT." description. Preferably, at least one line of description follows. Then we can venture inside with an "INT." shot and delineate the location further by adding to that. Take a look at these examples:

EXT. PARAMOUNT STUDIOS - EARLY MORNING

On Melrose Avenue, the last major studio actually located in Hollywood is open, but even the gate guard looks sleepy.

INT. PARAMOUNT STUDIOS, SKIP PRESS'S OFFICE - EARLY MORNING

SKIP PRESS, so-called writer, flops in his chair, feet on desk, head tilted back, SNORING. He's a wreck. Take-out remains are scattered on the floor. The coffee pot on a hot plate is smoking. He's been here all night. The computer SHRIEKS out an alarm.

(*Note the two lines between those scenes.*)

Unless it is necessary for dramatic purposes of the screenplay, stay away from writing a camera point of view (POV), like this:

SKIP'S POV

Also leave out "we see" descriptions such as this:

We see CAROL enter the ballroom, looking beautiful.

Try to leave out anything other than proper formatting that reminds the reader they are reading a screenplay. You want them to focus on the story.

Because Carol is a woman I know whom I find impressive, you might write in a POV for me, allowing the camera to dwell on her entrance, followed by a simple reaction shot on me:

CAROL enters the ballroom, more dazzling than ever.

Skip REACTS.

Let the director and actor decide how the actor reacts.

Do not concern yourself with defining individual shots unless you have a very specific reason for doing so, such as someone looking at an object closely. That would be described this way:

INSERT

The diamond. It sparkles like a captive sun.

Followed by:

RETURN TO SCENE

(If you return to the scene you were in before the INSERT.)

You could also use "RESUME SCENE" or "BACK TO SCENE" or nothing at all, just the next shot. Never let a shot heading be widowed at the bottom of a page, however. Move it to the next page, please.

As mentioned previously regarding the page from my script *Allure*, major sound effects are CAPITALIZED.

As also mentioned, the Cole-Haag book on screenplay formats was generally considered the standard reference but hasn't been updated for a decade. Again, I highly recommend that you get a screenwriting program to make your life easier. It will pay for itself by saving you extra work and these programs are regularly updated.

Skip's Tips

Your Name

A master scene script is the only one that you want to worry about writing. You simply describe the action as cleanly as possible, define each character with minimal superlatives, and write what each character says with few comments on how they say it. That way, the director and the actors remain your friends.

Hollywood Heat

When a concept is good enough, it never dies. The second script that I wrote struck the interest of Rona Edwards when she was working in development. She couldn't convince her boss of the script's worth, but years later, when I interviewed Edwards for a book, she remembered the script, asked about it, and optioned it. While producing movies such as *Out of Sync* (2000) on VH-1, Edwards kept waiting for me to rewrite my script. But then Will Ferrell did a movie called *Elf,* which was too much like mine, so I didn't write Rona's fave. In 2008, however, I did. Maybe by the time you read this, it will have sold.

On the following page is a title page properly formatted. (Note that although some people prefer to **bold the title,** the more prevailing standard is an <u>underlined title</u>.)

If you are a writing team, use an ampersand (&) instead of "and":

by
Joe Screenwriter & Jane Screenwriter

If you worked on the script separately, do it this way:

by
Joe Screenwriter
and
Jane Screenwriter

A writing team and another writer would read like this:

by
Joe Screenwriter & Jane Screenwriter
and
Nancy Goodfriend

Following the title page is a sample page (page 5) from *South China Sea* (a.k.a. *Fair Game*), written and sold by Michael Sean Conley and me. The inciting incident is presented, but the hero is not in this scene.

It's Not for Us

Although minimal is in, sometimes you have to use a "CUT TO:"—specifically a "SMASH CUT TO:"—in a horror movie such as *Scream*. This signifies an especially sharp and rapid transition, usually to something terrifying, such as a guy coming after you with a knife.

SAMPLE TITLE PAGE

My Screenplay
by
Jane Screenwriter

(Based on, if applicable)

Name
Address
Phone
E-mail
(Don't list a website unless it's about you or this script only.)

5

The powerboat approaches from out of the sun.

INT. GALLEY AREA IN SALON - DAY

Sandi starts the blender. It makes a horrible RACKET. A BEAT, then she frowns, hearing the RUMBLE of twin diesel engines. She looks out the open porthole toward the bow.

EXT. OFF THE YACHT'S BOW - DAY

SANDI'S POV OUT PORTHOLE as the W.W. II-vintage PT boat CUTS ENGINES to an idle and slides closer. Its torpedo launchers and .50-caliber guns have been removed. The Thai government's marine police <u>insignia</u> is on the bow.

There are four UNIFORMED MEN on board. One on the foredeck. One at the helm. A third beside him. A forth in a side turret aft of the bridge and forward of the day cabin.

INT. SALON - DAY

Sandi crosses to the ladder, passing an array of expensive underwater camera gear laid out on the dining bench.

EXT. YACHT AND PT BOAT - DAY

The PT boat has drawn alongside. Sandi frowns, studying the man on the bow, a muscle-bound blond Dutchman armed with a submachine gun. The other three men don't look Thai, either.

                              SANDI
                    (beat)
          Who are you?

The man GUNS HER DOWN in a fatal burst!

Jimmy turns at the staccato gunfire to finally see the PT boat goons. And his sister. Jimmy DROPS HIS BEER and rips the headset off in panic.

                              JIMMY
          SANDI!!

Sandy falls slowly onto the cockpit decking, dead.

You may be wondering why we say "DAY" or "NIGHT" with each new scene. When the film is shot, the scenes will likely be lifted out and filmed separately of each other, not in sequence. The underlined insignia is to draw attention to it. The "BEAT" mentioned with Sandy denotes that she pauses and then continues.

One more item that will also rarely fade from use: At the end of your script, you type, justified against the right margin:

FADE OUT.

(Note the period.) And then …

THE END

"THE END" is in bold. You'll be feeling bold when you finally wrap up the first draft of your script!

Winning the Daily Battle with the Hemingway Trick

When you're drafting out your first screenplay, don't worry too much about how many pages are in which act. Just write. Get the screenplay written. Try to set up a regular rhythm. If you can't write every day for the same amount of time, try to write on the same day each week for the same amount of time. Remember that each scene should have a beginning, middle, and end, just like the screenplay.

To help yourself resume the flow the next time, try stopping before you write the end of a scene. Ernest Hemingway had a little trick when writing novels. To make sure that he would be engaged with his work when he returned to it the next day, he would end his daily writing in the middle of a scene, even in the middle of a sentence. That way, he would have to start reading from the beginning of the scene to get back into it and finish it.

I'll often reread yesterday's chapter when writing a book, or read the last two scenes when writing a script, but when a story is hot enough I find that I'm usually still excited without having to end mid-scene. Whatever works for you, don't wear yourself out so much that you can't bear to write the next time.

And, remember, it's only a first draft. It won't really be a screenplay until you're done with enough rewrites to make your story shine.

The Least You Need to Know

◆ A good screenplay-formatting program can save you time, headaches, and the need to learn the format settings.

◆ Sometimes the only way to develop a marketable concept is to throw a few away.

◆ True screenplay treatments are double-spaced, written in prose style and in present tense. They cover all the main points of the story.

◆ Screenplay text looks best within the following margins: .75 inch on the top and bottom, 1.5 inches on the left, and .5 inch on the right.

◆ A "master scene script" without camera angles or dialogue directions for actors is the only one that you should try to write.

◆ Just write. Your first draft isn't really a screenplay until you are done with at least one rewrite.

Chapter 17

Navigating the Rewrite

In This Chapter

- First drafts
- Scene length
- Collaborators
- Who should read your script
- Rewrites and polishes
- Rewrite it better

You might find that a first-draft screenplay is like a child learning to walk. The important thing is that it makes it across the room, not that it does a perfect pirouette that makes everyone applaud. Would you make an exhausted-but-happy baby get up and keep going? You wouldn't, which is why I advise writers to set a first draft of anything aside for a couple of weeks, so they can gain distance and perspective uncolored by the enthusiasm of accomplishment.

When you begin the rewrite of your screenplay, you have to act like a benevolent-but-stern parent, with an eye toward making your child capable, sure and able to thrive on its own. Great scripts are like that; their maturity, worth, and "good breeding" are obvious. People who understand effective rewriting know what Mark Twain was talking about when he said as a teen-ager he thought his father was the stupidest man in the world, then at 18 he was amazed how much his dad had learned in a few short years.

Skip's Tips

There's an old adage called Keep It Simple, Stupid (KISS). If you can't easily describe your screenplay, you may be in trouble. It's the same with novels. In his *How to Grow a Novel* (St. Martin's Press, 1999), Sol Stein says, "All of the most successful novels I have edited over the years have had stories that could be synopsized in a single paragraph." Does that sound like a screenplay "log line"?

To create a great screenplay often takes a long time and many rewrites. I repeatedly tell people how M. Night Shyamalan said he didn't know Bruce Willis's character in *The Sixth Sense* was dead until "about the fifth or sixth draft."

Why First Drafts Are Drafty

I've found that beginning screenwriters inevitably "think on paper." In the heat of writing scenes, getting lost in them, being fascinated by the leading man or lady, or relishing in the stunningly clever viciousness of their villain, they write things in scenes that they have not yet thought through thoroughly.

Guess what? Highly paid veterans do, too. *S.W.A.T.* writer David Ayer showed me the first draft of that movie. It was 238 pages long. While you're in the midst of creation, it makes perfect sense to write that way. Swept along in the creative flow, we're just watching scenes appear first in our minds, and then on our computer screen.

I know it's hard to rewrite a first screenplay, particularly if you've sweated over it for a long time. But rewrite you must. One of the biggest hurdles for beginning writers to get over is what I call the "one-baby" syndrome. When you have only one child, the entire world revolves around its welfare. The more children you have, the less important a bloody nose is—you just doctor it and go on. Beginning writers are so protective of their first work that their inevitable first question is: "I'd like to tell someone about my screenplay, but how do I know that they won't steal my idea?"

To which I always reply: "You don't." I might tell them how I'm convinced that at least one of my screenplays (one I co-wrote with Linda Blair, of *The Exorcist*) was stolen and made into a movie that flopped. At one point, because of some odd events, I wondered whether *Shakespeare in Love* was perhaps derived from the first story of mine that was optioned.

You can drive yourself crazy worrying about negative possibilities. What really matters is that, if you write a screenplay that's good enough to be financed and filmed, it gets treated like a rare treasure.

Skip's Tips

A plot hole in a screenplay is something dangerous. The very life of the script might drain out if that hole isn't fixed. It could be a small hole that the viewer barely notices, or one so big that you could drive a Mack truck through and that will result in a collective groan from a theater audience if filmed as written. Sometimes rewriting won't catch a hole—you don't "see" it until you hear the script read aloud by actors.

Your Name

When drafting out screenplays, I've seen writers (including myself) usually end up with one or more of the following problems:

- **No pearl in this oyster.** You write a screenplay that isn't marketable in the first place. No amount of hot sauce will make it taste any better. You're left with a hollow shell.

- **Surfing in shallow water.** Incomplete research is done before writing the screenplay, resulting in shallow scenes and speeches that won't play well with audiences.

- **Rudderless ship.** The screenplay wanders away from the strong main current of the story and drifts along, lost. (That's why you need a Shaping Force to keep it on course—see Chapter 14 for more on this.)

- **Horse latitudes.** Like shipmates adrift on a windless sea, characters drone on endlessly but never advance the story.

- **Sinking leaky boats.** Scenes are repeatedly launched before they are ready, sinking the entire enterprise.

- **Titanic indifference.** Ignoring a major problem, the script churns onward blindly toward oblivion, resulting in a massive loss of life.

- **A drunken captain.** You're writing a screenplay about an unlikable hero or heroine that no one trusts or wants to emulate. (Trust me, I've seen a lot of drunken captains.)

You might be that rare prescient person who comes up with story lines and subjects that the rest of the world just doesn't quite "get" yet. John Lennon said that if he wrote a song his friends liked immediately, he thought something was wrong with it.

It was the songs that people had to take a while to assimilate that he wanted. I've come up with story ideas that weren't popular until years later. I had to deal with the current marketplace and prevailing "common wisdom." Most likely, so do you. If your script is tightly written and people tell you they'd like to see the movie, but it gets rejected, it just might not have found its "time" yet.

It's Not for Us

If you can't solve a script problem and decide to get some professional mentoring, research the gurus thoroughly. A pro might see something that you don't because he or she is not as immersed in the story as you are, but he or she also might be stuck in noncurrent methods. I once went out of my way to see someone speak who had written a book about second acts. All I heard about was political gripes and Joseph Campbell. I brought this up with my discussion group. One fellow who had worked in story development for Pixar panned the guy's book and said: "The first new thing I learned was on page 67."

When you're a practiced screenwriter, you'll have far fewer holes in first drafts. Due to the collaborative nature of the business, however, you'll simply have to get used to rewriting because (rightly or wrongly) every person influential in getting your script on film will have ideas that you will have to at least consider while defending your own ideas.

Make a sign and put it on your wall that says "Film is a collaborative medium." Even if you write a script and shoot it yourself, that will remain true unless you're the only actor and run all the equipment.

I used oceanic references earlier because I often feel at sea while engaged in the rewrite process.

Good screenwriters are like good sailors. They master their craft. They learn the tides and currents but know that such things are changeable and tricky. When they have survived enough Hollywood "voyages," they feel confident of weathering just about anything. And sometimes, they know it's better to stay in port and let the bad weather pass, or to abandon some voyages altogether.

Scene Length and Readability

Think now for a moment about the reader, the first person who might see your script. Even if you get a producer or director to read your script directly, busy people read a lot of screenplays, take a lot of phone calls, and cover all types of material. If you have long speeches and scenes longer than three minutes, they'd better be so fascinating that they'll capture the attention of super-busy executives. The material has to move quickly and succinctly from one scene to the next. Long passages of text rarely help. And when professional readers are tired, they'll take to scanning the dialogue to follow the story.

Hollywood Heat

One of the first influential people I met in Hollywood was director/producer Richard Donner. He told me that the first draft of *Superman* (1978) that he received from Mario Puzo was more than 500 pages long. The author and screenwriter of *The Godfather* (1972) received story credit and shared screenplay credit with David Newman, Leslie Newman, and Robert Benton. Puzo might have felt he that had leeway because of winning two Oscars for screenplays based on his *Godfather* novel.

Have you seriously studied dialogue exchanges in great movies? Once while watching Alfred Hitchcock's classic, *Psycho*, it occurred to me that Janet Leigh would deliver a line, and then the camera would be on Anthony Perkins and he would deliver a line. No matter how much you love great lines, it's still a visual medium.

On the other hand, if there's a real reason for the placement of a long speech, it could be a highlight of the film, like the endless "shrimp" conversation in Forrest Gump that ultimately led to the Bubba Gump Shrimp Company, which made the fortune of the lead character. (There were a lot of varied pictures during that speech, though.)

Any time a main character is involved in a long conversation or delivers a long speech, it's usually a turning point in the film or a summation, like Jimmy Stewart delivers in *Mr. Smith Goes to Washington* or Gary Cooper delivers in *Meet John Doe* (both by Frank Capra, who loved long speeches).

The first thing to look for as you mark up your script with red ink is length—length of scenes first, and length of speeches second. You might also use a checklist like this one:

- Is this scene necessary at all?
- What is the essence of this scene?
- Do all parts of this scene contribute to its essence?
- Does every character in this scene contribute to its essence?
- Do the beginning, middle, and end of this scene follow a 1:2:1 ratio? (You might not need that ratio, but it's an interesting guidepost that I've found often works.)

◆ Can this scene be written with less dialogue, or no dialogue at all?

◆ Does the end of the scene propel the reader into the scene that follows?

The more scenes you write, and the more ways you try to rewrite scenes, the more likely you are to develop an integrity about what works and what does not, with a complete loss of ego about utterly destroying something that you might have spent hours creating. William Faulkner called it "killing your darlings." When you reach that point, your chances of becoming professional are much more likely than they have ever been.

Skip's Tips

Successful people in Hollywood don't wait around when someone buys his or her idea. They stand up, shake hands, and leave before the buyer can change his or her mind. Use the same technique in writing scenes. Don't try to get cute and add extra unnecessary touches. At the point where the scene peaks, instantly move on to the next scene.

Your Name

Collaborators and Craft

When you begin your screenwriting career, you might feel uneasy about your own ability. That's normal. That's one reason why we see so many screenwriting teams. Another reason is that, in television, scripts are often worked on by a staff of writers. Most TV writers live in Los Angeles, and it's unlikely that you can collaborate with a TV writer as a neophyte. So, when I discuss collaboration, know that I'm talking about only screenplays for feature films or a movie for television.

When you prove your writing ability with an excellent feature screenplay of your own, you may be able to engender the interest of a proven screenwriter. They'll likely want to meet or work with you in person, but in our electronic age, you can work with a collaborator no matter where you live.

My best advice is that you find a writer or writers who are of equal or better ability than your own. Equal experience is important, but not crucial. I know of an Oscar winner who collaborated with a barely proven writer of ability. A word of caution if you work with a pro, however. *Learn the lingo.* If you don't know the difference between a *rewrite* and a *polish* or what a "page one rewrite" is, you might feel foolish if the professional mentions having to do one of those.

Script Notes

According to the Writers Guild of America Minimum Basic Agreement (MBA), article 1.B.7/1.C.2, a **rewrite** is defined as follows: "the writing of significant changes in plot, story line, or interrelationship of characters in a screenplay/teleplay." A **polish** is this: "the writing of changes in dialogue, narration, or action, but not including a rewrite." If any producer tells you anything different, that person is wrong. But be prepared for a producer to ask you to do a full rewrite and call it a polish so he or she will pay less (it's a common practice).

Collaborators who aren't professionals need to realize why certain things shouldn't be in a scene. When working on the rewrite of the first cowritten screenplay I sold, I cut about 85 percent of a 1½-page speech that came from a minor character. My cowriter was beside himself, but it was the first script he had written. It was the fourth one I'd worked on, and I was already an optioned and sold scriptwriter.

If you're not a pro and neither is your partner, write a script you can both live with and then do a reading of it. You'll both learn things about what works with an audience that you didn't see when hashing out the scenes together.

Who Should Read Your Script and Why

The only people whom I let read my screenplays are people I trust, usually other professionals, who I know will give me their honest opinion, whether I agree with them or not.

Rewriting makes the difference with screenplays. I still cringe when looking at the first drafts of my old scripts, even though my very first screenplay, a first draft, got optioned. Proof of the pudding? It didn't get bought (an exercised option) or made.

When you wrap up a rewrite, you want it to be the very best that you can deliver at that moment in time. The great thing about screenwriting is that you will continue to improve the more you write and the more you read great screenplays and watch great movies with a screenwriter's eye. Movies are

It's Not for Us

Please do the writing world a favor and don't open your criticism of other people's work with "Let me play the devil's advocate here." Why are you supporting the devil? After you've heard that cliché enough times, your immediate reaction is an urge to strangle someone. I've never heard it from seasoned writers—instead, they ask why you took a certain approach, or they offer an alternate "What if?"

the most collaborative of all the arts, but they are made by collaborating professionals. You might want to follow Clint Eastwood's example. When he first began his Hollywood career, he took pains to learn how everything worked on a movie set, to find out what every job was about. It helped him grow as an actor and to learn what producing and directing were all about. He was working with professionals, Hollywood veterans eager to share what they knew. The trick is getting yourself into regular association with such pros.

I almost gave up writing once because of a playwriting workshop in Los Angeles. The woman who hosted the workshop was the wife of a prominent comedy talent manager, and I thought that she might know her business. After we did a reading of a play of mine, however, the workshop leader's best friend (who had not sold any writing in years) shredded it. I almost gave up writing. Less than a month later, a stage director called me about wanting to do a professional reading of the play, he liked it so much.

Wherever you live, if you get involved in writing workshops, make sure that they aren't just social clubs in which the organizer is trying to "rule the roost." Find out what the professional credits are of the people involved. Sit in on a couple meetings before you join, particularly one in which a critique is taking place.

Normally, the following people are not the best candidates to read and comment on your screenplay: your mom, your roommate, your significant other, and your teacher or professor. Unless you live in a major metropolitan area, rarely are college professors successful screenwriters themselves. If they were, why would they be teaching full-time? If you think that your professor is particularly insightful based on your class experience, you might still ask about his or her own background before you ask that person to take a look at nonclass work.

When you've made your screenplay as good as you can, the only people who should read it are (a) people at a staged reading of the script; (b) people who are in a position to buy it or get it sold; (c) well-qualified script consultants who will give you an expert opinion based on years of successful Hollywood experience; and (d) agents or managers who might represent you.

The Difference Between a Rewrite and a Polish

The Writers Guild of America Minimum Basic Agreement (MBA) has a very specific definition of a rewrite and the key phrase is this: "significant changes in plot, story line, or interrelationship of characters." This means that if a producer who is "signatory" to the Guild (agrees to follow their rules) meets with you after reading your rewrite (the only screenplay that I hope you submit) and wants significant changes made, he or she is asking you to do a rewrite, work that the Writers Guild says you should be paid to do.

Of course, by WGA rules, you also should be paid a minimum of 10 percent of the final purchase price of the script before you're asked to write anything. If someone wants changes "in dialogue, narration or action" that does not significantly change the plot, story line, or similar element, this is a polish, not a rewrite.

Hollywood Heat

Being rewritten by others is a source of endless discussion among members of the Writers Guild of America. It can be so touchy that some screenwriters refuse to do it. Do a search with "rewrite" at the WGA site, and read all about it. If you are offered the chance to do a rewrite and are willing to do it, but you don't know how much to charge, find out about WGA minimums at www.wga.org. There are rules about the original writer being given chances to do rewrites. Find out if that took place—this could apply to you.

What changes are "significant"? Here's an example. The *Fair Game* script that I wrote with Mike Conley was optioned by the producers of *Red Scorpion* (1989), who asked us to change it from a Caribbean setting to the South China Sea because they thought that the Prime Minister of Malaysia was going to finance it. They paid for the rewrite, and we did it. When their option expired, we got the script back and no one bit on it for years. I did a polish on my own, changed the name to *South China Sea*, and a friend of Mike's sold it.

Unfortunately, the major trend these days among independent producers is to get writers to work for nothing. They offer to try to "set up" your script (meaning, to get it financed) if you will sign an option agreement in which you give them the right to shop it for up to 18 months, all for the princely sum of $1. And they usually don't even pay you the dollar! If that isn't bad enough, some producers will also ask you to do a rewrite—a rewrite, not a polish—for nothing, based on their "notes." They will do their best to convince you that if you are merely willing to write these changes, you'll end up with a better script that they can sell.

It's entirely up to you how you want to handle producers. If the producers have a decent track record, they might get a "free option" screenplay financed. On the other hand, I say, doesn't it make you wonder why they don't have any money with which to option your screenplay? I've usually found that producers who don't pay don't get paid.

Problematically, even pro screenwriters are being asked to do free rewrites these days. In the August 25, 2002, edition of *Variety*, Writers Guild of America West President Victoria Riskin opined: "Executives and producers take advantage of the goodwill of writers. No one else would think of asking another profession—doctors, plumbers, architects—to work without getting paid." Still, this kind of chicanery goes on all the time, and most producers push it to the limit.

You have to be tough to make it in Hollywood.

It's Not for Us

In Hollywood, ego kills projects. In 2001, I did a paid "page one" rewrite of a script for someone. I changed a great deal and gave it a new title. The assistant to the producer of a hit TV show thought it would make the basis of a great new series. Then the guy I rewrote for got greedy and wanted only his name on it. I let him and the producer's assistant know that wasn't okay with me. That was the end of the deal and he couldn't do anything about it.

Resources for Better Rewriting

There's an old Hollywood saying: "Great scripts aren't written; they're rewritten." These days, there is a veritable industry in place to help you rewrite, for a fee.

Lew Hunter, while still working as cochairman of the UCLA Screenwriting Program, did evaluations of screenplays for around $1,000. He used the money for his grandchildren's college fund. I told him that some of his peers were charging as much as five times as much, and he was stunned. I hope that he raised his rate.

Skip's Tips

If you can't decide who to ask for help on a rewrite, pick the person who can most easily take or leave your business, or who you simply like. They're likely the most reasonable and professional. Or you could e-mail me and ask me what I think of them. If I know about them, I'll tell you. Or maybe I'll help you myself. You can find me at www.skippress.com.

If you pay anyone for helping you with a rewrite, I advise you to do that only after you've rewritten it yourself. If you use people based in Hollywood, ask point-blank about their credits and what help in marketing they might offer once you've followed their rewrite advice. It is beneficial if they have a regular newsletter that is actually helpful and not just an advertisement for further services. The more helpful people are, the more likely they'll offer sound, objective advice.

A number of books offer advice on rewriting, but barring experiencing the actual process, the best thing you can do is try to find various versions of the screenplay of a movie and read them. I also highly recommend the *Shooting Script* books from Newmarket Press, which feature the final screenplay and discussions from the filmmakers and writers on how it got that way.

The Writers Guild of America offers a free online mentor program administered by its members, who can advise you on writing and rewriting. Check it out at www.wga.org. Some of them are working writers, some aren't, but they're all members of the Guild.

The best way to learn what works in rewrites is the script-to-screen experience. That's another reason I urge writers to get into making their own films, particularly in our digital age.

I once wrote and coproduced a safety video called *A Woman's Guide to Firearms*. (It was still being sold in DVD form on Amazon.com as I wrote this book.) I was not a shooting enthusiast when I started. In fact, I didn't own a gun. I researched the video by taking a firearms safety course from the two top marksmen in the United States, Mickey Fowler and Mike Dalton. I did some other research and then wrote the script. When it was done, the producer and originator of the video called me and said: "We've got a problem."

I cringed because I'd just gone through that with the executive producer of another video, Jan Stephenson's *How to Golf*. Although I had put together that video, bringing in the director and Jan Stephenson, the exec had asked me to rewrite the script in a way that I thought was unethical, and so I took some money and profit points and walked away from the production.

I listened to the "notes" from the firearms video producer, all of which were technical details and not nearly as serious as he believed they were. Instead of putting up a voracious defense about my "baby," I convinced him that if it didn't work for him, it surely wouldn't work for our ultimate audience. In a documentary on a complex subject, we had to be clear.

If I'd let my ego or past bad experience get in the way, I might not have stayed on the show all the way through production and editing. The video won a Silver Medal at the New York International Film Festival and was favorably reviewed in *People* magazine.

Here's a more famous example of how experience makes a big difference. I had the honor of meeting Nia Vardalos at a party before *My Big Fat Greek Wedding* became a big hit. The project started as a one-woman show that Tom Hanks's wife Rita Wilson (who is part Greek) loved. Produced for only $5 million, it became a blockbuster, the most successful romantic comedy of all time.

In Nia's original screenplay, she started with flashbacks that showed her and all her siblings being born. There were a lot of scenes that meant a lot to Nia, but would not to the audience. Working with experienced director Ed Zwick, she did a lot of trimming and tightening to get the story moving. They kept a small flashback montage of her early life, to explain the Greek American quirks and her personality, but not many minutes onscreen. Had Nia not been so egoless in the rewrites (after all, she was also the star), the movie might not have been the masterpiece it became.

The best way to learn how to rewrite is to work on a script all the way through production. If you don't have that luxury, I hope that some of the notes I've given you here help. If you don't think they do, let me know how you think I should rewrite them.

The Least You Need to Know

- You'd better get used to rewriting; if you start working as a screenwriter, you'll be doing a lot of it.

- Screenwriter and author William Faulkner's advice about rewriting was to "kill your darlings." He meant unhelpful scenes and characters, and he was right.

- Try to collaborate only with a writer or writers who are of equal or better ability.

- Ultimately, the only people who read your screenplay that matter are those who are in a position to buy it, get it sold, or pay to have it made.

- The best way to perfect rewriting is through the script-to-screen process.

- In Hollywood, ego kills projects. Check yours at the door.

Chapter 18

Polish Makes Perfect

In This Chapter

- ◆ From script to screen
- ◆ Learning from the pros
- ◆ Tools for perfection
- ◆ The completed product

So you write a first draft, and you do a rewrite. Then you find a producer who likes your script, and there's a sale. That's how it works, right?

Not usually. Unless you're the reincarnation of Ben Hecht (who won the first writing Oscar), you'd better think of a screenplay like Harry Winston thinks about jewelry. You perfect each piece until you just can't make it any better. Then you polish it up until you can't make it shine any brighter. (Who's Harry Winston? The company that provides a lot of the jewels you see on display at the Oscars.)

So you have this polished script and a producer takes it on. Then you work together and do another rewrite. Maybe the producer is a Writers Guild signatory and will treat you according to the rules. Then the producer has a meeting at the studio and is told, "We need to find a writer."

Huh!? Who wrote the original? This happens all the time because of various needs or perceived needs once a picture is seriously being considered for financing.

When you are polishing up your screenplay, you need to seriously think of minute details, like who might be right to star in the lead roles. You should also have some idea of whom these people have worked with in the past and would want to work with again. Why? Because the first thing that producer will ask is: "Who do you see in this?"

> **Skip's Tips** _____
>
> *Your Name* If you're not online, this tip won't help you. Let's say that you want Mel Gibson to star in your film. Want to see whether he has worked with a certain director? Look up Gibson's name at the Internet Movie Database (www.imdb.com), and then scroll to the bottom of the page and type in the director's name at the "Mel Gibson and _____" box.

What It Takes to Get a Script Onscreen

For what it's worth, every screenplay I ever sold was rewritten at least four times. Maybe I should have continued with rewrites, because to date none of them have made it onto the screen. I say that because the great "dead psychiatrist" twist in *The Sixth Sense* apparently showed up during the "fifth or sixth rewrite" according to writer/director M. Night Shyamalan. *Cast Away* was supposedly rewritten 35 times.

Selling a script is one thing. Getting one made changes your situation altogether. You get asked to do rewrites, and you can get pigeonholed as having a certain specialty. For example, Carrie "Princess Leia" Fisher apparently made $100,000 in a week for "punching up" the female dialogue in a screenplay. Richard LaGravenese had years without filmed credits but during that time was the hottest rewrite man in Hollywood, making six figures per week. He was even thanked by Julia Roberts in her Oscar acceptance speech for the unaccredited work he did on *Erin Brockovitch*. When you get that kind of acknowledgment, you are great at polishing scripts and very highly paid.

Many writers work on scripts but are unaccredited, due to Writers Guild rules. (Look up all Ben Hecht's uncrediteds on www.imdb.com.) When you get a chance, buy a bound movie script—not a script in a book, or those you download from the Internet (which are often illegal transcripts that violate copyright laws). Sooner or later, you'll find a script that lists all the writers who received Writers Guild credits on the movie.

Final-draft scripts from real studios often have a page in the front that lists a number of colored script pages in order of the revision number. In order, after white comes blue, pink, yellow, green, gold, and then back to white (and who knows what shades after that). That is how production companies keep track of script changes. The changed pages are a code that tells people which draft of the script they are working from. You don't need to worry about using any color but white at this point, so I won't bore you with the code details. But you may be wondering, why are there so many writers on studio movies?

Skip's Tips

If you want to know the full story of how onscreen writing credits are determined, read the Credits section at the Writers Guild of America site. You can download and/or read many useful documents at www.wga.org. They periodically change, and so make sure you have the latest information.

I once befriended a producer named James Nelson (*Borderline*, 1980) and worked with him on trying to get a property of mine sold. One day he told me that he had the rights to the Bob Wills story. Being from Texas, where the King of Western Swing music hailed from, I grinned. Nelson said Jack Nicholson wanted to play Bob Wills. I wondered out loud what was stopping the movie from being made. Well, Nicholson insisted that the screenplay be written by Thomas McGuane, who had been a writer on *The Missouri Breaks* (1976), a Western starring Nicholson. I only knew that McGuane was married to actress Margot Kidder, so again I asked what was the problem. "McGuane won't start on the script for less than $250,000," Nelson said, "which I don't have."

Thus began my education into the vagaries of Hollywood. I knew that, at one point, Bob Wills had been so popular that he sold more records than Bing "White Christmas" Crosby and appeared in a number of Hollywood movies. He was a notorious Lothario; reportedly, 300 crying women appeared at his funeral. But with no McGuane script, no Jack Nicholson, and no movie. And that's how it often goes with A-list actors and producers.

Let's say that you write a script good enough to be purchased, but it's your first script, and the director who gets involved wants to rewrite it. It could happen. Or, the producers might hire writers who they trust to take a pass at the script.

The studio executive will most certainly want extra writers. Eager to accommodate their stars and cover every base in every ballpark on every studio lot, executives have lists of writers they work with or want to work with. They will have a certain amount of development funds to "get the script right." And frankly, they're covering themselves. If the movie fails, they can say "Hey, I hired the best people in town!" And so it goes, sometimes on and on and on for years. It's called "development hell."

David Saperstein, whose unpublished manuscript became the movie *Cocoon* (1985), told me that five writers were hired at various times to adapt his novel. The fifth one, Tom Benedek, called Saperstein and said he didn't like any of the previous drafts; he simply planned to adapt the story the way it was laid out. And Benedek got the sole screenplay credit.

Most writers don't get that lucky.

If you've done a rewrite or several on your script and are satisfied with it, set it aside again for a couple weeks or a month. Watch a number of movies that you think might be similar to your movie. Then come back to your script and read it again. If you see things that you would like to tune up, that's where the polish comes in. It's also very helpful to see how the script sounds when read, and that's why there's a whole chapter on doing that in this book.

Learning the Ropes from the Writers Guild of America

To write professionally, it makes sense to pay attention to the working professionals. Many beginning screenwriters ignore the Writers Guild of America (WGA) until they earn the number of credits necessary to join. That's a mistake, particularly because of all the free resources available from the Guild. If you sell a screenplay to a producer who is signatory to the WGA, that means that the producer cooperates with the stipulations of the WGA's Theatrical and Television Agreement. That's the kind of producer you want to do business with, because they're more likely to play by established rules.

So check out the Guild; it's more easily joined by getting involved, and the best way to start is by availing yourself of the many publications from the WGA, both in print and online. One of the best places to start reading is the Credits Manual for film (another exists for television).

The WGA Theatrical and Television Basic Agreement is more commonly called the Writers Guild Minimum Basic Agreement, or MBA. If you are a Guild member, the Working Rules prohibit you from working for a company that is not signatory to the MBA. The companies have to sign an application to become signatory, so check to see that they did that; call the Guild's Signatories Department to find out. To join the

WGA, you must sell material to a signatory company. You'll have to prove that you made the sale to join, so keep copies of all e-mails, letters, phone logs, and checks.

What does this have to do with polishing scripts? Because if you're working for a signatory producer, you must be paid for a polish. Also, unfortunately, many producers bend the rules, and expect you to do a full rewrite that they call a polish. You should get some idea of what kind of work goes into getting a script ready for the screen.

Then there are all the other writers, and onscreen credits. Let's say that you sell your script and qualify for membership in the WGA, but other writers are hired to rewrite your script. Will you still receive a screenplay credit or a "story by" credit? That's why you need to know the rules. Most new writers don't and then are dumbfounded when they learn that the script they sold doesn't have their name on it in the theater.

Skip's Tips

When you are writing a "master scene" script, the scenes are not numbered, and shots such as "ANGLE ON GEORGE" are mostly left out. When a script is prepared for production, a "shooting script" is prepared that has all these things. Credits on a film are determined according to content of the shooting script.

If you work with a producer who is nonsignatory to the WGA's MBA, you're on your own (or with your lawyer or agent) in getting the credits you want. If you do work with a nonsignatory and disagree with its assessment of credits, try convincing the company to use WGA arbitration procedures to work things out.

When a project is completed, the company that made the movie submits materials to the Guild so that a Notice of Tentative Writing Credits (NTWC) can be issued. The Guild determines who gets writing credits and who does not. If the writers who worked on the project do not agree with the NTWC, they can protest. If a protest is lodged, an arbitration can be held. When an arbitration of credits is called for, all source materials—book, play, whatever—must also be submitted. Every possible aspect of contributory material is covered; it's quite a task.

If you don't agree with all the materials submitted for consideration, you can request a prearbitration hearing. When the materials are verified, they are looked at by the Arbitration Committee (consisting of three WGA members), who only know each writer in question by a letter of the alphabet. Each committee also has a consultant available to answer questions; the consultant is a WGA member with substantial experience as an arbiter. None of the arbiters know who the other two arbiters are, which keeps the whole affair as collusion-free as possible.

Because this method of determining credits evolved over time and was developed by professional writers, they've thought of everything. Let's say that you have enemies and don't want them judging you wrongly (gee, another writer with an axe to grind?), you get a chance to look over the "Arbiters List," which shows who all the eligible arbiters are. You get a chance to delete names of people who you think might not treat you fairly or who would be prejudiced toward you. The Guild doesn't ask for a reason why you make a deletion—that's your business.

When each member of the Committee has studied all the available material, they all report their decisions to both the Guild and the consultant assigned to the committee. A Guild credits employee then notifies each writer involved.

Hollywood Heat

Rumors about which writers worked on which scripts fly fast and furious around Hollywood. For example, it was wildly rumored that Robert Towne "really" wrote *Good Will Hunting* (1997), despite the fact that Matt Damon and Ben Affleck won an Oscar for their script! All Towne did, apparently, was offer them advice over lunch. One thing is certain, however. Experienced and trusted screenwriters can make great amounts of money to "fix" certain aspects of a screenplay. As one A-list writer who does a lot of fast rewrites and polishes told me, the money is "ridiculous," as in, six figures a week.

So how do members of a committee determine who gets credit? Says the Credits Manual: "Any writer whose work represents a contribution of more than 33 percent of a screenplay shall be entitled to screenplay credit, except where the screenplay is an original screenplay. In the case of an original screenplay, any subsequent writer or writing team must contribute 50 percent to the final screenplay."

Skip's Tips

If you do your homework and learn some of the rules, you'll impress producers with your acumen about the business. Most beginners don't even know the Minimum Basic Agreement exists, much less what the details are. If you can speak to it, producers might think twice about trying to get around the rules, whether they are WGA signatory or not.

The Credits Manual defines original screenplays as those "which are not based on source material and on which the first writer writes a screenplay without there being any other intervening literary material by another writer pertaining to the project." Got that? If you write your script without basing it on any other existing literary material (something someone else created), you're in good shape toward getting screenplay credit.

Still wondering why I'm telling you about screenplay credits when you're waiting to hear about polishing your screenplay? It's because beginning screenwriters are stunningly naive about show business. If you get your script in good enough shape, you might **never** have to be involved in an arbitration. It might resonate so well with everyone who reads it that they want to shoot what you have written and not bother with thoughts of other writers. Believe me, it can happen, but only with the very best scripts. When you polish up your work, that's the kind you want to end up with.

Dialogue, Subtext, and Other Tools

As you may have noticed, I mention the Internet Movie Database a lot. If you've tried it by now, you may have noticed that almost every popular movie has a section of Memorable Quotes from the film. That could be because Amazon.com bought IMDB.com some time back and sells videos of the films as well as books that correspond to the movie on the site (via a click to Amazon). People remember and quote lines of dialogue more often than any other element of film. How many variations of "We don't need no steenkin' badges" from *The Treasure of the Sierra Madre* have you heard in your life? This despite the fact that the film is more than 50 years old! How many times have you heard "They're here!" trilled out as someone arrived at your door, emulating little Heather O'Rourke as Carol Anne Freeling in *Poltergeist* (1982), or "Show me the money!" from *Jerry Maguire* (1996)?

Great lines of dialogue are what we repeat while socializing, and, as writers, wish we'd written. Unfortunately, most writers don't know where to start in creating memorable dialogue or improving existing dialogue during a rewrite or a polish.

You'll hear a lot about "writing like people talk," but the great playwrights and screenwriters mostly do not write normal, everyday dialogue. Rather, they write elevated dialogue that might sound like normal speech but is actually a higher level of thought than everyday life. The best screenwriters write in levels; in a family film there will be jokes for the adults the kids might not get. "Something for everyone" is the kind of thing you perfect in a polish, and it's an old practice. Shakespeare had to make sure the "groundling" commoners in his audiences understood what was going on. At the same time, the Bard wrote double entendres that only French-speaking people understood.

Most of the time, when I used to share my "elevated" rap about dialogue, I would get great arguments from "the way people really talk" writers. Then David Mamet came along with his plays and screenplays, and suddenly I didn't look like such an idiot.

I grew up being fascinated by film dialogue, whether it was Jimmy Stewart speeches in Frank Capra movies that I saw on television, or even the comic blustering of John Travolta's Tony Manero in *Saturday Night Fever* (1977).

Hollywood Heat _____

The great Gary Cooper was a handsome leading man who **appeared in** some of the most heroic films of all time, including *Sergeant York* (1942, for which he won the Best Actor Oscar) and *High Noon* (1952, for which he earned another Oscar). Cooper's frequent hesitations in delivering his lines were a source of comment and envy among fellow actors, some of whom imitated his easygoing delivery. Once, a reporter asked Cooper about his style. The trademark wry smile spread across his mouth, and "Coop" revealed his secret: "Well," he said slowly, "I'm just trying to … remember my lines."

What dialogue do you quote? Matt Damon's Will Hunting talking about why he shouldn't work for the NSA in *Good Will Hunting* (1997)? (Whew, talk about a long speech. If he could get away with that and win the Academy Award, maybe he could be elected president, after all.) Or is it "Show me the money!" from *Jerry Maguire*?

The best authority on dialogue I ever met is Sol Stein, former publisher of Stein and Day; author of many books, including the million-selling *The Magician;* and a founding member of the Playwright's Wing of the Actors Studio. Stein was the editor of fellow Actors Studio playwright Elia Kazan, a writer/director who had a major impact on Hollywood with films such as *On the Waterfront* (1954). He was a playwright for 15 years before he became a novelist, both of which helped prepare him for teaching the first university dialogue course in the nation, in 1990 at the University of California at Irvine.

Stein taught his students something simple but profound, that "dialogue is a new language and not recorded speech." To illustrate this principle, he would take an interchange of four boring lines and make them sparkle by changing one line at a time. He later detailed these methods in "The Secrets of Good Dialogue" chapter in his book *Stein on Writing*, and then he expanded upon it in *How to Grow a Novel* (St. Martin's Press, 1999). The essence of the 12-week course that he taught at UCI became a "Dialogue for Writers" audiotape that is free to anyone who tries any of his software programs. See www.writepro.com for details.

"What counts in dialogue," Stein told me, "is not what is said, but what is meant. Whenever possible, it should be adversarial. Characters reveal themselves best in dialogue. Dialogue helps to show rather than tell a story."

As you look through your script, you might well remember Stein's admonitions that "characters reveal themselves best in dialogue" and that good dialogue is "not what is said, but what is meant." Many successful screenwriters and playwrights share these sentiments. By "not what is said, but what is meant," Stein is talking about a concept known as subtext. You know what the character really means, despite what is being said. How do you achieve subtext? Playwright Jeffrey Sweet, author of *The Dramatist's Toolkit* (Heinemann, 1993), under the billing "creative consultant," wrote the screenplay for the TV movie version of Hugh Whitemore's play *Pack of Lies* (1987). Sweet says that he looks for the most important word in a passage and then tries to take it out. When the audience fills it in anyway, the result is subtext. The first chapter of his next book, *Solving Your Script* (Heinemann, 2001), is about the power of the unspoken word. (For more information, see his website at www.jeffreysweet.com.)

> **It's Not for Us**
>
> When you write something "too on the nose," that means you've written unimaginatively. Viewers like to be surprised, not bored by clichés. Think less in terms of authenticity and more in terms of surprise. Which is more interesting, a lumberjack drinking himself to sleep, or one who stays up late reading *The Theory of Relativity?*

My favorite example of not-so-subtle subtext is when a teenaged Lauren Bacall in *To Have and Have Not* (1944) tells Humphrey Bogart's Steve how to whistle. When she says that he should just put his lips together and blow, we know what she's talking about, and it sure ain't whistling. Scenes with sexual tension are the easiest ones in which to insert subtext. Sexual tension can be telegraphed with a look, but what do the words really mean?

When Claude Rains as Captain Louis Renault in *Casablanca* (1942) exclaims in Rick's club that he is "shocked, shocked!" at the gambling taking place, we know that he isn't really. He's putting on a show for the German occupation forces. The subtext tells us a lot about the dynamics of World War II Casablanca.

During a rewrite, you work on the structure of your script and the plot. By the time your rewrite is done, you should be relatively satisfied with the story line, the turning points, the act breaks. Think of it this way—you've built the skeleton, laid on the muscles, rigged up the nerves and blood vessels, and engaged the brain. With the polish, you're making the skin perfect, painting the eyes, and getting the hair and smile just right. And then you teach the kid to walk.

Rather than launching from page one and attempting to polish up your dialogue and the overall context of each scene in succession, pick a couple of your favorite scenes, hopefully crucial ones, and work on polishing them. When you've improved your best scenes, the lesser ones will more easily come up to the quality level of your best, now improved scenes.

While I don't follow a checklist in polishing scenes, if I did it would read something like this:

Skip's Tips

Your Name

Here's another hard-learned tip. You probably can't remember any memorable bit of dialogue that has more than a single thought in it. Go ahead, make my day. As you go through your dialogue, see if you have a character trying to express more than one thought in a single piece of dialogue. Simplify it to one thought; how many movie lines that you've repeated express more than one thought?

1. What does this scene say?

2. How does this scene serve the dynamics of the story?

3. What are the characters in this scene saying?

4. What's really on their minds?

5. What are the beginning, middle, and end of this scene?

6. How does the end of this scene propel us into the next one?

7. Is this scene memorable apart from the overall movie?

8. Will anyone admiringly repeat any of these lines after leaving the theater?

Sometimes great scenes turn on a line that epitomizes the essence of the interaction of the main characters. A fellow who was a reader for movie star Bruce Willis told me that Willis once got so frustrated trying to find a good screenplay to produce he finally blurted out: "Just find me something cool to say!"

Hollywood Heat

YOUR NAME

Robert E. Thompson was nominated for a WGA Screen Award, Best Comedy Written Directly for the Screen, for *Hearts of the West* (1975). It's a hilarious look at an aspiring writer getting skewered in Hollywood. The film stars Jeff Bridges as Lewis Tater, a Midwestern farm boy dying to be a "real Western writer" who stumbles into the chance to star in 1930s Westerns. Andy Griffith as Howard Pike rewrites Bridges's script, *Hearts of the West*, by changing only the name of the writer. The film pays homage to Republic Pictures Westerns and paints a perfect portrait of naive writers in Hollywood. And guess what? There was another movie called *Hearts of the West*, in 1925.

In one script I worked on, when the apprehended femme fatale is facing a gun wielded by the male hero she thinks she's fooled, she exclaims in shock, "But I thought you fell in love with me!" He replies wryly, "I didn't fall for you, Laura. I just looked over the edge." It was my cowriter's favorite line.

How You Know When It's Ready

What you want to end up with is an unchallengeable script. You want a screenplay that people will remark upon years later by saying something like, "That script? Wow. We just shot it." That means they bought it and made it the way you presented it to them.

The problem is, that's almost an impossible task. Pro screenwriters chew their fingernails over rewrites and polishes. Every time I've felt puffed up about the bulletproof nature of a screenplay, my ego has been carpet-bombed shortly thereafter by some agent or producer. And when I've thought that a script is as good as I can do at the moment and don't have a clue whether someone will like it or not, I've mostly received positive responses. By the time you've done the best you can do with a script, you've usually lost all perspective of its worth.

When you've gotten comments from people you trust and have rewritten your script, you might want to make a list and decide who provided you with the most positive or helpful comments. Don't ask these people to reread the screenplay after you've done the rewrite. Wait until you've put a polish on it.

Skip's Tips _____

Should you write accents in dialogue, such as Robert (southern accent)? Well, are you going to write it that way every time that character speaks? That could get tedious to read. Also, actors will often mess with or ignore inflections you write. You probably should write something in the action direction (not in a parenthetical). You can also use words in dialogue that are common in that dialect. For example, the word "darlin'" is a Southern U.S. term, as is "y'all" for "you all." Try to be authentic without being intrusive to the actor's job.

And when you've done that polish, other than doing a spell and format check on it, don't read it again yourself. You could run the risk of "grinding." You'll start nagging at the edges of scenes, messing with them when they don't need to be messed with. Just print out that polished script and set it aside. When you feel that the time is right, pick it up and read a scene or two. If you like it, then ask a seasoned pro to give it a read.

If you get a "Wow, I'd really like to see this movie," that's great, from anyone. Here's the response you want from a professional, like an agent, a director, or a producer:

"Who have you shown this to?" they'll ask.

And you'll mention whomever you feel like mentioning. What they mean is "Has anyone else in Hollywood who could make this movie seen your script?"

Then if you have the right answer, they'll say something like this:

> "Well, if you wouldn't mind, I know somebody at [insert company or agency name here] that I'd like to take a look at this."

That's when you know it's ready—when a professional is willing to put his or her reputation on the line to get your work read.

So polish it up and make it shine, and hopefully one day you'll be buying jewelry from Harry Winston.

The Least You Need to Know

- Studio movies often have too many writers because producers and executives want to please all the major players involved and cover all possible weaknesses in the script before filming; if the movie bombs, they can lay blame.

- Everything you could ever need to know about how screenplay credits are determined is available in the Credits Manual from the Writers Guild of America, both in print and online.

- Great dialogue and great scenes are often marked by the subtext (hidden meaning) of the words and actions onscreen.

- Many great scenes turn on a line that epitomizes the essence of the interaction of the main characters.

- Good speeches (even if only a line) usually revolve around a single thought.

- Don't ask someone to reread your screenplay after you've done the rewrite. Wait until you've put a polish on it.

Part 4

Post-Script Possibilities

Come behind the scenes to learn what the skilled professionals in a "production company" do with your screenplay after it's rewritten. Plus, we'll show you how to improve your script merely by having people read it. Learn up front what happens once a script is purchased, so you won't need a shoulder to cry on. We'll explain how the film industry works and dive into the subtle and not so subtle nuances of writing TV movies, short films, and even your own independent feature film.

Chapter 19

What a Reading Can Show You

In This Chapter

- ◆ Hollywood's theatre tradition
- ◆ How to find actors
- ◆ Organizing a reading
- ◆ Writers' gatherings
- ◆ Finding pro writers to help you

Writers get the wrong idea about how to get their scripts made. I hear from them all the time asking about how to get a certain actor to read their screenplays. They've done enough reading or watched enough talk shows to know that actors love to chat about how important they were to getting a project done. The truth is that major actors usually help only people they know from their struggling days, or people close to them. Many people who have had Hollywood success started together in the theater, like the Steppenwolf company or Second City in Chicago. As an example of theater connections, the movie *The Big Kahuna* (1999), directed by John Swanbeck and written by Roger Rueff, who also wrote the stage play, came about because actor Kevin Spacey liked the material and wanted to help a friend.

Every actor starts somewhere. Even if you don't live in Chicago, Los Angeles, or New York (where Spacey and friends live), there may be a professional theater company near you. With digital movies being made cheaply, material that could be shot in one room, such as *The Big Kahuna*, or even something with minimal locations gives you a better chance than ever of getting your movie made. One way to get that process started is a reading, just the way they do it in the theater.

The Theatrical Tradition in Hollywood

I first began to realize how things really work when I was casting a one-act play I'd written. I was at a Super Bowl party and was introduced to an actress who was a star of a soap opera. Because I didn't watch soaps, I had no idea who she was, but she asked if she could read my play. I got a copy to her, and she called and said she'd be happy to do it. I asked our mutual friend about her, who assured me that the actress would draw a lot of publicity for the play, and perhaps even get it reviewed in the *Los Angeles Times*.

We staged two of my one-acts, and we did get a review in the *Times*, but that was due to a personal contact of the star of the other play, who persuaded the *Times* reviewer to stop by. Sure enough, though, the actress in the first play was the one whose picture was featured in the review.

Movie actors often return to the stage because they aren't doing so well with their films. Actress Melanie Griffith told a reporter that the reason she took a part in the musical *Chicago* on Broadway was because no one would hire her as a film actress any more. She blamed it on "a few lines in her face." Whatever the reasons are, great actors often fade from the public view, and getting on a stage, where they might get favorable reviews, could make them attractive to Hollywood again.

Actors in Los Angeles love to do nonpaying roles in equity-waiver theater for several reasons:

◆ They get to work with up-and-coming writing talent, and they know that writers often become directors, or writer/producers in television.

◆ If they are known as situation comedy performers, they can do a drama and show off another side of their abilities.

◆ When they are not working, they can generate some publicity for themselves and drum up some paying work.

◆ It can be a whole lot of fun.

If you don't live in southern California or write plays, you might think you're out of the loop on this theater angle. What matters is that the same principle works anywhere. If you live in Keokuk, Iowa, and write a screenplay, you might find that actors will flock to you for the chance to participate in a reading. I don't know much about actors in Iowa, but I do know the Iowa Writers Program is one of the best in the world.

It's Not for Us _____

Don't make any promises, and don't lead anyone on. If you have a reading of your script, no one who participates should believe that by being a part of the process, they will be promised anything down the line. As a beginning writer, you simply won't have the power to make that commitment. Lasting friendships begin with honesty. Make friends and keep in touch.

Hollywood Heat _____

Actors can be forgotten quickly in Hollywood, even when they are legends. When she was older and had not worked in more than a year, superstar Bette Davis actually put a full-page ad in *Variety* to alert casting directors, directors, and producers that she was available for work. Such ads are looked upon as desperate measures among most Hollywood folk, which is precisely why they do plays and readings in small theaters in Los Angeles.

How to Find Actors for a Reading

If you're located in a very small town, you could get yourself in trouble by using locals for a reading, if you've patterned some of your characters after people that some or all of the readers will know.

But guess what? Hollywood is a small town, too. It really is. In a city of millions of people, the relevancy of the John Guare play that became a movie, *Six Degrees of Separation* (1993), continues to amaze me. I tell people that if they do some research, they might be amazed to discover whom their friends and relatives know or can reach. In fact, when I taught at the UCLA Extension Writers Program, the largest program of its kind in the world, researching extended contacts was an exercise that I gave budding writers.

Now, you might think that it was easy for them, living in Los Angeles, but many of them had never met a movie star or producer and didn't know anyone who worked in "the business." When they did the prescribed homework and began explaining that they had written a story and wanted a professional to read it and comment—did their friend/relative know anyone?—they were stunned with the positive results. At least, most of them were.

Let's assume for a moment that you live in an area where a troupe of actors can be found. They're probably doing "showcase code" (informally, "Equity-waiver") theater (99-seat and under venues), which means that they look high and low for plays that they can afford to license for a production, that they think the public will be happy to pay to see. (Equity refers to Actors Equity Association, a union representing stage actors.) And so, they are not terribly likely to want to do original material from unknown playwrights.

All those actors, it would be safe to say, have some Hollywood dream, whether it's a realistic dream or not. So, if you contact the group to arrange a reading of your screenplay, they may be more interested than they would be if you had a stage play.

If there isn't a theater near you, how about a college with a theater department? It doesn't matter whether the students are all young and you've written older characters. Remember, most movie stars are relatively young, and so are the majority of movie-goers, so having young actors read your work might make you rethink some roles in a way that will make your screenplay more commercial.

Skip's Tips

Don't just blindly call a theater and ask about arranging a reading. Go to one of the plays the theater puts on, and ask around at intermission. Try to get an idea about the personality of the dramaturge before you bring up your project. "How do you find your plays, anyway?" you might ask. People met in person are much friendlier.

If you contact a theater group, the normal person to contact is the *dramaturge*. This is the person who initially reviews all material for performance. If there is no dramaturge, there will be a theater director, but don't just blurt out what you would like to do over the phone. Tell this person that you have a project you need help with and that you would like to buy him or her lunch to explain. A free lunch is almost always appealing for a struggling actor, which most people in theater are, sadly enough. You don't have to be coy about your intent—it's simply better to explain something in person. The worst thing that could happen is that the person will say no or, after reading your script, turn you down.

If there's no theater company nearby, or no local college, unless you have a reason for having a high school drama club read your screenplay, your next best bet is a commercial venue such as a Barnes and Noble or Borders bookstore. I'd advise you to find any place that has a built-in, regular "audience," as well as refreshment facilities such as a coffee or snack bar. Although you might rather support a local bookstore than a chain, I mention Barnes and Noble because they all have a Community Relations Coordinator whose job it is to promote events. Also, if you're having a screenplay reading, that gives the bookstore a chance to sell the many books that it has about Hollywood and screenwriting, including this one. If aspiring actors know that they can be seen "performing" in a public place, they're more likely to get involved.

If you have a circle of friends whose reading and speaking abilities you trust, whether they are actors or not, you might be able to pull together a reading that works. I also suggest, if appropriate in your community, that you place an ad in a local newspaper to broaden your chances for better actors.

Keep this in mind—ultimately, this reading is for you. You want people who will contribute to the process and read the screenplay without injecting their own peculiar personality quirks. You want people who will be there to support making your screenplay better, not to get all the attention focused on them.

Here's an important part of your reading. You need a *narrator*. Whether or not you actually have a narrator featured in your screenplay (which most screenplays don't), you need someone who will read the set directions with some life in their voice. You might choose to take on this role yourself, but I would advise against it because it may conflict with your objective view of the reading process.

Try to find a narrator who is insightful and has a voice that is easily heard. The last person you want is a droning, monotonic Ben Stein type of actor who will sound bored while reading the description. You need someone who might sound just a little excited when Indiana Jones runs ahead of the gigantic rock. But not too excited—sort of like Steven Spielberg.

Although I've found that it's much better to watch a reading of your script without also participating as a reader, I would suggest that at some point you get some acting experience of your own, in a formal setting. You might want to look into helping with a production at the local theater, or auditioning for a role. Take an acting class locally. People are much more willing to trust and help folks with whom they've shared substantive experience. If you've ever been on a sports team or struggled through a traumatic experience with a group of people, you understand my meaning here.

Writers sometimes complain that actors don't understand what they have written, but when they do complain, I often find that the writers don't understand acting.

Acting ability will also come in handy if you ever come to Hollywood to "pitch" your material to a producer or studio executive. That's when you'll wish you took an acting class, if you didn't.

Lastly, you might want to consider arranging for someone to direct or produce the reading with you. If that sounds like a bit much for the reading of a little old screen-play, you probably haven't had much experience in theater, where the writer has final casting approval and complete script approval. A stage director runs readings of plays, while the writer sits by quietly, watching. An arrangement like that will give you something called "altitude," and you might find that your script gets treated with more respect.

Organizing a Reading That Works

As you are lining up your actors, make sure that you set a date that will give you enough leeway to make all the necessary arrangements that I'm about to suggest. As you might have suspected, I don't advise simply sitting around in chairs over pizza and Pepsi. The more quality you put into the reading, the more quality you'll get out of it.

I suggest that you find a way to videotape the reading. If aspiring actors don't have any footage of themselves at all, they might appreciate a short snippet from the reading to use in promoting their acting. You will also see things in reviewing the videotape that you probably won't see while the reading is taking place. And who knows? What if one of the actors at the reading goes on to superstardom? Wouldn't you like to have a video of a young Matt Damon reading from your screenplay? I'm guessing that it would be good blackmail material!

With the relatively low cost of digital video and computer editing equipment these days, there's another angle to consider. If your script isn't that expensive to turn into a feature, someone seeing your reading on video might want to finance the movie.

At the very least, audiotape the reading for your own benefit. Playing back someone delivering the lines as you rewrite later might help in making the dialogue more fluid.

If you have more than one actor in mind for certain parts, you might have to audition. If you've never done it, don't worry about it—just do it. Trust me, actors run into much worse characters than you in their careers. Select a pertinent scene from the script, and print out or photocopy plenty of copies. Meet the candidates in a clean, well-lit place if you don't want them in your living room, and be professional and courteous without making any commitment until you're convinced. The more professionally you treat the process, the better the results you will get.

Make sure that everyone selected to be involved in the reading has a character description and some background notes from which to formulate a mindset before the reading. Unless you know and trust the actors, do not give them a copy of the screenplay before the reading. When actors audition for a part, they do what is called a "cold reading." They are expected to perform from a script on the fly, without studying it beforehand. That way, the casting director can watch for glimpses of the craft that the actor brings to the work, or doesn't. Actors will be given a scene to study for a few minutes, at most, before the reading. When you're doing a reading of your screenplay, you want it to be a process of discovery for everyone involved. As actors read the lines, injecting their own unique look and personality, everyone forms mental pictures of the movie, in an organic fashion quite different from someone silently reading a script.

Hollywood Heat

Whether they came from the theater or not, with top Hollywood writers, screenplay readings are common practice and a major social event. Equally a success on Broadway and in Hollywood, Neil Simon began writing in the early days of television, working on programs such as *Your Show of Shows* (with Sid Caesar) as a staff writer. In television, shows are always read around a table before they are rehearsed so that adjustments can be made. The same thing happens in the theater. Thus, every time Simon came up with an original screenplay, or an adaptation of one of his plays, he always staged a reading of the script.

It's probably best if you give your narrator a copy of the script beforehand, as long as you can trust that person. Should you ask the narrator or anyone else to sign a confidentiality agreement? That's up to you and your legal adviser or agent. However, it might make you look too rigid and formal, which is something that actors generally disdain.

After you've finalized your cast, make sure that you have a few extra people on the list that can both serve as an audience and fill in on some parts if an actor or two doesn't make it to the reading. There's nothing more disheartening than an important actor not showing up on the day of a reading. Even if other actors can double up on key roles and do different voices as necessary, it's a distracting bit of business that you don't want to have as a part of your reading. (This is the voice of experience speaking here.) You'll also find that the actors will feel better if they're a bit pampered, so if someone is around to bring them little snacks and drinks and such, it's a more congenial atmosphere, and the reading will not be broken up by people getting up to help themselves.

Script Notes

Sides are pages from a screenplay that are given to actors when they audition for a part. Often while filming a movie, actors who are not leads do not receive the entire screenplay. They merely get pages containing their performance, perhaps with some background information. This helps maintain confidentiality about the project.

A couple of days before the reading is set to take place, phone everyone to make sure that they have the event marked on their calendars. This gives you an opportunity to make any last-minute adjustments or to answer any questions that may be lingering. If you call a week before the reading, your participants might forget. If you call the day before and they don't feel prepared, they might panic. You need to do everything you can to maintain an atmosphere of calm preparation.

The day or night that the reading takes place, give everyone ample time to get loosened up and grow familiar with each other, if the actors don't already know each other. Make sure that everyone is comfortable and has everything they might want to snack on or drink (check beforehand for diet peculiarities).

Hollywood Heat

If you live in Los Angeles or go there for any extended period of time and want to connect with playwrights who know all about readings, contact the Alliance of Los Angeles Playwrights (ALAP). Among the events ALAP sponsors are an annual Reading Festival and the Playwrights Expo, which bring together Los Angeles playwrights and dozens of representatives of local and national theatres. ALAP is an all-volunteer organization chaired in 2003 by Jon Dorf, whom I helped when he moved to L.A. from Philadelphia. To join ALAP or learn more, see its website at www.LAPlaywrights.org.

When you begin the reading, introduce the narrator, if the actors don't already know him or her. Explain that the narrator will read the slug lines (locations) as well as the descriptions of the action. Make sure that everyone knows where the restrooms are, and ask that they take care of business before the beginning of the reading. Make sure that it's okay with everyone to read the script straight through without a break. After all, they sit through most movies in one sitting. If you're videotaping or audiotaping, you may have to change tapes at certain times, and so a short break then wouldn't hurt the flow of the reading.

Just before you start, explain that although you would like the script to be read without interruption, you're willing to provide short clarifications if someone has a question during the reading. When you're ready to start, turn it over to the narrator. Let the fun begin, fade into the background, and pay attention. Just make sure that the narrator starts by reading the title and your name. That will set the right tone and promote respect for the work. And everyone will smile at you—for now.

You might want to have comment sheets that people can fill out to help you sort out all the opinions. Even if you're taping the reading, people have things on their minds that they might not reveal except on paper. If you use this follow-up, give them the opportunity to get the answers to you later. That way, if they think it's a pain in the butt to fill out a questionnaire, they can conveniently forget.

Make sure that you leave plenty of writing space on a questionnaire and have plenty of pens and pencils available. Pencils with erasers are better so that people can change their minds neatly. You might want to know something like the following:

- ◆ How did you like the screenplay?

- ◆ Did you find the story compelling?

- ◆ Did any particular character appeal to you? If so, why?

- ◆ Would you pay to see this movie in the theater?

- ◆ If you would not pay to see this movie, what could be done to improve it so that you would feel you got your money's worth?

- ◆ How does this movie compare to other films you've seen lately?

- ◆ Any other comments?

When the reading is wrapped up, thank everyone and tell them all that you'd be happy to discuss your screenplay with each of them privately, particularly if they liked it and know someone who might help bring it to the screen. This last is an old sales technique called "prospecting at the close." When it's delivered with self-deprecating humor and sincerity, it can work wonders.

It's Not for Us

PASS

Don't take it personally. If people don't like your script at a reading, don't get upset or explain what you were trying to say. If they didn't get it, that's the way it is. Your rebuff will be countered with, "If it ain't on the page, it ain't on the stage." Just write down their comments and thank them for sharing them. If someone is truly offensive, though, kick him or her out. You don't have to take it.

If you run a reading well and your script is of at least passable quality, you'll probably find that you've made some new friends. If the script has really impressed people—particularly if they're aspiring actors—you could make some good friends.

If you've read this section this far, you're probably of a mind to do a formal reading. For those not so inclined, I hope you and your buddies ordered enough really tasty pizza and didn't drink too much beer.

Writers' Conferences and Other Irregularities

I've spoken at a number of writers' conferences around California and across the country, and I can tell you that they all operate in much the same way. The people who speak there (including myself) are generally doing one or more of the following:

- ◆ Selling a book or books
- ◆ Looking for consultation clients
- ◆ Getting paid to appear
- ◆ Enjoying a new venue as they (hopefully) build their reputation as a guru

Hollywood Heat

> Hollywood is too small of a town. In early 2000, I had lunch with a producer and her friend to talk over a possible project. The friend and I kept telling each other that we looked familiar, and then she mentioned the WGA event "Words into Pictures," which she produced. Suddenly, I remembered dating her once and reminded her of the details. This is one example of why—despite all stories to the contrary—people in Hollywood generally try to be nice to each other and not burn bridges. You never know when you'll run into someone again.

We'll have a section on mentors and gurus later. I don't like being considered a guru, even though people all over the world ask me questions on daily basis, via e-mail, phone, or the occasional letter. I'd rather be writing something original, but when I see a need that isn't being completely filled, I'll get involved, as I did with this book and my *Ultimate Writer's Guide to Hollywood* (Barnes & Noble Books, 2004).

The very best one-stop shop to finding a writers' conference near you is on the Internet, at the ShawGuides, Inc., site, at www.writing.shawguides.com. This compilation of writers' conferences from across the United States and throughout the world on the site allows you to search through hundreds of events. You can search by your area of focus, such as "screenwriting."

The data isn't perfect. For example, I spoke for three years at the Aspen Summer Words festival, but ShawGuides did not list me even though I was always on the program. When I first checked it, ShawGuides listed the head of the Aspen Writers Foundation as Jeanne Small, although the new executive director at the time was my former UCLA Extension Writers Program student, Julie Comins. Still, ShawGuides is free to browse. It will also give you a listing as a writer/speaker, but it will then send you a lot of e-mails about paying for an expanded listing.

Skip's Tips

If you don't live in southern California but would like to go there for a conference, your best bet is the annual Screenwriters Expo, put on by *Creative Screenwriting* magazine publisher Erik Bauer. The first event in 2002 drew 3,000. I have appeared at it telling a packed room about my "shaping force" and how it applies to their writing career.

If you're of a mind to enter a screenplay contest after you've had a reading and fixed up your script even more, there are lots of them out there. Visit www.moviebytes.com for more information. One of my clients, James Ossi, has won dozens of contests with his scripts, as you'll see on the website.

Getting Advice from a Pro Screenwriter

Pro screenwriters have usually done many readings of their own scripts. As I mentioned previously, some top pros like Judd Apatow have readings with other writers with whom they worked as staff writers on TV shows. If you want to meet a Writers Guild of America member to give you advice on readings or anything else, you can get in contact with them via www.wga.org/agency/MemAgency.asp. There's no guarantee they'll get back to you, but usually they will—pros do that.

Whether you're looking for a conference or a contest or a pro to help, I hope that you find the information that you need to make your script saleable, whether it comes from a mentor or from the feedback that you get from a reading. Just remember whatever anyone tells you, it has to make sense to you, or it isn't helpful.

The Least You Need to Know

- Actors will often do nonpaying roles, even a screenplay reading, if there's potentially something in it for them.

- Hollywood is a small town; you may be closer to a helpful contact there than you think.

- A screenplay reading should be well organized, planned well in advance, and professionally conducted. After all, it's for you.

- Local theater groups are good sources for actors for readings, but don't be afraid to hold auditions.

- Before a reading, share your full screenplay only with the people reading the lead roles.

- Never hesitate to ask a pro; they were all amateurs once!

20

Why the Screenplay Is Merely a Blueprint

In This Chapter

- ◆ About movie budgets
- ◆ How scripts get changed
- ◆ Star power
- ◆ After the purchase
- ◆ Script resources

I never saw a screenplay that was filmed exactly as written. I heard that *Million Dollar Baby* was, but I wasn't privy to the process. The fact is, no matter how good you think your script is, after it's sold, the collaboration starts. Actually, it will probably start before you sell it, if your agent or manager gives you rewrite suggestions. Film is the most collaborative of all the arts. You might as well tattoo that 13-letter word, *collaboration*, on the inside of your eyelids right now because you'll likely see a lot of it when you sell a script.

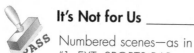

It's Not for Us

Numbered scenes—as in "1. EXT. SPORTS BAR - NIGHT"—are what you see in a shooting script. Software programs put the numbers in automatically, and some older books tell you to write them that way. Don't do it. Disable the software feature if it does it. A script isn't formatted that way until pre-production of the movie begins.

After a script is purchased, it's a serious commitment. Someone will spend a lot of money to get it made. If it's a digital movie you make yourself, it will probably cost as much as a good used car to get to the finished product. If it's a very low-budget movie with Screen Actors Guild (SAG) actors using one of their Low Budget Agreements (see www.sagindie.org for details on SAG producer agreements), it will still cost as much as a house in many instances. The average homeowner spends decades paying for a house that costs as much as that kind of film. That's one reason why I advise writers to think of a screenplay as the blueprint for a house. Someone has to line up all the contractors—that's the producer. You need a construction supervisor, or contractor—that's the director. There will be an inspector—that's the representative of the guaranty bond company that ensures the movie will be made and that investors' monies won't be lost. Then there are the various workers and vendors who do specific jobs. For example, you might think of the art director like the interior decorator of the home.

You, screenwriter, are the architect. Would the architect be necessary after the blueprint is in hand? Not necessarily. And that explains why the writer often gets shoved aside when the film or tape starts rolling. To help prevent that from happening, you need to learn as much about the filmmaking process as you possibly can.

What You Should Know About Movie Budgets

The Blair Witch Project (1999) was made for only $1,800, right? Or was it the official $22,000 figure? I don't know exactly how much the original footage cost. A lot of rumors were floating around when the film made such a splash. I do know that the filmmakers had the help of Louise Levinson in drawing up a business plan that raised the money needed to get the film in shape to be picked up for distribution. Levinson is the author of *Filmmakers and Financing: Business Plans for Independents, 2nd edition* (Focal Press, 1998) and writes advice columns on the web. See www.moviemoney.com for more details.

I also know that the original *El Mariachi* (1992), written and directed by Robert Rodriguez, was made on a budget of $7,000, with a final cost of $220,000 after post-production. Rodriguez chronicled the process excellently in his book, *Rebel Without a*

Crew: Or How a 23-Year-Old Filmmaker with $7,000 Became a Hollywood Player (Plume, 1996). Look up his "10 minute film school" interview and a lot more at www.exposure. co.uk.

The Blair Witch Project grossed in the neighborhood of $150 million, and *El Mariachi* made more than $2 million, and those are the U.S. figures only. Both these inexpensive films in their own way changed how Hollywood looked at filmmaking, at least for the up-and-coming generation. *Blair Witch* was made from an outline, while *El Mariachi* was scripted during and largely funded by Robert Rodriguez's stay in a hospital as one of the subjects of a cholesterol-reducing drug test. What matters is that both projects were made by the people who conceived them. If you're writing a screenplay only to sell, a budget might not be a major consideration for you, but you should at least have some idea of how much it costs to make movies.

Skip's Tips

Preproduction is the process that occurs when the money is in the bank to make a movie and the project is moving forward. The script is set and casting is in progress. If someone tells you they are in preproduction and the money isn't in the bank, they're not in preproduction.

Rodriguez went on to make the very successful *Spy Kids* movies and *Once Upon a Time in Mexico*, making him an A-list director. He still maintained his economic sensibilities, however. When he made the third *Spy Kids* for under $29 million, he was a studio hero.

As a writer you need an economic sensibility. I remember reading a friend's outlandish science-fiction/fantasy script years before computerized special effects were common. I told him that the script was okay but that it would be difficult to make because it would cost so much for the special effects. He was insulted and said that they would find a way to make it.

Maybe today they would find a way (if the script had been better). Generally, I tell writers today to write the script with little consideration for budget because anything a writer can conceive can be filmed, thanks to computers. But there's a catch.

The caveat to the advice of "Just write!" is this: If you have written a thoughtful character piece, set in a small town, but at the end you have a giant UFO landing like something out of *Independence Day*, that might not work. You've mixed genres badly. That scene will be the first thing cut from the film, for budgetary reasons. Computer-generated images are expensive. The equipment is expensive. The artists who operate the equipment are expensive. You'll be left with your characters staring in awe at the night sky as blinding rainbow lights are bathed across their faces, simulating a UFO.

Skip's Tips

If someone wants to make your film but asks you to take less for the script due to budgetary considerations, you might want to agree, but only if you can get "gross points" (a percentage of the profits before expenses are deducted). If you can't get that, you're dealing with someone who's greedy. Take your script elsewhere.

The real truth for screenwriters with regard to being concerned about budgets is simple: Just write, but keep the type of action consistent throughout the script.

If you write an action film, many of the scenes will be equally expensive. If you write a self-contained film such as *Clerks* (1994), which covers one eventful day on the job of some guys working at a convenience store and a video store, the cost per scene will be roughly consistent. If you don't write with a mind toward who might star in the movie and who would pay to make it, you're leaving questions open you might have to answer later.

Just remember this: Producers and studios lie about how much they spend on a film, usually saying they've spent more (or much more) than they really did. It's that old thing called bragging—you have to eat everything Hollywood feeds you with a grain of salt. Still, it's important that you understand at least rudimentary elements of budgeting. For example, if you are certain that you have a great TV movie script, it's doubtful that a TV network will spend much more than $3 million making your film. If you have elements in the script that will throw the film over budget, they have two choices if they want to make your movie:

1. Spend more because it's worth it (not likely).

2. Cut that part out of the script, or substitute something less expensive (highly likely).

The next time you watch a video of a movie that you think is somewhat like your film, look for consistency of content. I've found that people who get caught up in wild flights of fantasy that would take a lot of computer-generated effects to film usually haven't written a story worth a damn. Instead, they get caught up in the wild scenes in their mind. If you write a feature film script that's spectacular enough, though, the budget will be one of the least considerations.

How Your Cowboy Villain Became an English Terrorist

So you've written a Western. It's a different Western, and it has to be, because not many Westerns get made anymore. But you have something really different—a gunslinger that can't be killed because he's a vampire. He rules a town with an evil hand. We'll call it Darkness Gulch (it used to be Happy Valley). Then the girl arrives in town, and she's packing a pistol. We'll call her Mean Matilda. She doesn't like men. She's been traveling the West, gunning down famous gunslingers such as Biter Bill, and now she's come for him. Only Matilda doesn't know that he's a vampire, you see; she just knows his evil reputation.

Now, Bill might just sneer and shoot her right between the eyes, but she's very beautiful and, well, he's kind of taken with her, partner. He decides to put off his evil ways for a few days as he tries to cover up reality and woo her. And, dang if ole Matilda don't fall for it, shucks—until, that is, she finds out that he's not only a vampire, but the varmint that shot down her father, the very creep she's been gunning for all this time.

Your script—we'll call it *Dark Lust in the Dust*—is well-written and just quirky enough that a producer buys it from you. But no one wants a Western. Then for some reason, suddenly there's a renewed interest in Westerns because one is a big hit on television (it happens about once a year). Then the producer learns that the government of Thailand is offering concessions to filmmakers who will film there and put poor Thai people to work. This means the producer can make more money shooting in Thailand. About the same time, the producer learns that an English actor who once was riding high on a hit TV series, and who left the series early to raise elephants in Bangkok, is looking for a comeback vehicle. The producer does some quick calculations and figures that your script can now be filmed for one third of the original projected budget. And your horses become elephants.

Darkness Gulch becomes a beat-up neighborhood in Bangkok called "Wo Lookout." That's where a vampire runs an elephant racetrack. And, on top of that, the hero is a disgraced member of the British Secret Service, a really nasty ex–James Bond type, who plans to take over the city. Bail Bond, that's his name. And Matilda becomes Juicy Jones, the best undercover detective on the force, the only woman who can ride an elephant and win.

And when the producer explains this to you, you're absolutely dumbfounded. What happened to the great sweeping vistas of the Old West? They've been replaced by the ruins at Angkor Wat. What happened to the beautiful black horse with red eyes?

They put a red fringe bridle on the elephant. And so it goes, straight across your screenplay.

"Ludicrous!" you say. "I can't allow it!"

"Happens all the time," I reply calmly. "Get used to it."

Hollywood Heat

Behind-the-scenes Hollywood information can lead to screenwriting sales. *Lust in the Dust* (1985) was written by Philip John Taylor, an acquaintance of mine in the late 1980s. This spoof Western with the tagline "He Rode The West … The Girls Rode The Rest! Together They Ravaged The Land!" featured Tab Hunter as Abel Wood. Taylor told me that his script had been inspired by an earlier Hunter film called *The Burning Hills* (1956), a serious Western written by Irving Wallace from a Louis L'Amour novel. With Natalie Wood as the female lead, it seems that there was so much hanky-panky going on around the set that the crew nickname for the production was "Lust in the Dust."

Skip's Tips

"The back end" is a term that refers to box office revenue. If you get lucky enough to get paid "on the back end," that means you will be a profit participant. But, most likely, this will happen only if you own a percentage of gross points (gross profits). Make sure you have a good lawyer.

If you want to work as a screenwriter, you have a couple of choices: write something so spectacular that no one would think of changing it, or be flexible about changes, particularly those that have to do with budget.

This doesn't mean that you have to sacrifice artistic integrity altogether. You merely need to be willing to bend; you don't have to break to get your screenplay made. Of course, if you feel that strongly about it, you might be better off making it yourself.

And remember, this is show *business*. Do you want to be in business, or not?

Star Power Changes Screenplays

A friend of mine wrote a screenplay that got a lot of attention. He was being mentored by a very successful screenwriter, and so that helped, but my friend always had great ideas, from the time I first knew him as a teenager.

Through his mentor, my friend met the husband of a well-known film actress—an Academy Award nominee. And, small town that Hollywood is, another friend of mine did the novelization of the screenplay this actress starred in at about the same time. The actress's husband was a television director looking to direct his first feature film. Naturally, he didn't expect it to be a high-budget film, and, relationships being relationships, the director didn't want to take advantage of his wife's star power. Besides, my screenwriter friend's script did not feature a strong female lead.

But it was a fine action screenplay with a simple but great "What if?" premise.

Because of the script circulating in relatively high-level circles in Hollywood, it came to the attention of a very well-known male actor, and a notice appeared in "the trades" stating that this actor was scheduled to star in my friend's script.

Suddenly, a pretty good script set to be directed by a television director as his first feature film became important. My friend became very important. While word of his talent was already circulating, announcements in *Daily Variety* and *The Hollywood Reporter* about the project made him suddenly very hot as a writer. The reason was simple: star power.

And the actor made a good choice. The script by David Ayer was *Training Day* and Denzel Washington won an Academy Award.

Hollywood Heat

When the Internet got hot, some superstar-headed production companies aggressively sought to cultivate writers on their own, whether the screenwriters were agented or not. One of those companies was Saturn Films, founded by actor Nicolas Cage and producer Jeff Levine. They put up a website and solicited inquiries. After their *Shadow of the Vampire* came out, however, Saturn Films quit accepting scripts from unknowns. You'd be better off now creating a hot video game, and the companies would find you.

It's difficult to get a true star to read a script. Here's why. If you don't know them, they don't want to waste their time. They know that Hollywood stardom can be fleeting and that "You're only as good as your last picture." This means that they're often neurotic about what their next movie will be, particularly if box office results on the last one were disappointing. They want money, not promises. Then there's the Hollywood benchmark called "pay or play." Some stars insist that the money to make the movie is in the bank before they will even read the script. They take down payments on their services, just as writers hope producers will "option" their scripts for 10 percent down against the full 100 percent when the movie is financed. If the production of the film falls through, stars keep the pay or play money. Why? Because they've marked out a place on their schedule during which the movie is supposed to be filmed.

Does that sound greedy? Well, actors often struggle for years before their break-through film. They are made promises that are broken, suffering like writers. So, when they make it to the top, they don't want their time wasted. How can you blame them? When they put their name on a project, suddenly it can become very hot, and all the financing may fall into place quickly.

If you can somehow manage to get a top actor interested in your screenplay, you might become an A-list Hollywood screenwriter, like my friend. Just know this—with few exceptions, you will have to get to them through channels that they trust, whether it be official business friends, Hollywood professional friends, or long-standing family or college friends. Remember, they could be "bankable," meaning that a studio or financier knows that if that particular actor stars in a film, it is virtually guaranteed a certain return at the box office, and so they will finance the film with much more ease.

Don't bother trying to get movie stars to read your script if you don't have a personal conduit to them. Usually the only stars interested in seeing scripts from unknown screenwriters are those who have established their own production companies. If serendipity strikes and you happen to make the acquaintance of a popular actor, great. Just don't walk up and introduce yourself and hand him your script while he's eating.

Even if you manage to get a star to not only read your script but also like it, if that star does not have production experience or does not own a production company, he or she still must convince an agent to like it, which could be difficult. The agent would rather field offers, and actors with pet projects are notorious for failing badly, as John Travolta did with the awful *Battlefield Earth* (2000).

It's Not for Us

I almost sold a true story to Sean Connery's production company, about an MI-6 English intelligence agent who stopped World War III from happening. Problems began to arise when I told Connery's producer partner that I knew the writer of *Training Day*. They wanted me to set up a meeting or phone call with him to see if he would write the script of "our" story. Although they hadn't even optioned the story, I told Dave Ayer about it and he said they should call his agent. They didn't want to do that, because they'd have to make an offer. Unfortunately, this kind of thing is typical. The project fell apart and not long after, so did Connery's company, Fountainbridge.

How a Purchased Script Gets Read

When producers read a script with an eye to buying it, the first thing they think of is casting. They know what stars are available to work and when. Next, they think of their own markets, the studios where they do business, the cable networks looking for original material, and on down the line. If they know that certain stars are available and they've worked with them in the past, they might call the stars and tell them about the project, or even have a meal with them.

Hollywood is built on relationships, probably no more than any other billion-dollar business. Because of its nature, these relationships are broadly interesting to the general public. When Joe Roth left his executive position at Disney in 2000 and started a company that he later named Revolution Studios, the first star he made a deal with was Julia Roberts, the most popular actress in the world. And the first movie they made together was a box office bomb by most people's standards.

Hollywood people get swept up in the "wow" of it all and forget about things like good scripts the public would care about. But it's often fast and loose in Tinseltown. No producer should be discussing a screenplay before securing the rights by optioning the material, but producers do that all the time. When they start promoting a screenplay to secure financing, however, they must have it optioned, or the person they promote it to might option it out from under them.

The third thing producers think about when reading a screenplay (or in some cases, maybe the first thing) is who will direct the movie. They know the work of many directors and have worked with some. They know what actors the directors have relationships with and what studios like those directors.

If you want to play producer some time, get the Members Directory of the Directors Guild of America. You'll find hundreds of directors out of work who will be happy to talk to you. (See www.dga.org for details.)

Next comes the budget. Just as a producer will ask a writer who should star in the screenplay, a studio executive will want to know who might star and whether this person knows about the project; what director is interested, if any; and what the proposed

Skip's Tips

If you wonder whether or not a certain actor or director has a lot of clout among the powers that be in Hollywood, look them up on the "Star Power" area of www. hollywoodreporter.com. It will cost you a few bucks to do so, but the education is worth it.

budget is. If the producer has any qualms about the script, the executive (if interested in the project) will also discuss who can rewrite it, and whether that writer is available.

All of these factors are the basic things that producers think about when they read a script. Other things come into play, such as money-saving possibilities. If a country such as Ireland or a state like Kentucky wants productions shot in the area, it might make it very attractive for producers to film, giving them tax concessions, lowered or nonexistent filming fees, and a film commission that acts like government-level "gofers" to ensure that the producer gets whatever the producer wants. Many television shows and films are made in Canada, for a number of reasons. When the American dollar is stronger than the Canadian dollar, that also represents cost savings. The technical personnel are qualified, which helps. The last time I checked, American producers shooting in Canada got 18 percent of the budget kickback when the production was completed.

In return, the Canadians get a certain amount of "Canadian content" in addition to the benefits to the local economies where the productions take place. Canadian content means that a certain number of main characters, writers, and others must be of Canadian heritage or residency. Other countries do similar things. When other countries' currency is worth more than the U.S. dollar, however, shooting in states other than California is what Hollywood companies often do.

Like other countries, states in the United States want movies to showcase the beautiful geography of the region so that tourists and other filmmakers will want to come there. It's a win-win situation.

Skip's Tips

As soon as you make some money screenwriting, set aside some of it in a savings or investment account labeled "Forget You Money." Hopefully, you'll reach a point where you have enough money saved up to say, "Forget you," to a producer or development executive who offends you with suggested changes. You might have another word for it.

Here's a real example of how scripts can get changed to fit producers' needs. The script of *The Big Easy* (1987), written by Daniel Petrie Jr. and named after the nickname for New Orleans, Louisiana, was originally titled *Windy City* and set in Chicago. It made more sense economically at the time of *The Big Easy* to shoot in New Orleans. And another Petrie script, *Beverly Hills Cop*, was originally set to star Mickey Rourke and then, when that wasn't feasible, Sylvester Stallone. Isn't it amazing that they settled for that "nobody," Eddie Murphy?

(I know those stories because Dan Petrie Jr. was an agent for me at International Creative Management when I had my first movie treatment optioned.)

This is why the core of your story—your premise—and your plot needs to be so strong. Most good movies do not have to be location-specific, and changing characters to suit available stars may often actually add to the film's flavor. If you as a screenwriter are inflexible about such things, you might be looked upon as being "hard to work with," which will not help your career. It's a fine line, trying to maintain your standards and the integrity of your story, while still doing what you can to contribute to the collaborative nature of getting your movie made.

Experience helps, and you'll get that experience if you're as flexible as possible. Just don't be a pushover. There are so many insecure people in show business that if you maintain an air of composure and certainty, it might rub off. Even on you.

Script Resources That You Should Explore

It would greatly behoove you to do all you can to read as many versions of successful scripts as possible. Try to read the script that sold and all other versions of the screenplay, right on through the "shooting script" and versions published in books.

You can buy screenplays over the Internet at sites like www.scriptshack.com. Scripts are available at free sites such as www.script-o-rama.com and many others. Don't try to get everything for free, though. You can save a lot of time if you buy screenplays from sites like www.scriptfly.com. When they are selling scripts, the quality is usually much more reliable, with a larger selection. The last time I checked, Script Fly offered over 3,500 titles. These days, "Hollywood" in some ways means any place where films are made. For example, I have written Hollywood articles for an international audience in several magazines, and have been a regular contributor for the U.K. magazine *Scriptwriter* (see www.scriptwritermagazine.com for details). And guess what? Writers I hear from all over the world have the same problems you do!

The Least You Need to Know

- Movies such as *The Blair Witch Project*, *El Mariachi*, and *Clerks* were made cheaply but grossed millions. The catch is, the writers were also the directors.

- A screenwriter's only budget consideration should be in keeping the type of action consistent, budget-wise, throughout the script. If you're unwilling to cut or amend your script to suit the budget, you may get cut yourself.

- If you want your screenplay filmed the way you wrote it, write something so spectacular that no one would think of changing it.

♦ Don't bother trying to get movie stars to read your script if you don't have a personal conduit to them, unless they have their own production company actively looking for material.

♦ When reading screenplays that they might produce, producers will consider factors that may never occur to the screenwriter. You should learn about producing.

♦ To understand how screenplays are changed between sale and production, screenwriters need to read as many versions of successful scripts as possible.

Chapter 21

The Real Role of the Screenwriter

In This Chapter

◆ Smaller screen viewers

◆ Is the auteur truly the film's author?

◆ After a script is bought

◆ How Hollywood is changing

In the first edition of this book, I stuck my neck out and wrote: "The screenwriter is God, at least to the movies. Just like authors of novels, and just like the playwright in the theater, the screenwriter is the one on whom everyone else depends, without whom there would be no movie." I figured I would catch some heat for that, but I didn't care, because it's true.

Why would I expect repercussions for such a statement? Well, Mel Brooks once said, "Hollywood can nice you to death" to explain how people will rarely tell you how they really feel, fearing to alienate you should you become powerful later on. Despite this, screenwriters for a long time were looked upon as people whom, to paraphrase Groucho Marx's comment about women, "should be obscenely talented but not heard." (Of course, S. J. Perelman probably wrote the "obscene but not heard" line.)

Like God, the screenwriter often goes unappreciated, until the producer who thinks that he's God needs a rewrite done. God help the screenwriter. On the other hand, if you were an A-list screenwriter, I wouldn't be surprised to see a producer get on hands and knees and pray for your assistance.

As I wrote this edition, there was a months-long labor strike by the Writers Guild of America (WGA), west and east. The WGA ended up with a much better deal on DVD revenues, Internet profits, as well as jurisdiction over new media and residual formulas based on the gross revenue received by distributors. Previously, reruns of TV shows were being released on the Internet, making millions in ad revenue for the networks with little profit for the writers. In the costly strike, the writers gained control they deserved and forced producers and executives to give them more respect by demonstrating a salient fact—Hollywood shuts down without them.

We're in transition in Hollywood at the moment, with the old gods of producing and directing and distribution hanging fitfully by carefully manicured fingernails from a trembling, crumbling Mount Movie. As more members of that polytheistic pantheon fall to Earth, they are replaced by simple scribes holding a screenplay in one hand and a digital camera in the other. The latter legions have one mantra: "It all depends on the script." No one will fool them about where that screenplay came from—the writer. And nothing keeps them from putting up their own filmed work on the Web, either.

Independent moviemaking is simply catching up to television, where writer-producers rule. Networks want people whom they can depend on, to create hit shows, write them, and get them made. That holds true even with reality shows—those are written, whether it appears so or not. Perhaps because most screenwriters who make a living writing scripts (most don't) get their checks from television, that general attitude has bled over into the film arena. Writers are increasingly also directing, and the trend keeps growing. This chapter suggests ways to join the digital revolution, but it's mostly about attitudes: those of moviegoers and fans watching screens at home; those of other people in "the industry" toward screenwriters; and the changing attitudes that have resulted due to new technologies.

Writing for Smaller Screens

Every time things change in Hollywood, the patron saints of the establishment bemoan the passing grievously. I remember the hue and cry that went up years ago when a major Hollywood movie palace on Hollywood Boulevard was renovated, splitting it into two theaters. This was when cineplexes were first coming into vogue.

It was done purely for financial reasons because audiences simply weren't filling the big theater. With the ability to show two films, revenues went way up. Down the Boulevard, the classic Mann's Chinese Theatre added an annex and some people complained, but the additional dollars allowed the main theater to stay profitable. Now studios have arranged movies to be downloadable the same day they are released to theaters. It all comes down to the bottom line: where to find the bucks.

Hollywood Heat

There are three billion-dollar entertainment businesses in southern California. The first is Hollywood. The second is in the San Fernando Valley. It's the pornographic film business. More than 10,000 porn films are made per year in southern California in an industry employing tens of thousands of people, including the "actors." When mainstream film production suffers because of migration to Canada and states offering incentives for production, many mainstream production personnel quietly take work making porn movies. The other billion-dollar entertainment business is video games. Are some of the video heroines fashioned after porno stars? Take a look at *Grand Theft Auto: San Andreas* and you tell me.

The Kodak Theatre and the Academy of Motion Picture Arts and Sciences' building on Hollywood Boulevard were part of a billion dollars spent to spruce up the old town. It's a great thing to see *The Producers*, a musical derived from a movie, at a refurbished Pantages Theater, or the opening of a Disney family film at the El Capitan with Disney characters doing a show before the movie.

One block south on Sunset Boulevard, moviegoing has become (as I predicted almost a decade ago) a theatrical experience. At the Arclight Theatre (see arclightcinemas. com) all seats are reserved, there's a café bar where you can have drinks and dinner, and a cinema store to let you take a memento of a favorite movie home. That is great, because such a presentation tends to make movies special again.

Some people think that they have to write down to the normal moviegoer, and that's where they err. The fact is, the average person in the cineplex is more story-savvy than ever before. They want something that challenges their intellectual acumen, thrills them with improved images, and makes them think about their lives and relationships. And they want something special.

Unfortunately, many ill-informed, self-styled film gurus will try to get beginning writers to worship style over substance, and movie storytelling suffers. I advise people to write to the people in the cheap seats, but *NEVER* write down to them.

If you don't think that moviegoers are generally smart, if you believe that you can simply write some variation of old tired themes and succeed, I'm afraid you're in the wrong business. Successful films of recent vintage scream otherwise. Each new movie Pixar comes out with tends to become one of the top animated films of all time, and they are class personified. *The Sixth Sense* (1999) offered a new look at the spiritual nature of life. While promoted as a horror film, it was not, and it became one of the top 10 successes of all time because of its innovative storytelling. *My Big Fat Greek Wedding* is now the most successful romantic comedy of all time. Who wants to see a movie about a plain Greek American girl? Everybody, including people in other ethnic groups who have felt underrepresented in Hollywood movies! The huge success of *Little Miss Sunshine*, which was about overcoming family foibles and helping the least of us, is another example of being in touch with common folk.

So here's the point: Although you may think that you are writing for sophisticated Hollywood executives who want the same old thing with some new twist to pack 'em into the theaters, the opposite is true. To achieve outstanding success, you're actually writing for sophisticated movie audiences in the cineplexes. They watch TV too much, but increasingly they do that because TV writers live and die by ratings, and thus have to cater to what the public likes. Your ultimate audience has seen a jillion movies, and they've followed a jillion more video game scenarios. All this means the first script you sell might have to be stunningly good to stand out. If your script doesn't sell, don't complain. To make a breakthrough, you have to be superior to everything else out there. *And* you have to get a little bit lucky, like Nia Vardalos did when Tom Hanks's part-Greek wife Rita Wilson came to see Nia's one-woman show. Screenwriting is the same as any other business. To get your foot in the door, you must exhibit a lot more effort than you do once established. You have to get "on the radar" of someone who counts in Hollywood, and even then it's hard. First-time screenwriter Michael Arndt, who won an Oscar for *Little Miss Sunshine*, was broke at the time he sold it for $250,000, and the movie took five years to get made mostly due to financial reasons.

Skip's Tips

When you're planning your script, see what's playing at your local cineplex, and determine the premise of each film. Check back each week for a month, and see which ones remain; then analyze the premises again. If you're clever, you can also do this with trailers you can view online. It's likely that the ones with staying power, superstars or not, came from the best-written screenplays. You can check box office results in other areas at sites like www.boxofficemojo.com.

Is the Auteur Theory Still Viable?

Differences between the Writers Guild of America and the Directors Guild of America usually boil down to a simple phrase: "A Film By …." I never did agree with that credit, but then, I'm a writer at heart. I know that directors work hard making a movie. They're in charge of the set and usually the post-production process as well, but "A Film By …" is a denigration of the writer in my mind. Who knows whether the WGA and DGA will ever settle the agreement, but with more writers directing (thank you, digital) and WGA efforts like billboards featuring famous screenwriters, we're getting there. And as more writers direct, they're not so anxious to adopt the "A Film By …" credit. In television, where the writer/producer rules and directors are often hired on a show-by-show basis, directors never ask for "A Show By …" credit, even though as many people collaborate. In film, it's easier to see a director's vision, but unless they also write and produce the film, how can they truly claim creation credit?

The "auteur theory" that the director is the author of a film has never helped anyone in Hollywood except directors. It has created bad blood between people who contribute to getting a film on the screen. And it has served to demean screenwriters and lessen their contributions. When press kits are compiled to use in promoting a film, they usually contain biographies of the main actors, the producers, and the director, but rarely the screenwriter. That's not right, but as an aspiring screenwriter you need to know what you're up against.

In recent years, the WGA has tried to counter that by arranging "Meet the Screenwriters" public relations junkets featuring writers such as Callie Khouri, who wrote the wildly popular "chick flick" *Thelma and Louise* and directed *Divine Secrets of the Ya-Ya Sisterhood* (2002). Coupled with the boom in interest in screenwriting and the continuing expansion of the publication of screenplays and writers directing, it appears that screenwriting is coming into its own as a respected art form.

> **Skip's Tips**
>
> *Your Name*
>
> A movie in Hollywood that has staying power is said to "have legs." Those legs refer to the power of word-of-mouth, the people in the theaters who get up and go tell a friend about the show they just saw and enjoyed. (I hope your career has "legs.")

Here's the truth about "A Film By …": after your first film is made, if it is a success, you might be able to convince someone to let you direct your next screenplay. I've known many writer/directors and seen this process work time after time. I provided

Michael Rymer with the material for his first filmed feature, *Dead Sleep*. He rewrote an NBC TV movie, then turned down sale offers to film his script *Angel Baby* and directed it himself. That transformed his career, and in recent years he's been one of the mainstays of the revised *Battlestar Galactica* TV series. Stories like Michael's are why I urge beginning screenwriters to think long-term by thinking like a filmmaker, not just a screenwriter.

In most cases, being both a writer and director (and/or producer) is by far the best of both worlds. It takes longer to achieve, but the rewards are geometrically greater, particularly in the remuneration department.

What Happens After a Script Is Bought

When a production company or studio takes on a script, if the project doesn't come to them via a producer, the first thing that it must do is figure out which producer will helm the production. That's not a consideration if the company is a sole proprietorship. When the producer starts working the script, he'll list possible casting and directors, and figure out potential locations and studio needs. How much will be shot on location, and where? Will the film require a lot of computer work? How much takes place at night, and how much during the day? All these things and more go into figuring out a budget, which is probably compiled with the help of a program such as Movie Magic Budgeting and Scheduling (see www.writersstore.com for more information) or Gorilla Film Production software (fabulous for indie productions; see www.junglesoftware.com and also check out the demo on this book's CD). However they form the budget, they might do two different estimates—one for a low-budget movie and another for a high-budget film with major stars. Naturally, the optimum scenario for the producer is the high-budget version because the production fees will be higher, and so might the long-term profits. Also, studios will put a lot more money into promoting high-budget films.

Here's why it matters that you know about these things. As a screenwriter, what the budget of your movie might be affects how much you could be paid for the script. If it's a low-budget film and your first sale, you might expect only WGA minimum or a little more.

If the film has major stars in it, the budget could go to $80 million or more. A rough general rule of how much a screenwriter is paid is from 2.5 percent to 5 percent of the production budget. This means that for a film of $40 million or more, you could expect a paycheck of more than $1 million. Even if you get only half that, that kind of money explains why so many people are writing screenplays, trying to grab the platinum ring on the Hollywood merry-go-round.

When the producer has a budget and a rough schedule calculated, financing is secured and then the producer and director select a casting director to work with. Casting directors have become very important in Hollywood over the past decade and can be crucial in attracting A-level talent to a project, almost as much as a director. Hollywood depends a lot on word-of-mouth and reputation, and if a successful casting director hires onto a production, that can say a lot about the quality of the script.

Hollywood Heat

Some producers are role models for the fine way they treat writers and other behind-the-camera personnel. Although he was once sued by a screenwriter, Clint Eastwood nevertheless has a reputation for taking great pains to see that writers are well-paid. Even better is George Lucas. When he was running low on funds while making *Star Wars*, Lucas offered net point participation to some crewmembers. They took it, probably not expecting to ever see any money. Lucas not only proved "normal" expectations wrong, but many of the crew became millionaires.

Next comes a director of photography, usually the one the director prefers. Just as certain artists are known for a certain style, so are cinematographers.

Why isn't the producer considered the "author" of a film? After all, the producer finds the script, hires the director, works with the director and casting director, or even secures the lead stars. The producer gets the financing in place and makes the distribution deals. The producer has to see that the filming schedule is finalized, that wardrobe is taken care of, and that props and any special needs are provided for. More likely than not, it's the producer who brings the script supervisor onboard. (The script supervisor keeps track of the position of the script at the end of every shot and keeps the producer apprised of how many pages of the script are filmed each day. You can learn about training in this position and other film production jobs at www. cinemaartstech.com.)

And what about transportation, catering, and where the "dailies" of that day's filming are shown for the cast and crew? Ultimately, that's the producer's responsibility.

If certain scenes do not require on-camera appearances of the leads or other actors, they will be shot by a "second unit" director and crew. In some cases, a producer might also serve as second unit director. Doesn't that give him (or her) even more ammunition for claiming authorship of the film?

Last but not least, who sets up the publicity and advertising? Who selects the poster for the film and makes the arrangements for the shooting of the electronic press kit (EPK; a video documentary with the stars and director talking about their movie, with the screenwriter almost never on-camera)? Wouldn't that person be the producer? Yes, it would.

It's Not for Us

Don't sign away everything because you think you must. The Writers Guild stresses that writers maintain their "reserved rights," which includes merchandising rights, publication rights, and interactive rights (video games). They stress that to buy the writer's reserved rights, the acquisition must be covered in a separate document. Don't buy the "Oh, that's just boilerplate material" contract argument.

Does that give them more credence as the author of the film? Well, let's examine it. The authors of books usually do the promotion as well. We know that the actors aren't the authors of a film, but then, characters from a book can't speak, can they? Directors can speak on-camera and so can producers. Can screenwriters speak? Who knows? We rarely see them.

I'm being more than a little sarcastic here to illustrate the enormous amount of work that a producer does to get a film made, compared to the director or even the screenwriter. I find it strange, though, that in the entire time I've been in and around Hollywood, no producer has ever claimed to author a film. Still, I'm sure you see now why writer/producers rule in television.

Back to the other folks who get a film made. The "D of P" (director of photography) usually has his own crew, and so does the film's editor, who can often "save" a film that is in trouble after shooting or discover (via smart edits) a view of the film that has not been envisioned by the writer, producer, or director. For example, it was widely rumored that the innovative end of *Pulp Fiction* (1994), in which we return to the opening scene with Honey Bunny (Amanda Plummer) and Pumpkin (Tim Roth) holding up the restaurant, was an editing glitch and was not written into the original script. We return to the scene in the opening of the film despite the fact that we are seeing John Travolta again after seeing him get killed. If the rumor was true, was it the idea of editor Sally Menke, or did it come from writer/director/producer Quentin Tarantino? Maybe you know the answer; I'm still wondering. (I do know, however, that too many Tarantino movies like *Kill Bill* seem more derivative than original, so I can buy into the *Pulp Fiction* editing story.)

Experienced producers can also have a major effect on the movie storyline. For example, screenwriter Scott Michael Rosenberg wanted a warm, family ending to his *Con Air* (1997), but the reigning king of action movie producers, Jerry Bruckheimer, had another idea. Bruckheimer insisted that the movie close on Steve Buscemi's vicious convict character, Garland "The Marietta Mangler" Greene, now escaped, gambling inside a Las Vegas casino. The closing scene came on the heels of Nicolas Cage as Cameron Poe being happily reunited with his family. The producer convinced the screenwriter, leaving audiences with a chill reminiscent of the phone call to Jody Foster's Clarice Starling from Anthony Hopkins's "Hannibal the Cannibal" at the end of *Silence of the Lambs* (1991). And when I heard Disney was doing a movie version of their Pirates of the Caribbean Disneyland ride (boring unless you're a little kid), I didn't take it seriously until I heard Bruckheimer was producing. I'll basically see anything Bruckheimer produces, and the *Pirates* movies have made billions. Is he the author of his films?

If you want to be the next Quentin Tarantino, write a script as good as *Pulp Fiction* and handpick great actors like he did, with a little help from synchronicity. When Tarantino first met with John Travolta about the movie, he happened to be living in an apartment that Travolta had lived in when starting out in Hollywood. The roles played by Amanda Plummer and Tim Roth were written with them specifically in mind.

> **Skip's Tips**
>
> *Your Name*
>
> Even if your script isn't purchased, it might make a good "sample." That means that it illustrates the quality and (we hope) inventiveness of your writing. A great sample can get you assignment work, which is by and large the most lucrative area of feature film screenwriting. It's almost always what gets people their first TV writing jobs, too.

And if you go to film your own script, remember that actors really need you. John Travolta had been a superstar who had fallen when *Pulp Fiction* came his way. His fine performance put him back on top, and the movie vaulted Quentin Tarantino into comparisons with other "do everything" Hollywood legends such as Orson Welles.

It all starts with the screenplay, though. Many people contribute to the awesome collaboration that goes into getting a film made, but no activity would ever take place without the engine of the script pushing the project forward.

Steven Spielberg once announced publicly that he could make a film without much of a script, that it wasn't that important to him. Well, maybe so, but Spielberg himself turned to directing after being unhappy with the filmed result of a script that he co-wrote with Claudia Salte (writing as Chips Rosen), *Ace Eli and Rodger of the Skies* (1973). He told me that personally, and I have it on tape, and so I have to believe him. It all starts with the writing. And you don't even want to hear the stories about all the writers on *Minority Report*.

As a beginning screenwriter, you will probably be in awe of "real Hollywood people" for some time. That's only natural, but remember that almost no one in Hollywood could build a notable career without great scripts. Whoever the author of a film may be, the script came from a writer.

Don't you dare forget that.

It's Not for Us

Despite my horror stories and those of others, don't assume that Hollywood is largely a pit of vipers. You'll find that once people know your work, you'll be accorded a generous amount of respect. Getting them to know and respect your work is the trick.

How Hollywood Is Changing and What You Can Do to Help

If you intend to make a serious attempt at a screenwriting career, I urge you to not attempt to launch it when you have written only one screenplay, no matter how good you think that screenplay may be. According to the Writers Guild of America, only slightly more than 50 percent of its members are "employed slightly" on a yearly basis—this out of a membership base of around 10,000. The good news is that working WGA screenwriters are at all-time high growth levels, due to the expansion of cable television outlets and, recently, the explosion in content "ported" to the Internet. Just remember, not getting paid for TV shows seen on the Web was a big reason for the 2007 writers strike, so who knows how this expansion will ultimately pan out for writers? About one third of WGA members are employed by television, but the vast majority of those writers are living and working in southern California. If you do not live in Los Angeles, your chances are lessened. If you move there to make it, you'll probably need more than one screenplay to break in.

Now, here's your real problem. A successful producer, Tony Bill, once told me that great scripts are worth their weight not in gold, but in platinum. That is still true, but there are tons of people out there writing tinsel screenplays.

I'm a screenplay consultant, and I get a lot of scripts that will never sell in their original form. In contrast, I once chaired a panel at a weekend event put on by Gary Shusett and Sherwood Oaks, on pitching (verbally selling) screenplays. Most of the attendees were students of the Los Angeles Film School (see www.lafilm.com), which is a one-year full immersion program in filmmaking. Every single person who practiced his or her pitch on me had a screenplay that could sell with some work. It was the best group of stories at a pitch event that I'd ever heard. Most of these people knew not only screenwriting, but also filmmaking.

The most successful screenwriters are generally those who are the most educated about the business of Hollywood. They don't read one book and rely on it; they read a library. They study old films and new films until screenplay structure becomes second nature to them. They work hard at improving their craft while keeping up with new developments and dreaming up new innovations.

These days, it is feasible to acquire the equipment necessary to film and edit a digital movie for well under $10,000. Given how the prices of electronics drop, this situation will only improve in coming years.

If you're inclined to look into the idea of digitally filming your own script, do some reading first. One good place to start is *Videomaker* magazine, which you can read all about at www.videomaker.com. The company that produces this publication, York Publishing, also puts on conferences in various parts of the country at which vendors appear and persons knowledgeable about all aspects of filmmaking (not only video) speak on various subjects. Having attended one of these events in Burbank, California, I'll vouch for their tremendous worth.

Many organizations around the country offer membership and help to aspiring filmmakers. Some of them are geared toward "guerrilla" filmmakers, while others offer a more traditional approach (like filming on 16mm and eschewing digital video). I'll simply advise you to do an Internet search and see what you come up with, or check with your local or state film commission for suggestions.

Organizations based in Los Angeles, New York, Chicago, Dallas, and major cities in Florida—where most productions and commercial productions take place—are more likely to provide you with the information and guidance that you need. A couple of Internet-based resources you might look at are ...

- **Indieclub.com.** A site designed to enable filmmakers' networking capabilities. At this writing there were more than 14,000 members and 77 local chapters around the world.

- **Mandy.com.** A site based in the UK listing jobs and opportunities. You can post up to two resumés and a cover letter and get free weekly job listings sent to you via e-mail. (For a small fee, you can get daily jobs sent.) You can explore everything from student productions to full paying positions.

I'd also recommend Guy Magar's directing workshop, which gives you the basics in a jam-packed weekend. I've taken the workshop myself and everyone I've referred to it has appreciated it as much as I have. See www.actioncut.com for details.

It's Not for Us

Don't think that you could never produce or direct a film because you don't know the nuts and bolts of filmmaking. There are always people available to teach you, even on the set. "Line producers" get films made for producers, and first-time directors almost always have an experienced person to show them the ropes, usually a skillful director of photography.

Before launching into filmmaking, you might want to do a career plan. Take your screenwriting seriously enough to think that you might be able to do it full-time. Even if you never direct a film, the more complete your education is about the filmmaking process, the more likely you are to write a marketable screenplay.

If you can't make it to a school or workshop in a major city, check out the CD-ROM guide entitled "How to Make Your Movie: an interactive film school" (see www.interactivefilmschool.com). Three-time Oscar winner Walter Murch called it the "best, most complete and innovative filmmaking guide I have ever seen, in any format." Or, if you have an Apple computer and are getting started in editing with something like Final Cut Express, you might have a look at the tutorials available at dvcreators.net. And to make great web movies and interactive multimedia presentations to help sell your project, the best software I've found is MediaWorks (see www.mediaworkssoftware.com), which helps you do just about anything, including podcasts. Whatever you do, start putting some pictures together instead of just words—your screenplays will improve.

Here are some additional steps that might help transform you from screenwriter to writer-director or writer-director-producer:

1. Make a list of all the script projects that you would like to write in the foreseeable future.

2. Divide them up into low-budget ideas and high-budget ideas. Hint: the low-budget ones don't have big car chase scenes and city blocks blowing up.

3. Pick the high-budget one that you most like and that you could most easily see big stars appearing in.

4. Pick the low-budget idea that you like the most. Low-budget ideas generally have only a few locations and a minimal cast of characters. For example, stage plays these days generally have a cast of six or fewer, to accommodate the usual

skimpy budgets of regional and equity-waiver theaters across the country. Most low-budget films have no more than six main characters, and usually only two or three. (*Clerks* is a good example.)

5. While you work on selling your first script or writing your second, when you feel a need to change pace, start working on your low-budget script. When you sell your first script, you'll most likely be asked what else you have available. If you just happen to have a script ready that would be inexpensive to film, you might be able to talk someone into giving you a chance. And if you make that film work, you'll move up to a whole new Hollywood plateau.

Meanwhile, help yourself and other screenwriters by getting involved in the process even if you're an extra. Take my word for it, being involved in a production is a lot of fun, and you'll be amazed at what you'll learn. It's so much fun, in fact, that while you're doing it, you don't even think about who is authoring the film.

The Least You Need to Know

- The screenwriter is God in Hollywood, but it's hard to convert producers and directors to your religion.

- The cineplex patron and home theater viewer, the ultimate "end user" of screenwriting, is a lot savvier than most people believe. Never write down to the normal movie patron.

- To break in as a screenwriter, you must exhibit a lot more talent and effort than you do after you're established.

- The Hollywood battle over the simple phrase "A Film By …" between writers and directors is not likely to end soon.

- Producers expend more effort in getting a film made than just about anyone, but they are never considered the "author" of a film.

- A great number of great directors began as screenwriters, and many great screenwriters know how to make movies.

Chapter 22

Writing for Television

In This Chapter

- ◆ TV movie seven-act structure
- ◆ The TV queue
- ◆ Network and cable preferences
- ◆ Miniseries and other forms
- ◆ Reality shows
- ◆ Should it be a book?

Until you are an established writer, to write for American television, you probably need to live where those shows are made. Namely, Canada, Florida, New York, and other places, but the majority of the shows that air in the United States are made in Los Angeles. The studio facilities are here, the actors are here, and the beaches are here. And if you don't think beaches are important, you never saw *Baywatch* and haven't watched *The O.C.* or *Falcon Beach* on the ABC Family Channel.

If you want to write hit sitcoms, you definitely need to live in Los Angeles and be under the age of 30. Isn't age discrimination illegal!? Sure it is, but since when did that stop Hollywood? A group of TV writers have sued over getting older but not getting work (see www.writerscase.com for details). As of this writing and the last edition of this book, the case was unresolved. So stay tuned for possible changes.

The best way to break into television is via sales of original screenplays to channels such as Lifetime or the Disney Channel. HBO and Showtime are still reserved for the "big guns" and will probably remain so for the near future. Still, there are opportunities to be exploited. When new cable channels crop up and do well, sooner or later they want to make their own movies, to distribute in theaters as well as on their own airspace. And they can triumph; when Robert Duvall produced and starred in *Broken Trail* as a two-part miniseries for cable channel American Movie Classics in 2006, it had higher ratings than *any* network, broadcast or cable. Developments like this are good news for writers.

Hollywood Heat _____

Algo's Factory ("Algo" being short for "algorithm") was a kids' science show broadcast on UPN, a sort of latter-day "Mr. Wizard" (an early TV hit). I was a staff writer in the first season. Created by Perfectly Round Productions in Wichita, Kansas, and shot in Minneapolis, Minnesota, all the shows were written by writers in California who never had a joint staff meeting and never met the producer. All the shows were written and e-mailed in, with some discussions over the phone. As the Internet grows and computer technology becomes more spectacular, more shows are being done in this way.

The TV Movie and the Seven-Act Structure

Movies made directly for television started with the "Movie of the Week" and was soon known as an "MOW" (em-oh-dubya) in Hollywood. There aren't "Movies of the Week" any more, so generally a film made by a TV network is simply a "TV movie." That bit of history aside, here's my first introduction into how they are acquired. A former agent of mine asked me if I had any screenplays that would fit a certain star who had a TV movie "pay or play" deal with a network. First, she explained "pay or play." The star was paid to reserve her time and would get the money whether or not she did any of the three movies on her contract within a specific time. Then the agent told me that if I did have a script, I would get only $60,000 for it. "But hey," she said, "$60,000 is $60,000, and that's double WGA minimum." Better than doing word processing for a law firm, which is how I made my living at the time. I said I might have something. "Great," said the agent. "Just make sure that you use the seven-act structure, okay?"

I agreed, then went scrambling around to find out what she was talking about. Seven acts! Good lord, Shakespeare used only five! Then I sat down and thought about it.

It didn't take a genius to divide a two-hour TV movie into 15-minute segments and calculate that an act might end every time we saw a commercial. I got my hands on some scripts so that I wasn't just guessing when I typed out "End Act One" on a certain page.

If you have a good screenplay that's suitable for a cable channel or even one of the major networks, no one will shoot you for not putting it in the format of a TV movie, but you might as well know what that format looks like.

Hollywood Heat

Sabrina the Teenage Witch was a hit comedy on ABC before moving to the Warner Brothers Network. Originating from an *Archie* comic book character, *Sabrina* began as a 1996 movie on Showtime, a cable channel that is also part of Viacom, the company that produced the show. If you also saw the movie that inspired the show, you might have noticed that Salem Saberhagan, the animatronic robot black cat, was much less realistic than the computer-generated image (CGI) cat in the movie. Why didn't they use the CGI for the show? Very simple: they couldn't afford it on a weekly basis.

Let's use the pilot script of what became the most successful show in the world as an example. I haven't changed this example in three books because I really liked the pilot script. It was set in southern California and featured a lot of sunshine and water. That's right, *Baywatch*, the show that made Pamela Anderson a star. TV shows often have some kind of black-and-white illustration on the cover page. If you're trying to sell an original screenplay as the lead-in to a series, that's the toughest sale in Hollywood because usually the only people who get a chance to do that are people who are established television writer/producers. If you have a really good illustration and logo to include on the cover page, it's probably okay to include it, but unless you can prove you can produce that series, I wouldn't bother. The *Baywatch* illustration was a lifeguard stand in the foreground, with lines that could be heat waves or ocean waves behind it. The *Baywatch* (two words) logo was to the right, superimposed on a setting sun. Nice work.

Like a stage play, the *Baywatch* script (revision 11/8/88) featured a CAST LIST (centered, middle of the page) with two sections: SERIES LEADS and RECURRING CHARACTERS (both flush left), listing character names IN ALL CAPS two tabs in from the left. Similarly, on the next page was an EPISODE CAST (centered, middle of the page) for the first episode (the two-hour movie), again listing their names IN ALL CAPS two tabs in from the left. On the next page was a SET LIST (centered, middle of the page). INTERIORS (centered, middle of the page) were listed on the first page, with EXTERIORS (centered, middle of the page) on the next. The LIFEGUARD HEADQUARTERS were divided into the eight sets there (MITCH'S OFFICE, and so on), indented two tabs over from the left. All other LOCATIONS including the exteriors (such as SANTA MONICA PIER) were listed line by line, flush left.

The first part of a TV movie is sort of a reverse denouement called a "teaser." It's a few-minute lead-in to the show that establishes the main character(s), perhaps the main location, and what's going on. The format on the title page begins: "Title" TEASER EXT. LOCATION—ANY MORE SPECIFIC PART OF LOCATION—DAY OR NIGHT. Then comes a space and the first line of the script. Like a normal screenplay, the first page is not numbered. (The scenes of this draft are numbered to the right, but don't worry about doing that with your script. Write unnumbered "master scenes.")

The *Baywatch* teaser starts with lifeguard Lieutenant MITCH TAYLOR tutoring a new lifeguard, EDDIE KRAMMER. We also learn about Mitch's mentor, AL DEMPSEY, who figures prominently later. This is followed by a crisis in a lifeguard tower as a PCP-crazed man sets it on fire, and other lifeguards rush to the rescue while Mitch and Eddie try to remedy the situation at the scene. They are barely able to get the man out of the burning tower in time to save him, and after other lifeguards (establishing their characters) arrive and help subdue the man with a choke hold, Eddie has learned graphically that there's a lot more to lifeguarding than being a good swimmer.

And then we go directly to the high-energy MAIN TITLE MONTAGE that we saw every week as each new episode of *Baywatch* appeared. Writers ask me about montages and I generally try to dissuade them from writing them, because they don't do them the way Eisenstein (who invented them) intended. A main title montage on a TV show is not usually a montage with an emotional arc, however. It's just a flashy visual setup to inspire you to watch the show.

The teaser ends in the middle of page eight. The rest of the page is blank space. Act One begins on the top of page nine this way: ACT ONE. Again, no title line. From there we simply add a blank line and then start the script again normally. Act One ends at the bottom of page 26 with a FADE OUT: END OF ACT ONE. As with any feature-length screenplay, within Act One the story and characters have been set up. With TV shows and movies, however, there is always some sort of "cliffhanger" type of action that makes the viewer want to come back after the commercial to see what happens. In the *Baywatch* script, a girl named WENDY HARRIS has been saved by CPR and mouth-to-mouth resuscitation by lifeguard CRAIG POMEROY, but there's something going on with her psychologically, or at least there appears to be.

To compare a seven-act TV movie to a normal, three-act screenplay, you might consider that the teaser and Act One would comprise the normal first act, while Acts Two through Five would comprise the normal second act. Acts Six and Seven make up the normal third act. Each act ends the same way, format-wise—FADE OUT: END OF [NAME OF ACT].

The new act always begins on a new page. In the *Baywatch* script that I'm using as an example, Act Two begins on page 27 and ends on page 38. Act Three begins on page 39 and ends on page 57. Act Four begins on page 58 and ends on page 74. Act Five begins on page 75 and ends on page 88. Act Six begins on page 89 and ends on page 104. The script is 113 pages long, with Act Seven beginning on page 105. Both Act Seven and the opening Teaser are roughly of the same length. Other than what I've mentioned, a TV movie script page looks exactly like a regular screenplay, following the same rules. It's usually no more than 110 pages.

Skip's Tips

Try it before you knock it. It's easy to deride TV movies and series. For example, the slang term for the *Baywatch* series was "Babewatch." The truth, however, is that most TV movies are written by experienced writers who have structure down cold. You'd do well to study some.

In contrast, a one-hour TV show (usually 52 to 56 pages) follows this format:

Teaser

Act One

Act Two

Act Three

Act Four

There are also commercials after each of the previous items, followed by the end credits.

By the end of Act Five, we know what Wendy's problem was that was hinted at when Act One ended. She is suffering from sexual molestation by her stepfather, JACK HARRIS. The midpoint change (teenage Wendy's budding friendship with married lifeguard Craig) comes at the end of Act Three, when he finds her in his lifeguard tower with a picnic lunch. The normal screenplay turning point toward the end of Act One (that sends the story in another direction) comes at the end of Act Two in this seven-act script. The second turning point that would be toward the end of Act Two comes at the end of this script's Act Four, when Wendy's father locks her in her room. In Act Six, Wendy's stepfather is confronted by Craig about the sexual molestation.

Episodes of *Baywatch* almost always interwove A, B, and C story lines. By my estimation, the A story line in the pilot MOW is Eddie learning what lifeguarding is about and our look into the lives of all the lifeguards. The B story line is the "episode" story of molested and confused teenage beauty Wendy. The C story line is the passing of the mantle of lifeguard legends. As Act Seven of the movie opens, lifeguard mentor Al Dempsey goes fishing off Malibu with HOBIE TAYLOR on an excursion fishing boat. At the end of the act, however, a fire in the galley of the boat causes the boat to explode. Naturally, all the lifeguards must rescue the fishermen. When they arrive on the scene in their boat, Al, the legend, is trying to find his buddy, Hobie. When the lifeguards arrive, Al doesn't let them take over. Worn out, he hyperventilates before diving but manages to help Mitch get victims out of the capsized boat below, only to be trapped himself. Mitch gets Al to the surface, but too late. Al is dead.

The denouement of the film is Al's funeral. It lasts a page and a half, with a half-page eulogy to Al from Mitch that nicely summarizes a lifeguard's life.

Why am I telling you about an old show like *Baywatch*? Because, thanks to the never-say-die efforts of David Hasselhoff, it was rescued from cancellation and became the number-one international hit.

It's always surprising to me to see which American shows are popular in other countries. In 2003, I met a Chinese American who came here with his family at age 14. His favorite TV show growing up was *Small Wonder*, a syndicated sitcom about a teenage girl robot. Although it wasn't broadcast in mainland China, pirated videos of the show were the number-one hit on the black market.

I remember being dumbfounded at a Los Angeles party of Australian film professionals when I learned that *Baywatch* was number-one not only in Australia, but also all over the world. After reading the tight pilot teleplay by Michael Berk and Douglas Schwartz (writing team), with the story by Michael Berk and Douglas Schwartz, and Gregory J. Bonann, however, I'm not surprised that the show sold or that it became such a success. And I'm just as certain that if you wrote a script with that kind of content today, you might get it on television. Fox's *The O.C.* seemed, to me, like *Baywatch* away from the beach.

The TV Queue That Supposedly Doesn't Exist

I knew a screenwriter who had his first feature made. His second sale was a writing assignment of a TV movie set in Texas. As it usually goes with things in TV, budget was a primary consideration. One of the reasons my friend got the job was because he worked cheap. Even then, however, he was not a writer known to the network on which the TV movie aired, and so the producer had to fight to keep the writer on the project. It helped that, because of the budget, despite the fact that it was set in Texas, the movie was cheaper to make in the writer's native Australia, with Australian actors doing American accents! That was one of the first times I'd heard about "having TV-Q" as a writer or actor, but it makes sense. Like sitcoms wanting writing staffs under age 30, the TV queue is legally not supposed to exist, but it's been around as long as I've been around Hollywood.

Skip's Tips

"Having TV-Q" means that the public will watch a program based on a certain actor's appearance alone. For screenwriters, it means that they're on a network's approved writer list. Whether based on the idea of people forming single-line queues outside a theater or someone taking a "cue" before doing something, this discriminatory practice exists, even though it's not supposed to, legally.

With a feature film, the sky could be the limit, profit-wise. TV movies or miniseries, however, have only a limited numbers of showings and sales of prepackaged videos and DVDs. Execs know how much revenue (roughly) will come in from commercials, so they set prices for the script and other things, and that's that. Whereas I generally advise writers not to try to get their scripts to actors without production companies, in television it can be a good idea.

The catch is, do those actors fit the "greenlight" list of a network? For example, a TV movie starring one of the stars of any hit show would probably guarantee high ratings and having them involved would help you get a TV movie made. They'll be jumping to features as quickly as possible, though—just look at what happened with the young cast of *That '70s Show*.

It's Not for Us

Full-length screenplays to debut a new TV series are not done much any more. "Backdoor pilots" are not completely dead, but normally only a simple one-hour episode or a half-hour sitcom is shot. Networks may fund a sample show and no more until they see what kind of ratings it pulls.

You can't see a "TV-Q" list because they supposedly don't exist. Unless you know someone inside a top agency or a network, try selecting actors with hit TV shows, comedy or drama, or those who repeatedly show up in TV movies. To find out how to reach an actor, try the site www.whoRepresents.com, which was free as I wrote this book. You can also contact the Screen Actors Guild (SAG) National office. You can find its contact information on the web at www.sag.org but don't try to locate an actor via the site. The Actors to Locate number is the one that you want to use to find out a SAG member's representative, at 800-503-6737. Callers from the eastern United States who cannot access the 800 number can call 212-827-1444.

When you reach an actor's agent, they probably won't want to hear from you unless you have a legitimate offer of paying work for the actor. So, simply say that you have a script perfect for the actor, and ask whether that actor has a production company. Remember, if you don't have an agent and the agency that you are calling also represents writers, it might take you on and make commissions on the actor, you, other people they put in the "package," and a 10 percent "packaging fee."

Again, it's tough to sell a screenplay to television. You'll most likely have to either sell your script to a production company that does TV movies, or find an agent to do that for you.

Plotting by Network or Channel

If you're serious about writing a movie for television, plot it by networks and the kind of films that they usually do. Even the main broadcast (free) networks have their own unique signatures. CBS, for example, has traditionally skewed to older audiences. Or, if you have a movie set in World War II, your agent might be able to sell it to the History Channel. You'll have to do some homework. Then you need to find an agent who sells to TV.

Hollywood Heat

YOUR NAME

If you hear the terms "CBSP" and "NBCP," they refer to the in-house production companies of the various networks, which increasingly make as many TV shows and TV movies as possible, cutting out the independent producer. (CBSP would be CBS Productions.) Many producers got rich in earlier years by supplying content to television, but when the "financial syndication" (a.k.a. "fin-syn") rules changed due to legislation, networks were able to get around what had formerly been in place to prevent monopoly abuse. The face of television (and the opportunities for TV moviemakers) dwindled until cable channels opened things up a little. Now cable channels make a lot more TV movies than the "free" U.S. networks.

Check your *TV Guide* or favorite TV website to see what movies are coming up that you think might be cousins to your screenplay. Watch at least the beginning, but definitely the end. As you've probably noticed, in the United States, credits on TV movies are shown at the end. You'll probably see only the logo and the name of the production company, or maybe several companies. If you're not sure what you saw, you can most likely find a listing for the film on www.imdb.com. Then you'll have to search through a print directory or use an online subscription service such as ShowBizData.com or hcdonline.com to look up the contact information for the company or companies that made the movie.

After you talk to them, if they won't take an "unsolicited submission" (roughly, something not submitted by an agent) ask them what agencies in town have the best TV writers. You might get a referral or at least some useful information.

You can learn about fall TV schedules in advance by subscribing to *Daily Variety* or *The Hollywood Reporter*. Both have extensive special issues that cover things like this. Each weekly print magazine has production charts as well, usually with contact information on relevant production companies, so that's another way to keep up on both what's being made and by whom.

The Hollywood Reporter, at www.hollywoodreporter.com, lists the entire fall schedule on its website via the "Charts button" (on the left when this was written). Other listings in the Charts area are only for paying subscribers. *Daily Variety* offers both film and TV production charts and is searchable. Click on TV Production under "Charts & Data" on the left at www.variety.com.

The Writers Guild has full TV production company contact information available to its members via its website at www.wga.org. There is a way to access the information even if you are not a member (and I won't tell you how) and non-SAG writers can write for network shows, but I won't go into that here. You need to read everything you can on the WGA site because it's a great education, and you may even be able to join as an associate member (read the site to find out how).

It's Not for Us _____

You can't do everything via free areas of the Internet. If you pinch pennies, you might choke your career. I tell writers repeatedly to subscribe to trade publications and online directories, or to buy print directories. I can't tell you how many times I've mentioned a certain production company and received an e-mail asking "Got a website link?" I don't answer.

Even though many cable channels are making their own movies now, it's still most likely that you'll need a credit or two before you'll be considered suitable for networks that aren't one of the top six (ABC, CBS, Fox, NBC, WB, and UPN). There are always exceptions to every Hollywood "rule." I know one writer on the East Coast who, via a manager in Santa Ynez, California (two hours north of Los Angeles), sold a feature to Disney and another to Showtime via actress Mimi Rogers's Millbrook Farms production company. As usual in Hollywood, anything can happen. TV movies sales usually occur via the normal channels and methods, and you generally must first prove yourself as a writer.

A Long Form Is Not What You Fill Out to Sell a Miniseries

Anything longer than a one-hour show on television is known around network circles as a "long form." Most people will never get a chance to write a miniseries in their lives, but I may have figured out a way you can do it. Try one of the following:

Skip's Tips

If you really want to write for television, read A Friend in the Business: Honest Advice for Anyone Trying to Break into Television Writing, by Robert Massello (Perigee, 2000) or The TV Writer.Com Book of Television Writing (2006), a book by veteran TV writer Larry Brody, available at his website, www.tvwriter.com. Larry also has quite a collection of writers and resources on his site.

1. Become as good a writer as Peter Barnes. He wrote *Arabian Nights* (2000), *The Magical Legend of the Leprechauns* (1999), and *Merlin* (1998), working with Hallmark Entertainment.

2. Become Simon Moore. He wrote *Dinotopia* (2001), *The 10th Kingdom* (2000), and the miniseries of *Gulliver's Travels* (1996).

3. Buy Hallmark Entertainment from Robert Halmi Sr. The company produced the minis listed with Peter Barnes, as well as dozens more programs. Find a popular legend or great story of mankind that has not yet become a miniseries, and film it.

4. Take over Stephen King's body and "field offers."

5. Write a thick, best-selling novel and field offers.

6. Forget fiction and take the Ken Burns route, making extended documentaries about great American subjects. Just don't pick one Ken Burns is doing.

7. Get to be a famous actor like Robert Duvall with your own production company, and make projects you care about. Even then, after you've been #1 in the ratings, you might still have your next project turned down. (Duvall and his producing partner wanted to do a miniseries on the Pony Express after #1 *Broken Trail*—it got turned down!)

You're not amused? I've insulted your original miniseries without even seeing it? Sorry. Maybe you've scripted a major historical event (a fave miniseries subject). The first miniseries was from a best-selling book, *QB VII*, in 1975. It seems like I've been hearing writers mention their original miniseries since that time. How many of them sold? As I recall, sadly, zero.

> **Script Notes** _____
>
> In England, "limited series" are made. The BBC or another channel will contract for a limited number of episodes (for example, 12) and then simply end the show. That idea used to be anathema to U.S. networks, but things are changing. After all, Americans having been adapting British shows successfully for decades. Why not use their programming habits, too?

The Reality of Reality Shows

The way television fluctuates from year to year, all the reality shows like *Survivor* may be gone from the airwaves by the time you read this book. I once wrote and produced "how-to" videos and I have scripted reality television show credits. Still, I didn't rush out to try to sell a reality show when they became hot.

What most people don't realize is that most of the popular reality shows in the United States were inspired by shows from other countries. The long-running *America's Funniest Home Videos* came about when Vin de Bona saw a popular show in Japan.

The one thing a network or production company will want to know is who will *deliver* the show week to week. If you're not a filmmaker or videomaker and can't do that, you'll have to connect with someone who can. People who make reality shows are often from news-gathering or "industrial" video backgrounds and are used to scrambling together coherent shows.

Depending on the show, you might use a dual-column format to write the scripts. Final Draft (www.finaldraft.com) created Final Draft A/V for this purpose. If you don't know what a dual-column format script looks like, check out the software on the site.

Unless you create a massive hit like *Survivor*, reality shows don't pay much more than a working person's wage. If you're one of the creators and the show does well, however, you're suddenly "in the club" in Hollywood and people will return your phone calls. It's likely that you will need to be a filmmaker, though. Martin Kunert and Eric

Manes are two of the hardest working people I know. Their *Fear* on MTV was the number-two show after *The Osbournes*, but I got the idea they viewed it as a stepping-stone to more feature films. Just like most TV shows, if you want to work in reality, the reality is you probably need to live in Los Angeles.

If you want to see an example of an amazing reality show company, take a look at 44 Blue Productions at www.44blue.com. They're a great success story.

If the Idea's That Good, Write a Book

In my first *Writer's Guide to Hollywood*, I surprised some people when one of the first chapters was titled "Maybe You Should Write a Book." That sentiment hasn't changed in the four years since I wrote the first edition of that guide to selling to Hollywood, and I kept it up with the *Ultimate Writers Guide to Hollywood* for Barnes & Noble, but I added "Or Maybe a Comic Book" because of the huge success of comics and graphic novels turned into Hollywood movies.

A long time ago, when I heard that New York publishers came out with around 50,000 books per year, with half of those fiction, I compared that to the roughly 500 movies made by Hollywood each year. That 500 compared to 50,000 means that you have roughly a 50-to-1 better chance of selling a story in book form than you do selling a screenplay. The publishing business has suffered a bit in the last couple of years, but it still offers better odds than does Hollywood.

About the same time I was writing the first edition of this book, I joined an online comedy writers group. One of the other members wrote a book about the troubles he was having with boys who wanted to date his teenage daughters. It was a great read, very entertaining. After I left the group, I learned that the book called *8 Simple Rules for Dating My Teenage Daughter* had become a TV series.

In books, you get to write about things such as characters' thoughts, which you can almost never portray onscreen. You can take your time developing the background of an area or a person, using paragraphs of words that would get your screenplay round-filed in Hollywood. And what do you think those actors do while they're waiting around on the set? A lot of them read books.

You might think that you have to publish a book in hardcover to get it taken seriously in Hollywood, but that isn't so. My three *You Solve It Mystery* books for young adults appeared only as paperbacks, and yet they were optioned by a media billionaire's production company in Beverly Hills. Even electronic books (e-books) have a chance.

When I received an e-mail stating that the electronic version of my *How To Write What You Want & Sell What You Write* was a finalist in the first annual Eppie Awards for electronic books, I began trading e-mails with the person who had notified me. Within weeks, she and her e-publisher were in negotiations about the film rights to one of her e-novels with a very high-profile Hollywood company.

If you become a successful screenwriter and a member of the Writers Guild of America and the WGA goes on strike, guess what? You can't work until the strike is settled, unless you are one of the producers of the movie or show. No one will complain about you writing and selling a novel. If your book's successful, you'll get the money from the book sale and the money for the film and TV rights, and you can probably talk them into letting you write at least the first draft of the screenplay. Hollywood respects authors. If you start off writing screenplays and then write books or novels, you might have a print editor say to you: "You write so cinematically!" I still laugh at that one.

I personally prefer writing novels, then movies, then TV. Given that, I'll probably end up a TV mogul. Maybe in my next life ....

The Least You Need to Know

- In most cases, only established writers write movies for television, but there are always exceptions.

- TV movies are rarely longer than 110 pages, with a seven-act structure that includes a "teaser" at the beginning.

- TV movies and one-hour episodes often have an A, B, and C story line. Some have a D story line as well.

- Networks insist on stars with "TV-Q" (popularity) to star in their films.

- Writers of TV movies are also judged by TV-Q and are either on an approved list or not.

- You will probably never get to write a miniseries unless you write a book first, which isn't a bad idea, anyway, because it vastly increases your odds of selling a big story.

Chapter 23

Filmmaking Your Way to Hollywood Success

In This Chapter

- ◆ Blame it on MTV
- ◆ Download logic
- ◆ Short films
- ◆ Filming your own scripts

More than 100 years after the beginning of film, we return again to the short film. In these digital days, it is possible to create your own short animations or movies then very quickly post them on a web page for the world to see. In December 1999, Matt Stone and Trey Parker, the creators of *South Park*, made a deal to create 39 original two- to five-minute animated shorts for Shockwave.com—a deal that they never could have made with a TV or film studio. They were given control and ownership that simply wouldn't have been allowed in traditional media. I created and wrote an original animated web show for a site called WireBreak.com during the dotcom boom of the late 1990s. I had high hopes that we could turn it into a cable TV series.

Then came the "dotcom meltdown" and WireBreak lost its financing and let go its staff. Ah well, it was a good payday and a fun project. And typical in Hollywood. Nevertheless, the viewing of short films on the Web is endlessly popular in 2008.

Blame It on MTV: How Short Films Affect Screenwriting

I'm old enough to remember the time in movie theaters when there was always an animated cartoon before the movie or double feature. The first movie experience that I can recall was a Woody Woodpecker cartoon in which Woody battled his nemesis, Buzz Buzzard, with some barrels of oil. Years later, when I first came to Hollywood, I got a hand-drawn portrait of Woody from the wacky woodpecker's creator, Walter Lantz. I still treasure it. Shortly after that, when I was making the rounds as a singer/songwriter in Los Angeles, I had an idea that I tried to talk some film-making friends into doing. I wanted to make short, funny musical films the length of an average song and convince movie theaters to play them. But no one was interested.

I was thinking in the wrong medium. A year later, Music Television (MTV) was launched on its own cable channel, and the era of the music video began. MTV offered something new and primal, with an emphasis on youth and sex. (A combination that generally always works.)

> **It's Not for Us**
>
> Even though you can learn a lot about putting together effective moving pictures by watching MTV, VH-1, and various things posted to YouTube.com, don't write specific song titles into a script or put them into you short film without permission. You might not be able to secure a license to use that song, and your effect might be ruined.

Whether or not you grew up watching MTV, it serves you well to study filmmaking styles of music videos. The people making and starring in those today will be helming and starring in feature films tomorrow. In 2002, the megasuccess of movies starring rappers, like *Barbershop* (Ice Cube) and *8 Mile* (Eminem) opened Hollywood's eyes. Britney Spears didn't do so well with *Crossroads* (2002), but she's not a rapper, is she?

Remember the exercise of writing a silent film to learn movie structure? Try that sometime with music videos. Turn on the DVR and turn off the volume. Record some videos that you think are particularly interesting, and then play them back slowly, writing scripts for them as you watch. The good ones will tell a story in pictures and jam a lot of information into a relatively small space. That's not the same as something on YouTube, which usually isn't done with nearly the detail of a music video.

If you want to succeed at writing action films, studying car commercials might be better, or any great sequence in a major action feature. Take a look at the heart-stopping chases in a film like *The Italian Job* or any of the *Bourne* movies and you'll see what I mean.

Downloads, Debuts, and Short Films

It used to be that the clear leader for short film exhibition was AtomFilms.com, but they've been eclipsed for some time now by YouTube.com. If you make a film and put it on YouTube and it catches on by viral marketing (meaning, people see it and pass it on), you could become very popular very quickly. Almost as important is linking a video to your page on MySpace.com or Facebook.com. If you have a lot of MySpace friends, and they link your video, and their friends link it, word gets around very quickly. Try going to MySpace and searching for any famous dead movie star you can think of—he or she probably has a page, because Hollywood execs have caught onto the vast marketing potential of MySpace.

On the Web, you can reach viewers that you simply never could have reached via previous media routes, except perhaps local public access cable channels. In the last edition of this book I said I liked iFilm because a former student of mine, Alexander Orrelle, won the Sundance Online Film Festival 2001 with his animated short "Freeware" and showcased on iFilm. He's since gone on to start the only animation company in Israel, www.crew972.com. These days, if he was showcasing something, he'd put it on YouTube.

Skip's Tips _____

If you decide to make a short film, make sure that you have someone involved who knows lighting well, and use a good cameraman. You also need the sound recorded as well as possible, separate from the camera if you can. If your script is good and you have an eye for talented actors, you could be on the road to Hollywood success, but not if your footage has terrible lighting and scenes are out of focus. And the sound better be clear, too.

Short Animated Films

When I began writing my series for WireBreak.com, I was faced with a dilemma. There was no preexisting format for short films. No *storyboard*, no template, no book, no article posted on the web. Should I write the script in the format of a 30-minute situation comedy for TV? Would an industrial (audiovisual) format, with dialogue on one side and action in the opposite column, be more appropriate?

Script Notes

A **storyboard** is a must if you make a film, short or long. Think in terms of the panels in a cartoon strip, and you have the right idea. With even rudimentary sketches of the scenes that you want in your film, you can much more easily show people what you're trying to achieve. Computer software also is available to create a storyboard. I've always liked Storyboard Quick (see www.powerproductions.com), but an even better product is FrameForge, billed as "the closest thing to shooting live." (See www.frameforge3d.com for info.)

I settled on standard feature-film screenplay format. When I turned in the scripts, no one complained or even mentioned the format, so I suppose that what I did was suitable. I was writing for presentation in the limited-action Macromedia Flash format, however, and there were some preexisting examples of that to learn from on the Web. Just know that when you write animation, the rules of screenplays change slightly:

◆ In animation, you are God. You write every single thing that happens on the screen, including angles that you think are necessary.

◆ In animation you also write the way your actors say their lines. An actor will go in the sound studio and record the lines, with (most likely) a director on hand to coax them into the best delivery.

◆ Although there is still a beginning, middle, and end, the longer the short film becomes, the more chance there is for a "B" story.

Due to the prevalence of 56K modems when I started writing my scripts for WireBreak.com, I decided the optimum length of shorts on the web was around two minutes. That was a manageable download for any speed Internet connection. Now, when most people have broadband Internet access, most shorts are two to seven minutes. I'm not sure why this length seems to prevail, but I suspect it has to do with the size of a video and storing it as, for example, a QuickTime movie.

Longer live-action shorts (with real actors) are generally made to be screened at film festivals in hopes of winning competitions. They are almost without variation under thirty minutes in length. To really get noticed as a filmmaker in Hollywood, you need to at least make a short live action film. (Unless, that is, you plan a career in animation.) When I started mapping out my own short films, I concluded that my mentors should be filmmaking stars of the early days of Hollywood, like Buster Keaton. In the United States, you can catch great silent films such as Keaton's *The General* on the American Movie Classics (AMC) channel in their "One Reel Wonders" segments.

Hollywood Heat

In June 2000, the Board of the Academy of Motion Picture Arts & Sciences (AMPAS) modified its eligibility rules. It stipulated, "A film cannot appear on the Internet before its theatrical release and be eligible for an Oscar." The logic was that an Internet transmission was more like a television broadcast than a feature film. To get around this hurdle, iFilm.com teamed up with AMC Theaters to create the iFilm@AMC Cinema Series theatrical showcase for short films. The arrangement to show a short twice daily for three consecutive days to a paying theater audience satisfied the AMPAS requirements for Academy Award eligibility and allowed short films to then be broadcast on the Internet. iFilm later partnered with Spike TV and continues to be very influential.

Filming Your Own Feature Script

If you want to create live-action films, I suggest the Apple route, simply because they're easier to use and FinalCut Pro is the favorite in Hollywood. Macs also tend to last a lot longer than PC systems, which makes up for their normal extra cost. You can learn to edit easily on a Mac starting with the free iMovie, and then moving up to Final Cut Express and finally Final Cut Pro Studio.

Of course, whether you choose PC or Mac, that's a debate for an entire other book. I wrote an entire chapter about digital filmmaking resources in my *Ultimate Writer's Guide to Hollywood*. I'll leave it to you to determine what kind of computer and digital equipment you use. Try to get professional advice before buying. You can get a broadcast-quality camera for a few thousand, but there might be someone whose camera you could borrow. If you don't know what the terms 24P or HD mean, you need to learn; look them up and get an education in what you

Skip's Tips

If you plan to make a short film, do yourself a favor and attend a digital video convention before you commit to any computer platform, software, or digital video camera. Manufacturers bend over backward to get their latest and greatest products on display and will eagerly answer all your questions. Plus, you'll be offered substantial convention-only discounts.

need to know. However you choose to shoot, anyone can quickly calculate that, for less than $10,000, you can have the equipment necessary to become a filmmaker. If you buy computer equipment and rent a camera, it's $5,000 or less.

Here are some online resources I'd suggest to help you get started in filmmaking:

♦ DV.com (www.dv.com), which has a newsletter and online forums.

♦ As they slowly take over the planet, Google offers interesting possibilities in the video department. Have a look at video.google.com and don't forget to click "About Google Video" at the bottom of the page.

♦ Independent Feature Project (www.ifp.org), with chapters in several U.S. cities, is the best organization of its kind for getting independent feature filmmakers started.

♦ Los Angeles Film School (www.lafilm.com) takes a "full immersion" approach in its one-year program to turn people with ideas into professional filmmakers.

♦ RESFEST Digital Film Festival (www.resfest.com) is a showcase of the best of digital filmmaking, touring major U.S. cities.

♦ *Videomaker* magazine (www.videomaker.com) offers a free monthly e-mail news-letter for video production enthusiasts and they put on conventions, too.

For a long time, I wrote a Hollywood advice column for writers in the UK. See www.scriptwritermagazine.com for details on what screenwriters and filmmakers are doing in England and Europe—you never know what you might pick up on that could be imported into your area. You can also check in with me at www.skippress.com with any other questions and I'll try to help you if I can.

The Least You Need to Know

♦ Hot new filmmakers usually start on YouTube these days, but on MTV you can study music videos and see cutting edge and usually expensive short films.

♦ One good way to learn to write effective short films is by taping music videos and watching them with the sound off as you try to write a script that matches the video.

♦ Two websites, YouTube and MySpace, are the best places to get your own short films noticed internationally.

◆ A great short film with enough exposure on the Web can quickly lead to a studio or network deal.

◆ In writing short animated films (and all animated films), you must write all the details, as if you are God creating a world.

◆ It's possible for anyone with the proper training to become a moviemaker; to be a good one they need a great script, even with short films.

Part 5

It's All in the Details

There are some things that you learn only by working in Hollywood. Herein lies a map through the Movieland jungle, replete with descriptions of snakes, quicksand, and ridiculous Hollywood practices. For example, you must use two brads (not three) when binding your script, and not just any brads, either. You'll learn about amateur technical mistakes, screenwriting gurus, and Tinseltown bozos. We'll give you the bona fide tour on selling scripts, tell you how to plan a screenwriting career, and in an article included on this book's CD, even cover working with a pesky co-writer. All aboard!

Chapter 24

Sweating the Small Stuff

In This Chapter

- Two brads, please
- Elegant simplicity
- No funky fonts
- Quirky perqers
- How old are you?
- Persistence wins

This chapter will (I hope) answer the dumb questions that you might not know to ask as a screenwriting "newbie." The idea is to provide you with elements of screenwriting etiquette that will keep you from being branded an amateur when you submit your script. I hope you'll read the whole thing. Of course, if you've been around Hollywood a while you might not need to, but then why would you read my book? You won't believe some of the things I'm going to tell you, but you might get a few laughs at Hollywood's expense.

On occasion, I get a chance to rewrite a screenplay. I've been so busy in the writing advice business that for several years I haven't had much time to write speculative screenplays. Nevertheless, I occasionally get a job rewriting one, which I welcome.

Because of all the people I hear from, which is sometimes 1,000 e-mails a week from around the world, I hear about current preferences at production companies and other things that I might not be privy to if I were simply submitting my work to established contacts. I've also spoken at the Screenwriters Expo as long as it has existed, and regularly moderate panels for Sherwood Oaks College in Hollywood. With all this going on, I pick up useful information, so in this chapter I'll try to share as many of these "inside tips" that I think you need.

Two Brads, Not Three

Here's the drill. Now that you have the drill, make three holes in your screenplay on the left side. Okay, I'm just kidding, but unless there is a sea change of major proportions in Hollywood screenplay protocol, print your screenplay only on three-hole 8½×11-inch paper, or use a three-hole punch to make three equally spaced holes along the left side of the script.

When you print out a completed screenplay on three-hole paper and you bind it with brads and start reading it, you'll see why you need to leave plenty of room on the left. If you don't, you'll find that reading along the left side is cramped. Pages read will not lay down easily. If you submit a script like that to a busy agent, development executive, or producer, they might get tired of holding down pages they've turned and chuck your script in the trash, the round file, the waste bin, the deep six.

The idea is to do everything that you can to conform to the standards so that readers think about only the content of your screenplay. You don't give them a chance to get distracted. Several companies make the brass fasteners, known in the business as *brads*. If the ones you use are brass-plated but feel flimsy, they bug people in Hollywood. Seriously, it's odd but true. The solid brass brads feel more substantial, so those are the ones that I use. In North America, brads can generally be found at any major office supply store, such as Staples or Office Depot, both of which have websites. I mention this last because many European screenwriters these days want to present their work to American studios with the "proper" binding on 8½×11-inch paper, not the two-hole punched A4 standard used in Europe. If you can't find what you need locally, I know you can find it via the Writer's Store, which has a great store in Los Angeles and a website full of supplies and resources at www.writersstore.com.

I'll tell you why to only use brads in a moment. Meanwhile, do not use any of the following to bind your screenplay:

- **Banker's clasps.** Long, thin, stainless steel fasteners often used as money clips.

- **Binder clips.** Black, hollow prism shape with two wire "handles."

- **Thick cardstock covers.** Particularly the kind with built-in prong fasteners.

- **Bulldog clips.** Silver spring-loaded clips with circular, thumb-size "handles."

- **Chicago screws.** Solid aluminum posts $\frac{3}{16}$ inch in diameter that screw into $\frac{3}{8}$-inch aluminum heads.

- **Ideal paper clamps.** Looks a bit like three steel triangles formed from one piece of wire.

- **Loose-leaf rings.** Metal rings that clasp together in the middle.

- **Prong fasteners.** Flat, stainless-steel strips with pointed ends that are held in place on the back with prong compressors.

- **Regal clips.** Thick, steel wire paper holders that roughly resemble the face of an owl.

- **Self-adhesive fasteners.** Identical to prong fasteners, with an adhesive strip on one side so that a compressor isn't needed.

- **Spiral binding.** Usually done with a clear front cover.

- **Solid-spine binding.** Favored by large offices with a plastic spine created by heat sealing.

- **String or anything else.** Use brass brads!

Skip's Tips

Your Name

If you're in doubt about what a "normal" Hollywood script should look like, printing and binding-wise, just ask a working screenwriter. Ask one of the mentors online at www.wga.org if you don't believe me. If you order a script from a place that sells screenplays, it will probably have a cardstock cover to protect it while shipping. Agencies use cardstock, too. Most working screenwriters I know, however, use no covers at all, just a title page.

You're probably thinking I'm nuts by now, but one of my clients sent me a screenplay that was written out in hand on lined paper, with each paper inside a plastic protector. The "script" was in a three-ring binder. I'd never seen anything like it. So here's another rule for you: although there are three holes in the paper, use brads only in the top and bottom holes. When people like a screenplay, they want to share it with others. Although you as the writer hold the copyright, meaning that they are supposed to ask your permission to photocopy your work, no one does.

They simply run it through the copy machine. To facilitate the ease of this practice, people in Hollywood like scripts with two brads and no fasteners. Whatever you do, don't use too long brads whose points slide around and snag clothes and other things.

Script Notes _____

A staple is a small piece of wire used to bind a synopsis or treatment in the upper-left corner. I'm sure you know what a staple is, but that's all you need to use. If you use brads, use a small one, ½ inch or so. School report binders with clear plastic covers are okay, too, for synopses and treatments.

You might assume that, to keep people from catching their fingers on the bent-over brads in the back, you should bend the pointed ends of the brads under. No. That makes the script lay funny on top of other scripts. You need the prongs to lie flat. Do *not* clip off the ends; those can cut fingers. I've found it useful to use a small rubber mallet: lay the script on a flat surface, and tap the brad prongs flat, hopefully without denting the round head on the front. Sounds goofy, I know, but most screenwriters I know use some variation of this method.

Even though I've mentioned logos and artwork being printed on title pages of network movie scripts and TV shows, leave them off your covers. Leave them off your title page. If you *must use* cardstock covers, use a light, nonobtrusive color. I use white when I use covers, but pale blue and light tan are also common.

Hollywood Heat _____

I wrote a script named *Gold Bricks* that got optioned immediately by an actress who wanted an old boyfriend to produce it. He said that he would, but he didn't. Back to selling my script, I headed over to the main script copying place in Hollywood, Barbara's Place, on Santa Monica Boulevard. I found a shiny gold plastic cover and had the shop print the title on each cover. I sent producer David Permut a copy, and he called after reading the first 40 pages. He liked the writing a lot, he said, even though he almost didn't read it because the crazy gold cover was very amateurish.

Whatever you do, make sure the script you submit looks fresh. If you've been in a producer's office and seen the title handwritten with a felt-tipped pen on the spine of the script, don't do that for them—let them do that. A producer would think that a spine-marked script had already been read elsewhere and that you didn't even do him the courtesy of printing up a new script. The last thing any producer wants to see is a script that's been "around town." That's why they'll ask, "Who's seen this?"

Simple Is Elegant

Hopefully my little thesis has shown you something about tastes in Hollywood offices. Now let's talk about the people. The development executives that I know tend to dress casually but conservatively. The women wear chunky black dress shoes with low heels. The men wear conservative but hip shoes (I've never seen any wingtips). Yes, even Bruno Maglis like O. J. Simpson wore, if they can afford them. Offices may be piled high with scripts, but they're generally fairly neat and the furniture has simple lines. Producers' offices can be quite the opposite, very colorful and eccentric. It's not uncommon to see expensive jukeboxes or video parlor games against a wall.

With development executives, the overall impression that I'm generally left with is that they have so much going on in their lives—so many scripts to read and so much "coverage" to generate—that they disdain anything out of the ordinary. Tricks and gimmicks generally don't go over too well. If you're thinking of putting on a grizzly-bear suit to hand-deliver your script about a man chased by a grizzly bear, with a blood-red grizzly paw print on the cover, good luck. Your script probably won't get read, and a security guard might shoot you. (Well, probably not, but you won't make friends.)

For all the offensive material it occasionally produces, Hollywood is very much about making the right impression. That's why authors get more respect; they're "serious" writers. Every time I've been in an office to pitch a script, I've seen books that are under consideration stacked on shelves off the floor. Scripts—even those from major agencies, which you might assume are the best—are piled all over, often against a wall on the floor. Scripts that have received great coverage or scripts that the company has in production or is putting in production will be on the executive's desk. Their priorities, like anyone's, are based on what they consider important. For some reason in Hollywood, many people think books and novels are more "important" than most scripts, even though a script would have to be written to make a movie. The cachet of a book (nonfiction) or novel (fiction) is that they are "market-proven" just by the fact of being published. If you send in a script that is properly formatted, the right length, in a plain envelope, with the receiving person's name spelled correctly, you're more likely to be viewed as "could become important." (That's assuming they're expecting your script.) If you try a bunch of tricks, importance probably won't happen.

Even though Hollywood puts wild and crazy images on the screen, and celebrity antics fill the tabloids, screenwriters breaking in generally must follow very conservative rules of production-company etiquette when your work is presented for the first time.

Even when companies are prosperous and the men can afford expensive suits, they're usually all Armani. And expensive designers make the simple black dresses that the women wear. Conformity and uniformity are constants in Hollywood. When you've seen enough of it, you realize just how much it is show business.

That also applies to writers who appear at "pitch" events. I've seen people show up wearing ten-gallon cowboy hats, dressed like mountain men and Heidi the Swiss maid. It usually doesn't work (despite how Diablo Cody was dressed when she won the Oscar for *Juno* in 2008). The usual impression is "kook who can't write." The only exception I know to that is John Milius, who would show up at meetings with crossed rifle belts, like a bandito from an old movie. But he was selling scripts in the 1970s and 1980s so that doesn't count.

When you get your first chance to meet someone in person, you can impress him or her by simply being businesslike. Just about anyone can afford to print a simple script on white paper and send it in a manila envelope. (No, they don't insist that it come in a manila envelope; just don't draw little doodles to get attention.) And it's generally assumed that beginning screenwriters fit the profile of the "starving writer."

It's Not for Us

Even if you spell people's names right—a big thing in Hollywood—you never know what might be seen as bad taste. I once sent a Mesoamerican novel by Laura Seraso that I thought would make a great movie and video game to Moctesuma Esparza, famous for *Selena, Walkout,* and other Hispanic-themed films. The book had a great villain named Tlapalel who was based on a real historical character. When Mocte called me I said, "So you liked it?" Not hardly. "Skip!" he began, "My son is named Tlapalel!" His historical interpretation obviously didn't match that of the author.

If you get a chance to meet someone in person, this emphasis should be on your writing. I try to dress neatly and cleanly, and almost always casually. Your grooming is your own business; if you're selling a script called *Megadeath Below Hell*, you might want to wear appropriate clothing. Even then, most people I know prefer fresh breath. If you're ever in question about which way to go in Hollywood, think simple. Scripts from very successful writers are very simply presented. Good writers show up for meetings on time, are usually soft-spoken (until they start passionately presenting a story), and don't do anything to make other people's lives more complicated. The "simple is elegant" approach works.

The Funky Fonts Don't Fly

These days, so many fonts are available for computers that we have complete software programs that do nothing but manage fonts. Just as I once used a shiny gold cover to try to make a script stand out, I've seen many beginning screenwriters use a special font on title pages or within a script, in an attempt to make something look prominent. Don't do it—you'll just look amateur.

Use Courier 12 pitch. I know, I know. New York looks bolder. You prefer Times or Times New Roman. Some people have given me long dissertations about Courier being a dinosaur from the days of the typewriter, but that's the point. They'll tell me that they prefer reading pages that have a justified right margin, so why can't they do that with character description? I've heard it all. The fact is, readers like scripts that look like they could have been typed on a typewriter (and some readers will ask, "what's a typewriter?"). Courier New is just fine, if your program doesn't have Courier. Any Courier font is generally okay.

Never, ever, have I heard a professional, working screenwriter question the use of Courier 12 pitch. I have rarely seen a sold script that was written in anything but Courier 12 pitch. People will tell me about John Irving's script for *Cider House Rules* being written in the Helvetica or *American Beauty* by Alan Ball being written in Times. So what? Both of those writers were known entities; beginning screenwriters are not. Don't rock the boat, use Courier.

There isn't some Courier cabal that gets a kickback every time someone uses that font. Properly formatted screenplays in Courier 12 generally work out to a minute a page, in screen time. Properly formatted manuscript pages generally work out to a certain number of words per page, double-spaced (250 per page is my general rule). Some purists will explain that Courier 12 yields ten (10) characters per horizontal inch and six (6) lines per vertical inch and Courier New doesn't, so you shouldn't use the latter. Maybe so, but no one will reject your script for using Courier New, and some software programs have their own particular version of Courier. Close is good enough.

Shane Black and Other Quirky Perqers

I once belonged to a writing workshop that met every month at some NBC offices in Burbank. The television network didn't officially sanction the workshop, but that didn't stop us from calling it the NBC Writers Workshop. Maybe that's why a lot of top names would show up to give us tips about breaking into Hollywood.

One night, Shane Black arrived to talk about screenwriting. I wondered what an actor was doing talking to us about writing scripts. I knew Black only from his appearance in *Predator* (1987). I loved that film, and I also knew the executive producer, Laurence Pereira. I didn't read the trades in those days, so I didn't know that Black had just sold two scripts that would be made into films in 1987, *The Monster Squad* and a little something call *Lethal Weapon*, which would make a superstar of Mel Gibson. With sales that followed, Black quickly became one of the highest-paid writers in Hollywood, receiving up to $4 million for a script.

I spoke to Black briefly that night about *Predator*. When he said he'd sold *Lethal Weapon* to a director I knew, Richard Donner, I was intrigued, so I began following his career. I wasn't the only screenwriter interested in what Black was writing. I began reading the trades after the NBC Workshop, and one day my eyes bugged when I saw that Black had sold a script for $1.75 million (the biggest sale in 1990). I got one of his scripts and read it. The same self-deprecating humor that I'd seen that night at NBC was all over some pages.

What Black did differently was throw in descriptive paragraphs that spoke directly to the reader. For example, he might describe a house lavishly and throw in a line such as, "The kind of house I'm going to run out and buy after you buy this script." Some of the descriptions of the character Riggs in *Lethal Weapon* were darkly amusing, given the suicidal tendencies of that character, but when Black "spoke" to the reader, it made you empathize with the script and wonder about the screenwriter personally. The problem for screenwriters who tried to emulate this style was that Black originated it. It was his own unique voice, which was refreshing to readers who had never seen such a thing. Plus, Black is a fine screenwriter, so his quirkiness was not bothersome. His descriptive method didn't always work for others who didn't have his writing skills.

> **Skip's Tips**
>
> A writer's "voice" comes about for two reasons: writing and rewriting enough words to learn the craft, and certainty gained due to other's appreciation of your work. Rather than attempt to emulate other's styles, keep writing and rewriting until your own uniqueness blooms. Have faith; it will.

That's the way it is in Hollywood, or any other major industry, for that matter. If you're good enough, you get the perquisites, or "perqs." Hot screenwriters will be granted their eccentricities just like a movie star. With his script *Adaptation*, Charlie Kaufman took oddity to new heights, creating his brother "Donald" and inserting his own personal struggles into an adaptation of a hit novel called *The Orchid Thief*. Kaufman happens to be a hilarious and very talented writer, though, so don't try him at home. Writers with less talent may not be as readily appreciated, no matter how cute their quirks.

Every writer wants to do something to stand out, to make a mark, or even to get very rich. Just about anyone who arrives in Los Angeles can find a way to get in a door for a meeting, but smarmy comments in a script or dressing up in a bandoleer and sombrero won't guarantee success. You'll have to back it up with the writing—the plot, dialogue, and character development in your screenplay. Remember, every time you read about some eccentric Hollywood person or event, it's in print because it's news that sells newspapers and gets people to watch TV. For 99 percent of all screenwriters, only the script matters.

Hollywood and Ageism

If you're entering a screenwriting career later in life, meaning after the age of 30, you might hear rumors that older writers find it hard to get work or sell scripts. Unfortunately, in television (where most WGA writers work), that can be true, particularly in situation-comedy land. You may recall that I mentioned the "older writers" case in the television chapter. If you're groaning right about now, let me share with you what I've observed about feature writers. I'm over the age of 40, but I've never had anyone ask me my age except in the book business. It has just never come up.

I know of a writer who sold a screenplay to Will Smith's company, Overbrook Entertainment, at age 58. He said that no one ever mentioned his age. In 2006, a woman in New York had her first film made at age 84. This is rare, however; usually older people who sell scripts have been working in Hollywood a long time.

People who been working in Hollywood for decades like Alvin Sargeant (writing *Spider Man* movies in his 70s) defy the "older people don't work" mantra via sheer talent, but I've seen people break into the business at an age much later than most people think possible. One of the people who contacted me after reading my *Writer's Guide to Hollywood* was a woman in her 50s living in Santa Fe, New Mexico. She was an excellent writer, and I tried to help open some doors for her. On her own, though, she got a job writing some episodes for a Cartoon Network series. And that's why I love the Internet. In cyberspace, with e-mail, no one can tell how old you are. The essences of the ideas come across. You can send someone a script and let it stand on its own, with no consideration for your age on the other end.

Even on the phone, it's sometimes hard to tell someone's age. And you know what? In the end, it really doesn't matter. If it's on the page, it'll make the stage. Will Smith bought a script from someone old enough to be his grandfather, and Smith has been more successful at the box office in recent years than any other actor. If you're an older screenwriter, don't worry about Hollywood ageism. A lot of older writers do not work because they are inflexible about their ideas. They refuse to grow with the culture.

You probably know of the very popular social networking Website, Facebook.com. Odd as it might sound, people over 50 have signed up for it and MySpace in massive numbers. Approximately one-third of Facebook users are between 35 and 54, while around 40 percent of MySpace users are in the same age category. Like MySpace, Facebook is very effective for networking yourself with other creative people.

> **Skip's Tips** _____
>
> If you're a writer of grand-parent age looking to break in, I'd advise you to write films or TV movies that kids love. It's one area of Hollywood that doesn't seem to care so much about age. I've repeatedly done studies on this over the years and sent the results to any-one who requested a look.

As the Baby Boomer generation gets older, they are much less likely to judge by age. The Boomers' generation was the one that loved a Roger Corman movie called *Wild in the Streets*, whose big line was "Don't trust anyone over 30." Now, with most successful producers a part of the Baby Boomer generation and gray all over their heads, they don't feel that way any more. And when you have great older actors like Robert Duvall defying the odds and coming in #1 with a TV miniseries, people pay less attention to age. Just write a great script, and people won't even look up to see the wrinkles in your face until they read "THE END."

Persistence Makes Perfect

I could write about Hollywood "rules" until the last film in the last theater on Earth runs the final credits, and there would still be successful exceptions, even to the Courier 12-pitch screenplay standard. You can read about rules, talk about rules, and listen to rumors until your eyes are permanently bloodshot. It's better to spend your time perfecting your craft and learning how the film industry works when you're not writing.

I met a writer named Dwayne A. Smith after he sold a script called *Joe's Last Chance*. I'd read about the sale in *Variety* and noticed that he popped up on an Internet news-group that I frequented. When we traded e-mails, I shared a story with Dwayne that I'd heard about Burt Reynolds and Clint Eastwood. Supposedly, they'd both gotten fired from their contracts at the same studio on the same day. They began comparing notes after they both became superstars and figured out that it had taken each of them about 15 years to make it. Dwayne said that's how long it took him, too, and he added that he'd been reading my posts on the newsgroup for years. On his Wordplay site (www.wordplayer.com), Terry Rossio said he quit worrying about making it when he realized that anyone in just about any profession usually takes at least 10 years to establish his or her career. While I believe that cream rises to the top, that doesn't necessarily mean that someone always skims it off and consumes it. Keep writing and perfecting your voice, and someday you'll be singing your own opera. But you have to be in it for the long haul. Hopefully, if you know the etiquette and protocols, you can get there faster.

The Least You Need to Know

- Use only solid brass brads to bind your three-hole punched script—one in the top hole, one in the bottom, none in the middle—and no washers to secure the brads.

- Screenwriters breaking in should generally know and follow very conservative rules of production company etiquette.

- Use only Courier 12 pitch type in your screenplay. Courier New or another type of Courier is also okay.

- Highly successful screenwriters such as Charlie Kaufman have unique voices in their screenplays, but they are allowed such "perqs" only because they are great screenwriters.

- Hollywood ageism exists, but talent, persistence, young thinking, and the use of the Internet all help overcome it.

- Often enough, it can take a decade or longer to make it in Hollywood, so for cream to rise to the top, it must be persistent.

Chapter 25

Fixing Amateur Technical Mistakes

In This Chapter

- ◆ Flashbacks, anyone?
- ◆ Talking on the phone
- ◆ Voiceovers and other noises
- ◆ Cute usually isn't
- ◆ Who needs actors and directors?

Now that we've gone over some of the ins and outs of dealing with Hollywood, let's talk about some of the amateur mistakes that will get your script rejected. I've read a lot of scripts in my time and at least once a month I'll consult on someone's script. I don't know why people make the same mistakes except for simply lacking information. So if you ever send me a script to read, I hope that your reading this book first allows me to think only of the great story you're telling.

I've taught writing at all levels, from grade schoolers in small towns to post-college courses at the UCLA Extension Writers Program (the largest of its kind in the world) and online at WritersWrite.com (at the time I taught, the largest website for writers in the world). And with my own online screen-writing course available on three continents, I've pretty much seen it all. Beginning writers seem to follow the same patterns over and over. If they don't want to write screenplays, they generally start off with children's books, poetry, or short stories. If they write screenplays, those are usually jammed with dialogue and are better suited for the stage, not a motion picture theater.

There's a lot to learn about screenwriting. After 15 years of writing and selling scripts and all sorts of other things, I'm only now beginning to feel like I can consistently write a screenplay that I'll love. That's why I hope to help you avoid clichés and keep your script from being tossed in the trash.

> **It's Not for Us**
>
> A major thing to keep in mind with any script is the exchanges of dialogue. Sit down with someone you like some time and mentally clock how much is said by one person before another says something. Similarly, if one character onscreen talks for too long, it leaves the other actors standing around with nothing to do.

Flashbacks and Foolish Foibles

I hope that, when you outlined your script, you did at least a rudimentary background sketch of all your main characters. I hope that you worked out their "back story" well enough that you know how they will react in almost any given situation, often in ways that the audience does not expect. If you did not do this you might find yourself writing a lot of flashbacks to "explain." Instead of doing that, when preparing your script, try considering the following elements to better understand the characters you're writing:

> **Skip's Tips**
>
> Buy yourself a baby names book, whether you expect to be a parent or not. Or, get some software that displays the meaning of names. You'll come up with characters whose names suit them. For example, "Skip" is a Norwegian word for a leader on a ship.

- **Name.** Come up with a full name, and delve into the origin of those names. A well-named character affects audiences on a primal level. Did you know that *Luke*, as in "Luke Skywalker," means "light"?

- **Nickname.** If your character is Southern and a big person, chances are good that someone called them "Tiny" at some point. A girl nicknamed "Darling Sugar" tells us that she's probably spoiled.

- **Position in family.** A middle child has a very different outlook on life than a firstborn or "baby" of a family.

- **Family stability.** If the character's family moved a lot in youth, it might make the character do anything for security.

- **Religion, or lack of it.** Don't always go with the standard religions. The superstitious Santeria-following slugger in *Major League* was a breath of comic fresh air.

- **Phobias and fixations.** Things that your character is "stuck on" can be a tremendous source of entertainment. For example, the father's constant use of Windex in *My Big Fat Greek Wedding*.

- **Hidden past.** This could be a hidden former identity, or simply some past embarrassment that your character doesn't want revealed.

- **Sexual preferences or habits.** You should know this, whether we see them having sex or not. *Wedding Crashers* and many hit comedies revolve around this area.

- **Undisclosed agenda.** If you don't know what each main character wants most out of life during the time period of your screenplay, you've done yourself a disservice.

I'm sure you can think of many other items to list. What's important is that you have a storehouse of information on your characters that you do *not* put onscreen. Most beginning screenwriters don't take enough time to work things out before they write. Thus, they "think on paper," using flashbacks to reveal troubling elements of a character's past. If they already knew their characters intimately, they would figure out a way to reveal specifics about the person without bouncing back to the past. How? We'd learn about characters via their *actions*.

Expert handling of flashbacks is done with a very specific purpose, often to deal with a single important element of the story. When they are done well, as in *Rashomon*, *Somewhere in Time*, or *Memento*, flashbacks build to an emotional crescendo that is resolved in the last act. When they are not done well, they can confuse or even lose the audience. That's why experienced filmmakers often use black-and-white or sepia tones in flashbacks, so the audience can easily follow.

I've rarely seen a beginning writer handle flashbacks well. Simply writing "FLASH-BACK" as a script direction might make it clear for the reader what's going on, but the person in the movie theater doesn't have that luxury. Try to write without them so that the flow of your story is not broken up.

My favorite example of how one long flashback can fill in a satisfying story hole is the Paris sequence in *Casablanca* (1942). If you haven't seen it, do. If you've never seen a flashback-within-a-flashback-within-a-flashback see if you can find a video or DVD of *Passage to Marseille* (1944) directed by Michael Curtiz. Curtiz directed *Casablanca* and most of the cast of that movie return in *Passage to Marseille*, which again stars Humphrey Bogart. Moving on up the timeline, the extensive flashbacks in *Angel Heart* are done well, and *Reservoir Dogs* shows Quentin Tarantino knows how to do flashbacks.

A semi-flashback story structure that is easy for the beginner is something you'll hear referred to as a "frame narrative" or "bookending." I call it a circle. The beginning and ending of the movie "frame" the story and serve as bookends to support it. *Sunset Boulevard* used this technique, and so did *American Beauty*. Both of those films had a narrator who spoke at the beginning and end and the whole film was told from the narrator's memory. It's a structure that audiences seem to enjoy. Technically, a flashback is a vision seen in a flash and then we are visually slammed back into the present action. Hence the "flash." If it's quick, you don't have as much risk of losing the audience.

Hollywood Heat

Even as a movie title, a flashback can be troublesome. *Flashback* (1990) seemed like a clever idea, telling the story of yuppie FBI agent John Buckner (Kiefer Sutherland) rousting 1960s hippie radical Huey Walker (Dennis Hopper) out of the underground to bring him to prison. Unfortunately, it came off like a watered-down version of *Midnight Run* (1988). When well-known critic Leonard Maltin reviewed it, he gave it a very low rating, a ½ star.

Don't You Just Love Watching People Talk on the Phone While They're Eating?

Here's an exercise for you. If you live with someone, sit down some time and watch them talk on the phone. See if you can stand it for at least 30 seconds. (If they're naked, it doesn't count.) I'll bet you won't make it 20 seconds, unless you're a part of the conversation they're having. Nevertheless, I see scenes in screenplays all the time with people having long conversations on the phone. Thankfully, I don't see antiquated techniques like a split-screen of both sides of a conversation at once any more, unless it's a spoof of older films.

Like a flashback, unless you have a very good reason for having a phone conversation in your script, …

A. Keep it very short.

B. Leave it out altogether.

C. Come up with some unique presentation that we haven't seen before.

The extensive use of cell phones has helped revive this stagnant device; letting you do things like taking your detective character throughout a crime scene while talking on the phone, but beginners often use phone scenes to convey information that could be better done with moving pictures. Because you can be mobile while talking on a cordless phone and even more so with a cell phone, I don't mind seeing them used onscreen. When you have constant phone conversations by someone in a fixed place, however, it can kill the flow of the movie.

Nevertheless, on occasion someone finds an interesting way to use a phone call that is riveting. When the killer calls in the *Scream* movies and we hear his menacing voice, we share the terror of his victims. And *Phone Booth* (2003) was an entire movie built around a phone conversation!

Try going over your script to see if you can have your character learn something or discover something *without* a phone, even a cell phone. After all, driving while talking on a cell is now illegal in some U.S. states. Must you use "I gotta take this" to get a character out of a scene? I'll bet you can come up with richer ideas.

Skip's Tips

The word "villain" comes from the word *villa*, or "country estate." Maybe that's why so many movie villains are rich. Remember that all villains consider themselves to be the hero of their movie. Actors love to play bad guys because they're generally so much less restrained. Who is more fun to play, the lady owner of the Dalmatians whose name you don't remember, or Cruella de Ville?

Now here's another staple of movies, particularly in ensemble films such as the *American Pie* movies: eating scenes. One screenwriting guru, UCLA Screenwriting Department cochairman Richard Walter, hates watching people onscreen having conversations over dinner and advises against writing them. When I first read that bit of advice, I wanted to agree, but then I thought of a number of great eating scenes I'd enjoyed.

The stimulating *My Dinner with André* (1981), directed by Louis Malle, took place almost completely over dinner in a nice restaurant. And who could forget the "Who do you and your girlfriend make out to, Mathis or Sinatra?" conversation in *Diner?* Or the food fight in the cafeteria in *Animal House* (1978)? Or Bill Murray's repeated attempts to seduce Andie MacDowell in the restaurant in *Groundhog Day* (1993)? Or the lack of a tip that leads to splitting a winning lottery ticket in *It Could Happen to You* (1994, a.k.a. *Cop Tips Waitress $2 Million*)? Or the alien hatchling popping out of someone's stomach during a meal on the mining ship in *Alien* (1979)? And who could forget *American Pie* movies where they do other things with food. You get the point, don't you?

And how about the all-time funniest dinner conversation, when Meg Ryan showed Billy Crystal how women can easily fake a convincing orgasm in *When Harry Met Sally* (1989)? I still laugh out loud when I think of how the director, Rob Reiner, cut to his mother, Estelle Reiner (playing "Older Woman Customer"), at the end of the scene so that she could say to the waiter, "I'll have what she's having!"

> ### It's Not for Us
>
> Don't settle for a meal scene in your movie until you have one that is memorable. In this day of inexpensive digital movies, it's easy to write in a dinner conversation, but if it isn't unique, you might feed your audience a sleeping pill. For example, in the hilarious *Dude, Where's My Car?* (2000) the funniest scene in the film ("And then?") came when the main characters were simply trying to order drive-through Chinese.

For every Hollywood "rule" that someone puts forth, people can come up with numerous examples of something opposite working onscreen. With all the scenes I just mentioned, there's a central reason why they worked. Just know this: if you write great enough scenes, you can some times make your own rules.

Memorable meal conversations in movies speak to the central issue of the film.

My Dinner with André was about having a deep, earnest conversation about the examination of life. Perfect to do over dinner.

Diner was about the coming of age of a group of friends in Baltimore, Maryland, in 1959. The singers used to put their girlfriends in the mood for love fits the theme of the film.

The food fight in *Animal House* is perfectly illustrative of a bizarre, out-of-control fraternity on a college campus.

As Bill Murray keeps repeating the same day in *Groundhog Day*, he is able to glean information from Andie MacDowell (who isn't in on knowledge of the time loop) that makes her like him. What it takes for Murray's miserable character to become likable is the theme of the film.

It Could Happen to You, a.k.a. *Cop Tips Waitress $2 Million*, based on a true story, is about selfless giving and values being more important than money.

The plot of *Alien* revolves around a bizarre species that parasitically destroy human life, so a hatchling ripping out the man's stomach is a microcosm of the aliens' overall plan.

When Harry Met Sally stems from the age-old question of whether an attractive man and an attractive woman can simply be friends without evolving into a sexual relationship. When Meg Ryan fakes her orgasm so convincingly, it invites Billy Crystal to think of her sexually, but it also adds to his confusion over what their long-term friendly relationship is really all about.

Waitress, a charming 2007 independent feature, had various pies the main character made as a running commentary on relationships in the movie, and it largely took place in a diner.

I think that memorable meal conversations in movies work only when they speak directly to the central issue of the film. Maybe that's because the stomach is central to a human being's survival.

If you can come up with a better idea about how to make a dinner conversation scene work in a movie, I'll buy you dinner. Of course, you'll have to convince me first.

Voiceovers as Sleep Aids

Just like the ubiquitous phone conversation, I often see *voiceovers* abused in screenplays from beginners. Why does this happen? They probably saw a lot of Disney nature films on the Disney Channel. It's sort of the movie equivalent of the children's stories that beginners serve up in some of my writing classes. When you think of what purpose a voiceover serves, isn't it usually as a narrator? That's the only time I use it.

The exception may be when you transition between scenes, and someone from the previous scene is still talking in *voiceover* (V.O.) as the new scene begins. That's an editing device that smoothly furthers the flow of the story. If using these things doesn't flow naturally, I'd recommend that you merely cut cleanly between scenes, with no dialogue carryovers.

A number of classic films use a narrator voiceover in opening the film with it and then coming back to it at the end. Examples are *To Kill a Mockingbird* (1962), *Sophie's Choice* (1982), *Stand by Me* (1986), *The Shawshank Redemption* (1994), and *Big Fish* (2003). All those films had something in common. They originated in literature, with two of them from Stephen King.

> **Script Notes** _____
>
> A **voiceover (V.O.)** is usually when a character is speaking but is not physically present in the scene. The notation **off-screen (O.S.)** usually denotes that the person is physically present but cannot be seen within the framed shot. Either one should be typed just to the right of the character's capitalized name, as in "SKIP (V.O.)" or "SKIP (O.S.)." Most screenwriting formatting software lets you add them automatically. A variation to these is when the character is present and commenting on actions he or she performed or is performing; in this case the person is almost always the narrator of the story.

They're also all coming-of-age stories narrated by someone looking back at memorable, life-changing events in their own life or someone with whom they were close. Novels are generally deeper and more thoughtful than screenplays, and using a voiceover to open and close a film helps convey thoughtfulness, particularly when the story is told in reflection. A circle tale told well leaves us with the feeling that things work out all right after all.

Another type of effective voiceover is in film noir, such as the Humphrey Bogart movies derived from Raymond Chandler novels. The hard-boiled detective's ironic commentary was used so much, however, that using it in a film now almost seems like satire. *L.A. Confidential* opened with a great voiceover by Danny DeVito, but he got whacked not long into the movie! If you can find a way to make voiceover work, as in the original *Blade Runner*, go for it, but you'll probably run into people who want to take it out of the script.

> **Hollywood Heat** _____
>
> If you don't have a DVD player, you might not have seen the Ridley Scott director's cut of *Blade Runner* (1982). Unlike the theatrically released version, in the DVD the voiceovers of Harrison Ford as the detective Deckard are gone. The missing narration is compensated by more moving pictures. For example, when we see the advertising slogan on a passing blimp while Deckard waits for a seat at a noodle bar, it's longer than in the original. Of course, I enjoyed Ford's resonant voice narrating the denouement as he flew out of the city with the beautiful android played by Sean Young. How about you?

Some films by their very nature call for a narrator who will appear at appropriate points throughout the film—a movie with animals and kids, for example. When a voiceover is used in that context, it's pretty much an acceptable convention. You'll have to use your own judgment on how you go about using or not using voiceovers. If you use it too much, readers will think you're an amateur. How much is too much? I don't know; I haven't read your script.

Cute Is for Babies

I wrote a script once about a Swedish au pair coming to live with a professional southern California couple who needed a caregiver for their small child. I was inspired after meeting some beautiful Swedish au pairs at a party one Christmas. They told me that there were thousands of young women from Sweden doing this kind of work in the Los Angeles area. My movie centered on misunderstandings that arose with the husband working at home in his garage recording studio and his lawyer wife away at the office. Temptation, temptation.

I had the script completed four days after I got the initial idea. *The Swedish Touch* was mostly set in one house, making it cheap to shoot, and the number of characters was minimal. The screenplay never got filmed, even with successful actors like Linda Blair attached to it. I never figured out why until several years later. Shortly after I wrote the *Writer's Guide to Hollywood*, I began contacting producers, after several years away from the business. I found a producing team who liked the script. They wanted to change the punk rock band in the original script into rappers, which made their lust for the beautiful au pair even more controversial. I tried to revise the script, but never seemed to get it just right. Then one day I realized what was wrong.

The baby boy, Bryan, was the culprit. Here I was writing a sex comedy about lust and temptation and cross-cultural sexual mores, and right in the middle of it was a small baby boy that the au pair looked after.

That just didn't work. Bryan was cute, with very minimal lines, but he didn't belong in that environment. And without the kid—who managed to get moved to Grandma's house so that he was out of the way at certain times—who needs an au pair? So there went the movie. No one ever brought up this point to me, but I'm sure that I'm right about it.

It's Not for Us

PASS In an effort to be different, you might try mixing up genres and keeping your script as unpredictable as possible. Different is appreciated in Hollywood. Too different is not. If your screenplay could not be placed on an established category shelf in a video store, you're probably in trouble. It's best to learn to paint within the lines before you go wandering around outside them.

It's one thing to write a movie such as *Baby Boom* (1987) in which yuppie executive Diane Keaton has to change her lifestyle to accommodate an inherited baby. That movie was cute (even though it was a box office disappointment). Unlike my script, no elements of the movie clashed with the presence of the baby. When Keaton falls for a man from the country played by Sam Shepard, it's warm and fuzzy, like a Rock Hudson and Doris Day movie from the 1950s.

Since then, I've realized that writing for a definite age range is the best way to go. Also, you need to be consistent throughout with a theme. If you're going to write a family movie, you need to keep certain elements (like naked au pairs) out of it.

Cute is for babies, not sex-charged young professionals. Just as you can get in trouble mixing genres, inappropriate elements can mess up your movie.

Who Needs Actors and Directors, Anyway?

When your script goes into production, if you remain the main writer on the project, you'll experience a reading of the screenplay. If it's the first time you've heard your screenplay read out loud, you'll be stunned at how they laugh at things that you didn't mean to be funny and don't get jokes that you think are a scream. Scene transitions that are perfectly logical to you will seem confusing to others. Actors will ask about their character's motivation in scenes, or maybe the entire screenplay.

Skip's Tips

If you've never taken an improvisational acting class, you should. If you can't find an improv company in your town, read *Improvisation for the Theater: A Handbook of Teaching and Directing Techniques (Drama and Performance Studies), 3rd Edition,* by Viola Spolin, edited by Paul Sills (Northwestern University Press, 1999). Writers need to understand how actors think; this book will help.

Before that happens, the director will give you notes on your script and suggest changes. Some directors will even try to steal the project from you entirely and ask the producer to do a rewrite. (I had a production completely ruined like that not long ago, despite the fact that I introduced the director to the producer!)

Or, you might write such a good script that no one wants to mess with it. They'll defer to you, compliment you on your work, and ask what you're working on next. They'll see you as a long-term asset. And you will be a one in a million.

At some point in your screenwriting career, you'll probably wonder what kind of crazy pills actors and directors take, where they get them, and why they swallow so many. Get over it. Filmmaking is the most collaborative art on Earth, and unless you write, produce, direct, and star in your own films, like Woody Allen, it's unlikely that you'll be able to get around the reality of working with others. That's why I reassure writers who get peeved at some note from a reader or development executive trashing their script.

It's all part of the collaborative process. I'm constantly reminded of that old Native American saying: "Sometimes you eat the bear, sometimes the bear eats you." If you let the process get to you and get angry about things you don't like, that's bear teeth clamping down.

There are 13 letters in the word *collaboration*, but that's unlucky only if you make it so. The best thing that a screenwriter can do is get inside the heads of the other people involved in making a movie. If you can't negotiate "notes" from others or, say, don't want to change an element in the script to fit a high-profile actor who has been cast, you're simply not cut out for filmmaking. Even top novelists get edited.

The good news is, in most cases, the more successful you become the nicer and more accommodating people are. No matter what you've read in the tabloids, the majority of people in Hollywood are consummate professionals with unique skills. They struggled for years to make it and will empathize with you.

Top film professionals will go out of their way to explain why they feel a certain way about a scene or a line of dialogue. Argument and bitterness generally arise only out of insecurity, and you get that more often from people who haven't made it than you do from people happy with their careers.

If you run into trouble, hang in there. Keep smiling and keep learning. There's an old saying in Hollywood that you see the same people on the way up as you do on the way down, so you might as well be nice to everyone. It's a hard thing to remember sometimes—I certainly haven't always done it—but it's as good an axiom as any in Screenland.

The Least You Need to Know

♦ Beginning screenwriters should try to stay away from the use of flashbacks until they can use them effectively.

♦ Phone conversations too often break up the action. Either come up with some unique presentation that we haven't seen before, or try to use something other than a phone call.

◆ Memorable meal conversations in movies often work well when they speak to the central issue of the film.

◆ Narrator voiceovers in movies are best used in coming-of-age stories narrated by someone looking back at life-changing events.

◆ Inappropriate elements in a screenplay can cause as much script trouble as mixing genres.

◆ Film is the most collaborative of all arts, so it is important for a screenwriter to learn as much as possible about the way actors and directors exercise their craft.

Chapter **26**

The Mentor Merry-Go-Round

In This Chapter

- ◆ Guru world
- ◆ Are they experienced?
- ◆ Legitimate resources
- ◆ Festivals and pundits
- ◆ Online oracles
- ◆ Real schooling

According to the great Chinese historian Szuma Ch'ien, there was a meeting between the Chinese philosophers Confucius and Lao-tze (author of the *Tao Te Ching* [*Book of the Way and of Virtue*]). Lao-tze (also known as Lao-tzu) was 87 when the meeting took place. Confucius was 34. The elder philosopher told the young inquirer that a man of great achievement is simple in manners and appearance. He advised Confucius to get rid of his pride and his many ambitions, his affectation and extravagant aims, because his character gained nothing from any of them. Confucius later told his own pupils that meeting with Lao-tze was comparable to meeting a dragon, the most revered creature of all of Chinese philosophy.

There is another Lao-tze story that I find more interesting. Lao-tze was a librarian, a man of simple tastes who valued rural life. Impressing rulers or important officials was never important to him, even though he did impress them. When he wrote poetry, he tested it by giving it to the flower lady on the corner. If she liked it, he thought that it was good. I've found that the best screenwriters and filmmakers, at least the late great ones I met like Ernest Lehman and Robert Wise, created for the simplest of viewers and the keenest of intellects at the same time. Perhaps because they had such an expansive worldview, they were the most gracious of people, as well.

Skip's Tips

Your Name

The true test of a teacher is not his credentials, but his students. Some people are simply better at observing and teaching than anything else. Find out what a potential guru's students have accomplished, and you have a clue to the teacher's real worth.

In finding help to improve your screenplays, do not limit yourself to Hollywood. Look for sincerity. It denotes honest character, the thing we all want. I've gleaned story advice from novelists, publishers, and even my mother. Sincerity seems uncommon these days. Screenplay how-to books and services have become a cottage industry, and some people make a large living traveling the country to tell people how to write and sell screenplays. It's a bit ridiculous, because of how many American feature films get made each year. I show up at occasional conferences, but I would rather be at home with my family, writing my own stories or being paid to write them for someone else. I do what I do for writers, writing books and giving mostly free advice, simply because I love writing and hope for better stories from others. I advise people about writing all kinds of things, not just screenplays. My feeling is that if I help improve the culture by helping writers, I can contribute to a better world. Hollywood is not, unfortunately, a very accurate reflection of society.

The Galloping Gurus

When I consider experts in any field, I wonder if they could make a living doing anything other than giving seminars and doing consulting work. Too many self-styled gurus have jumped on the advice bandwagon in recent years—enough, in fact, that I wonder how many people are left to watch the parade.

I get challenged about credits occasionally, but inevitably the person doing it has some hidden agenda, such as a stalker who tried to trash me all over the Internet until I found out that he had a book that competed with my first *Writer's Guide to Hollywood.* When I discovered who he was and where he lived, I didn't call my lawyer, even though he was guilty of libel. I simply announced on a newsgroup that I knew who he was, and he shut up. Not so surprisingly, his credits weren't as substantial as mine. But then, as Lao-tze said, "Reversal is the nature of the Tao."

The next thing I look for in an expert is humility and humor. Truly knowledgeable people are too fascinated with the work they do and the wonder of life itself to be full of themselves. When I encounter arrogance or an inability to laugh, I know that I'm dealing with an insecure person who is covering up. Sincerity is one thing; a too-serious person who doesn't laugh much generally won't enlighten your life with wisdom.

My next criterion in the worth of a screenwriting guru is whether that person seems to always have a show on the road. If so, he or she is in the seminar business, not the writing business. If someone comes to your city with a seminar and then returns within six months, wouldn't you have to assume that this person makes a living running seminars?

I nevertheless listen to all the gurus, but I also have readers from all over the world who share their experience. Many of them are on my Yahoo! discussion group and talk about gurus there regularly.

I once heard talk around Hollywood about forming a consultants organization to certify qualifications for helping writers, something like a U.S. Better Business Bureau certification. If you have any thoughts about such an organization, or about your own experiences (good or bad) with screenwriting gurus or consultants, please check in at skippress.com and let me know. Meanwhile, there's a pretty good collection of consultants now online at www.storylink.com. The site was put together by the always dependable Writers Store in Los Angeles. Check out the site; you'll find me there, too.

> **Hollywood Heat**
>
> A great many Hollywood screenwriting successes have friends or co-writers who, if not actually writing or ghostwriting with them, act as professional sounding boards for their material. A woman whose name is on a substantial prize in filmdom had a co-writer, and so did a man who had a weather vane in the shape of the Oscar that he won on the top of his house in Malibu. How do I know? I've met them.

Book Writers and Real-Life Experience

I've seen two types of writers of advice books (and not only in the screenwriting field). The first and worst type is a person looking to make a name, get noticed in the media, and gain followers hungry for direction in life.

Unfortunately, there are a lot of lost souls out there, and too many people are ready to keep them lost while professing to do just the opposite. Once I knew a salesman wanted for tax evasion in Canada. Supposedly he was an actor, but he never seemed to work much at that. I knew him because he married a friend of mine. After their daughter was a couple years old, he abandoned my friend, her son from another marriage, and his daughter to take up with a lady who wrote love advice books and did seminars all over the country. The lady's ex-husband also dished love advice in books and seminars. The guy I knew was her third marriage.

I wondered why she couldn't make her marriages work. I also wondered why the lady dedicated several subsequent books to the irresponsible salesman/actor. After the first edition of this book came out, I got an e-mail from the salesman/actor. He was divorced from the love expert and had written a book on nutrition and beating cancer. He'd also written a screenplay. I read the script, but only because he'd once gotten a brother of mine a job at a time he really needed one. It was as much political screed as screenplay. I challenged him on that, and he launched into a diatribe against a political party. Ah, experts.

I met Tony Robbins once when he was living in a tiny apartment near the beach. He told me that his mission was to interview all types of successful people, find out what they do that works, and then write a book about it. It sounded logical, but it never occurred to me that someone would turn other's people advice into an advice-dispensing empire. Later, I found out that he'd simply copied the methods of Napoleon Hill, of *Think & Grow Rich*.

As I said, I've been taken in by the best, but at least I escaped them. This brings us around to screenwriting advisers. I have one criterion in judging the worth of what they offer: *Do I put into use and remember what they teach me?*

I've read a lot of pop psychology books, as well as books of wisdom that have survived the ages. If I don't find a use for the advice contained in a book, I consider it worthless. Maybe it's worthwhile to someone else, but not for me.

Whether or not the writer has racked up big screenplay sales doesn't matter to me. Christopher Vogler, author of *The Writer's Journey* (Michael Wiese Productions, 1998), to my knowledge had never sold a screenplay before he developed his assessment of the Joseph Campbell myth structure that so ably speaks to screenwriters. But then, Campbell had never authored a great novel or even a short story, as far as I know. Even though I know the Campbell material absolutely does not apply to some stories, I use, remember, and refer back to the material when it is applicable.

The same holds true for Syd Fields's "paradigm" screenplay schematic, Robert McKee's "expectation gap" for characters in scenes, Blake Snyder's "save the cat," and Lew Hunter's idea that with most good scripts, you know what's happening by page 17. Lew also has a good take on what "sex and violence" really means in screenplays, discussed in his *Screenwriting 434* (Perigee, 1994).

If you can't use it, lose it, and that goes for anything in this book, too. Some gurus will make you think they know the "only" way. They'll provide vague promises of access, and others will tell you the "rules" that supposedly everyone follows. There is no only way, and there are no "everybody" rules. The best teachers give you tools that you can use to make screenplays that sell. And that's really what matters to beginning screenwriters.

Sherwood Oaks Experimental College and Other Legitimate Resources

A friend of mine told me a story about how he supported his wife's decision to get into the filmmaking program at the American Film Institute (AFI). The program cost $15,000 a year for two years, and she had always wanted to do it. "Sure," he said, "if you can get accepted." He knew that it was very difficult to get into the program and thought that she would probably be turned down. To his amazement, she was accepted. His assessment had been correct; his wife had simply heavily impressed the faculty. With most top film programs in Los Angeles, it's difficult to make the cut.

The good thing is, if you live in southern California, there are many easier opportunities to gain a working knowledge of the film and television business. I cover a lot of them in my *Writer's Guide to Hollywood*, but I have some favorites that are accessible to the general public.

The first organization that I like a lot is one founded and directed by Gary Shusett:

Sherwood Oaks Experimental College
7095 Hollywood Blvd. #876
Los Angeles, CA 90028
Phone: 323-851-1769
Fax: 323-850-5302
E-mail: sherwoodoak@aol.com
Website: www.sherwoodoakscollege.com

This organization offers regular weekend seminars and weeklong seminars at various locations in Hollywood and Beverly Hills. I'm often a moderator on panels. At many of these events, you can meet working producers, the decision-makers of companies, not just a reader sent to listen to pitches.

Hollywood Heat

The first class that I took at the old Sherwood Oaks Experimental College was taught by a lady who had written a number of *Classics Illustrated* comic books, which I'd first discovered in my great-grandfather's house. I treasured these illustrated Cliff's Notes–like comics when I was a kid. To me, anyone who had written for them was akin to a legend. As it turned out, her adroitness at distilling the most important elements of thick classic novels made her perfect for adapting books into screenplays. As a result, she worked a lot, and when she began teaching, she had a lot of useful information to pass on.

Gary Shusett was a former schoolteacher who simply saw a need for a part-time school to help people break into Hollywood. I first came across Sherwood Oaks in the 1980s, as did a lot of other people who are much more successful than me. For example, James Cameron studied screenwriting at Sherwood Oaks, which is why he and people like him are quite willing to come back and speak to aspiring Hollywoodians on occasion. Although Sherwood Oaks is always careful to note that "Guests are subject to availability," having participated in some of their panels and events in recent years, I can assure you that you get the real thing—a chance to meet real Hollywood players that you might not gain access to on your own.

Skip's Tips

There are two types of screenwriting seminars: how-to-do seminars and how-to-sell seminars. The how-to-sell events that are worthwhile have people present who can buy your work, usually on the panel. If those people aren't from companies that have made films in the last year, the event might not be worth it.

Another favorite is the UCLA Extension Writers' Program, which offers 450 individual courses annually as well as certificate programs. I spent a year teaching at Extension, the nation's largest university-related writing program. Extension is affiliated with the university but supports itself, which allows it to bring in teachers who are working professionals who may or may not have university degrees or teaching credentials. Admissions are open, so all you have to do is pay the price of admission and show up for class. One of my readers, Mirko Betz, moved here from Germany, took a screenwriting course at UCLA Extension, and sold his first screenplay to director Roland Emmerich. Any time I've read through the catalog I've seen a lot of familiar names (familiar to anyone working in Hollywood). If you think you might spend some time in Los Angeles and try the program, contact:

UCLA Extension Writers' Program
10995 Le Conte Avenue, Ste. 440
Los Angeles, CA 90024
310-825-9415 or 800-388-UCLA
E-mail: writers@uclaextension.edu
Website: www.uclaextension.edu

Festivals, Weekends, and Panels of Pundits

When I helped put together the first Hollywood Film Festival, I advised the founder of it to set up shop in the Hollywood Roosevelt, a classic hotel named after President Theodore Roosevelt, just across from the Mann Chinese Theater on Hollywood Boulevard. It was simply the only venue on Hollywood Boulevard that made sense. Also, the first Academy Awards had been held in the Blossom Room of the Roosevelt, and so having the first Hollywood Film Festival there was a nice way to honor a fine tradition.

I chaired two panels at the weeklong festival, one on film and another on television. I invited recognizable Hollywood players that I knew personally, including Robert Katz, producer of *Gettysburg*, *Selena*, and other impressive films. I held my breath as each event began, not knowing whether anyone would show up. To my relief, several dozen attendees came to each event, and I didn't embarrass my guests, who gave freely and willingly of their time to offer advice.

Robert Katz was asked by one member of the film panel audience why he, a busy producer, would take the time to show up at a new event such as the Hollywood Film Festival and speak to a room of only a few dozen people. Katz's reply was frank. He informed the questioner that it had not been that long since he himself had been a member of the audience, script in hand, trying to get someone interested in his project. He remembered well the passion he had felt and the frustration he had experienced in trying to break in. Katz simply wanted to make it easier for others than it had been for him.

"Giving back," I heard several panelists murmur in concurrence, nodding their heads in affirmation.

"Besides," Katz continued, "we need you." He explained that all the top agents in the world submitting scripts were no guarantee that producers would find the stellar screenplays and top properties that they needed to keep their careers in high gear. That's why most successful producers he knew attended events such as the Festival, hoping to meet that special writer who has a story that audiences will pay to see.

Script Notes

A **film festival** is organized to showcase films and provide filmmakers with the possible prestige of winning a prize. For screenwriters, these are good to attend because you meet people currently involved in the filmmaking process, and most festivals now hold script competitions. Check www.moviebytes.com for information on such contests at festivals. You can also keep track of film festivals around the world by logging onto www.filmfestivals.com.

There are *film festivals* all over the world. I've never been to Cannes or Sundance, simply because I've never had a film to sell. That's the main focus of all festivals, even Hollywood. Filmmakers show up with finished product, hoping to get it noticed, and possibly strike a distribution deal. I learned that when I began attending the annual American Film Market in Santa Monica, California, where buyers and distributors from all over the world arrive to make deals with filmmakers. For this reason, at most festivals, writers are, as usual, secondary. One of my readers has won or placed highly at several film festival script competitions but has yet to get the script even optioned by someone. A former student of mine won the first Sundance Online Film Festival short subject competition, but it didn't get him any work. Besides, I'm not sure that the reader *coverage* done on screenplays submitted to festival competitions is done by Hollywood professionals, since most festivals take place outside Hollywood.

So good luck with festivals, but I can't promise they'll help you unless you show a film there. Then it might get sold.

Online Oracles and Internet Interpreters

Because I'm a well-known provider of "inside" information on Hollywood (which really means only that I'm involved in the business and paying attention), and because I constantly hear from hopeful screenwriters around the world, I've had various entreaties in the past few years from people who want me to help them sell access to Hollywood.

These folks, all of whom I've liked well enough, wanted my "blessing" on the services they offered, which generally consisted of the following:

◆ Potential access to industry movers and shakers, due to their personal experience with the same

◆ Script *coverage*, which, if positive, would be passed on to said movers and shakers for possible consideration

◆ Advice (for a price) on improving submitted screenplays

Sometimes I got evasive answers about who the contacts were and what interaction they'd had. Always, the price for the services was more than the normal $50 or so paid to a freelance script reader by producers. And in some cases, people who had been agents or producers made me wonder why they weren't making money doing *that* instead of a website.

In a previous edition of this book, I mentioned FilmTracker.com, a site that purported to provide access to hundreds of top production companies and agencies that might contact writers directly if they saw a log line that looks interesting.

> **Script Notes**
>
> **Coverage** is what a producer has done to tell him whether he wants to read a script for possible purchase. If your script coverage will not go before a producer, it's worthless, and you shouldn't pay anyone to have it done. Coverage done at studios is kept on file seemingly forever. If you submit your script to another production company on a studio lot after being rejected, you should probably change the title to ensure a fresh read.

Unfortunately, after I refused to let a person from Madonna's production company into a discussion group I had on that site, the site owners decided Madonna was good and I was bad. Why? Because even though I had helped the site owners for two years for absolutely nothing, Madonna's people were paying to access the site. I had also arranged for the site to provide contact information to a software maker, with the idea that users of the software could update their contacts via the site. They never fulfilled that agreement.

Be very cautious of promises made by online offerers of Hollywood access. In a decade of dealing with them, I've rarely found them to be worthwhile. If you have any questions about any of them, check in at my discussion group, Skip's Hollywood Hangout, at Yahoo!

Schools and Other Institutions

There are film schools all over the world, and no matter whom I mention here, someone is certain to give me grief over not mentioning some alma mater. Let me just say this. The main universities important to screenwriters in Los Angeles are the University of Southern California (USC, a private school) and the University of California at Los Angeles (UCLA, a state school). Naturally, tuition at UCLA is less expensive for anyone who is a California resident. I won't speak to the relative worth of either; they both have graduates with remarkable track records. And I know professors I respect at each school. See usc.edu and ucla.edu for more information.

Another Los Angeles school that's a Hollywood staple is the American Film Institute, which also has occasional programs in other parts of the country. For details, have a look at www.afi.com.

If you intend on becoming a filmmaker and can afford to study a year in Los Angeles, you might consider The Los Angeles Film School. This is a "full immersion" facility that teaches Hollywood skills in the way Berlitz teaches languages. According to its website, the school has five operating principles:

1. Small, hands-on classes

2. A faculty of professional filmmakers

3. State-of-the-art facilities

4. Keep the rights to your films

5. The cost of education

I know some of the people on the faculty, but I'm not associated with the school. In fact, someone with a competing book to mine is one of the instructors. Having been impressed by its students, however, I recommend it. Following is contact information:

The Los Angeles Film School
6363 Sunset Boulevard
Hollywood, CA 90028
Toll Free: 877-952-3456
Local and International: 323-860-0789
E-mail: info@lafilm.com
Website: www.lafilm.com

This is a real life participation school; as of this writing, classes are not available online.

If you are reading this and growing indignant about my not mentioning the Raindance Workshops in London, a New York film school, or your own favorite institution, sorry. I write about other resources in my *Ultimate Writer's Guide to Hollywood* (Barnes & Noble, 2004). If you want to be included in the next edition of this book or that one, let me know.

However you learn about screenwriting, I hope that you remember that old line from Mark Twain, and don't let your schooling get in the way of your education. In Hollywood, the latter never ends.

The Least You Need to Know

- With gurus, first ask whether they can make a living doing what they're telling you how to do.

- Gurus who keep their show on the road are in the seminar business, not the screenwriting business.

- My primary criterion in judging the worth of what any guru offers is this: *Do I put into use and remember what they teach me?*

- If you come to southern California long enough to attend events at industry-centric schools, you can easily meet and interact with industry pros.

- Most film festivals are great places to meet filmmakers, but winning a screen-writing competition at one rarely helps you.

- The main three university-based programs for screenwriting in southern California are USC, UCLA, and AFI.

- No matter where you study, the business of screenwriting is a continuing education.

Chapter 27

The Truth About Selling Scripts

In This Chapter

- ◆ Do query letters work any more?
- ◆ Use the telephone
- ◆ Effective e-mails
- ◆ All about gatekeepers
- ◆ Internet impact
- ◆ Do it in person

It's still a jungle out there with regard to selling scripts. It's an Amazon jungle, with creatures stranger than pink river dolphins selling Hollywood consultations. A forest of former "development executives" regularly try to figure out a way to make a living via Hollywood, not *in* Hollywood. It's even worse after a strike, because so many people have lost their jobs. It's not widely known outside of Tinseltown that many personnel at production companies are working for free, hoping they can break in. Whether they are interns, or "trust-fund babies," or someone with a supportive spouse or significant other, they're usually running to stay in place, hoping for a miracle. Kind of like an aspiring screenwriter, you know?

Here's what you need to do to sell a screenplay: *Write a great screenplay.* That's the same thing I've always said; it's easier to sell scripts once you've sold one, so when you break in you really need to stand out, if you want to do business with the big players. If you show obvious talent in a commercially viable screenplay and find companies whose personnel will resonate with your particular subject matter and storytelling style, you'll get noticed. The rest depends on making friends, persistence, timing, and luck, in that order. As long as you know your own strengths and write commercially interesting screenplays (the kind people will pay to see), you're in the running.

Even if you write quirky or truly weird scripts that you think no one will like, there might be an independent filmmaker who would think you're great. The trick is in finding those people.

Hollywood Heat

Sometimes a script floats around Hollywood for a long time. People know about the script. Maybe the writer has even made some money on an option. Nevertheless, even though the script is admired, it's not made into a film. That's what happened to scripts such as *The Electric Horseman, Unforgiven,* and a number of other great ones. I heard producer Mace Neufeld say one time that he was putting a film in production that he had been trying to make for 22 years! If you're not willing to be in the game for the long haul, this isn't the business for you.

How to Keep Your Query Letter Out of the Round File and Your Project on Their Mind

People often come to screenwriting with a literary mindset. They've written short stories or novels or plays and believe a manuscript is always submitted with a query letter attached. In reality, a query letter is sent asking an agent or editor or publisher or dramaturge (theater) to request the manuscript. It's the same way with Hollywood. A query letter offers a bit of description about the project, in the hope that it will convince someone to ask to see it.

Should you send a letter to a Hollywood agent, director or producer? It's a very good chance that no one will read the letter. It's the electronic age, and that's how Hollywood does business. Most busy people have Blackberrys, iPhones, and other "always connected" devices. I'm of the mind that you should not send a print letter at all, but call instead or e-mail. The same holds true for faxes; they're still used, but more often than not, as an "e-fax." Every time I think the query letter is completely dead with regard to effectiveness in Hollywood, someone who sent in query letters and got good responses will write me. That's okay; I'm writing about norms here, not exceptions.

Scriptblaster, a website operated from Australia, has had good results sending short e-mail messages describing client's projects to 1,000 Hollywood producers and agents. I'm not affiliated with them in any way, nor have I used the service, as I don't need to. I've simply received reports of the mass e-mail marketing getting reads requested. They have success stories on their site, but I don't recognize a single project; see if you do. And frankly, if you had those e-mail addresses, couldn't you do the same yourself? A subscription to www.hcdonline.com would get you that many addresses and a lot more.

> **It's Not for Us**
>
> Do not waste your money getting a query letter to anyone overnight or by special delivery. Do not use any kind of special envelope to make it get noticed. In Hollywood, scripts are sent by messenger from place to place. How letters arrive doesn't matter—they just go in the pile unless they contain a check. (And *don't* send a check!)

If you do write a query letter, e-mail or "snail mail," you need to keep the following elements in mind:

◆ *Who* you're writing to. *Never* send a "To Whom It May Concern" letter or any letter that looks like it has gone to several people. Find out who receives scripts, and learn how to spell that person's name. If you're sending a print letter, use decent stationery if you can afford it, or at least something other than photocopy paper. If you send an e-mail, do not automatically assume that every recipient can read HTML style e-mails or e-mails with stationery or JPEG pictures attached. Plain text, please.

◆ *What* you're trying to sell. Get right to the point. Say what your script is about. This is why you need to know your own log line backward and forward. Your "What if?" question might come in handy here.

◆ *Why* you chose to write to them, indicating that you've done some research (and you'd better have really done it). This could be as short as: "Since I know you've been so successful with teen horror films …" or something appropriate to that company.

◆ *Who* you are. If you have any credits at all, any particular qualifications for writing your script, any prizes for your writing, or whatever, say so succinctly.

If you've won several contests or placed well in them, you only need mention the best-known one by name.

♦ *When* you will be available to talk about the project, if someone is interested. If you'll be in the city soon, say so. If you work during the day and can give out your work number, do so. If you have a cell phone, provide that number. People in Hollywood pick up the phone. The younger generation (most development people are under 30) also fire off e-mails. Try to be as "reachable" as you can without sounding desperate. You can put your contact information in a "signature" at the end of your e-mail, or refer to your website (like www.skippress.com) in the signature.

With all of the previous points to consider, your printed letter should be on no more than one page. It looks better if it's no more than ¾ of a page.

An e-mail should be even shorter, no more than what you can read on a computer screen without "scrolling down." In fact, unless you specifically know that the person you are e-mailing is willing to see e-mails from people they don't know, your first e-mail should do nothing more than ask if you can tell the recipient about your property. *Never, ever, ever, no way, no how,* should you send an attached file of your work unless the recipient specifically requests it. If you do that, most will automatically delete that e-mail and every other e-mail you send.

I doubt that one person in ten will read a query letter longer than a page. The average agency—particularly any agency listed in well-known contact books such as the *Hollywood Creative Directory*—gets *thousands* of query letters every year. Forget tricks, chocolates, and dancing delivery people—it's been done.

When someone says they want to read your script, ask whether a printed script or an e-mailed script is preferred. Many people will read an e-mailed script these days.

Okay, here it comes, the sample query letter. I'm not going to get cute with you because I don't think that you should try to be cute. Charming, maybe. Smart, sure. Not cute.

I will assume that you are sending your letter on nice stationery.

It's a small touch, but if you have printed stationery or something that comes off your printer that looks professional, you're better off. It at least shows that you're spending some money in an attempt to be professional.

Should you compare your movie to some others, as we've discussed earlier in this book? In the last edition, I said: "No, you should not—not in a query letter. They see that kind of comparison all day long. They're sick of it." Well, Hollywood changed again. Now you'll see combination descriptions in "the trades." In mid-September 2003, Michael Fleming reported in *Variety* that New Line, in a mid-six-figure deal, bought the pitch "Titans," which was described as *The Breakfast Club* meets *Lord of the Rings*. Fleming said the film was "a coming-of-age story of a group of teens who just happen to be the future gods of Mt. Olympus." If your movie can be described that succinctly and has the commercial potential of "Titans" you'll probably sell it. Meanwhile, here's a sample query letter for you, using a property of mine.

ME THE SCREENWRITER [Stationery heading, possibly centered]

Date

Sandra Somebody
The Beverly Hills Agency
555 Canon Drive
Beverly Hills, CA 90210

Dear Ms. Somebody:

For many single women, turning 30 can be traumatic.

For Mirabella Flowers, it's enough to drive her crazy. She's stuck in Gallup, New Mexico, wondering if her Prince Charming will ever arrive. The night of her thirtieth birthday, he shows up, but he might be an alien.

Not an illegal alien. An alien from another planet.

I read the *Spec Screenplay Sales Directory* and noticed that you've been particularly adept at selling romantic comedies like mine.

My script, *Walking After Midnight*, was a finalist in two national competitions and a semifinalist in two others as a stage play. When two working Hollywood professionals told me it should be a screenplay, I wrote the script.

You can reach me at the number or e-mail below, at your convenience. I hope you'll take a look at it.

Sincerely,

Me the Screenwriter

Address
Phone number
E-mail
Website

I center my contact information to make it catch the eye, but you might choose another design. Just keep it businesslike.

Guess what? I rewrote the query letter from the last edition. I shortened it and left out details that didn't matter. All I needed to say was that she's turning 30 and Prince Charming could be an alien. They would either like that concept or not.

I know your next question: "How long should I wait after sending my letter before I follow up?" Usually, if you don't hear from your addressee within six weeks, you're not going to hear. Cross that name off the list and move on to the next one. If you're convinced that this simply is the perfect agency or production company for you, and if it has been six weeks or more, you might post a very short, polite follow-up—even a postcard—but don't get your hopes up. Just send the letter and hope for the best. If you don't get the best, find it elsewhere. As an aside, in the United States you can pay less than half a dollar and get a "proof of delivery" tag on your package and then track its delivery on the Internet. With FedEx and other delivery services you can do the same thing, but most writers I know use the U.S. post office. Do *not* send your script "Certified" or some other "official" way that is usually reserved for legal documents. That will spook a lot of companies.

Hollywood Heat

> Although I later interviewed him for *Boy's Life* magazine, I had no idea how many people wanted to contact Steven Spielberg until the first time I sent a query to his production company, Amblin, located on the lot at Universal Studios. I got my letter back with a stamp that basically said, "We don't know you, so we won't even open your letter." That had never happened to me before. I quickly discovered that it is a standing policy at top Hollywood companies.

Sooner or later, if you keep at it, you'll strike gold with a query. Don't get too excited, though. They still have to like the script. If they're an agency, they have to sell it.

The Telephone as Weapon of Choice

Although it might seem intrusive to pick up the phone and call someone you don't know, I can't tell you how many times I've seen people in Land Rovers, BMWs, or SUVs cutting through L.A. expressway traffic with one hand on the wheel and the other holding a cell phone to their ear. They might as well graft it to their ear, Hollywood people use the phone so much.

Personnel at many production companies change regularly. They move from one studio to another, depending on projects. They might even switch area codes. (That doesn't apply with cell phones, but it's unlikely a Hollywood person who doesn't know you will instantly give you their cell number.)

You need to get to know southern California area codes because they matter to some people in Hollywood. For your reference, 213 is downtown L.A. (not many production companies there). If a company is in Beverly Hills, that's 310. Hollywood is 323, and 818 is the San Fernando Valley (as in Burbank, where Warner Brothers and Disney are located, with Universal nearby). If a company is in another area code, it might not matter. If you saw an 805 number would you shy away? If so, you could be ignoring director Ivan Reitman's company in affluent Santa Barbara.

Skip's Tips

Many companies offer free trials around the winter holidays. The *Hollywood Creative Directory* (www. hcdonline.com) might allow free access for a month. *Variety* often gives away a free month, when Hollywood news is slow. Take it, and do research on companies. When you know who you want to see your script, use free trials and free services for the marketing you'll do in the New Year.

Your phone number and address might matter to some. Try and see. If you find that a few people don't call you back in Peoria, maybe you need to set up an L.A. address and phone number somehow or an 800 number so they can call you at no charge.

Normally, when a production company moves, it will have an answering machine that will give you new numbers (including fax) but that does *not* record messages. So keep a pencil ready when you make your calls.

It takes some effort (albeit minimal) to get the post office to forward mail. Your query letter might get forwarded but your script might not. Verify the address before you mail your package. There are forwarding services for e-mail, but who uses those? See why I say the telephone is the preferred way to contact people in Hollywood?

So here's the deal. Get your hands on some contact information from the myriad sources available, and make some calls. Ask for a specific person, state your name, and say what you have to offer. Ask if this person is willing to look at unsolicited material. If you get a cold "no," just politely say thanks and hang up. If that person says "sometimes" or gives you an opening, you'd better have a pitch ready. You'd better know the log line of your script cold, but don't read it aloud. It has to sound natural, something they could easily repeat.

If you get a pause on the other end and something like, "Hold on a second," that means one of two things: There's a rookie answering the phones who doesn't know the rules, or you've garnered someone's interest and that person wants to see if a higher-up or partner wants to hear about your screenplay. If, after hearing about it, the person says that he or she wants to see your script, ask whether you should mail it or e-mail it. If it's by e-mail, all the better—nothing like striking while the iron is hot. Usually, most people can read a Microsoft Word file, or even an Adobe PDF file. The latter could be better for you because they can't tamper with the file unless they have certain software. Just don't be surprised if they ask for a Final Draft or Movie Magic Screenwriter file. If you don't have your script in the format of a popular script-formatting program, don't worry. A printed script is more portable and preferable to read—it just can't get there as fast.

E-mails and Other Specious Species

When e-mail was a relatively new item in Hollywood, people went crazy with the novelty of it. I sent an e-mail to producer Gale Anne Hurd, and she picked it up on the set of her movie in South Dakota. I was stunned when her assistant called me within an hour of my sending the e-mail.

Since that time, the bloom has killed the rose. People in Hollywood have suffered through the same virus and spam e-mail abuse as everyone else. They'll answer e-mail because it's quick, but some of them are *very* protective of their e-mail addresses. The main thing to know is that just about everyone in Hollywood has e-mail. They're checking it on their laptops, their Palm Pilots, their cell phones, and their desktops. They're swapping e-mails all day long. To get them to read your e-mail when they don't know you, you need to know a very simple trick:

The subject line of your e-mail must compel them to open the message.

I do *not* mean using ALL CAPS. That's considered shouting in cyberspace and is very rude. I'll personally delete almost any e-mail from anyone with an ALL CAPS subject line. Older folks seem to love to use it, though, so I'll pause for a second to see whom the e-mail is from; if I recognize the sender or the subject looks interesting, I'll take a look.

Don't use subject headers such as "The Greatest Script on Earth." That one will be deleted. Using the example of my script, I could use something like "Is Her Prince Charming an Alien?" That might prompt a few people to open the e-mail, or it might make them think it's a Viagra ad. I'd probably use something like "Script query." Then I might use the "is he an alien" line in the body of the e-mail and continue the text like this:

> *That's what Mirabelle Flowers is wondering on the night of her thirtieth birthday as she waits for her friends to show up to throw her a "surprise" birthday party.*

(Note: These italics are merely for emphasis. Use only plain text in e-mails until you know someone has HTML capability.)

Then I'd explain who I am, tell why I picked the agency or production company, mention something about myself if there was anything I felt worth mentioning, and then close the message. If I had a web page where the entire synopsis could be read, I might list the URL in a "signature" line below my name and I would make sure I told them the synopsis was available at the website. I would keep the entire e-mail to no more than 10 to 12 lines if possible. If someone has to scroll down the screen very far to read what you've sent, my feeling (based on experience) is that they probably won't. If you're mailing these people but they're not expecting your e-mail, I would explain where you got the address. I would also add a line toward the end that "I hope this is no intrusion, and please accept my apologies if it is. This is a one-time mailing."

The good thing about e-mail is that it doesn't have to be answered immediately. It's not as intrusive as an unexpected fax, and it's as easy to trash as a mailed query letter.

They can also claim that they've had troubles with viruses and spam and never got your e-mail, so if you know how to do a return notification with your message, do it. They might click on it and let you know that they received it.

Last but not least, save copies of your e-mails with full headers (those things that give a unique signature to each e-mail message— check your software program help area or manual). I hope that it never happens to you, but you might need them as evidence.

It's Not for Us

Just as with e-mails, some companies can be sticklers about receiving faxes from people they don't know. There's a legal reason for that. Fax machines keep records of numbers they send a fax to, and these records can be used in court to prove access. Don't send a fax unless you know that it's okay to do so.

Pitching to the Gatekeepers: The Usual Channels Are There for a Reason

I ran into producer David Permut a long time ago, when he was producing *Blind Date*. A script of mine impressed him, and I was invited to his offices to pitch. His assistant at the time, Katie Jacobs, went on to become a producer, as have many other people who have worked for Permut.

Similarly, when I first met producer Jennie Lew Tugend, she was the point person for producer/director Richard Donner, right after he made *Superman* but before he made *Lethal Weapon*. Her comments were always insightful, and we've remained friends ever since.

> **Skip's Tips** _____
>
> Development people read a lot of scripts on weekends, trying hard to find a movie worth making. If they don't find something good sooner or later, they're out of a job. Use an old trick. Call them on Monday morning after 10:00 before their boss arrives. Or go in and pitch to them early on Monday. If they didn't find anything on the weekend, they're more likely to want to talk to you.

Your Name

Both Jacobs and Tugend were development people then, the folks who (if they liked a query or a pitch) were the first ones to read a script. Over the years, despite a few (emphasis on few) instances of rude front office personnel, I've noticed two things:

- Smart development people become smart producers, often rather quickly.

- Writers who circumvent the existing structure are screwed because the producer will give the script to his reader first.

Perhaps because the Joseph Campbell myth structure is so well known in Hollywood these days, the people who are the "threshold guardians" of agencies and production companies are looked upon as opposing forces that one must conquer. The exact opposite is true. In many classic stories, the first threshold to new and unknown territory is passed by providing the guardian with a secret password. In your case, that would be your very good screenplay. You must impress the development person.

That means you need to know how to pitch your story. There are various levels of pitching:

- Over the phone, to get someone to request your material.

- In writing via letter or e-mail, which we've covered.

◆ At a "pitch event," at which you'll usually have no more than five minutes to get across all the important points of your story. If they like it, they'll request to see the material.

◆ In a formal pitch at someone's office. You'll probably have at least 15 minutes and if they like what they're hearing the meeting could go longer. You're winning if they invite someone else to come hear your pitch while it's going on or after you've finished pitching the initial person.

You wouldn't pitch a screenplay in a formal office setting unless there is some odd reason why they would want you to pitch it. They'll probably just want to read the script. Of course, if they like it but want changes and are unsure of your ability to come up with new ideas about it, they might invite you in to discuss that.

Let's just say you get someone to read your screenplay. What happens if the development person or reader likes your script and checks "consider" or even the rare "recommend" on it? Well, unless the producer gave it to them to read, the development person "found" your property. If it goes into production, that person is likely to make a lot of extra money and get an "associate producer" credit. Suddenly this person is not a development person any more. Now he or she has a higher position in the company and is on the way to being a producer.

That's why a lot of people in "development" are doing it for free these days, hoping they'll find something that will get produced, get a credit and a fee, and move on to producing more movies.

So, if you talk to someone in development who sounds cross, that person has either had a hard day or doesn't like your pitch. Don't worry about it. Just wish him or her a good day and go on to the next one. You might be talking to someone who will be an important producer some day.

And here's another tip. Most likely, when you go to a pitch event, the "lowest person on the totem pole" from any given production company will probably show up. Don't expect to see a movie star or even the president of the company there unless it's a Hollywood event put on by Sherwood Oaks. Exceptions are when there are only a couple of people in a production company, or even a sole independent producer.

Before becoming a successful writer, I made a living doing word processing for law firms and working as a legal secretary. Maybe that's why I never saw receptionists and readers and development people as the first line of defense to breach on my way to winning the war of Hollywood. I could truly empathize with their long hours and short pay.

Many people I met in development are now producing movies. Being nice is good business, to say nothing of good living. Generally, the nicest people in Hollywood are the ones at the top. It doesn't hurt to practice getting there.

How the Internet Changed the Access Codes

Hollywood companies have experimented with finding writers and material via websites. Hollywood Literary Sales (www.hollywoodlitsales.com), a site put together by Howard Meibach, the author of the *Spec Screenplay Sales Directory*, has an arrangement with the Escape Artists production company at this writing. Most companies of any stature, however, have turned away from the Internet and spec screenplays because they found it so hard to locate a good one with that method.

Skip's Tips

You can look up the street address, phone number, and e-mail contacts of just about any company that has a website via a "Whois" search. If you don't know what that is, do some research on the Internet or try a "net tools" site like www.samspade.org.

Many companies have registered domain names but do not maintain websites. They merely use the domain name to set up e-mail addresses. Or, they might have a site but do not list e-mail addresses. However, if you know only *one* e-mail address within that company, you can figure out the listing of other names. For example, if you know that John Smith is jsmith@warner.com, it's likely that Mary Smith is msmith@warner.com. Just a little tip.

I was years ahead of most people in Hollywood advocating the use of the Web. (I wrote a business computing column for three years.) Suffice it to say that the Web has revolutionized this business and will continue to do so in the future. It may make lasting changes in the way Hollywood does business, from top to bottom.

If you really make a connection with someone, though, you might find you're trading text messages on your cell or some other device like a Blackberry. Hollywood people are usually on top of the latest electronic craze, and so perhaps you can use that to advantage when getting in touch with them.

and-Blood Contacts Are Still the Most Sexy

make this as short and sweet as possible: the best way to gain access in Hollywood *in person*. If you don't live in southern California, get there, at least for a big have some business cards ready. And nothing fancy, just contact information.

Make sure that you're well groomed and that your breath doesn't smell, and start meeting people.

Hollywood Heat _____

I have a good memory for faces and names, but once it failed me. I was at a party in the Hollywood Hills when I handed a beer from a refrigerator to a guy behind me. We got to talking and I asked him his name. "Peter" was all he would tell me, even though I asked his last name. Finally I realized that I was talking to Peter Yarrow of Peter, Paul, and Mary (a folk group popular long before my time). It was the first in a long list of celebrities I met who introduce themselves only by their first name. Keep that in mind in Hollywood.

In showbiz parlance, meeting people in a large gathering is called "working the room." Most people will have business cards, but some might have only their name and phone number (that's considered chic by some). The secret is simple: be yourself and don't push it. If they like you, it might lead to something. You might even make a friend. If there's no chemistry, move on. If you don't immediately hit it off with someone, chances are you never will. And that could be your guardian angel tapping you on the shoulder and telling you that there are better horizons ahead. Good luck!

The Least You Need to Know

- The most effective query letter is less than a page long and tells people what you're trying to sell up front.

- Other than person to person, the telephone is still the preferred means of communication in Hollywood.

- When you call a production company or agency, ask for a specific person, state who you are, and say what you have.

- The secret of an effective e-mail query is that the subject line of your e-mail must compel someone to open the message.

- The development person you try to circumvent today could be the producer you try to sell to tomorrow.

- Learning how to effectively communicate the specifics of your screenplay could be the key to selling it.

- In a people business like Hollywood, the very best way to gain access is *in person*. If you don't live there, get there, even if only for a weekend.

Chapter 28

Plotting Your Screenwriting Career

In This Chapter

- ◆ Your next script
- ◆ L.A. or not L.A.?
- ◆ The big picture
- ◆ Agent myths
- ◆ Somebody who knows somebody
- ◆ Effective post-screenplay resources

Almost always, you need a great script to break into the business. That means you start with a great premise, create a tight plot, develop compelling characters, don't overwrite dialogue, and put fascinating and unexpected twists into scenes. You'll need to be a person who does a lot of reading and watches a lot of films, because successful screenwriting is both a craft learned and one absorbed via the osmosis of immersion in great film stories.

One currently very successful screenwriter was previously a lawyer. Interestingly enough, a lot of lawyers do well in Hollywood as writers and then move on to being writer/producers or writer/directors. This friend of a friend rented the top 50 movies of all time and got the scripts for each of these films. He went about it in the way a lawyer does exhaustive "discovery" before a trial. He watched all the movies, scripts in hand, and virtually absorbed great movie stories. Then he began writing.

You must be dedicated to learning to gain the tools necessary to the craft. If a German friend of mine can come here from his home country, take one class at UCLA on my advice, and sell his first screenplay, don't you think you could? He got a little lucky by babysitting the kids of the best friend of a successful producer, but the script was worth buying.

If you don't have such luck, you might need someone touting your writing. If you can't find a professional agent or manager, try this. I know of a writer who finally broke in after his wife took over as his manager and began making phone calls for him. After a couple of years of part-time effort, she made a deal for him, and he's been working constantly ever since. Hollywood is a small town. When you get known as a good writer, everyone wants to know you.

When to Start Your Next Script

If you've completed your first script by the time you get to this chapter, I'd hazard a guess that you'll make it as a screenwriter, at least in some capacity. Screenwriters who work a lot write fast, and they write well. They are brimming with ideas. If you have done the best you can with your first script, start another one. What if you impressed a producer with the story of your first script but it was too much like something on the market? If he or she asked you what else you had, how would you feel if you had to say "Nothing at the moment"? One of my readers won a big national contest on MTV for a short film he made, then had nothing else to pitch all the top people he met in town like Peter Abrams, an old friend of mine who produced *Wedding Crashers*. Be smart, write a *lot*.

I often speak at writer's conferences and other events. One question I often get—and this includes e-mails from all over the world—is "How do I know they won't steal my idea?" One fellow even asked how he could be assured I wouldn't steal his idea! I replied that I had 50 projects of my own, and I was pretty certain that they were all as good as his, whatever it was. I have so many stories and ideas I usually just go on to something else when one doesn't work, but I find a lot of writers are not so prolific. That's too bad, because most working writers I know have lots of ideas. If you sell your first script, or if your first script impresses someone but that person doesn't want to buy it, the first question you'll have to field will be, "So, what else you got?" (Probably those exact words.) If you're serious about screenwriting, you'll think of it like going on a major expedition. You'll want to be as well equipped as possible.

I think that you should have at least three fully worked-out scenarios from which to pick your next script, if not a dozen. I mentioned earlier in this book that prolific writers throw away ideas or even whole scripts, or shove them in a drawer somewhere until a time when they're in a position to use them. You really must think in terms of quantity. Your ideas might not all be good ideas but more like chaff to sort through to get to the golden wheat of great ideas.

It's Not for Us

Never settle for "good enough." Make each script the absolute best that it can be. The more you write, the better you'll get, but if you don't maintain high standards for yourself—such as a movie you'd pay to see—your chances of impressing others are lessened. In this day of computers, you should have no excuse for not doing another draft to perfect your screenplay. *Cast Away* supposedly took 35 drafts to get right.

You might think of trying a different genre with your second screenplay. Hollywood will try to pigeonhole you into one category. Of course, if you're content writing in one genre and think it's your strong suit, don't worry about it. Just write more than one script so you won't ask me if I'll steal your idea when you send me that e-mail.

Do You Need to Live in L.A.?

Although I know people who do not live in Los Angeles and yet sell screenplays (even their first screenplay), I can't imagine not living in southern California while trying to make it in Hollywood, at least for a year. Besides, where else can you brush up against movie legends, or even break bread with them as an unknown? Despite my own ups and downs and heartbreaks in Hollywood, the good has far outweighed the bad.

One day I parked my car at the curb to have breakfast at Nate 'n' Al's Deli in Beverly Hills, and Fred Astaire turned the corner and said good morning to me. Another time in Century City, Burt Lancaster sauntered by, grinned broadly, and said hello. My mother and stepfather were visiting from out of state once, so I took them to dinner at the world-famous Magic Castle in Hollywood. Danny DeVito stopped at our table and pretended to be the maître d', asking if our meal was okay that evening.

(Danny had read a script of mine and recognized me, but my folks didn't know who he was!) A few years ago, I took my son Haley to a party one night at the Hollywood Roosevelt and he spent two hours talking with Nia "Greek Wedding" Vardalos and her husband Ian Gomez. Nia told me "Your son was the life of the party!" It can be a great town.

Hollywood Heat

YOUR NAME

Hollywood, particularly television, can be amazingly lucrative. A show that runs for three years usually makes millionaires out of the writer/producers involved. Unfortunately, the schedule is deadly, and values can get distorted. I've known top TV people who are multimillionaires, but they work like madmen and seem personally emotionless—it all goes into the scripts. And I personally knew a TV producer who got fired from his million-dollar-a-year job after a fit of pique and, not long afterward, committed suicide. If you think that you're going to take off in Hollywood, you'd do well to get your personal life very well grounded first.

I'll bet you're thinking, Skip's been in the business a long time, so he knows people. While that's true, the real point is that this is where the stars, producers, directors, and studio people live. If you're out and about in certain areas, you'll see them going about everyday life. It's not hard to say hello or strike up a conversation. It really isn't.

Skip's Tips

Your Name

If you want the shortest route to making it in Holly-wood, bring some skill other than writing, and go to work for a production company. You'll make 10 percent less than comparable jobs in other industries, but you'll get to know people. Use the Internet for job information. For example, look up these websites: www. showbizjobs.com or www. entertainmentcareers.net.

I met director/producer Richard Donner by saying hello in a grocery store parking lot. As mentioned previously, great seminars take place in southern California all the time. The Learning Annex also offers classes for less than $50, taught by top industry people. As an example, my friend Paul Mason, former head of production at Viacom, did a class on producing at The Learning Annex and had Sid Sheinberg, the legend of Universal Studios, as his guest. There is always something going on here that can forward your career. And tell me where else in the world you can be skiing in the morning, surfing in the afternoon, and then watching a movie at the magnificent Mann's Chinese Theater in the evening or even a screening of a new film at a movie studio?

Do you need to live in L.A.? Maybe not. As Web-based and digital solutions proliferate, New York, Toronto, Vancouver, even Austin, Texas are places you can have a film career, but nowhere is so much media concentrated as Los Angeles. Even if you can give it only six months, I urge you to try it.

The Big Picture Is Not Just a Movie

Most people I know think too little of themselves, and they have myths built up about Hollywood. Maybe that's because actors on a movie screen are five times larger than the normal person. Or, they read tabloid stories and books about the seedy side of the entertainment business, which, frankly, can be a veritable garden of weeds. Lives can indeed get destroyed, but the last time I checked, there was a major heroin problem in Plano, Texas, a town north of Dallas where I used to live.

If you show up in Los Angeles on impulse, knowing no one, you have my sympathies. Remember, this is show *business*. It's a billion-dollar business that dazzles people around the world. Despite the glitter tales, the people that I see make it have a well-thought-out plan from which they work. They don't depend on a muse, a stroke of luck, or a pot of gold at the bottom of the Hollywood sign. They methodically go about trying to make a career work. Even then, in the darkest hour before their dawn, they're prepared to pack it in. Michael J. Fox had sold his furniture and was ready to go back to Canada when he got the part on *Family Ties* that made him famous. Nia Vardalos couldn't get much work and so turned to doing a one-woman show to make money. When Rita Wilson saw *My Big Fat Greek Wedding*, that show turned into a *lot* of money. The stories like that are legion. I've personally been homeless in Los Angeles, with no job and sleeping in my car.

You can get around the troubles with a plan. If you live in southern California, you probably already know what to do. If you don't, you might want to do something like the following:

1. Find a way to give yourself at least six months. If you have a full-time job that provides a good living, see whether you can take a sabbatical. Three months isn't enough. Within six months, you should be able to know whether you want to pursue Hollywood.

2. Arrive with a good, dependable car, or the funds to buy one. Los Angeles has recently opened a reliable subway system and has decent buses, but you need a car.

3. Expect to pay a lot of money for rent—not as much as New York, but more than most parts of the country. For an idea about rent, check the *Los Angeles Times* or the *Daily News*. You can find them at www.latimes.com and www.dailynews.com.

4. Working professionals tend to live and congregate in North Hollywood, Studio City, Burbank/Toluca Lake, Los Feliz, the Hollywood Hills, West Hollywood, Beverly Hills, West L.A., Santa Monica, and Venice. To get a good idea of what's going on among young professionals in Los Angeles, read the *L.A. Weekly* at www.laweekly.com.

5. Use every contact you have to get help setting you up in Los Angeles—friends, relatives, alumni associations, and fellow workers. Have a written plan. When you meet people who are working in the business, offer to buy them lunch or breakfast to get their advice on your plan. Rely on getting advice; people love to give it as long as you are appreciative and not too pushy or dependent.

6. As soon as you arrive, spend some time learning where writers spend time. You can attend events at the Writers Guild of America and Directors Guild of America, whether you are a member or not. The same goes for the Academy of Motion Picture Arts & Sciences and the Television Academy in North Hollywood. It amazes me that some people are here for a year or more before they know that.

7. Be a friend. People appreciate having someone to have coffee with and commiserate. Friends help friends in this business, sometimes over more talented people.

Script Notes _____

Humility is a word that has only this to do with screenwriting: there are a lot of talented writers in Hollywood. If you arrive thinking that you're the most special scribe since William Shakespeare and that your writing doesn't need improvement, you're destined to land face first in mud. Learn humility, and keep learning.

8. Give freely of your time. I know people who have gotten hired by production companies after walking in and offering to read scripts for free. Others volunteer for worthy causes and meet people. Familiarity breeds trust in this business.

9. Keep a sunny disposition, and don't get down on yourself. Be sincere and persistent. There are too many people ready to put you down; don't do their job for them.

10. For every hard-luck story you tell someone, they have one just as bad, or worse. Be ready to take a decade to make it, and don't be surprised if everyone takes at least five years off their real age!

For someone on a six-month mission to make it in Hollywood, I suggest that you divide your time into writing, meeting people, learning the town (and I don't mean only the geography), and having fun. I look at the big picture, and I'm in the game for the long haul, but I've met some of the best people when simply enjoying myself.

Skip's Tips

Your area code is something that people pay a lot of attention to in Hollywood. If you don't live in the 213, 323, or 310 area codes, you might get a grimace at a party. The 818 area code (where I live) is acceptable enough but not as hip. So is the 626 area, or 805. It's just geographic desirability, nothing more, nothing less. Want to get around all that? Get an 800 number, and no one will know where you live.

The Truth About Agents

Here's the big truth about finding a Hollywood literary agent. Most writers get an agent by being referred by another writer or maybe a producer.

Agents are busy, and they don't want to waste time trying to figure out whether someone is worth representing. If they are successful, they have a stable of clients who are working regularly, and they concentrate on those writers. If someone whose opinion they respect refers someone, though, they will take the time to study that person's work.

Most writers I know get as much work on their own, if not more, than their agents do for them. That goes for book writers as well as screenwriters. Agents are good at making sure that contracts benefit the writer and at getting more money, particularly enough to cover their agenting fee.

Generally, agents at the big agencies—Creative Artists, Endeavor, International Creative Management, the William Morris Agency, United Talent Artists—won't be interested in you until you've made some noise on your own. That usually means a screenplay sale. The only way around that is if someone who is already a client—or someone whose opinion is respected by an agent at one of those agencies—refers you, or by winning a major contest such as the Nicholl.

When you first start out in Hollywood, you're better off contacting independent production companies directly to get them to read your material. That's the main advice I gave in my *Writer's Guide to Hollywood* first edition, and it was still true 10 years later in my *Ultimate Writer's Guide to Hollywood*. Keep trying to meet working writers, and ask them to read and refer you (while offering to do something for them in exchange). Don't think that an agent is your instant ticket to success. Until you make a sale, and even well after that, the primary burden will be on you, so get used to it. I hope that you get lucky and find that perfect agent right away, but for most writers, that isn't what happens.

Somebody Who Knows Somebody—How It Usually Works

I continually hear this phrase—"He (or she) knew somebody." Well, how does anyone know somebody? The best way is an introduction. The second is a social occasion. The next is a public event where you know that you have at least a shared interest. Last but not least is simply introducing yourself.

I was standing in a photocopy shop in Sunset Boulevard one day when I noticed that the fellow next to me was looking over some copies about something to do with play-wright Tennessee Williams. Without really looking at the man closely, I remarked that I'd interviewed Mr. Williams once for a magazine and found him to be a gracious, interesting interview. Then I realized that I was talking to distinguished English actor Michael York. Like most celebrities, he was uncomfortable at being approached with little hurrah, but being the gracious man that he is, York had a bit of a conversation with me about the tribute that he was participating in for Williams.

I later learned that he had starred in an original Williams play on Broadway. Being the bold person that I am, I asked Michael whether I could send him a screenplay of mine sometime. It turned out that he and his wife had recently moved to Los Angeles from Monaco, and he said he'd be happy to read something. He gave me an address and, amazingly enough, optioned the first thing I sent him.

Sometimes you are simply physically close to someone. I met a lady named Loretta Crawford because she lived in the apartment below me in Los Feliz. I discovered that Loretta had been married to a fellow named Henry Crawford in Australia, at a time when almost all Australian filmmakers were learning their craft at Crawford Film & Television. She had a company called The Australian Connection that helped Aussie showbiz people get a toehold in Hollywood. She knew everyone from Australia, it seemed: Mel Gibson, Olivia Newton-John, and Peter Weir. A few years later, I helped Michael Rymer, who later married Loretta, find the material for the first script he sold. I still hear from them on occasion.

Talented people can sense other talented people. I've seen it happen over and over. People at parties tend to gravitate toward other people of like mind. If you're upbeat, sincere, and genuinely interested in others, it comes across. While I know that it's hip to be cynical and full of sharp quips as a screenwriter, most of the successful ones I know don't sport the attitude.

Which brings us to the subject of co-writing. Two of the screenplays I have sold were co-written, and the script most recently optioned was co-written. As you make the social rounds in Los Angeles, you might find yourself considering co-writing with someone. If you chose to do that, you'd be in good company. The great Billy Wilder wrote most of his best scripts with I. A. L. Diamond. Can you imagine Matt Damon writing *Good Will Hunting* without Ben Affleck?

If you find a co-writer, or at least some writers to spend time with, try to find people with as much talent as you. How do you gauge that? By your own estimation, and what other people (not your co-writer) think of your own work. The other thing that counts is (obviously) flexibility. The best writing teams know what their weaknesses are as well as their strengths. But I could go on and on about this, perhaps even a separate book.

Effective Post-Screenplay Resources

I've often spent too much time helping other writers and not enough helping myself. I know that's true, because old friends of mine have sold screenplays for more than a million dollars and won Oscars, and I'm not living in a house in Pacific Palisades or the Hollywood Hills like they are. But every time I hear a writer say that I've helped, often from around the world, I can't help but grin.

Skip's Tips _____

Staff writers spend a great deal of time swapping stories around a table. Some times, it can really pay off. Writer/producer Paul Mason told me that Mel Brooks never wanted to let anyone know he was out of work, so he would hang out at the "writer's table" in the Universal commissary. When asked what he was working on, Brooks would joke "Springtime for Hitler" and make up bits of story. Finally someone (Paul thinks it was Larry Gelbart) said: "That's getting pretty good. You should write it." It became *The Producers*, first a movie and then the winner of numerous Tony Awards as a Broadway musical.

I sincerely hope that, in this book, I've provided you with the tools to embark on a fulfilling and lucrative screenwriting career. If I have helped you, let me know. If you have ideas about other things you'd like help with, let me know that as well.

If you have never taken a course in screenwriting, have a look at my site, www. skippress.com. I'm always offering courses that can help, and I answer your questions and look over your work personally. Hundreds of writers from around the world regularly participate on my free Yahoo discussion group, so you can also get help there.

 This time, there is an accompanying CD with this book, and I'm thrilled we were able to offer this to my readers. You'll find software demos and files that you should find very helpful. If there is anything you wish was on the CD that wasn't, or in this book that wasn't, I'm always open to suggestions, so please e-mail me at skippress@ yahoo.com.

Whatever you choose to do, I wish you great success with your screenwriting career. I hope I've helped you some with this book, and thanks for picking it up.

And so we fade out, leaving you to fade in, with pictures that thrill and dazzle us all. Write on, screenwriter!

The Least You Need to Know

- ◆ You have to write better when breaking into Hollywood than you do when you're established.

- ◆ For most people, it's advisable to live in L.A. for at least six months to get a screenwriting career started.

- ◆ Never let yourself be viewed as a "one-trick pony." Have at least two or three projects ready to sell at any one time.

- ◆ The big agencies won't be interested in you until you've made some noise on your own, meaning a sale.

- ◆ Writers first starting out in Hollywood are better off contacting independent production companies directly.

- ◆ My course, "Your Screenwriting Career," has helped many writers successfully launch a screenwriting career.

- ◆ You'll make your own luck, but good luck, anyway!

Appendix A

Script Formats

Script formats are a source of continuous discussion among screenwriters. One would think, after more than 100 years of a worldwide film industry, there would be some inflexible standard, but how could there be? In Russia, you might see an English language script written in any size and font type; for example, Times New Roman 18. Scripts there are printed on A4 paper, as they are throughout Europe. Writers in England pay more attention to Hollywood formatting standards, but they (and most Europeans) have difficulty finding American style 8.5×11-inch paper to print scripts on that they intend to sell to Hollywood companies.

Wherever you live, I highly suggest you invest the money in one of the top screenplay formatting programs. With such software, you can change between paper sizes and from one type of script to another with a few short keystrokes or moves of your computer mouse. My personal preference is Movie Magic Screenwriter from Write Brothers (see www.screenplay.com).

The standard Hollywood print reference for feature film screenplay format used to be *The Complete Guide to Standard Script Formats—Part I: The Screenplay by Cole/Haag*. The problem is that book was last printed in 1999 and things change whimsically in Hollywood.

If you'd like a handy one-sheet reference, get the Screenplay Format Guide from www.scriptbuddy.com (see Store on the site). I also recommend the book *The Hollywood Standard: The Complete and Authoritative Guide to Script Format and Style* by Christopher Riley (Michael Wiese Productions, 2005).

If you simply cannot afford any kind of formatting software, a 1-inch top and bottom margin is okay, but a more precise (and possibly standard) margin would be 1.12 inch at the top and 0.75 inch at the bottom, with .5 inch from the top of the paper to the page number, and .5 inch from the bottom of the paper to footers such as (CONTINUED). This type of footer indicates that a scene is continued on the next page, but its use is falling out of favor. Personally, I use a .75-inch margin on the bottom of the page.

As I mentioned previously, the left margin should be 1.5 inches because scripts in Hollywood are copied onto or printed on three-hole paper with brads used only on the top and bottom holes. (A script from England on A4 uses 4 holes.) A left margin smaller than 1.5 inches might make a script hard to read once your script is bound. Generally, the right margin should be .5 inch from the edge of the paper, but in popular formatting programs and templates, the default margins are set at 15 and 75 on the program's viewable menu formatting.

I advise using a 12-point Courier font, or Courier New. Whatever you use, it should be a fixed-pitch font with 10 characters per horizontal inch and 6 lines per vertical inch, *not* a proportional font. And *never* use a justified right margin.

On the second page, the distance from the top to your page number should be three carriage returns, or .5 inch. Then a single blank line separates the page number and the body of the script, which begins at .75 inch. Numbers should align aesthetically past the right margin, with a period after the number and no "Page Number" spelled out before the numeral.

Try to get your hands on scripts from recently filmed movies and you'll see what formats are currently being used. Just don't expect them all to match.

Again, save yourself this kind of headache and let the computer programs do the formatting for you.

And don't forget—the story matters more than the format.

Now I'll show you acceptable formats in the following pages, using the same one-page scene in different styles. Remember, though, this book is not printed on 8.5×11-inch paper while screenplays are. So pay attention to the numbers I mention.

FADE IN:

EXT. MOVIE STUDIO - DAY

SKIP SCREENWRITER (39ish) walks in the gate of a studio. The HOLLYWOOD sign can be seen in the B.G. As Skip is passing, a STUDIO GUARD (60s) stares, then yells at Skip and hurries toward him. Spooked, Skip takes off running.

(A character seen the first time is CAPPED. B.G. stands for "background." Try to give some idea about a character's age.)

EXT. WRITERS BUILDING - DAY

Skip hustles up the steps in and into the building, YELLING as he runs in the door.

(Noises, gunshots, explosions and other Special Effects [noted as SFX] and Computer Generated Images [noted CGI] are also CAPPED. People compiling a production budget use these notations in figuring out filming costs.)

INT. SKIP'S OFFICE - DAY

SKIP
(breathless)
Why is he chasing me!?

(Character names are roughly five tabs in at about 35. Dialogue appears two tabs in at 25. Parentheticals are one tab left of a character name but such directions are generally better left to actors and directors to determine.)

The guard steps in Skip's office and holds up a studio identification badge.

CLOSE ON BADGE - Skip holds his own studio ID badge.

RESUME SHOT

Now wearing the ID badge, Skip gives the guard a tip. The guard keeps his hand out. Skip gives him a larger tip.

Note that I used "CLOSE ON" above for what has traditionally been called an "INSERT." Only use such things when it's important to see an object or a picture, etc. "RESUME SHOT" or "RESUME SCENE" traditionally was noted with "BACK TO SCENE" which some still use. You need it to show you're away from the close shot.

If you use a scene transition, such as:

CUT TO:

It should be aligned against the right margin. (Note the colon that follows any indication of scene change.) These are generally left out these days because it is considered obvious that the scene has changed when we see a new location listed below a scene. One that has a particularly good use, however, is:

DISSOLVE TO:

That transition has traditionally been used to show that time is passing between scenes, but the meaning has been somewhat lost with today's script readers.

When someone speaks off-screen but is in the scene, write it this way:

STUDIO GUARD (O.S.)
Hey, you!

O.S. is an abbreviation for "off screen."

When someone speaks off-camera but is not physically in the scene, write it this way:

SKIP (V.O.)
I knew it would be a weird day …

V.O. is an abbreviation for "voice over."

Remember, O.S. is physically present but not seen. V.O. might be narration by a character we see, but that character is *usually* telling the story in retrospect. If the character is describing something currently happening in a scene in which that character is present (like the overheard thoughts in *What Women Want* with Mel Gibson and Helen Hunt), you could use V.O. as a notation or simply write:

SKIP (HIS THOUGHTS)
I feel like an idiot!

You might put the thought-but-not-said dialogue *in italics* to make it clearer that the character's lips are not moving. In *What Women Want* script I saw, however, the women's unspoken thoughts about Gibson (he could hear the thoughts, others could not) were not italicized. You could also write:

SKIP
(thinking)
I feel like an idiot!

If you wrote it that way without italics, though, the reader might think the character is thinking of something *then* saying a line. I'd suggest doing what the writers of *What Women Want* did to show the content of thoughts.

Now let's look at writing location in scenes. The traditional method has been to write scenes so that we know whether it takes place outside (EXT. for exterior) or inside (INT. for interior). If it's neither, just write what it is, such as:

EXT. SPACE STATION

There is no day or night 50 miles above Earth.

If you went inside that space station, however, you would be in an interior location so you would write:

INT. SPACE STATION

Here's another oddity. When transitioning from locations in a continuous sequence of events, it has become common in recent years to forego traditional EXT. and INT. and use something like the following:

EXT. MOVIE STUDIO - DAY (CONTINUOUS)

SKIP SCREENWRITER (39ish) walks in the gate of a studio. The HOLLYWOOD sign can be seen in the B.G. As Skip is passing, a STUDIO GUARD (60s) stares, then yells at Skip and hurries toward him. Spooked, Skip takes off running.

WRITERS BUILDING

Skip comes running up the steps, chased by the guard.

SKIP'S OFFICE

Skip dashes in, catching his breath.

The idea in using such description is that we are within one big "set" (the movie studio) and that it is a given there are various places where shots take place, and they all take place during the same time (like "DAY"). Thus they are continuous.

In reality, each shot has to be "set up" separately. Before computers became commonplace, shots were handwritten on thin cardboard strips, kept in a holder so that each shot of the day (or the entire movie) could be followed at a glance.

I and other writers I know still rarely use CONTINUOUS because each shot will have to be lit for DAY or NIGHT. It makes sense to use it, however, in something like a car chase where we are going back and forth from inside a car to what it looks like outside the car. For example:

EXT. STREET - DAY (CONTINUOUS)

DETECTIVE BOB and DETECTIVE BILL drive fast in pursuit of a red convertible.

Bill is fighting off a wasp inside the car.

The red convertible takes a hard right, the cop car follows.

The wasp bites Bill on the nose!

Each line would be a different shot and location, wouldn't it? I'm sure you see the problem in clarity of notation.

You could also write it this way:

EXT./INT. STREET/CAR - DAY

An unmarked police car drives fast in pursuit of a red convertible.

Inside the car, DETECTIVE BOB and DETECTIVE BILL are nervous. Bill is fighting off a wasp.

Again, there's a problem in clarity if you try to shorthand the switch between shot locations, but just as CUT TO: is generally left off in showing transitions between scenes, we get notations like CONTINUOUS, and we have to live with them.

This is a book about writing feature film screenplays, and there's no room to cover two-column audio-visual scripts (often the format of reality shows) and other types of screenplays. That's why you need a formatting program. Screenwriter 2000 offers different formats for screenplays and stage plays as well as three types of sitcom formats and a novel format. Just for grins, though, I thought I'd show you what the first scene I started with might look like in one of the sitcom formats, to show you how very different the mediums are. If you want to write sitcoms, you need to live some place where sitcoms are made (like Los Angeles) and concentrate on that intensely. Have a look:

<u>ACT ONE</u>

<u>SCENE ONE</u>

INT. MOVIE STUDIO - DAY

SKIP SCREENWRITER (39ISH) WALKS IN THE GATE OF A STUDIO. THE HOLLYWOOD SIGN CAN BE SEEN IN THE B.G. AS SKIP IS PASSING, A STUDIO GUARD (60S) STARES, THEN YELLS AT SKIP AND HURRIES TOWARD HIM. SPOOKED, SKIP TAKES OFF RUNNING.

EXT. WRITERS BUILDING - DAY

SKIP HUSTLES UP THE STEPS IN AND INTO THE BUILDING, SLAMMING THE DOOR BEHIND HIM.

INT. WRITERS BUILDING, SKIP'S OFFICE - DAY

SKIP

(BREATHLESS)

Why is he chasing me!?

THE GUARD STEPS INSIDE AND HOLDS UP A SECURITY BADGE.

STUDIO GUARD

Got one of these?

CLOSE ON BADGE - IT'S SKIP'S STUDIO I.D. BADGE.

RESUME SHOT

Obviously, in most sitcoms Scene One would take place in one location (like Skip's Office). But note the differences:

(a)   Scene description is ALL CAPS.

(b)   A "parenthetical" is also ALL CAPS.

(c)   Dialogue is double-spaced.

If you want to write sitcoms, study scripts to see how it is done. There are many things to learn about script formatting and every writer has his or her own style. For example, I've always used one dash instead of two:

EXT. SKIP'S PLACE - DAY

Instead of what script format programs insert:

EXT. SKIP'S PLACE -- DAY

(You'd probably be better off with two dashes as a standard.)

When a character starts talking and then is interrupted by an action in the location or a page break in the script, you need to use a CONT'D (for CONTINUED), this way:

SKIP

Why are you chasing me!? I didn't …

The guard hands Skip an I.D. badge.

ON BADGE - It's Skip's own badge.

SKIP (CONT'D)

… know I was a complete idiot.

So study scripts for format and save yourself headaches by using a software program. Good luck, and good formatting!

Web Resources

These links are essential Hollywood surfing. See my own site at www. skippress.com for more links. Meanwhile, you can get a great screenwriting education with this page.

www.allmovie.com   All-Movie Guide that includes movie information with companion music and game sites.

www.boxofficemojo.com   Site by Brandon Gray which provides copious financial data.

www.boxofficeprophets.com   A box office database.

www.everyonewhosanyone.com   Fabulous database including e-mail addresses to Hollywood people, publishing, and media worldwide.

www.filmindependent.org   Formerly Independent Feature Project West; best organization for beginning filmmakers in Los Angeles.

www.hcdonline.com   The Hollywood Creative Directory is the number-one contact database in Hollywood, updated daily.

www.hollywoodlitsales.com   Information about script sales and script coverage for $75.

www.hollywoodreporter.com   The Hollywood Reporter; daily Hollywood business news and other resources.

http://movies.groups.yahoo.com/group/hollywoodwriters   My own personal discussion group with hundreds of pro and aspiring writers from around the world engaged in daily discussion.

www.ifp.org   New York-based national resource for independent filmmakers with chapters in cities across the country.

www.imdb.com   The Internet Movie Database; the number-one source of free movie information with an available pro version.

www.mania.com   Movie, video game, and comic book news; check out Development Heck for screenplay deals.

www.moviebytes.com   Screenwriting contest news.

www.showbizdata.com   Includes contact, credits, and deal information.

www.variety.com   Variety; daily Hollywood business news with many free resources.

http://wgaeast.org   Writers Guild of America, East (for U.S. writers east of the Mississippi). Check out New Writers.

www.wga.org   Writers Guild of America, West; has an amazing amount of free information, mentors, and a newsletter.

www.wordplayer.com   Fabulous, free information and a discussion from a top Hollywood screenwriting team.

Index

Y-Z

On the CD

On this CD you'll find a number of demonstration versions of software for screen-writing and other writerly pursuits. You'll also find some demo software for budgeting and scheduling a feature film from your script, should you decide to go that route (and I urge you to contemplate it). Depending on the particular piece of software, it's for PC, Mac, and even Linux.

But first, these items from me, Skip Press:

What Moviegoers Want and Hollywood Often Ignores   A 2008 update of a study of what goes into successful Hollywood movies, what *really* makes them work, which I first put together in 1999 and previously updated in 2003.

Conquering Collaboration   An article originally written for *Scriptwriter* in the United Kingdom about how to successfully collaborate (or not) with another writer.

Navigating the Three Acts of a Screenwriting Breakthrough   A lengthy document about how I've used the story matrix that I teach in screenwriting to apply to my life and career. For me, it works well. See what you think.

How to Write What You Want and Sell What You Write   The first chapter of my book *How to Write What You Want and Sell What You Write*. 2008 will see the third reprint of the third edition of this book, which came out from two previous publishers. My current publisher is Barnes & Noble Books. This chapter advises you on planning out a career, not just a screenplay.

Interview with James Kelly Durgin   A lengthy interview with the head of Cinema Arts Tech, James Kelly Durgin, who has four decades of experience in Hollywood, commenting on what most beginning screenwriters don't know about creating a "film friendly" screenplay that will make their script much more likely to be considered by filmmakers. See www.cinemaartstech.com for info on his school.

Interview in "Shooting the Donkey"   An interview with me by Steve Kayser, the creator of the award-winning business newsletter "Shooting the Donkey." I was the original interviewee in this long-running celebrated series, thus making me the "First Donkey." I think you'll find the discussion of making a complex sale to Hollywood to be worthwhile.

Walking After Midnight   My screenplay, which has brought me a decent amount of money via being "optioned" but has not yet been made into a film. It's an example of an "indie" screenplay.

From some of my professional colleagues, you'll find:

Interview with Devorah Cutler-Rubenstein   A short interview with Devorah Cutler-Rubenstein, perhaps the most knowledgeable teacher of short filmmaking today.

Peacock Blues   The script for *Peacock Blues* written by Devorah and her husband Scott, which won the Chanticleer Discovery Program and was directed by Devorah for Showtime's *Stories from the Edge*. The film also won first prize and was voted Audience Favorite at the Moondance Film Festival.

PC Noir   The script for *PC Noir*, an award-winner that was written and directed by Dawn Natalia. For more information on Dawn and her work, go to www.filmaka.com/we_teammedford.asp.

Santa Croce   The script for *Santa Croce*, a short film that was the American Film Institute Director's Program project for Gavin Heffernan, who I met while he was still in college at McGill University in Canada. Gavin made his first feature film, *The Steaks*, for $800 while still in college and then made another well-received film before enrolling at AFI. View the *Santa Croce* website and read more at www.santacrocefilm.com.

The software demos for Mac, PC, and Linux include:

Celtx 0.997   This software is much more than simply screenplay formatting. See www.celtx.com for details.

Gorilla Film Budgeting and Scheduling software—"Take Total Control of Your Film"—which is a favorite of independent moviemakers everywhere. See www.junglesoftware.com for details.

A suite of various software applications for writers from Mariner Software:

- **Desktop Poet** facilitates easier poetry production
- **MacJournal** for journaling and blogging easily
- **Mariner Calc** spreadsheet software for writers
- **Mariner Write** for other writing needs, including novels
- **Montage** scriptwriting software for film, TV, *and* theater
- **WinJournal** for journaling and blogging easily

Hope you find all this worthwhile. If you have any comments or any trouble with anything on the CD, please let me know by sending an e-mail to skippress@yahoo.com.

Enjoy!

Skip Press
January 2008